SING ME BACK HOME

SING ME BACK HOME
Southern Roots and Country Music

BILL C. MALONE

UNIVERSITY OF OKLAHOMA : NORMAN

This book is published with the generous assistance of
The McCasland Foundation, Duncan, Oklahoma.

An excerpt from the poem "Owed to Johnny Gimble," by Garrison Keillor,
appears in chapter 10. It is copyright © 1994 and used by permission
of Garrison Keillor. All rights reserved.

Library of Congress Cataloging-in-Publication Data

Name: Malone, Bill C., author.
Title: Sing me back home : southern roots and country music / Bill C. Malone.
Description: First edition. | Norman, OK : University of Oklahoma Press, [2017] | Series:
     American popular music series ; 1 | Includes index.
Identifiers: LCCN 2016027506 | ISBN 978-0-8061-5586-9 (hardcover : alk. paper)
Subjects: LCSH: Country music—Southern States—History and criticism. | Folk music—
     Southern States—History and criticism.
Classification: LCC ML3551 .M256 2017 | DDC 781.6420975—dc23
LC record available at https://lccn.loc.gov/2016027506

Sing Me Back Home: Southern Roots and Country Music is Volume 1 in the American
Popular Music Series.

The paper in this book meets the guidelines for permanence and durability of the Committee
on Production Guidelines for Book Longevity of the Council on Library Resources, Inc. ∞

Copyright © 2017 by the University of Oklahoma Press, Norman, Publishing Division of the
University. Manufactured in the U.S.A.

1 2 3 4 5 6 7 8 9 10

CONTENTS

ILLUSTRATIONS

CREDITS AND ACKNOWLEDGMENTS

The essays in this volume have been reproduced with the generous permission of the institutions noted here:

CHAPTER 1: "'Sing Me Back Home': Growing Up in the South and Writing the History of Its Music" was first published in John Boles's edited volume *Shapers of Southern History* (2004) and is reproduced here courtesy of the University of Georgia Press, Athens.

CHAPTER 2: "Neither Anglo-Saxon nor Celtic: The Music of the Southern Plain Folk" was first published in Samuel C. Hyde Jr.'s edited volume *Plain Folk of the South Revisited* (1997) and is reproduced courtesy of Louisiana State University Press, Baton Rouge.

CHAPTER 3: "Blacks and Whites and the Music of the Old South" was first published in Ted Ownby's edited volume *Black and White Cultural Interaction in the Antebellum South* (1993) and is reproduced courtesy of the University Press of Mississippi, Jackson.

CHAPTER 4: "William S. Hays: The Bard of Kentucky" was originally published in the *Register of the Kentucky Historical Society* (1995) and is reproduced here with permission.

CHAPTER 5: "Stranger Passing through Your Town: Jimmie Rodgers and the Rambler Tradition" was first published in Mary E. Davis and Warren Zanes's edited volume *Waiting for a Train: Jimmie Rodgers' America* (2009) and is reproduced here by permission of Rounder Books.

CHAPTER 6: The liner notes reprinted in "The Blue Sky Boys: The Sunny Side of Life" are reproduced by permission of the Bear Family, Vollersode, Germany.

CHAPTER 7: "Albert E. Brumley: Folk Composer" was first published in *Bluegrass Unlimited* magazine and is reprinted here by permission of *Bluegrass Unlimited*. The song lyrics by Albert Brumley that appear in this essay are used here by permission of Brumley Music Group, Powell, Missouri.

CHAPTER 8: Liner notes reprinted in "The Chuck Wagon Gang: God's Gentle People" are reproduced by permission of the Bear Family, Vollersode, Germany.

CHAPTER 9: "Honky-Tonk: The Music of the Southern Working Class" first appeared in William Ferris and Mary L. Hart's edited volume *Folk Music and Modern Sound* (1982) and is reprinted here by permission of the University Press of Mississippi, Jackson.

CHAPTER 10: "Johnny Gimble: The Music Came Up from His Soul" was first published in *No Depression* 42 (May–June 2002) and is reprinted here by permission of *No Depression*. An excerpt from Garrison Keillor's poem "Owed to Johnny Gimble" appears in this chapter. It is copyright © 1994 and used by permission of Garrison Keillor. All rights reserved.

CHAPTER 11: "Texas Myth/Texas Music" was first published in the *Journal of Texas Music History* 1 (Spring 2001) and is reprinted here by permission of the Center for Texas Music History at Texas State University, San Marcos.

CHAPTER 12: "The Romance That Will Not Die: Appalachian Music and American Popular Culture" was originally published in Richard Straw and H. Tyler Blethen's edited volume *High Mountains Rising: Appalachia in Time and Place, an Anthology on Appalachian Culture and History* (2004) and is reproduced here by permission of the University of Illinois Press, Champaign–Urbana.

CHAPTER 13: "Elvis, Country Music, and the South" was originally published in Jac L. Tharpe's edited volume *Elvis: Images and Fancies* (1979) and is reproduced here by permission of the University Press of Mississippi, Jackson, as a special issue of the *Southern Quarterly*.

CHAPTER 14: "The Rural South Moves North: Country Music since World War II" was first published in R. Douglas Hurt's edited volume *The Rural South since World War II* (1998) and is reproduced here by permission of the Louisiana State University Press, Baton Rouge.

CHAPTER 15: "Country Music and the Academy" was first published in Daniel W. Patterson's edited volume *Sounds of the South* (1991) and is reprinted here by permission of the Southern Folklife Collection at the University of North Carolina, Chapel Hill.

CHAPTER 16: "Memories of Austin and Threadgill's" was first published in the *Old-Time Herald* 4, no. 3 (Spring 1994): 20–22.

SING ME BACK HOME

INTRODUCTION
Gathering, Reflecting, and Rethinking

The essays presented in this book represent a lifetime of loving, listening to, singing, writing, and thinking about country music. Running the gamut in style and type of publication, they first appeared in anthologies, music periodicals, academic journals, and as CD liner notes. The essays were written for both scholarly and popular audiences. Consequently, some essays have a full array of endnotes; others do not.

Select and generally small audiences have seen or heard the original essays; their presence now in this anthology will permit them, potentially, to reach a much larger readership. For years they have remained scattered, and some are no longer in print. Unlike my more comprehensive and encyclopedic *Country Music, U.S.A.*, these essays certainly do not address every aspect of country music's long and multifaceted history. In fact, one will find little attention devoted to the contemporary music scene. That story is told elsewhere, generally by people who have more affection and understanding for modern country music than I do. My goal, instead, has been to explore many of country music's historic styles and subgenres, evaluate some of its most compelling performers, and raise questions about its origins, defining myths, and relationship to other forms of music. As might be expected, a good deal of attention is also paid to those personal moments that define my own lifelong relationship with country music and explain why the music captured my affection many years ago.

For the most part, the contents of the essays have not been altered from the forms in which they first appeared. Since they were originally published as discrete pieces and for different audiences at different stages of my career, some repetition has been inevitable. For example, the reader may grow tired of repeated references to the Philco battery radio's entrance into our home in 1939 and of the sanctity that the event has attained in my memory. I have not tried to eliminate repeated material, feeling that the reader should be permitted to see what my thinking was at the time that each individual essay was written. On the other hand, the newly written introductions to the various essays indicate the ways in which my perspectives have sometimes shifted over the years, reflecting insights gained from more recent scholarship and from my own reconsiderations. Despite what the subtitle of one essay suggests, my involvement in the writing of country music history has been much more than a "thirty-year odyssey."

The only changes I have made within the essays are occasional corrections of factual errors. Death dates of various performers, on the other hand, and some other information that seems crucial to the music's changing history are generally given in the new introductions to the various essays. For each essay I have also listed relevant published scholarship that either was overlooked at the time of writing or has appeared since my work was originally published. In the final analysis, though, reading about country music will not be enough to attain a full understanding or appreciation of a phenomenon that not only has been central to my life but has also been embraced by millions of people around the world. The music has to be heard. Fortunately, much of the music from the pre–World War II years is now available on reissued recordings, produced both abroad and in the United States. The potential scholar can reach beyond these commercially available resources to find old 78 and 45 rpm records, LPs, and radio transcriptions, through visits to archives such as the Country Music Hall of Fame and Museum in Nashville or the Southern Folklife Collection at the University of North Carolina, Chapel Hill. As a matter of fact, the interested listener, whether scholar or casual fan, need travel no farther than his or her computer, iPod, or other digital resource to find examples of virtually every musical item mentioned in these essays. And on YouTube, the video-sharing website, one can not only hear rare or obscure pieces of music but can also see old film footage of radio barn dances, cowboy movies, and similar "rustic" fare. Most of the YouTube material is supplied by fans who have little motivation other than a sheer love for the music and a desire to share it with others, and with no thought of financial compensation.

My central hope is that these essays will provide a broader and more in-depth understanding of the genre to which I have devoted my life and might provoke readers to seek additional resources that give them a greater appreciation for—and pleasure in—listening to country music for their own enjoyment.

Mama and me (Maude and Bill Malone). This is where it all began.
My introduction to country music came from Mama.
Courtesy the Bill C. Malone Collection, Madison, Wisconsin.

CHAPTER 1

"SING ME BACK HOME"
Growing Up in the South
and Writing the History of Its Music

I was honored and delighted when Professor John Boles, a historian at Rice University in Houston and onetime editor of the *Journal of Southern History*, asked me to be part of a group of southern historians who were asked to describe how their personal histories contributed to the kinds of academic histories that they wrote. This essay was first published in *Shapers of Southern History* (2004), edited by John Boles. While my original decision to write a doctoral dissertation on the subject of country music was rather accidental and unexpected, the actual tone that the subject assumed, for good or ill, was powerfully shaped by my having grown up in a southern working-class home.

I AM NOT ONE OF THOSE TEXANS WHO DENIES HIS SOUTHERN ROOTS. You know the kind. They argue that Texas is an exceptional place that somehow escaped the sin, guilt, and hidebound traditionalism that marks the southern experience. This argument, of course, is central to the Texas Mystique. In country music scholarship, the denial comes from those who rail against the corporate Nashville establishment and instead stress the alleged freedom

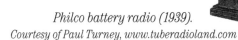

Philco battery radio (1939).
Courtesy of Paul Turney, www.tuberadioland.com

and experimentation of such Texas musicians as Bob Wills and Willie Nelson and the Austin Outlaws and argue that this spiritual and psychological expansiveness derives from the vastness of the Texas landscape and the diversity of its culture. This conception, it seems to me, is essentially a *West* Texas vision and is of course linked to the romance of cowboys and the limitless western range.

My little corner of sandy and red-clay East Texas soil, with its wide variety of deciduous and pine trees, was thoroughly southern until the oilmen, bankers, and developers came in and appropriated the land and its resources. It was settled by folks who began coming into the area before the Civil War from thoroughly southern places like north Alabama and Mississippi, Tennessee, and North Carolina. If they knew for sure where their ancestors came from across the waters, they seldom passed the information on to children and their offspring. Local surnames such as Browning, Maxfield, Starr, Boyd, Bogue, Nipp, Goode, Gilbert, Owens, and Malone suggest that they came from various parts of Ireland, Scotland, England, Wales, and even the European continent. The Foshees on my paternal side, for example, apparently arrived on the South Atlantic coast as part of a Huguenot French immigration. Some of the people claimed an Indian admixture, and my relatives were no exception. My mother spoke proudly of her grandmother's alleged Indian extraction. I suspect that most white people represented that glorious and untraceable mixture of ethnicity that virtually defined the South. Some of the white settlers brought slaves, and the culture that they created bore the marks of an interrelation between the two peoples—in folklore, foodways, religion, speech patterns—that had begun long before the trek to East Texas was made.

Most black people in our area lived nearby, only a couple of miles down the Willow Flat Road in the Clear Springs community. Blacks and whites frequently worked side by side, in the fields or at clearing off the land. White people often attended revivals at the black community, Clear Springs, in the Baptist and Church of God in Christ congregations, sitting in segregated sections. As a child, it was exciting to hear the music and watch the black church people dance, but for me, the most joyful aspects of the revivals were the stands that sold fried catfish and homemade ice cream. Yet I would never presume to romanticize this relationship. Even though some miscegenation occurred, and my parents could point out individuals who were the progeny of such relationships, we remained keenly aware of a social line that could not be crossed. White supremacy and racial segregation prevailed. Children easily absorbed the etiquette of racial relations and the hurtful attitudes that accompanied them. I remember one day when a fire broke out down in the pasture. A small cousin and I reflexively agreed, "I bet them niggers did it." The older folks had an even more malevolent heritage to deal with, because they still talked about a grim and grisly incident from the not-too-distant past, the burning alive of a black man on Tyler's courthouse square. In some ways that shameful incident paled before another local event, because it involved people that we knew. A man and his son, presumably drunk, went into a black home, began tossing an infant to and from each other, purely for sport, until the child died from a head injury. They were taken into custody but ultimately went unpunished.

We called our little community "Galena," and for a brief period around the turn of the twentieth century we even had a post office bearing the name. I don't know why or how the name was chosen. As far as I know, no lead deposits were ever found there. The name just sounded pretty, I suppose, although most people I knew pronounced it G'leener. One does find occasional references to a nearby two-room school, Elm Grove (pronounced Ellem Grove) or to the Wells' Gin Community (inspired by one of the names given to the cotton gin that long thrived there), and, recognizing a habit that was well-nigh universal among young and old, male and female, and blacks and whites, some observers called it "Snuff City." If a poll had been taken among local farmers selecting America's most renowned men, the name of the great snuff maker, Levi Garrett, would have ranked very high.

Located about twenty miles west of Tyler, and eighty miles east of Dallas, Galena consisted of widely scattered farmsteads that extended across the Smith and Van Zandt county lines. Paul Terry and Verner Sims, in their study of a similar community in Alabama, *They Live on the Land* (1940), had described such entities as "Open-Country Communities." Galena had no central or easily definable core, although at least three local institutions provided some social cohesion: the cotton gin that was located at the intersection of Willow Flat and Carroll Roads; the Elm Grove two-room schoolhouse; and the Tin Top Pentecostal Church. Cotton ruled the economy, and although a few semi-prosperous men owned their farms, most people lived as sharecroppers and tenant farmers, paying the owners a share of what they produced. When the Great Depression arrived in 1929, people in my part of East Texas already knew hard times and deprivation, a legacy of Civil War defeat and one-crop agriculture.

A rough equality prevailed at social gatherings—in church, at the cotton gin, at the little country store that functioned at the crossroads, or at country dances—but tenants and other poor farmers paid deference to their "betters" with respectful words and a tip of the hat. People always knew who ranked above and below them. If humble farmers recognized the existence of those above them on the social scale, they also knew that some white people deserved only contempt. Poverty itself was not a disgrace, because most people were poor. I don't remember ever hearing the word "trash" used to describe poor farmers. The preferred word was "sorry," and it was reserved for those who would not work, or who let their livestock run freely into their neighbors' fields, or who led morally contemptible lives.

I entered this world on August 25, 1934, the third son of Cleburne and Maude Owens Malone. I was born at home on the Bracken place (owned by a family in Tyler), in a little four-room, tin-roofed "boxed" house (with walls made secure by one-by-three strips of wood nailed over the cracks between vertically aligned one-by-twelve boards). A porch, or gallery as we described it, ran along the front of the house, about two feet off the ground, and just high enough that our dogs could find refuge there during rainstorms or the blazing heat of summer. Since the interior walls were unlined, Daddy placed cardboard on the walls of the "living room" to lend some insulation and protection against winter winds. A few pictures, some religious mottoes with inscriptions like "Only one life it will soon be past. Only what's done for Christ will last," and some hoary and long out-of-date calendars that had pleasant or comic illustrations, decorated the walls.

The floors had no rugs or linoleum, and the cracks were so wide in some areas that we could see the chickens scratching underneath the house. Only one room—the front room—had a ceiling. In the other three we could see the rafters, and the rain often seeped through. Our interior furnishings can best be described as modest and minimal: two beds, a few straight chairs (with seats generally made of closely woven binder twine), a kitchen table that Daddy had made, a small desk, a dresser, a sturdy high chair that was passed down from son to son, a kitchen pie safe (complete with built-in flour sifter), and a couple of wires strung up in the bedrooms where our meager supply of clothes hung. Privacy was hard to come by in this little house. My brothers slept with each other in one bed, and I slept with my father and mother in the other one. I do not recall where visitors slept, but I'm sure that pallets were often called into use.

My mother certainly spent too many precious moments bending over the big iron kitchen cook stove to regard it with any affection, but the rest of us felt it our home's most cherished centerpiece. Since the rigors of farmwork required it, meals were always substantial and, because we generally managed to maintain a garden, relatively balanced. We produced our own pork and poultry and sometimes had fried catfish or perch caught from Caney Creek down in the pasture or from Boyd Water (a locally named portion of the Neches River). Beef was highly prized but seldom consumed, largely because of the difficulty of preservation. During much of my childhood on the Bracken Place we had no icebox but instead wrapped a quilt around a block of ice and kept it in a firebox (where kindling for the fireplace was kept). We kept milk fresh by placing it in a tightly sealed syrup bucket, wrapping it securely with burlap, and lowering it into the well. At the time I did not comprehend just how much backbreaking labor and ingenuity had gone into the production of things that I took for granted. I only knew that the cornbread, fluffy biscuits, white gravy, sausage patties, pinto beans, homemade tomato soup, and Christmas pastries that graced our table when times were good were among the most sublime elements of country life.

My southernness and sense of history seem to have been Malone traits. My father, Patrick Cleburne Malone, named for a martyred Confederate general, was the son of Laura Foshee and Thomas Jefferson Malone, who in turn was the son of William Carroll Malone (named for a onetime Democratic governor of Tennessee). My parents were born in Van Zandt County, Texas—Daddy near the now-vanished community of Owlet Green, and my mother in the similarly defunct village of Primrose, not far from Edom. If opposites attract, then their union seems foreordained. He was quiet, and she was talkative. He generally held back his feelings but could explode into a furious rage. She was impulsive, and we always knew what was on her mind. He resisted going to church; she was passionately religious. He couldn't carry a tune; she was a wonderful singer. Both were intelligent and gifted individuals whose talents were unfulfilled or unrecognized, partly because of poverty and inadequate education but also because they lacked the will to seek new challenges. My mother longed to go places and see new things, but she never learned how to drive and permitted herself to remain confined most of her life to a relatively narrow strip of East Texas soil. My father spent most of his life as a farmer but could master any mechanical puzzle put before him. Yet he would take few risks and consequently remained a wage laborer all his life. The marriage was probably a mistake, but they stayed together for forty-eight years, until Mama died in 1971.

The house where I was born, and where I lived for the first ten years of my life, was about a mile and a half from the crossroads where the cotton gin and little country store sat. Daddy was a cotton tenant farmer, working the land with a mule and plow, and relying on the help of his wife and my two older brothers, Wylie and Kelly, for picking, hoeing, and other tasks related to farm life. The crop year began with a visit to Tyler and the general supply store—Caldwell, Hughes, Delay and Allen—where Daddy bought on credit needed merchandise for the coming year—cotton sacks, overalls, plow lines, bridles, and related material. After the cotton was ginned, he paid his bills and invariably found himself in debt, a situation that was carried over from year to year. Ours was a semi-isolated existence until 1939, when Daddy bought our first battery-powered Philco radio. I remember going to Dallas only once during the ten years that I lived on the farm, but if we could hitch a ride with some neighbor—usually Jess Starr, who owned an old beat-up truck—we might make it in to Tyler, twenty miles away, a couple of times a year (usually around Christmas-time or during the East Texas Fair). Through the blessings of rural free delivery we did receive newspapers, religious and political tracts, and the Sears-Roebuck and Montgomery Ward catalogs; and periodically a peddler made his rounds in the countryside, bringing us useful household items, candy, and gossip from the outside world. Otherwise, we were a true folk community that depended on its own resources and the time-tested traditions of our ancestors. Our lighting came from coal-oil lamps, our heat from woodstoves, and our water from a backyard well. The alum-infested water, however, was distasteful to drink and hard to wash clothes with. Mama caught some rainwater in a barrel, but she often went down to a spring in the pasture to wash our clothes. Wylie or Kelly would hitch one of the mules to a sled and transport the big black wash pot and our load of clothes down to the spring.

We permitted no blade of grass to grow in the yard but instead kept it swept clean with a rake and a home-made broom. I'm not sure that anyone ever stopped to think of why we did it—it was just one of the traditions we inherited—but swept yards were easier to maintain than grass-carpeted ones and would not harbor snakes. When we felt the call of nature, we made the trek to the outdoor privy, using pages from magazines or Sears catalogs as our toilet paper. On very cold nights, though, we had to resort to the appropriately named slop jar. As a consequence, bodily needs were too often repressed for much of the night. Medically, our treatment can only be described as substandard. We never went to the dentist and consulted a doctor only for the most severe ailments. Some of our neighbors occasionally visited old Mrs. Blackstock, who had the reputation of being a healer, someone who could cure complaints with her homemade concoctions or with appropriate scriptural incantations. One biblical verse, it was said, could even stop bleeding. My mother preferred to trust her own prayers, or those of her friends, but sometimes we had to resort to professional medical assistance. Dr. Montgomery occasionally drove his Model A Ford coupe down from Van to make house calls when we were seriously ill, but most problems were treated with coal oil, liniment, Alka-Seltzer, Grove's Chill Tonic, castor oil, or other patent medicines or home remedies.

One finds little romance, then, in those farm days in East Texas in the late 1930s and early 1940s. Life was often hard and lonely, but it was enlivened by periodic occasions of social intercourse—Christmas (the only time that oranges and apples entered the house), baseball games, fish fries down at Boyd Water, house parties (the commonly used designation for country dances, or what had once been called "frolics"), all-day singings, brush arbor revival meetings, quilting parties, ice-cream suppers, funerals, Sunday gatherings at Grandma Malone's, school closings, domino games (the new game of "42" was all the rage in the mid-1930s), and occasional trips to Canton for First Monday, a mule-trading day that has since become a giant flea market. Visiting, though, was the most common form of conviviality and even unscheduled trips were welcomed. I was always bemused when Miss Winnie Smith visited, because in her mind all useful philosophy came from the Holy Scriptures. During one of my childish frustrations, for example, she declared, "Just remember, Billy, as the Bible says 'if at first you don't succeed, try, try again.'" If a family's visit came at a time when the crops were "laid by," or when no urgent farm task was impending, the host family would often pack up the wagon and immediately follow the visiting family back home.

Hog-killing day was in many ways the most special occasion of all. On the days leading up to the event, Daddy and the older folks seemed to be watching the sky and judging the position and color of the sun. I suppose they were merely looking for the coldest day of the year, when the meat could be easily preserved, but somehow it all seemed magical to me. Neighbors and relatives typically gathered to share both the tasks and the fun. Sheltered from the most grim aspects of the day—the actual butchering of the hog—I instead reveled in the more festive aspects of the occasion, the grinding of the sausage, the preparation of the pork for the smokehouse, the rendering of the lard in the big black wash pot, and the making of the lye soap that was used in the cleansing of our heavy work clothes.

My father began each day by going out on the front porch, at about six o'clock in the morning, and hollering at the top of his voice, as if to announce to neighbors far and wide that Cleburne Malone was ready to confront the world. Like most southern men of his generation, he found his diversions outside the house, often in communion with other males—fishing, hunting, drinking, gambling, playing practical jokes, and spinning tall tales. The stories about Halloween were particularly fascinating, and they make accounts of today's trick-or-treating seem especially tame.

Setting fire to an outdoor toilet when it had an occupant or dismantling a neighbor's buggy or wagon and reassembling it on the top of his house were harmful enough, but using a "dumb bull" to frighten people was almost diabolical. Someone would remove the bottom from a wooden keg, stretch a rawhide tautly across the top like a drumhead, cut a small hole in it, and then pull a cord made of horsehair through the narrow opening. When rosin or a fingernail was rubbed against the cord, a horrifying sound akin to that made by a wild beast was produced. Fiendish young men delighted in taking a dumb bull to the woods, or making the terrible sound near some black family's home. Those who heard it were convinced that a panther or some other predatory varmint was lurking nearby. Of course, plenty of material existed to supply the wants of local storytellers. Ghost stories, family feuds, murders, and violent retribution were the stuff of enthralling tales. One such story involved our nearest neighbor, Aaron Smith (Miss Winnie's husband) who was shot to death by his brother-in-law outside his home, just across the pasture from our house.

Mama found her consolation in religion. Her life had always been hard. She was about a month old when her mother died, a victim of childbirth complications. Mama was virtually abandoned by her dad, an engineer for the Cotton Belt Railroad, and was reared by her paternal grandparents on a bleak farm in Primrose. She worshiped her grandfather, but too often he spent his meager Confederate pension on whiskey and kept his little family in dire straits. She had a love-hate relationship with her dad, recognizing his imperfections but nevertheless fascinated by his life as a railroad man. She never ceased to be thrilled by the sound and sight of a locomotive engine, and she may have thought of her absent father when she heard and sometimes requested songs like "Black Jack David" and "Rattlesnaking Daddy" that described rakish or devilish men.

Mama was raised a Methodist, but she and her grandmother were converted to Pentecostalism in about 1915 by an itinerant band of missionaries that came through East Texas. Regular church services were not always an option, but my mother prayed constantly, went to prayer meetings in her friends' homes, and often went down to the woods to pray alongside her friends or with her sister-in-law, my Aunt Erna. The Tin Top Pentecostal Church convened irregularly, with services conducted usually by local volunteers or by visiting evangelists. Pentecostalism was rough and scary in those days, and its adherents were convinced that both demons and angels peopled the world they inhabited. As I was growing up, my mother still talked about the time a wanderer remembered only as "Frenchy" (probably a Cajun) came to a revival meeting, made fun of the scene he saw around him, and pretended to speak in tongues. What seemed to be a blatant act of blasphemy cast both sinners and believers into an awestruck silence. When the man was found dead in his room the next morning, they were convinced that God had struck him down.

Shouting, testifying, glossolalia (speaking in tongues), and the various physically emotional manifestations that had inspired the term "holy rollers" marked the emotion-laden services. The music was wondrously spirited. Sometimes, only a guitar accompanied the singing, but often the music was performed a cappella, with the driving rhythm provided by tambourines and handclapping. The spirit could not always be contained within the walls of the church or confined by the limits of a church service. Heading home late at night after the congregation had been dismissed, Mama and Aunt Erna would shepherd their children through the dark woods (the shortest distance between church and home) and would continue to sing the cherished gospel songs at the top of their voices: "I'm in the way, the bright and shining way, I'm in the Glory Land Way. Telling the world that Jesus saves today."

Music, then, was also her salvation, as it was for me. She sang to dispel her loneliness, to voice her frustrations, and to praise her God. I don't know where she learned all of her songs, in those days before we obtained a radio. She knew a few pop songs, like "Red Wing," "San Antonio," and "Pony Boy," and some scattered verses of folk songs such as "Roll On Buddy" ("Old Diamond Joe, he was an old fool. He spent all his money trying to break Jay Gould"). She remembered most of her songs in fragmentary form, and probably learned them from friends and relatives. Like many rural people of her generation, she also copied down the lyrics of favorite songs in a school tablet or composition book. A sizeable number, such as the sentimental parlor songs "The Little Rosewood Casket," "Two Little Orphans," and "The Letter Edged in Black," came from "the Young People's Page" of the *Dallas Semi-Weekly Farm News*, in which people exchanged the lyrics of old songs. An even larger percentage of songs came from revival meetings or church-singing schools and were preserved in the paperback hymnals distributed at monthly singing conventions or sold in bulk quantity to rural churches. No songs were more soul-satisfying or emotionally uplifting to her than such items as "Farther Along," "No Never Alone," and "Leave It There." I realize now that the assemblage of songs in her repertory typified the music remembered throughout the rural South in the decades before 1920. These were the "old-familiar" tunes (a term used by the Columbia label to describe the old-time records in its catalogs) that made their way on to the early phonograph recordings and radio broadcasts when country music was in its commercial infancy.

Then came the Philco battery radio. It arrived in our household in 1939, bringing with it the awareness of another and more exciting world. The radio delivered auditory confirmation of the society we saw displayed in Sears-Roebuck and Montgomery Ward catalogs or in the Dick and Jane readers. It helped to dispel the loneliness and alienation that too often marked the lives of rural farm women. The radio's effects on my mother's life were incalculable, and she immersed herself in the soap operas, dramas, and comedies that were radio's standard fare. And it fed the imaginative universe that I inhabited, adding to my already fertile storehouse of make-believe with its stories and professional sports. Above all, it brought me into the universe of hillbilly music.

We began each day with the live hillbilly shows broadcast from Tyler, Dallas, Fort Worth, Shreveport, and Tulsa, and we brightened our noon-time dinners with the gospel music of the Chuck Wagon Gang or the Stamps Quartet. Each Saturday night, of course, we listened to the Grand Ole Opry from Nashville, and occasionally picked up a syndicated segment of the National Barn Dance from Chicago. Each weekday night we generally heard some Mexican border programming, from XERA and XEG—Cowboy Slim Rinehart, the Herrington Trio, Mainer's Mountaineers, and the Carter Family. Such radio hillbillies as the Shelton Brothers, the Callahan Brothers, Peg Moreland, the Chuck Wagon Gang, and Ernest Tubb were virtually members of the family. These entertainers fostered that illusion with their homey patter, down-home humor, and moralistic messages, and we were loyal to them. We bought their songbooks and

Mama's passion for the music of the "radio hillbillies" is shown in the picture postcard obtained from Ernest Tubb.
Courtesy the Bill C. Malone Collection, Madison, Wisconsin.

picture postcards, gossiped about them, and faithfully patronized the flour manufacturers, cough-syrup makers, laxative distributors, and other businesses that sponsored them.

My brothers have similar affectionate recollections of the battery radio and of the music it dispensed, and their guitar strumming and earnest renditions of songs like "The Last Letter" and "The Great Speckled Bird" enlivened our household at the end of the 1930s. Otherwise, their memories of farm life are not nearly so sanguine. They had gone to the fields almost as soon as they started school. They were eight and nine years older than me and bore most of the work as well as the hard discipline that Daddy meted out. His frustrations with poor crops, bad weather, boll weevils, and stubborn mules were sometimes taken out in bursts of rage at his wife and sons. Consequently, my brothers were restless, uninterested in reading, but anxious to see the outside world. They never graduated from high school and left home as teenagers on a few occasions to work briefly in Dallas and Wichita Falls. When he was seventeen, in July 1943, Wylie begged and cajoled my parents into letting him sign up for service in the Navy Seabees. As the baby of the family, and almost an only child because of our age differences, I was sheltered from the hardest farm work and grew up much closer to my mother than they did. My mother dreamed that I might become a preacher, and as a child I must have encouraged that hope with some of my play. I often put a bible and hymnbook on top of the high chair that Daddy had built, and regaled her with my earnest prayers, songs, and sermons.

With much time on my hands and no playmates, I often retreated to an imaginary world peopled with ideas and scenes inspired by my reading and the radio. One of my flights of imagination wrought considerable damage to our already-strained economic condition. One day after I watched our landlord's hired hands brand some of their cows, I decided to play cowboy. I found a long stick, ignited it from a fire under my mother's wash pot, and set out to do my own "branding." Our dogs Jake and Wimpey refused to cooperate, so I branded a cotton bale that was sitting in the backyard. Daddy had to take the bale back to the gin for re-ginning. I was an adult before I got up enough nerve to confess to him that the fire had not been caused by a spark from the wash pot.

My imaginations usually assumed more benign manifestations. My Neverland was a vast world that contained nations that fought wars against each other but also competed in all the big-time sports. I even made a map of this land, created countries both real and imagined, and bisected them with a vast river, the Satin River, which was large enough to host huge naval battles. I also conjured up a mythical family, the McLemore Brothers, who combined my chief interests. They were detectives who captured criminals, incarcerated them in their own prison, and in their spare time sang and harmonized over their own radio station, in a fashion similar to that of the Sons of the Pioneers. When World War II came, I began writing a history of the conflict, made up of both facts and a great mixture of fiction, and became a Chinese detective named Mr. Wing who solved crimes great and small. When Wylie went off to war, I peppered my letters to him with references to spy-catching, and signed them as "Mr. Wing." To the end of his days, when I was in my forties, my dad still liked to call me Mr. Wing.

Even before the war came, the forces of modernization were already intruding upon our lives. Rural electric lines did not extend past the crossroads at the cotton gin (probably because only a few white families like ours lived on that section of the Willow Flat Road), but the battery-powered radio had introduced us to sounds and experiences that came from far-off and often romantic places. Oil had been discovered in 1929 at nearby Van. Although no one among my relatives had ever prospered from the discovery, the event nevertheless affected our lives. Van built the most modern school complex in our part of East Texas and began consolidating most of the little rural schools in the region. As the one- and two-room schools were swallowed up, the communities around them surrendered their identities. Nearby Elm Grove had ceased to function by 1940, and so I trudged off the first day of school to catch the bus that would take me to Van. Although we had been forced to consolidate, the Van school nevertheless would not send a bus a mile and a half down the Willow Flat Road to pick us up. Bus service and rural electrification both ended at the Galena crossroads. I must confess that I missed school that first day, crying and holding back to the point that my brother Kelly, who had been entrusted with my care, also missed the bus—probably to his delight.

I also missed most of the other days that year and as a result failed the first grade. I simply was not prepared psychologically to take leave of my mother, which she wisely understood. One day when my teacher drove down into the country to inquire about my absences, Mama said to her, "Billy doesn't want to go to school, and we don't make him." By the time the next school year rolled around, I was more than ready to attend, and spurred on by my mother's tutelage had already learned how to read. My love affair with reading and books has never ceased.

When I finally settled into the regimen of learning at Van, I could look out through the windows of the first-grade classroom and see the future of Texas being dynamically dramatized by the pumps of the Pure Oil Company, as they busily extracted their precious supplies of black liquid from beneath the schoolgrounds themselves. Certainly I was not prescient enough to recognize the significance of what I saw, but I was literally witnessing the end of our way of life and the beginnings of modern Texas. By 1943 my family had become part of the host of rural folk who abandoned their lifelong moorings in the country to begin new lives as urban blue-collar dwellers. By this time Galena's population had already been severely depleted, a victim of migrations to the industrial and war plants of Dallas, Fort Worth, Houston, and the Gulf Coast and by the entry of its young men and women into military service. Daddy had even done two short stints as a wage laborer, in Wichita Falls as a construction worker and in Velasco at the Dow Magnesium plant, but had come back to make one last attempt at farming. His efforts failed, and that last Christmas on the farm was indeed bleak. The apples and oranges that usually came into our house only at Christmas were absent this time, and I remember getting only one present, a paperback book, which he bought for thirty-five cents at a drugstore in Van.

Wylie's absence in the Seabees meant one less field hand and an aching loneliness in my mother's life. Once the inevitable decision was made to leave, we borrowed Jess Starr's truck and set out for Tyler. Adding insult to injury, the truck caught fire near Carroll, and some of our meager store of goods were damaged or destroyed. We settled into a little rental house, also without electric lights, on the old Van Highway right on the edge of Tyler's western city limits. The entire time my family lived in Tyler, from 1943 to the mid-1950s, we lived at addresses defined by the linkages to rural communities surrounding the city. We moved from the Van Highway to the Old Garden Valley Road to the Old Longview Road, and we remained on the margins of Tyler society, socially and economically as well as geographically.

World War II revolutionized life for southern rural people. The economic and social consequences of the war generated new opportunities and new forms of wealth. The move to town, though, evoked varying responses and adaptations, often according to gender, age, and race. Many rural men, including my father and brothers, never fully adjusted to the pace, regimentation, and discipline of town life; they remained rural people in the city. Daddy and Kelly both worked briefly for Norman-Ford on West Erwin Street, a small plant that made prisms for bomb sights, but Daddy soon moved from there to the Gordon-Sewell wholesale grocery house, where he did back-breaking warehouse work. By the time we left Tyler for Dallas, about ten years later, he was working as a mechanic and shipping clerk for East Texas Auto Supply, making only a dollar an hour and still wondering if the move into town had been wise. Fortunately, C. E. Owen, the owner of East Texas Auto Supply who had invested heavily in the Lone Star Steel Company near Daingerfield, talked Daddy into buying one hundred shares of stock, at a dollar per share. Daddy's only speculative venture proved providential. Dividends and occasional sales of stock helped to finance my first years at the University of Texas in Austin.

My mother never doubted the decision to move to town. She ardently embraced the changes. Town life meant ready-made clothes, a telephone, a washing machine, and a refrigerator; it generated more opportunities to go to church and promised the end of her social isolation. Sometimes when Daddy reminisced about the past, and said, perhaps not too jokingly, that if he could get a mule and plow he would move back to the farm, Mama would quickly respond, "If you do, you'll move without me."

On Saturdays my mother and I generally took the bus into town. I might go to one or more of the five movie houses located on or near the courthouse square. Waiting for Daddy to get off work, we often sat on the benches outside the courthouse visiting with friends or listening to the religious arguments waged by old men, usually Baptists or Campbellites (the name usually given to members of the Church of Christ). Almost always, we ate a hamburger and drank a Barq's orange at a little café right off the square, bought broken and discounted peanut patties at a local candy factory, or went into the bowling alley on Spring Street to watch the bowlers and listen to the jukebox. Certain songs endure as vivid memories of that period: Gene Autry's "I'll Wait for You," Tex Ritter's "Have I Stayed

Away Too Long?" and Wiley and Gene's "When My Blue Moon Turns to Gold Again," all speaking directly to the loneliness felt by my mother as she thought about her boy far away in the South Pacific in military service. When Wylie left home at the end of his first furlough, and right before he went overseas, we sat in the bowling alley listening somberly as he fed nickel after nickel into the jukebox, playing only one song, "When My Blue Moon Turns to Gold Again." We then walked over to the old Dixie Highway, where he hitched a ride to Dallas that would take him off to an unknown fate. To this day he still talks about watching my mother as she walked down the highway waving to him until the car got out of sight. We did not know until some time later that he had overextended his leave and was AWOL (the military parlance for absence without leave).

Religion remained all-important to my mother. She listened faithfully to the radio preachers and went to the tent revivals when they came to town. The years immediately following the war marked the age of such charismatic evangelists as Oral Roberts, A. A. Allen, and Jack Coe, who attracted immense throngs with their messages of divine healing and biblical prophecy. An unending stream of events seemed to bear out the proof of the ominous sermons that they conveyed. The euphoria that accompanied victory over the Axis powers was soon dimmed by the rise of militant communism and the knowledge that the Soviet Union had developed an atomic bomb. A third world war no longer seemed unthinkable. The birth of Israel in 1948 only added to the conviction that the prophecies in the Book of Revelations were being fulfilled, that the end of time was near, and that Christ's return was imminent. Pentecostalism, in short, had come to town but was as scary as ever. Its messages could even be heard in some of the hillbilly songs that received airplay in the late 1940s. Roy Acuff, for example, sang "This World Can't Stand Long," the Bailes Brothers declared that "We're Living in the Last Days Now," and Molly O'Day agreed, with her interpretation of "Matthew 24," that the end was "nearing every door."

Except for having to make new friends, I was immensely happy with our move to town. My attendance at a country school called Dixie, just outside Tyler, somewhat cushioned my transition to town life. There I encountered a number of students whose family histories were much like mine. As a fat kid, of course, I always had to contend with a painful self-consciousness, but I found ready retreats in the radio, sports, popular culture, reading, and country music. A sports fanatic at the time, I bought every sport magazine that was available, memorized reams of statistics, and followed the exploits of the local Class C baseball team, the Tyler Trojans. Although I was usually very shy (and was in fact voted "Most Bashful" in my tenth-grade class at Dixie), I nevertheless loved to show off, particularly in spelling matches and singing. My debut as a solo singer came during a school assembly at Dixie, where in my boy soprano voice, I sang Tex Ritter's "Gold Star in the Window," a lament about a son killed in military action.

Since Dixie curiously had only ten grades, I transferred to Tyler High School in my junior year. In Tyler I encountered a considerably more class-differentiated environment, with kids from Dixie, Noonday, Chapel Hill, and other nearby country schools sharing classrooms with the sons and daughters of bankers, oilmen, and businessmen. It was not uncommon to sit side by side in class with the future rose queens and duchesses of the city's annual and elite Rose Festival. I didn't always spend my hours at Tyler High School (now John Tyler) productively (I spent too much time daydreaming about the Grand Ole Opry and the New York Yankees), but I was fortunate in having Miss Sara Marsh as my twelfth-grade English teacher and having the Carnegie Public Library available for browsing while waiting for Daddy to get off work at East Texas Auto Supply. Miss Marsh was the most demanding teacher I ever had—a comma blunder guaranteed an F even if the rest of your essay was perfect—but she sharpened my writing skills and encouraged critical thought. At the Carnegie Public Library I discovered Irving Stone's *Clarence Darrow for the Defense*, a biography that has won few words of praise from professional historians but which nevertheless shaped my sympathies for organized labor and radicalism. Very briefly, I toyed with the idea of becoming a lawyer, but only if I could spend all of my time promoting social justice and defending unpopular causes.

With my high school years ending, my thoughts were riveted on going on to college. At a junior year career day convocation, I had told one of the interviewers that I wanted to go to the University of Texas in Austin to become a history teacher. My parents, however, remained socially conservative, poor but proud, afraid of large ambitions, and reluctant to support any venture that might ultimately cause me disappointment or frustration. Perhaps they were also wary that I might breach the unthinkable but unspoken social code, "Don't get above your raisin'." Above all, they were leery of a venture that might be too costly for their working-class pocketbooks. My mother tried to talk me into taking a six-month course at one of the local business colleges in preparation for a career as a bookkeeper. That kind of career would enable me to wear a white shirt each day and live a much more secure and comfortable life than had ever been available to them. Besides, I could save some money and then go on to the university. Remaining stubbornly persistent, I was permitted to attend the local Tyler Junior College. On the first day of registration, my father dropped me off at 7:00 A.M. at the college on his way to work, but only after leaving me with these words of advice: "Son, don't sign up for anything big, like lawyer."

During my two years at Tyler Junior College, I buckled down to work with a passion that I had seldom displayed in high school. Somehow, this experience caught my attention as being much more serious than anything that had come before. Two of my teachers were immensely influential: Dr. Wiley Jenkins, who taught American history, and Dr. J. C. Henderson, who taught biology and chemistry. Actually, Professor Jenkins rarely taught history but instead spent almost every class hour talking in a pompous but endearing way about football and current events. Nevertheless, his comments whetted my interest in public affairs and sharpened my intellectual curiosity. Professor Henderson was a gentle human being and a marvelous lecturer. I had little aptitude for either biology or chemistry, but he impressed me with his ability to give an absorbing and highly detailed lecture from notes sketched on only one three-by-five card. Most important, both men were strong Democrats at a time when Tyler, and the nation, was shifting toward the Republican Party (today, the Democrats don't even bother to run candidates in Tyler). My encounter with an article included in a political science anthology—Henry Steele Commager's "Who Is Loyal to America?"—furthered my commitment to dissent and critical thought. The populist, New Deal philosophy inherited from my parents was gradually evolving into liberalism.

Although academic studies now consumed much of my time, my deep love for country music never wavered. The years that ran roughly from 1945 to 1956 marked the heyday of what we now call "hard country music." Even such "soft," quasi-pop singers as Eddy Arnold used instruments that seemed to evoke the ambience and sound of the barn dance or honky-tonk, and the music seemed redolent of working-class experience. Today as I listen to the recordings of that era, I hear how effectively the songs mirrored the aspirations and frustrations of people who were trying to adapt to new jobs and new ways of living. Electric amplification was becoming the norm in almost every style of country music, but fiddles and steel guitars abounded in virtually all performances. My brothers and I still described the music as "hillbilly," but the terms "country" or "country and western" (reflecting the concerns of those who longed for respectability) were becoming the preferred labels of both musicians and "music industry" representatives. Not only did the music still express the often ambivalent concerns of a culture in transition, it was also intruding into markets and regions where it had never before been heard. Recalling that era in one of his songs, when his own musical tastes were being shaped, Merle Haggard declared that "Hank and Lefty crowded every jukebox." He concluded with, "That's the way it was in '51."

Hank Williams also figured strongly in my life. As songwriter Dallas Frazier phrased it, "I never met old Hank but we were awful close." Hank had come to Tyler in about 1949 as part of the cast of the Louisiana Hayride, a Saturday night show that normally broadcast from Shreveport but which occasionally took its programs to other cities in KWKH's listening orbit. This particular night Hank, Kitty Wells, the Bailes Brothers, and other Hayride regulars sang from the stage of the Tyler High School auditorium. Even though Hank's songs soon became popular all over the nation and even moved into the repertoires of sophisticated lounge singers like Tony Bennett, it always seemed to me that he was a profoundly "rural" singer and that he understood the little anxieties and frustrations that troubled my teenage soul.

I heard all the performers, old and new, who sang on such radio barn dances as the Grand Ole Opry, Shreveport's Louisiana Hayride, and Dallas's Big D Jamboree, or whose records were played on such shows as Hal Horton's "Hillbilly Hit Parade" in Dallas. Disc jockeys like Horton, Tom Perryman in Gladewater, or Paul Kallinger down on the Mexican border still affected informal down-home styles, peppered their speech with rustic aphorisms, and conveyed the impression that they and the musicians they played on their shows were part of your family. Longing to know more about the stars and to learn their songs, I bought *Country Song Roundup* magazine and any other music journal that became available. Of course, I did not realize that I was unconsciously involved in research that could be of great use in my later formal study, so I tended to clip out certain interesting or appealing songs and then discard the rest of the magazine.

While new performers were always interesting to me, my preferences turned increasingly to older entertainers and their styles and to the roots of the music I loved. Fortunately, one of those legendary performers, the Grand Ole Opry's Uncle Dave Macon, came to Tyler in about 1949 as part of a tent show that also included Curly Fox, Texas Ruby, and comedian Lazy Jim Day. At about the same time we obtained our first record player, part of a radio console purchased from a railroad salvage store. Among the cache of 78 rpm records that I brought into the house was an album of songs by Jimmie Rodgers, the Mississippi Blue Yodeler, first recorded in the late 1920s and early 1930s, but whose recordings since his death in 1933 had largely lain dormant. Rodgers had been country music's first star and was now widely heralded as "the Father of Country Music." From this point on my search for the music of the pioneer performers, or for what I considered to be "real" country music, became virtually a crusade.

If I had any illusions about the permanence of the country music that prevailed during the early 1950s, I should have known better because of two events that occurred early in that decade. Rhythm-and-blues tunes by the likes of Fats Domino, Chuck Berry, Clyde McPhatter, Big Mama Thornton, and Lloyd Price dominated the jukebox at the Wigwam, the little student center at Tyler Junior College. While I devoted my nickels to such songs as "Jambalaya" and "I Don't Hurt Anymore," my classmates more often listened to such items as "Honey Love," "One Mint Julep," and "Work with Me, Annie." In July 1954 Elvis Presley made his first Sun record in Memphis, the first dramatic evidence that young southern whites were beginning to appropriate the rhythms of black performers and to incorporate them into other musical styles. By the end of the year Elvis was making personal appearances throughout East Texas and was drawing enthusiastic hordes of young fans. The full implications of these stirrings of social revolution, in both the habits of young white people and in the nature of American popular music, were not immediately apparent to me. As I set out toward Austin and the University of Texas in September, having completed the two years at Tyler Junior College, I probably felt that the kind of country music I knew and loved would last forever. Hank Williams was now dead, but hard country singers like Kitty Wells and Webb Pierce were still turning out their heart-wrenching laments of hard times and lost loves.

By September 1954, thanks to a thirty-five dollar a semester tuition fee and money derived from the sale of Lone Star Steel stock, I was in Austin and enrolled as a history major at the University of Texas. My parents never anticipated that my college stay would extend to eight years, through the bachelor's, master's, and PhD degrees, nor were they ever able to respond conclusively when relatives would periodically ask, "Is Billy about through down there at the university?" The inevitable second question was even harder to answer: "Do you think he'll ever do anything with all that education?" I'm not sure that I could answer the question either, but I was nevertheless having the time of my life. The move to Austin was liberating in many ways, even though I had no automobile and generally made the trip from home to the Capital City via Continental Trailways bus or by catching a ride with a student from Tyler. I encountered Mexican food for the first time, met my first genuine atheist (a graduate student who lived across the tiny hall in the garage apartment where I lived), spent countless hours at Home Drug drinking coffee and talking politics and literature, gloried in the athletic triumphs of the Longhorns, reveled in the rich resources of the giant University of Texas Library, and, of course, went to as many country music shows as my limited means and transportation would permit. Lest I be misunderstood, I also went to class faithfully and was fortunate enough to take two courses with legendary historian of the West, Walter Prescott Webb.

Any lingering doubts about Elvis Presley's effects on American youth and country music were completely dispelled on the night of January 19, 1956, when I saw him at the Austin Coliseum. I had gone to the Coliseum to see and hear my current hero, Hank Snow, but was appalled when his show was cut short in order to accommodate the huge crowd standing outside who had come to hear Presley. I was troubled even more when I saw the reactions made by many of the young women in the auditorium when Presley made his most blatant sexual movements. Old-fashioned prudishness, of course, explains my discomfort at the sight of women screaming and rushing the stage. In my double-standard way of viewing human emotions, I felt that women should not behave in such a manner or aggressively express their sexuality.

Otherwise, my negative feelings arose from the fear that Presley's style was endangering "traditional" forms of country music. His performances evoked positive reactions from his youthful audience, and the country music industry was already rushing to find other musicians who could successfully emulate his success. For a brief period my suspicions seemed confirmed, and fiddles, steel guitars, and hard-country singing styles began to disappear from jukeboxes, records, and radio shows. As traditional country music faded from public view, my own quest for older-sounding or roots-based musicians intensified. I delighted in any evidence that the older forms still thrived, or that younger musicians, such as George Jones and Ray Price, were able to create new and commercially viable sounds out of older materials. Like many concerned fans, I also retreated to bluegrass and found both musical and spiritual satisfaction in its acoustic-based high lonesome sound. I will never forget the thrill I felt when I first heard the Stanley Brothers singing "White Dove" and "Gathering Flowers for the Master's Bouquet."

Above all, I continued to express my affection for country music through my own singing, which did not begin in earnest until 1956 when graduate school contributed to the illusion that I had a lot of free time on my hands. I bought a used Stella guitar from a budding novelist and English graduate student Bill Casey, but until I learned to pick passably enough, I generally relied on other people for instrumental accompaniment. Singing at beer parties for countless hours, I wore out the fingers of good friends Tom Crouch and Willie Benson, who strummed as I sang. I took immense pride in knowing hundreds of songs, mostly sad ones such as "Unloved and Unclaimed," "Wreck on the Highway," and "The Knoxville Girl," and described myself as the Tragic Balladeer. Listeners often asked me, "Why is country music so sad?" mistaking my personal preferences for the total country song bag.

Sometime during this period my browsings in the Austin Public Library brought me in contact with the Folkways *Anthology of American Folk Music*, the most important body of reissued commercial folk recordings made in the twentieth century. Based on a collection amassed by Harry Smith and graced by his quirky and idiosyncratic liner notes, this assemblage of hillbilly, blues, gospel, and Cajun recordings from the late 1920s and early 1930s introduced a large number of young people to the world of American roots music. I was particularly impressed with the collection because it lent validity to hillbilly music by linking it to the word "folk," a term with immense snob appeal. I found some familiar names from my childhood, such as Uncle Dave Macon, the Carter Family, and the Skillet Lickers, and encountered for the first time such vital entertainers as Charlie Poole, Buell Kazee, Clarence Ashley, and Kelly Harrell. Like many other young fans and singers, I soon began singing songs—such as "Wagoner Lad" and "Engine 143"—that I had learned from the *Anthology*. To our additional delight, we soon discovered that many of these performers, who had either been unknown or presumed dead, were still alive and still capable of making good music.

Although I could always be coaxed into singing at a party or beer bust, my chief venue for music-making by the end of the 1950s was a little bar in North Austin called Threadgill's, a converted filling station that reputedly had received the first beer license in Travis County when Prohibition was repealed in 1933. The owner and genial host was a man named Kenneth Threadgill, who knew a storehouse of Jimmie Rodgers songs and other old-time pieces, and who could sing and yodel them with a sweet but bell-like clarity. Threadgill's was basically a working-class bar, but by the end of the 1950s it began to be caught up in what has since been described as "the folk music revival," first when a few of my graduate school friends (Stan Alexander, Ed Mellon, and Willie Benson) and I began singing there on a weekly basis and, next, when offshoots from the university folk-music club, including the now-legendary Janis Joplin, arrived a few years later. We sat around the big circular tables in front of the bar and, without the aid of microphones or electrical amplification, sang our hearts out until Kenneth Threadgill felt sufficiently caught up with his work to join us with a few of his favorite songs.

The folk revival began in earnest in 1958 when the Kingston Trio recorded their immensely popular version of an old North Carolina murder ballad, "Tom Dooley." Everywhere, young people began trying to learn the guitar, banjo, or some other string instrument and began experimenting with traditional or traditional-sounding songs. The quest for "authenticity" inspired some people to look beyond the Kingston Trio and other singers like them who seemed pale and superficial, and to search for *real* folk songs performed by *real* folk musicians. That search inevitably led fans to the old 78 rpm records of the 1920s and 1930s—that is, to the same kind of material heard on Harry Smith's collection—and to the contemporary musicians who were trying to re-create that tradition. In that same pivotal year of 1958 a trio of young New York–born musicians (Mike Seeger, John Cohen, Tom Paley) began their career as the New Lost City Ramblers, playing string-band tunes and ballads and love songs learned from old hillbilly records. Through Folkways recordings, numerous concerts in folk-music clubs and on college campuses (including the University of Texas), and a songbook that contained the bulk of their recorded songs, the Ramblers inaugurated a revival of old-time string band music that has endured in America.

I became absorbed in all of the elements of the folk revival and bor-rowed from everything I heard—anything that seemed old. All the while, I thought that what I sang was more "authentic" than most of what I was hearing. I was skeptical of any so-called folk singer who did not grow up in a southern working-class environment and was suspicious of anyone who did not realize that people like Ernest Tubb, Hank Williams, and Kitty Wells were the natural inheritors of the hillbilly tradition that was now in fashion. Consequently, when I sang I generally made a point of singing songs like "Driftwood on the River," "Mansion on the Hill," and other products of the modern commercial country music era. Everyone I knew abhorred the music of the Kingston Trio, the Brothers Four, and other acts that seemed to be little more than pale reproductions of music borrowed from the "real" folk. On the other hand, we listened avidly to the New Lost City Ramblers, and I even got to jam with them one night at Threadgill's during their Austin visit. We sometimes couldn't resist poking fun at these northern boys, who had only recently discovered *our* music, but we borrowed freely from their storehouse of recorded songs, bought their songbook, and carefully pored over the liner notes of their albums. The folk revival encouraged historical documentation, and record liner notes became valuable sources of information concerning early hillbilly recording sessions. The Ramblers usually listed the sources from which they obtained their songs, providing the names of recording artists and record release numbers. While we enjoyed New Lost City Ramblers performances, we longed to hear the music of the people who had inspired them—Charlie Poole, Gid Tanner and the Skillet Lickers, Dock Boggs, the Monroe Brothers, and other early hillbilly musicians—and at least a few of us yearned to know more about the culture that had produced this music. My research into this music was punctuated by a strong sense of personal pride, because I was convinced that I was delving into the culture of my own people and, in the process, lending dignity and worth both to their lives and to their contributions to the American musical legacy.

Despite my immersion in the music and culture of hillbilly music, it scarcely entered my mind that this passion could become the basis of an academic career. Another graduate student, Ronald Davis, it is true, was preparing a doctoral dissertation on opera, but that topic was eminently respectable. Most of my history graduate-student friends had embarked on political or economic studies, and few of them really enjoyed what they were doing. Topics like "abandoned short line railroads" or "Texas crude oil pipe lines" (the names of actual theses written at the time in the University of Texas history department) might make useful contributions to knowledge, but they could hardly engage the full emotional and intellectual capacities of the researcher. After I passed my preliminary examinations for the PhD in November 1960, I began a tentative search for a suitable dissertation topic, probably in the realm of southern labor history. No topic had firmly coalesced in my mind when I rode to Houston in December with Joe B. Frantz, my supervising professor, and a few graduate-student friends to see the Longhorns play Alabama in the Bluebonnet Bowl football game. I was already notorious in the history department for being a country music fanatic and had even written a few political parodies and topical songs such as "The Ballad of John Glenn." That notoriety, and the fact that I was able to sing just about any country song requested on the way to the game, seems to have prompted Professor Frantz to ask me the fateful question, "Why don't you write a history of Nashville Music Publishing?"

Frantz had only a casual interest in country music and probably thought that its cultural importance was marginal at best. But as a business historian (a specialty that he shared with his expertise in western history), he could only be impressed with the economic vigor that the music was then demonstrating. Energized by a new and aggressive trade organization called the Country Music Association (CMA), and by a group of emerging publishing houses and recording studios that prompted the description of Nashville as Music City, U.S.A., country music had rebounded from the blows dealt by rock and roll and was becoming an economic phenomenon that was respected around the world. I had mixed feelings about this economic success story. I was pleased that the men and women of country music were enjoying a prosperity that had long been denied them, but I was troubled by some of the diluted styles that had been passing as country music. I wanted to go far beyond the music-business history that Professor Frantz envisioned, to write a study that would encompass the full dimensions of the country music story, would delve into questions of identity and authenticity, and would demonstrate the vital link between the music and southern working-class people. I doubt that I ever mentioned my ambitious goals to Professor Frantz, but fortunately, in the years that followed, he never resisted my decision to write a general history.

My venture into formal country music scholarship, then, was clearly a consequence of events that occurred in the late 1950s and early 1960s. Almost nothing in my academic training prepared me to write about country music. I had no courses in anthropology, folklore, or music, and my history courses, although strongly concentrated on southern subjects, scarcely delved into the lives of plain people. Fortunately, I discovered the writings of Frank Owsley, Howard Odum, Bell Wiley, and W. J. Cash on my own. Cash's *Mind of the South* was revelatory because, although his purview was that of Piedmont Carolina, it sounded like he had an intimate insight into the lives and thinking of my own people. Without the folk-music revival, though, few people in academia would have recognized the legitimacy of the study and documentation of roots music, and without the resurgence of country music as a vital economic phenomenon Professor Frantz probably would not have suggested the utility of a study of the genre. More than likely, I would have become a southern political or economic historian and would have remained a frustrated fan of country music.

Although the immediate social context in which I lived made it possible for a country music history to be written, the chief perceptions and overall thesis of my work were shaped years earlier by my East Texas experiences. I could not separate the music from the memories of growing up poor on an East Texas cotton farm and finding escape and diversion in the sounds of hillbilly music. I could not forget the thrill of being awakened and energized early each morning by the radio sounds of a fiddle, steel guitar, and lonesome voice, or of hearing my mother express her loneliness through the words of a gospel song. Nor could I ever forget the importance that the music held for the working people whose sacrifices made it possible for me to attend college and to live a life of relative ease. Their story and that of country music were closely intertwined. That story did not cease when communities like Galena vanished. The music followed the people into the cities and into blue-collar life, and it now accompanies their children and grandchildren as they try to cope with suburban existence and ways of life that seem alien to me. Whether the music can survive this evolutionary process with any recognizable identity left intact is anybody's guess. Clearly, the questions of identity and authenticity that intrigued me forty years ago, when I diverged from the task assigned by Professor Frantz, continue to inspire and stimulate my scholarship. And it is immensely satisfying to have converted a lifelong passion into a field of academic study, and to be as ardently committed to it as I was in the beginning.

CHAPTER 2

NEITHER ANGLO-SAXON NOR CELTIC
The Music of the Southern Plain Folk

The material found here was first given as a lecture at a symposium at South-eastern Louisiana University in Hammond, in 1996, devoted to a retrospective of Frank Owsley's *Plain Folk of the Old South* (1949). The lecture later appeared as an essay in *Plain Folk of the South Revisited* (1997). Owsley, who had actually said very little about music in his ground-breaking study, was not alone among students of the South when it came to the subject of music. Most of his con-temporaries had either neglected the subject or had clouded its identity under a murky veil of romance or half-truths. My intent was to argue that the music, which was central to people's survival and aspirations, was a product of working folk's grappling with economic, geographic, and social change. It did not develop in some isolated corner of Appalachia among a people of pristine culture with an undiluted racial strain. While African American influence was profound, and inextricably linked to the culture of southern white people, I have clung to the definition of plain folk culture originally used by Owsley. This is a study, then, of the music made and cherished by white southerners. Southern working-class music history still calls for further research, but its story is gradually being well documented and told by such students as Edward Ayers, James Cobb, Barry Mazor, Nolan Porterfield, Tom Piazza, Patrick Huber, and Charles Hughes.

ONE CAN SCARCELY CONCEIVE OF AMERICAN MUSIC IN THIS CENTURY without thinking of the profound role played by southern-born white musi-cians. Beginning in the 1920s with Gene Austin, the pioneer pop crooner from Sherman, Texas, and Jimmie Rodgers, the yodeling ex-brakeman from Meridian, Mississippi, a continuing array of white southern musicians have participated prominently in the music culture of America. A few of them, like Gene Autry, Bob Wills, Hank Williams, Bill Monroe, Merle Travis, Willie Nelson, Johnny Cash, and Elvis Presley, have created major stylistic genres that are known around the world. The burgeoning of country music in our own time, when entertainers like the Oklahoma superstars Garth Brooks and Reba McEntire achieve media recognition that rivals or surpasses that of performers in any other style of music, provides dramatic evidence of the appeal exhibited by southern-born musicians. An article in the *New Republic* once described country music as "the voice of America," and although the essayist noted that performers from the North and Canada participated prominently in a musical genre that had become increasingly affluent and middle-class, it nevertheless seems significant that twenty-six of the thirty-one entertainers who were mentioned came from either the original Confederate states or from Oklahoma.[1]

The prominence of these southern entertainers, most of whom have working-class backgrounds, seems all the more remarkable when we recall that the music of their ancestors was scarcely known, or valued, by Americans at large or by the southern elites until the years running roughly from 1910 to 1917. In contrast, the music of black southerners had moved long before that time, in various manifestations, into the consciousness of Americans everywhere and had even become a powerful presence in the popular culture of Great Britain. Whether displayed in the caricatured forms popularized by the blackface minstrels or the "coon" songs, or in the irresistible rhythms of black ragtime pianists, southern music seemed to be African American music. Speaking of still another southern black-derived musical form, Anton Dvorak, the Czech composer, who first heard such music after he came to the United States in 1892, argued that the Negro spirituals represented the very essence of the American soul.[2]

John Lomax's *Cowboy Songs and Other Frontier Ballads* (1910) and Cecil Sharp and Olive Dame Campbell's *English Folk Songs from the Southern Appalachians* (1917) were the first significant collections of music that in any way reflected the culture of southern white folk.[3] These collections, however, touched only the geographic fringes of the South—the Appalachians on the east and the Texas Plains on the west—and they concentrated primarily on the music of those regions and only incidentally on the people who produced and preserved it. Lomax and Sharp were

*This picture of an unidentified fiddler and a banjo player
from Taccoa, Georgia, reminds us of the homegrown
sources of commercial country music.
Photograph courtesy of the Vanishing Georgia Collection,
Georgia Archives, Morrow, Georgia (STP 050).*

actually more inclusive in their treatment than most of the collectors who came immediately after them, and they did often identify their informants. Reading the commentary or head notes that accompanied Sharp's selections, one would know, for example, that Jane Gentry of Hot Springs, North Carolina, supplied him with sixty-four items, his single largest cache of ballads.[4] As had been the fate of the Negro spirituals in the late nineteenth century, the Appalachian ballads and cowboy songs were first made available to a rather small and educated group of Americans, and in versions made palatable to middle-class tastes by the classical concert styles of musicians like Howard Brockway, Loraine Wyman, and John Jacob Niles who had been trained at the Juilliard School of Music or other approved centers of high-art education. Confined to performances before women's clubs, music appreciation groups, college audiences, and other devotees of "serious music," this body of music reached the ears of few Americans, and in styles that were far removed from those heard in the communities where the songs had been collected.

Whether presented on the pages of a published song collection or in the repertoire of a concert musician, the music of the southern white folk seemed interesting but nevertheless in danger of extinction. Although Cecil Sharp asserted that he had found himself "in a community in which singing was as common and almost as universal a practice as speaking" and that he could get what he wanted from "pretty nearly every one . . . young and old," he still conveyed the impression that the best of their music would soon be gone, and that it was being replaced by inferior products of the street and music hall.[5] Collectors and concert musicians alike went about their work with a sense of urgency, feeling that the music and the culture that had sustained it were both dying.

While the seeming archaicism of southern folk music was one source of its appeal, its identification with a presumed racially homogeneous culture was an additional attraction to those who saw America's own supposed racial purity disappearing in the years surrounding World War I. The southern mountains seemed to be one of the last remaining repositories of Anglo-Saxonism in the United States, a quality that stood out in bold relief when compared with the nation's large cities and their hordes of blacks and "new immigrants" who were already changing American culture in dramatic ways. The suggestion that the allegedly backward southern mountaineers were really "our contemporary ancestors," a group of people whose dialects and folkways presumably provided evidence of the nation's pure Anglo-Saxon origins, was not likely to effect any significant political changes in American life.[6] But it was a romantically appealing image and a satisfying rationale for the preservation of the ballads and other remaining cultural artifacts of that society. The journalist William Aspenwall Bradley was so impressed by his sojourn in the southern mountains in 1915 and by the conservatism of life there as to remark that "wandering through the mountains, one now knew he might at any time meet a company of Robin Hood's men encamped in some sequestered cove."[7]

A few years later two of the pioneer promoters of southern folk festivals, Jean Thomas and John Powell, continued to view southern folk arts as survivals of early English culture. The self-styled "traipsing woman," Jean Thomas, who was a longtime court reporter in the Kentucky hills and the founder of the Singin' Gatherin', even saw the ghost of Anne Boleyn lingering in the songs that had endured in the southern hills. Thomas built a cottage, the "Wee House in the Wood," whose gateway and entrance were "modeled after the cottage entrance of Anne Boleyn." Her rationale, she insisted, was that Boleyn "was the mother of Queen Elizabeth and because many of our Kentucky mountain ballads and folk dances date back to the time of Queen Elizabeth, this replica of the English cottage has been built to recreate the scene where our balladry was cradled." Powell, a nationally known classical pianist and composer from Richmond, Virginia, was not nearly so prone to flights of romantic fantasy as was Ms. Thomas. He was one of the first collectors of southern folk music to argue that examples of such music survived outside the mountains and had in fact been preserved across class lines. Powell, though, was explicit in his assertions that southern balladry arose from an Anglo-Saxon past and that this purportedly superior racial component linked the upper-class southerners to their poor white neighbors. He argued further that "our only hope as a nation lies in grafting the stock of our culture on the anglo-saxon root," and that "familiarity with this noble inheritance would revive and confirm in ourselves those traditions and feelings which are the crown of our race and assure to us as well that supreme glory, a nationhood unparalleled in the annals of time."[8]

Terms like "Anglo-Saxon" and "Elizabethan" appeared frequently in discussions of southern folk music despite the fact that the English were not alone in the settling of Appalachia or other regions of the South. Students of Appalachian balladry, who far outnumbered any other kind of folk song specialists, seemed to assume that the mountains had been populated exclusively by Englishmen or that English-descendants had overwhelmed every other group who came to the region. Cecil Sharp, for example, recognized the presence of Scotch-Irish and border elements in the southern hills and nevertheless entitled his epochal book *English Folk Songs from the Southern Appalachians.* The musical influence of the Scotch-Irish people, the largest group to settle the backcountry South, seldom received mention in any academic discussion of southern folk music as late as the 1960s.

My doctoral dissertation of 1965 described the music of the white South as "Anglo-Celtic" in an effort to suggest that the music of the region drew

upon resources from all over the British Isles.[9] Some writers and academicians have since gone well beyond that assumption, though, and have
argued that Celtic influences lie at the core of plain-folk music and such
commercial descendants as country, bluegrass, and Cajun. We have been
assured on record-liner notes, in the public statements of a few country
musicians, and in at least one book that Celtic musical traits/styles can easily be discerned in the playing and singing of southern country musicians.
Buttressed by that faith, and emboldened perhaps by an enmity toward any
and all things English, or perhaps by the desire to deny the prominence of
black influence in country music, such observers imagine the strains of a
Celtic bagpipe whenever they hear the drone of a country fiddle or banjo.
They seek cultural legitimacy for modern country music by linking it to
an ancient tradition but instead obscure our understanding of it under a
murky veil of romanticism.[10]

The narrow perspectives of the early collectors and concert interpreters inhibited an understanding of the total picture of plain-folk music. The
music they valued, and which they adapted to the concert stage, seemed to
be an archaic expression of a stagnant or dying culture. By concentrating
on a special type of balladry—the remnants of those English and Scottish
items canonized in the late nineteenth century by the Harvard scholar
Francis James Child—they ignored the wide breadth of southern folk
music, and by emphasizing the secular material in the folk-song bag they
underestimated the extent and influence of the religious songs that lay at
the heart of southern folk culture. Above all, they neglected the largest
domain of plain-folk culture, that vast geographical interior of the South
that lay between the Appalachian Mountains and the Texas plains. Until
the publication of G. P. Jackson's epochal *White Spirituals in the Southern
Uplands* in 1933 and Arthur Palmer Hudson's *Folksongs of Mississippi
and Their Background* in 1934, no book-length study of the music of the
interior South had appeared.[11]

The commercial music industry, of course, had been making such music
available since the early twenties in radio broadcasts and phonograph
recordings, under such labels as "old-time," "old familiar," and "hillbilly."[12]
This music, however, did not conform very readily to the images of southern folk music conveyed earlier by the academic folklorists and concert

interpreters. One suspects that it was the taint of commercialism that did most to give academicians pause. True folk musicians, it was believed, were not concerned about money, nor did they seek economic rewards for their art. Of course, we really do not know what the academicians thought, since most of them tended to ignore the music of the radio hillbillies. The pioneer southern sociologist Howard Odum was one of the rare students of southern life who bothered to look at the music distributed on phonograph recordings and to take it seriously as a source for the understanding of the southern folk mind.[13] Probably more representative of the view of southern academicians was that of the historian Tom Clark, who, while singing the praises of the frontier fiddlers of Kentucky, could nevertheless refer to their commercial descendants as "the hillbilly rabble" of radio.[14]

It must be confessed that a handful of Yankees and even a few sophisticated city entertainers contributed to the making of the hillbilly music business, but most of the fiddlers, string bands, balladeers, and gospel singers who disseminated their art on radio broadcasts, phonograph recordings, and personal appearances came from the working-class South. And while their audience may have been diverse—extending in fact all the way to Australia and the frozen wilds of Alaska—its core came from what Arthur Smith, a cynical "dealer in sound-reproducing machines," described in 1933 as a "subterranean musical world" inhabited by "a great, unnumbered, inarticulate multitude" who were "interested, like children, in trains, wrecks, disasters, and crimes."[15] He of course was talking about the musical world of the southern plain folk.

Smith's condescending comments are not surprising. After all, he spoke of a culture that had never generated much sympathy or respect. Unlike the mountain South, this vast, interior South—the land of the plain folk—had supported slavery and the racial values that surrounded it and had contributed few soldiers to the Union army, thus eliciting little support from northern missionary or philanthropic groups. Long stigmatized as poor whites or rednecks, mainly by their more affluent neighbors, these people seemed never to have recovered from the war or from the economic dislocations that followed it. More important, they seemed to possess neither the ambition nor the skills to rise above economic distress, or the ability to overcome the catalog of well-publicized ills such as pellagra, hookworm, racial violence, religious bigotry, ignorance, and sharecropping that too often consumed their lives. They were responsible, it seemed, for the South's grossest political excesses and could therefore elicit the hatred of men like William Alexander Percy, the Mississippi Delta aristocrat who could say much later of his poor white neighbors, "I can forgive them as the Lord God forgives, but admire them, trust them, love them—never. At their door must be laid the disgraceful riots and lynchings gloated over and exaggerated by Negrophiles the world over."[16] Writing in 1917, the acerbic Baltimore journalist H. L. Mencken had bemoaned the collapse of the South's "great civilization," which had been despoiled by the "mob of peasants" who ascended from the wreckage left by the Civil War. The South had been inherited by "the poor white trash" in whose veins flowed "some of the worst blood of Western Europe."[17]

Musically, what had been the reality of life for those "lowly white folk" who lived in the "subterranean culture" described by Arthur Smith? Smith had been right about a few things. Contrary to romantic perceptions, the "lowly native white folk of the South" did not sing Stephen Foster songs, unless they were introduced to them in elementary-school songbooks. And they did like songs about disasters and outlaws. Those musical preferences were part of their British inheritance and were shared by their African American neighbors. Their culture, though, was considerably more complex than Smith, Mencken, or other critics suggested, and its reality was accurately summed up by neither its romancers nor its detractors. It was neither Anglo-Saxon nor Celtic, although elements from those traditions were present in its composite mixture. Southern folk culture and the music that emerged from it were anything but pure, and they certainly were not static. As blendings of cultures and influences, they represented a syncretic process that neither began nor ended when ethnic and racial cultures met in the colonial South; the process had begun on the borders of Great Britain and in West Africa, and it continued throughout the evolving social history of the South.[18]

Neither was the culture exclusively "folk," if one means by that a self-contained, socially ingrown society that drew exclusively upon its inherited cultural resources. This remarkably organic culture was built and preserved by a people who were sufficiently isolated and socially conservative to retain musical traits long after they had ceased to be fashionable elsewhere, but who were nevertheless remarkably receptive to new and externally originated musical influences, and prone to change them to fit their own tastes and styles. New songs and tunes were freely adopted, but styles of performance—which were deeply rooted in the culture of childhood—changed much more slowly. Sharp had noted in 1916 that when "the text of a modern street-song succeeds in penetrating into the mountains it is at once mated to a traditional tune."[19] Change nevertheless came both consciously and unconsciously.[20] Musical choices and styles of performance, as well as the definitions applied to songs, were shaped by the people's own aesthetic and moral criteria, at least until the early collectors, academicians, and commercial record producers suggested that some songs were more valuable than others. The early collectors sought surviving specimens of British material; the folk, in contrast, had embraced any kind of musical material that fit their social and aesthetic needs.[21]

A large body of British-derived material *did* survive among the southern folk, most often in fragmentary form but sometimes in much lengthier versions. Before this music came to America it had already moved frequently across regional and social boundaries and had been circulated by both professional and folk performers.[22] It came to America in the possession of the original settlers and in the repertoires of professional entertainers who arrived in this country with circuses, puppet shows, equestrian shows, and dramatic troupes. Southern folk culture was overwhelmingly oral, but it was no more resistant to the printed or written preservation of songs and ballads than its British forebears had been. The British folk wrote favorite songs down and pasted the broadside sheets to the walls of inns, alehouses, homes, barns, and cowsheds.[23] None of the broadside sheets seem to have survived among southern rural families, but favorite songs were laboriously written down in English composition books, five-cent tablets, or on loose sheets of paper ("song ballets"), and song lyrics were clipped from magazines or newspapers and posted on the pages of some old schoolbook.[24] Singers generally tried to perform or preserve a song exactly as they had first learned it (a marked difference from the practice followed by African American singers), but alterations in tunes and lyrics inevitably occurred, largely through faulty recollection or the imperfect comprehension of a word or phrase, but sometimes through the conscious decision to "improve" a song, tune, or dance. This inherited material, which varied from place to place, existed comfortably alongside the newer songs and dances, with young people generally being the crucial agents of change.

One can never know precisely who the principal makers of music were in folk communities, why they made music, or what effects their songs or performances had on their listeners. Gender roles, for example, cannot be conclusively determined. Performance, however, was governed largely by the etiquette surrounding the social hierarchical structure. Public performance—before a group larger than one's family—tended to be male-dominated and oriented most often toward the playing of instruments or solo dancing. Solo vocal performance, on the other hand, may have been female-dominated, and it tended to occur at home or in some other private setting, during work or relaxation, and was rendered usually for one's own personal enjoyment or that of family or a small circle of friends. In short, most singing was not perceived as "performance" at all.

Surprisingly few references to singing appear in nineteenth-century accounts of plain-folk life, except for some generalized observations about camp-meeting choruses, singing school performances, play-party refrains, or the group singing done around Civil War battlefield campfires.[25] Solo singing—lullabies to children, the individualized expression of private anguish, loneliness, or happiness, or an act of friendship or love for family or friends—may have been too personal to share with the casual stranger or observer who passed through the community.[26] Women certainly played crucial roles in the shaping of children's musical tastes and singing styles, and they may have been the chief preservers of ballads and other types of songs. Emma Bell Miles spoke only of the mountain women whom she knew in southeastern Tennessee, but her observations probably ring true for poor rural women throughout the South. Comparing mountain women with their men, who had "the adventures of which future ballads will be sung," Miles said that "the woman belong to the race, to the old people. . . . It is over the loom and the knitting that old ballads are dreamily, endlessly crooned."[27]

For both men and women, singing may often have been little more than a diversion or momentary release of emotional energy, or a means of soothing the spirits of a child. But the songs chosen, whether religious or secular, may have been vehicles for social expression or complaint.[28] For plain-folk women especially, singing, like the making of a quilt or the planting of a flower garden, could be a way of bringing a bit of beauty into a life that was often drab and colorless. In a patriarchal society that generally discouraged or repressed the articulation of private anguish, music also could exert a cathartic function, permitting the discharge of frustrations, pain, or rage. Alan Lomax argued that "the British folk songs most popular in the backwoods were not merely survivals from a body of lore handed on indiscriminately from overseas sources, but a selection from that lore of vehicles for fantasies, wishes, and norms of behavior which corresponded to the emotional needs of pioneer women in America. In fact, the universally popular ballads represented the deepest emotional preoccupations of women who lived within the patriarchal family system." Further evidence of the effects wrought by that system appear, he argued, "in the folklore of the Devil or the bogeyman," where "we can feel the bottomless fear aroused by ruthless, authoritarian father figures who have held women and children in thrall for centuries."[29] The bloody ballads and old lonesome tunes appealed across age and gender lines, and like the equally cherished violent fairy tales, they may have functioned as musical soap operas. Women, though, may have found a means to channel their aggression by singing about cruel mothers, hardhearted lovers, and spurned but murderous sweethearts.

The old ballads may have provided valuable, if unconscious, links to an important but slowly receding past, and important vehicles for the discharge of repressed emotions, but religious music was far more important in shaping the content, values, and style of southern folk music.[30] Music accompanied the dissenting Protestant sects who settled the southern backcountry, and it played an indispensable role in the implantation of evangelical Christianity in the South. Baptists, Methodist, New Light Presbyterians, and German pietistic groups conquered the southern backcountry with a democratic message that promised salvation for those who believed and with a body of music that borrowed freely from the rhythms of that sinful world that the dissenters hoped to redeem. From at least as early as the First Great Awakening, in the 1740s, when radical Baptists and dissenting Anglicans threw down their challenge to the established church and ruling hierarchy of Virginia, music was an indispensable weapon in the evangelizing of the South, making the region the greatest stronghold of evangelical Protestantism in the United States and bequeathing to the plain folk a body of songs and performance styles that have affected every secular genre of southern music.[31]

Religious music became an integral part of southern life, a constant presence from infancy to death. A southerner can escape neither religion nor the music associated with it. Most people learned to sing, or were encouraged to do so, in religious settings—in church, at revivals, or at singing conventions (the sites of the famous all-day-singing-with-dinner-on-the grounds)—and they learned the rudiments of harmony and the skill of reading music at church-sponsored singing schools and conventions where the shape-note method was taught, or by listening to the professional singers employed by the shape-note publishing houses.[32]

Southerners made their first contributions to the larger body of American music as early as 1805 when songs from the Kentucky camp meetings began to appear in pocket-sized songsters, and after 1813 when songs from those books reappeared in John Wyeth's *Repository of Sacred Music*, Part Second, a widely circulated northern songbook.[33] It is difficult to determine how early or to what extent southern singing styles affected those who heard them, but in the early contexts of the camp meetings and the shape-note publishing houses we encounter some of the most vital ingredients that shaped and defined the music of the plain folk: the easy confluence of secular melodies and religious lyrics (a tradition inherited from their British ancestors), the borrowing of African American styles and rhythms, and the employment of commercial methods of dissemination. The large throngs who attended the Kentucky revivals of the early 1800s thundered out spirituals in melodies that often bespoke tavern or street origins, lent them an emotional vocal color that may have been borrowed from the African Americans who were in their midst, and prolonged them (and made them easier to memorize) with techniques that also may have been borrowed from African American refrains and choruses. The songs, or others like them that were alleged to be products of the camp meetings, then appeared in printed songsters or tune books, where they began their task of permanently influencing the religious music of both northerners and southerners.

The southern folk religious repertory in the nineteenth century was a mélange of old and new practices, inherited from Great Britain or newly molded in the environment of America. Some congregations sang only the unadorned and musically unaccompanied psalms, utilizing only a few tested melodies, employing the practice of "lining the hymn," eschewing harmony, but embellishing the melody with odd vocal bendings and twists and extended notes that remained characteristic of southern backwoods singing. Long before the journey to America was made, British folk had contributed to the democratization of religious music by creating ballads that united popularly known melodies with spiritual or moralistic texts to describe the Christians' earthly travail or celebrate their joy, or warn the listener about the awful fate that awaited the transgressor. Plain-folk theology rejected the world and its vanity, but the folk could not forget, or resist the temptation to use, the secular tunes that had enriched their lives.

Coexisting with the psalms and folk spirituals, but soon supplanting them in the affections of the folk, were the newer composed hymns of Isaac Watts, Charles Wesley, and other professional composers, which spread with the revivals in the late eighteenth and the early nineteenth centuries. Powered largely by the enthusiastic singing of the Methodists, who took them to every corner of the southern frontier, such hymns as "Amazing Grace" and "When I Can Read My Title Clear" moved into the repertories of both white and black Christians. Laboring to make the songs even more singable, and striving to make them easier to learn, dissenting Protestants further democratized the performance of this music by altering melodies and adding refrains and choruses.

In the decades following the Civil War, a new variety of revival songs, described as "gospel" after 1875, entered the South in great numbers, accompanying the tours made by such popular evangelists and songleaders as Dwight Moody and Ira Sankey. In the South they became permanently enshrined in widely circulated songbooks. Written mostly by such northern songwriters as Philip Bliss, James McGranahan, and Charles Gabriel, these songs bore striking resemblance to the pop songs of the day with their sentimental imagery, evocations of pastoral simplicity, refrains, and singable melodies.[34] The alliance between pop and gospel only became stronger at the end of the century when the emerging Pentecostal movement successfully adapted the "worldly" sounds of brass bands, ragtime pianos, and jazzlike syncopations to their music. Ironically, while southerners labored to rebuild their war-ravaged economy and struggled to preserve the conviction that God was still on their side despite the humiliation of defeat, they often retreated to "Beautiful Isle of Somewhere," "Shall We Gather at the River," "Will the Circle Be Unbroken," and other northern-composed gospel songs to find solace and reassurance in a time of spiritual and social malaise.

Religious music did not simply offer emotional release; it also brought the business of music to the South. Whether motivated by spiritual zeal or by capitalistic enterprise, music merchandisers contributed to southerners many of their most cherished songs while also promoting innovations in performance style.

As new songs and styles emerged from the crucible of revivalism and from the sectarian competition that raged in the southern backcountry, singing-school teachers in the early 1800s came down out of Pennsylvania, through the Valley of Virginia, and into the lower South, holding ten-day schools where they taught the shape-note style of notation and the singing of four-part harmony. Publishers and songbooks representing the singing-school movement appeared as early as 1816 when Ananias Davisson published his *Kentucky Harmony*, one of the first "tunebooks" to appear in the South.[35] Often called "longboys" because their width exceeded their height, these cherished books became the nucleus of a regional publishing business that codified and circulated most of the South's religious music styles.

Although the most famous books emerging from the tradition, *Southern Harmony* and *The Sacred Harp*, exemplified the four-note fasola system, a style that had been familiar to Shakespeare, the shape-note business adapted easily and quickly to the seven-note do-re-mi fashion. Led by the Ruebush-Kieffer Company, which began operations in a Virginia town appropriately named Singer's Glen, the shape-note publishing business soon after the Civil War sent teachers and songbooks to every section of the South and laid the groundwork for the flourishing southern gospel business of our own time.[36] The most enterprising leader of the Ruebush-Kieffer empire, James D. Vaughan, from Lawrenceburg, Tennessee, ultimately made the most crucial innovations in the emerging gospel phenomenon. After the turn of the century he employed traveling quartets to popularize his songs and songbooks, and he made these performers and his business even more widely known through pioneering phonograph records and radio broadcasts.[37] With good reason, the *Singing News*, the premier journal of what is now called "southern gospel music," long carried Vaughan's photograph on its masthead.[38]

The early and continuing commercialization of southern religious music is a vivid reminder of the role played by popular culture and the marketplace in the lives of the southern folk. Songs, instrumental pieces, dances, instruments, comedy, and performance styles of popular or professional origin had moved constantly into the repertoires of the folk since long before they left the British Isles or Germany to begin new lives in the vastness of the southern frontier. The ultimate origins of the famous British ballads will never be known, but the most cherished of them all, "Barbara Allen," enjoyed a life in popular culture as early as 1666.[39]

In this country a wide array of traveling shows—equestrian, puppet, circus, dramatic, medicine, tent repertoire, blackface minstrel, and vaudeville—dispensed musical entertainment to city and village alike, while also constantly borrowing ideas from the folk culture in which it existed.[40] The cultural interchange that marked this relationship between town and country makes it next to impossible to determine precisely the origins of pre-twentieth-century forms of music and the styles with which they were performed. Music and dance often moved in a rather circular process of cultural transmission. A professional entertainer, for example, might pick up a catchy tune on the street, adapt it successfully into his stage act, and then reintroduce his altered version to the folk through his traveling show. Similarly, on an occasional jaunt into town, a country fiddler might learn a new tune from any number of sources, such as a circus brass band, a saloon piano player, a minstrel string band, or a phonograph recording displayed in a department store window. When the fiddler incorporated the tune into his own repertory, it began a new life as a "country" tune—that is, until some later professional entertainer "borrowed" it and reintroduced it to a "popular" audience, or until some folklorist "discovered" the tune and published it as a "folk song."[41]

New musical ideas journeyed to the rural South as inseparable products of the larger phenomenon of modernization. A powerful array of forces including the Civil War, the expansion southward of the nation's railway system, and the steady growth of cities after the war weakened the traditional hegemony of agriculture in the region, broadened the reach of the market system, and popularized the merchandise of the towns and the values of middle-class life.[42] As a colonial economy, the South had never had a popular culture that it could call its own. Even during the Civil War, when southerners consciously strove to produce an indigenous body of patriotic and nationalistic poetry, they more often embraced songs of northern vintage, such as "Lorena" and "Listen to the Mockingbird" and even adopted Ohio-born Dan Emmett's minstrel walkaround "Dixie" as their battle song.[43] The market/urban revolution of the late nineteenth century only increased the flow of songs, sheet music, instruments, and ultimately phonographs and phonograph recordings into the hinterlands of the South. When the commercialization of southern folk music began in the early 1920s, with the introduction of such music to a larger public through phonograph recordings and radio broadcasts, rural musicians already possessed a large body of music that came from the performances of blackface minstrels, tent performers, vaudeville entertainers, ragtime pianists, and other popular performers.[44] Songs of unabashed sentimentality, like "Little Rosewood Casket," "Put My Little Shoes Away," and "The Blind Child," coexisted happily with more lighthearted tunes like "Dill Pickle Rag" or bawdy saloon numbers like "Frankie and Johnny."[45] Even more significant, these songs moved, with little apparent sense of contradiction, into the repertories of rural performers alongside such venerable ballads as "Barbara Allen," "The House Carpenter," and "The Wife of Usher's Well."

Whatever their origin, the vocal songs, secular and religious, were clearly indispensable to the shaping of the total corpus of southern folk songs, and they continued to appear, often in fragmentary or greatly altered form, in the repertories of the radio hillbillies of the post-1920s era. We need to recall, however, that it has been in the area of performance style that white southern folk have made their most vital contributions to the music of the world. The multiplicity of sounds that form the southern style and set it apart from other regional expressions were a product of the total southern experience, and they were forged in a culture of interrelating ethnic, racial, religious, and commercial interaction. The church was a powerful shaper of values and a bottomless fount of songs and vocal styles. In the arena of public dance, white folk musicians learned to work with each other and, above all, to play for and strive to please audiences outside of their immediate families. The quest for an expanding audience broadened the repertories of musicians, sharpened their skills, and ultimately took their music to performing venues far removed from the rural South.

It is no accident that most of the rural musicians who made phonograph recordings and radio broadcasts in the early twenties were solo fiddlers or members of string bands who were not known for their singing. Most of them were heirs to the venerable frolic tradition of rural America and the British Isles, a tradition of country dancing celebrating rural harvests, religious and patriotic holidays, and the events that accompanied life's most important passages.[46] Evangelical religion might encourage guilt about the bodily pleasures of the dance while also questioning the morality and social utility of musicians who would squander their God-given time in the pursuit of frivolity, but dancing remained a passion in the rural South among rich and poor and black and white. Although the image of the drunken fiddler, along with the British-born legend of the musician who had sold his soul to the devil, remained strong in southern folklore and fiction, the fiddler was more venerated than scorned by rural southern folk. Undoubtedly, some fiddlers were mere wastrels, but their ranks also included respected politicians, judges, lawyers, preachers, and planters, as well as solid workingmen of all gradations—yeomen farmers, poor whites, free blacks, slaves. The fiddler reigned supreme at country dances held in houses great and small, and in the humble cabins of the slaves, from the Chesapeake Bay to the plains of Texas.[47]

The frolic tradition reaffirms the essential eclecticism of southern rural culture, and the varied sources of its music. The first fiddlers in colonial America (and the first recorded arrival in the South is that of John Utie, who came to Virginia in 1621)[48] unquestionably brought styles and tunes born in the British Isles and Western Europe. But on the southern frontier, or in the important cultural seedbed of western Pennsylvania,[49] they and their descendants came in almost immediate contact with other musicians, including fiddlers, from Germany, France, Spain, and Africa. As the geographical South expanded from its original base in the Chesapeake Bay to the last frontier of Texas, plain-folk southerners preserved their love for fiddle music and transmitted it to their children and grandchildren. White southerners clearly learned from one another, but they remained acutely aware of the presence of two other important bodies of fiddlers in the nineteenth century—African Americans and professional blackface minstrels. From both groups they absorbed songs and styles, as well as precedents for string band music, including the use of the five-string banjo as both a percussive and melodic instrument. The union of banjo and fiddle profoundly testified to the influence of commercial popular entertainment in the lives of the southern folk and was also powerfully emblematic of the fusion of African and European traits in their musical culture.[50]

Southern country fiddlers and the dancers for whom they played rejected no song or performance style that could successfully be transferred to the fiddle or adapted to the dance floor. Old World pieces of both folk and stage origin such as "Soldier's Joy" and "Fisher's Hornpipe" and homegrown tunes with similarly clouded identities such as "The Eighth of January," "The Arkansas Traveler," and "Durang's Hornpipe" competed for the affections of fiddlers with more recent tunes of minstrel, vaudeville, ragtime, and Tin Pan Alley origin such as "Listen to the Mockingbird," "Whistling Rufus," "Dill Pickle Rag," "Over the Waves," "Under the Double Eagle," "Ragtime Annie," and "Red Wing."[51]

The dances favored by southern country people displayed a similar history of cultural exchange across racial, ethnic, and social lines.[52] British settlers surely brought memories of Old World dances to the southern frontier, including not only dances that had been passed from parents to children but also steps that had been learned from professional entertainers or that had been imitations of courtly amusements. The group dances of the rural South, which usually included four or more couples, and which even some intensely religious people could tolerate because they involved no intimate frontal contact between dancers, were ultimately traceable to the interchange that went on between the upper-class English and French during the reign of King Charles II. Dances presumably of rural peasant English origin were taken to France in the 1660s, recodified in

French instruction books and given French names (such as cotillion and quadrille), and then transported back to England—and to America—by French dance instructors or others who had learned from them. In the United States some of the French vocabulary of instruction—such as allemande, promenade, and dos-i-dos—was preserved, but improvising Americans abandoned the books and instead employed a caller (who was often the fiddler himself) who shouted the movements to the dancers as they went through their paces. "Square dancing" (so-called because four couples constituted a square) thus began its venerated and enduring history as the dance of rural America.[53]

Individual step dancing also came to the rural South in a number of guises that prevent an accurate attribution of origins. The dances came in the repertories of professional stage entertainers (who invariably included solo dancing as part of their musical, comedic, or dramatic routines), in the pedagogy of the dance instructors, and in the possession of humble immigrants who learned them from God only knows where. In the United States the old dances were further preserved and modified and new ones were introduced and popularized, particularly by African Americans and by the innovative and perambulating blackface minstrels. Terms like "clog," "jig," "flatfeet," and "hornpipe," which may have referred to precisely differentiated steps in the Old World, were generally used indiscriminately in this country to describe any kind of solo step dance. The dance variations introduced by professional entertainers, although eagerly embraced by rural people, only complicate the task of dance historians. Whatever the source or fate of these dances, they persistently powered variations among fiddlers and other rural musicians who tailored their playing to fit the often-intricate movements of the steps and who preserved the tunes long after the dances themselves were forgotten. All country fiddlers today can play versions of tunes such as "Sailor's Hornpipe," "Durang's Hornpipe," or "Fisher's Hornpipe," but only rarely does one know that the term once described a solo quickstep dance performed by humble folk throughout the British Isles and by professional entertainers there and in the United States.[54]

When the components of its musical repertoire are reviewed, it becomes readily apparent that southern folk culture was neither homogeneous in its ethnic or racial composition nor static in its social development. This socially conservative culture, which changed slowly and often with dogged resistance, was nevertheless remarkably receptive to new and diverse musical ideas. By the end of the nineteenth century a broad array of songs, tunes, dances, and performance styles was available to the southern folk, often in substantially altered or modified forms. The origin of this musical material is irrelevant in assessing its relationship or value to plain folk musical culture. If a song, dance, or style resonated successfully with the aesthetic and social needs of the folk, the material became the property of the folk and was integrated into their culture.[55] Consequently, Old World ballads and dances coexisted amicably with northern-composed gospel songs, Tin Pan Alley parlor songs, and minstrel jigs and hornpipes. The European-derived fiddle preserved its dominance as a dance instrument, but by the end of the nineteenth century it had been joined in string bands by a variety of instruments that bespoke diverse ethnic and commercial origins—the African five-string banjo, the Spanish guitar, the Italian mandolin, the German harmonica and accordion, and the American-born autoharp, all of which were being made widely available by mail-order catalogs and other forms of commercial merchandising.[56]

Receptivity to musical innovation did not necessarily equate with social democracy or racial egalitarianism. The pre-twentieth-century South was a region plagued by the sins of racial injustice and economic inequality. Poor whites and blacks viewed each other with hostility even as they borrowed music from each other, and the social distance between rich and poor remained wide, and virtually impassable, even if musical styles sometimes crossed class barriers. Music could not empower the powerless, but it could give voice to the poor and lend dignity, self-respect, and emotional sustenance to their quest for survival. As the product of two centuries of migration across the southern frontier, and of successive and often traumatic adaptations to the changes that marked the transition from rural to urban-industrial life, the musical culture of the plain folk survived into the twentieth century to become the enduring inspiration for those who value traditional music. Under such guises as country, cowboy, Cajun, bluegrass, gospel, rockabilly, and southern rock, the music of the plain folk has moved around the world and has become virtually the musical voice of America itself. But that is another story.[57]

NOTES

1. Bruce Feiler, "Gone Country: The Voice of Suburban America," *New Republic*, February 5, 1996, 19–24.

2. For an overview of the musical contributions made by southerners, see Bill C. Malone, *Southern Music, American Music* (Lexington, Ky., 1979), and the music section of Malone, ed., *Encyclopedia of Southern Culture* (Chapel Hill, N.C., 1989).

3. John A. Lomax, *Cowboy Songs and Other Frontier Ballads* (New York, 1910); Cecil J. Sharp and Olive Dame Campbell, *English Folk Songs from the Southern Appalachians* (New York, 1917).

4. Sharp and Campbell, *English Folk Songs*, xi. Betty Smith has written a good account of Ms. Gentry's life and career in *Jane Hicks Gentry: A Singer among Singers* (Lexington, Ky., 1998).

5. Sharp and Campbell, *English Folk Songs*, viii.

6. The best discussion of the discovery of the southern Appalachians, and the consequent belief that they constituted a unique region of the United States, is Herbert D. Shapiro, *Appalachia on Our Mind: The Southern Mountains and Mountaineers in the American Consciousness, 1870–1920* (Chapel Hill, N.C., 1978).

7. William A. Bradley, "Song-Ballets and Devil's Ditties," *Harper's Monthly* (May 1915): 905.

8. Jean Thomas, *Ballad Makin' in the Mountains of Kentucky* (New York, 1939), 266; John Powell, untitled article in *Etude* 45 (May 1927): 349–50. David Whisnant describes people such as Thomas and Powell as "cultural interventionists" in his superb study *All That Is Native and Fine: The Politics of Culture in an American Region* (Chapel Hill, N.C., 1983).

9. Billy Charles Malone, "A History of Commercial Country Music in the United States, 1920–1965" (PhD diss., University of Texas–Austin, 1965).

10. Playing at a concert in Durham, North Carolina, on April 7, 1990, the old-time banjo player Dave Sturgill announced that he would play "Mississippi Sawyer" and said, "If you listen, you'll hear the sounds of the bagpipes." Historian Grady McWhiney has asserted that "even in the late twentieth century the continuity between the country music of Celts and Southerners is startling"; *Cracker Culture: Celtic Ways in the Old South* (Tuscaloosa, Ala., 1988), 120. In contrast, the leading scholar of ethnic music in the United States, Richard K. Spottswood, declared that "Irish music bears no relation to bluegrass and little more to southern country music as a whole"; Spottswood, *Bluegrass Unlimited* (May 1978): 47–50. The British folksinger Ian Robb argued that "for many people, the term Celtic is simply an ill-considered but convenient way to exclude English music. For them it is a geopolitical distinction, which outside of overtly anti-English songs has little to do with music"; Robb, "The British-North America Art," *Sing Out XL* (May–June–July, 1995): 80.

11. George Pullen Jackson, *White Spirituals in the Southern Uplands* (Chapel Hill, N.C., 1933); Arthur Palmer Hudson, *Folksongs of Mississippi and Their Background* (Chapel Hill, N.C., 1936).

12. For a general survey of the commercialization of southern white folk music, see Bill C. Malone, *Country Music, U.S.A.* (1968; rev. ed. Austin, Tex., 1985), and Archie Green, "Hillbilly Music: Source and Symbol," *Journal of American Folklore* 78 (1965): 204–28.

13. In *An American Epoch: Southern Portraiture in the National Picture* (New York, 1930), 201–203, Odum provided an extensive list of folk songs that came from both commercial and noncommercial sources, and he made no invidious distinctions between the two categories. His discussion of religious music (180–200) was exceptionally perceptive and sympathetic. Historian Daniel Joseph Singal, in *The War Within: From Victorian to Modernist Thought in the South, 1919–1945* (Chapel Hill, N.C., 1982), points to ambivalence in Odum and argues that he overlooked the "miseries of his own rural childhood" and tended to romanticize the people from whom he came (139).

14. Thomas D. Clark provided excellent vignettes of folk fiddlers in his history of the Kentucky River, *The Kentucky* (New York, 1942), but he expressed contempt for commercial hillbilly fiddlers (128).

15. Arthur Smith, "Hillbilly Folk Music" *Etude* 51 (1933): 154, 208.

16. William Alexander Percy, *Lanterns on the Levee: Recollections of a Planter's Son* (1941; rpr. Baton Rouge, La., 1973), 20.

17. H. L. Mencken, "Sahara of the Bozart," in *A Mencken Chrestomathy* (New York, 1920), reprinted in *The South since Reconstruction*, ed. Thomas D. Clark (Indianapolis, Ind., 1973), 551, 554.

18. For excellent discussions of the cultural, social, and ethnic intermingling that occurred in the British Isles prior to the settling of English North America, see Carl Bridenbaugh, *Vexed and Troubled Englishmen, 1590–1642* (New York, 1968), and David Hackett Fischer, *Albion's Seed: Four British Folkways in America* (New York, 1989). For discussions of similar interacting interrelationships in this country, see Mechal Sobel, *The World They Made Together: Black and White Values in Eighteenth-Century Virginia* (Princeton, N.J., 1987), and Alan Lomax, *The Folk Songs of North America* (New York, 1960).

19. No analysis has yet surpassed that of Alan Lomax, who discussed the conservatism of folk musical style in "Folk Song Style," *American Anthropologist* 61 (1959): 927–55, but Roger Abrahams and George Foss have contributed a useful discussion in *Anglo-American Folksong Style* (Englewood Cliffs, N.J., 1968). Sharp's quote is in Sharp and Campbell, *English Folk Songs*, ix.

20. Phillips Barry, whose analyses were among the most commonsensical of earlier folklorists, declared that "when we say that tradition—with due stress on its diversification—makes the folksong what it is, we are simply stopping short of a more nearly ultimate statement: the individualism of the folksinger, both consciously and unconsciously exerted, makes the tradition what it is"; Barry, "American Folk Music," *Southern Folklore Quarterly* 1, no. 2 (1937): 30.

21. It should be noted that the music chosen by folk entertainers has often included material shaped by the judgments and definitions of the folklorists and

other collectors of music. "Pure" folk musicians (that is, those who performed at the festivals or other venues favored by the folklorists) and "commercial" musicians (hillbilly, country) have often chosen to do material favored or suggested by folklorists. Similarly, during the folk revival of the 1960s, country and bluegrass performers like Johnny Cash and the Stanley Brothers sometimes performed music learned from the urban revivalists.

22. See A. L. Lloyd, *Folk Song in England* (New York, 1967).

23. Ibid., 25–34.

24. I recall from personal experience that this practice remained strong at least into the 1940s. My mother clipped songs from the "Young People's Page" of the *Dallas Semi-Weekly Farm News* and pasted them to the pages of an old schoolbook.

25. See, for example, Joseph T. Durkin, ed., *John Dooley, Confederate Soldier: His War Journal* (Washington, D.C., 1945), which describes a Confederate soldier and ballad singer, Archibald Goven, who was clearly of poor-white extraction. Another Confederate soldier, James M. Williams, described "psalm singers" who made the night "hideous with their horrid nasal twang butchering bad music"; John Kent Folmar, ed., *From That Terrible Field: Civil War Letters of James M. Williams, Twenty-First Alabama Infantry Volunteers* (Tuscaloosa, Ala., 1981), 13. The distinguished historian of Confederate soldiers and other plain folk, Bell Wiley, said that soldiers gathered often about the campfires or in winter huts to sing songs like "Home Sweet Home" or "Lorena"; Bell Irvin Wiley, *The Plain People of the Confederacy* (Baton Rouge, La, 1944), 18.

26. This shyness or emotional reserve may explain the awkwardness sometimes displayed by the folk singer before the folk-song collector.

27. Emma Bell Miles, *The Spirit of the Mountains* (1905; rpr. Knoxville, Tenn., 1975), 68–69.

28. The lyric content of the songs favored by the southern folk in the eighteenth and nineteenth centuries remains one of the most neglected areas of folk-music scholarship. The execution of such a study is hampered by our inability to know precisely when, where, and by whom the songs were sung. Nevertheless, good beginnings have been made by Dickson D. Bruce Jr., *And They All Sang Hallelujah: Plain-Folk Camp-Meeting Religion, 1800–1845* (Knoxville, Tenn., 1974); Bruce Collins, *White Society in the Antebellum South* (London, 1985); and Bill Cecil-Fronsman, *Common Whites: Class and Culture in Antebellum North Carolina* (Lexington, Ky., 1992).

29. Alan Lomax, *Folk Songs of North America*, 169.

30. One of the first scholars to recognize the cultural value of southern religious music was Howard W. Odum, who noted that such music "not only brought forth the sweep of social heritage and individual memories but touched deep the chords of old moralities and loyalties"; Howard W. Odum, *An American Epoch: Southern Portraiture in the National Picture* (New York, 1930), 180.

31. Although neither scholar talks much about music, John Boles and Rhys Isaac provided excellent interpretive accounts of the Protestant evangelization of the South: Boles, *The Great Revival, 1787–1805: The Origins of the Southern Evangelical*

Mind (Lexington, Ky., 1975), and Isaac, *The Transformation of Virginia, 1740–1790* (Chapel Hill, N.C., 1982). Studies of religious music are much more common, but unfortunately not all of them are published. See, for example, James C. Downey, "The Music of American Revivalism" (PhD diss., Tulane University, 1969); Timothy Alan Smith, "The Southern Folk-Hymn, 1802–1860: A History and Musical Analysis, with Notes on Performance Practice" (MA thesis, California State University–Fullerton, 1981); Richard H. Hulan, "Camp-Meeting Spiritual Folksongs: Legacy of the 'Great Revival in the West'" (PhD diss., University of Texas–Austin, 1978); Bruce, *They All Sang*; and Jackson, *White Spirituals*.

32. The seminal work on the shape-note tradition is Jackson, *White Spirituals*. It should be supplemented with Harry Eskew, "Shape-Note Hymnody in the Shenandoah Valley, 1816–1860" (PhD diss., Tulane University, 1966), and Buell E. Cobb Jr., *The Sacred Harp and Its Music* (Athens, Ga., 1978).

33. Hulan, "Camp-Meeting Spiritual Folksongs," xxv, 47–49, 91–93.

34. There is no good comprehensive history of nineteenth-century gospel music, but the outlines of the story can be found in biographies and in a few reminiscences of the gospel composers: William G. McLoughlin Jr., *Modern Revivalism* (New York, 1959) and *Billy Sunday Was His Real Name* (Chicago, Ill., 1955); James F. Findlay Jr., *Dwight L. Moody, American Evangelist, 1837–1899* (Chicago, Ill., 1969); Kathleen Martha Minnix, "God's Comedian: The Life and Career of Evangelist Sam Jones" (PhD diss., Georgia State University, 1986); Charles Hutchinson Gabriel, *Gospel Songs and Their Writers* (Chicago, Ill., 1913); Phil Kerr, *Music in Evangelism* (Glendale, Calif., 1939).

35. Rachel Augusta Harley, "Ananias Davisson: Southern Tunebook Compiler" (PhD diss., University of Michigan, 1972).

36. The official journal of the Ruebush-Kieffer Company, and the leading publicist of the do-re-mi shape-note style, is discussed in Paul M. Hall, *The Musical Million: A Study and Analysis of the Periodical Promoting Reading Music through Shape-Notes in Northern America from 1870 to 1914*" (DMA dissertation, Catholic University of America, Washington, D.C., 1970). See also Grace I. Showalter, *The Music Books of Ruebush and Kieffer, 1866–1942* (Richmond, Va., 1975).

37. Jo Fleming, "James D. Vaughan, Music Publisher" (SMD dissertation, Union Theological Seminary, 1972). Another influential alumnus of Ruebush-Kieffer is discussed by Joel Francis Reed in "Anthony J. Showalter (1858–1924): Southern Educator, Publisher, Composer" (EdD dissertation, New Orleans Baptist Theological Seminary, 1975).

38. Published by Maurice Templeton and edited by Jerry Kirksey, *Singing News* is a monthly publication located in Boone, North Carolina.

39. The famous English diarist Samuel Pepys heard the ballad sung by the actress Mrs. Knipp on January 1, 1666. We will probably never know how old the song was at the time she learned it, or how it came into her possession. *The Diary of Samuel Pepys*, 11 vols., ed. Robert Latham and William Matthews (Berkeley, Calif., 1970–1983), vol. 2, pt. 1, p. 5.

40. I have written an extended discussion of the popular influence: "Popular Culture and the Music of the South," in Bill C. Malone, *Singing Cowboys and Musical Mountaineers: Southern Culture and the Roots of Country Music* (Athens, Ga., 1993), 43–69. I have also written about the most popular songwriter of the late nineteenth century, William S. Hays, who composed many songs that eventually moved into the folk and country music repertoires. See "William S. Hays: The Bard of Kentucky," *Register of the Kentucky Historical Society* 93 (1995): 286–307.

41. There is no better example of this process than the history of the famous fiddle tune "Listen to the Mockingbird." The Philadelphia songwriter Septimus Winner heard the tune being whistled by a black man, Richard Milburn, on a street near Winner's office sometime in the 1850s. Winner appropriated the tune, added sentimental lyrics about the death of a young maiden, and then saw it circulated widely throughout the United States by blackface minstrel troupes. The song became very popular in the South and is now known almost exclusively as a virtuoso fiddle piece in which fiddlers imitate birdcalls.

42. The market economy expanded into the southern backcountry at an irregular pace and at different periods of time. Steven Hahn provides a model for other potential students in his excellent case study of northern Georgia, *The Roots of Southern Populism: Yeoman Farmers and the Transformation of the Georgia Upcountry, 1850–1890* (New York, 1983). Thomas D. Clark speaks of the emerging network of international credit that enveloped all rural southerners after the war in *Pills, Petticoats, and Plows: The Southern Country Store* (Norman, Okla., 1944). Edward L. Ayers provides a masterful survey of the integration of the entire South into the national economy during the late nineteenth century in *The Promise of the New South: Life after Reconstruction* (New York, 1992). The industrialization of the South has been well discussed in a number of books, including David L. Carlton, *Mill and Town in South Carolina, 1880–1920* (Baton Rouge, La., 1980); Ronald D. Eller, *Miners, Millhands, and Mountaineers: Industrialization of the Appalachian South, 1880–1930* (Knoxville, Tenn., 1982); Crandall Shiflett, *Coal Town: Life, Work, and Culture in Company Towns of Southern Appalachia, 1880–1960* (Knoxville, Tenn., 1991); Jacqueline Hall et al., *Like a Family: The Making of a Southern Cotton Mill World* (Chapel Hill, N.C., 1987); and James C. Cobb, *Industrialization and Southern Society, 1877–1984* (Lexington, Ky., 1984). For a more extensive bibliography of industrialization, see the notes to Ayers, *Promise of the New South*. The other side of the coin, the disintegration of southern agriculture, has been discussed by many scholars, including Gilbert C. Fite, *Cotton Fields No More: Southern Agriculture, 1865–1980* (Lexington, Ky., 1984); Pete Daniel, *Breaking the Land: The Transformation of Cotton, Tobacco, and Rice Cultures since 1880* (Urbana, Ill., 1985); and Jack Temple Kirby, *Rural Worlds Lost: The American South, 1920–1960* (Baton Rouge, La., 1987).

43. The South's struggle to create a body of music and poetry of its own can be seen in the plethora of paperback songsters produced during the war. The ones I have seen are located in the Harris Collection, Hay Library, Brown University,

Providence, Rhode Island. Richard B. Harwell discusses the massive outpouring of southern songs during the Civil War in *Confederate Music* (Chapel Hill, N.C., 1950).

44. Evidence of early country music's debts to such performers is found in the invaluable compendium *Country Music Records: A Discography, 1921–1942*, comp. Tony Russell (New York, 2004), and in the record collection *Minstrels and Tunesmiths: The Commercial Roots of Early Country Music* (JEMF recording 109), produced and edited by Norm Cohen, the most important student of folk music's indebtedness to the pop tradition.

45. A major study of the sentimental songs that moved into the folk tradition is sorely needed. William C. Ellis made a useful beginning in "The Sentimental Mother Song in American Country Music, 1923–1945" (PhD diss., Ohio State University, 1978).

46. See chapter 1, "Southern Rural Music in the Nineteenth Century," in Malone, *Singing Cowboys*, for a more extended discussion of the frolic tradition.

47. One of the first and best accounts of a southern country dance, and a suggestive statement about the wide range of people who were attracted to such affairs, is "The Dance," in Augustus Baldwin Longstreet, *Georgia Scenes* (1835; 2d ed., New York, 1859). For other references to frolics, see the notes to Malone, *Singing Cowboys*.

48. Earl V. Spielman, "Traditional North American Fiddling: A Methodology for the Historical and Comparative Analytical Style Study of Instrumental Musical Traditions" (PhD diss., University of Wisconsin, 1975), 191.

49. Samuel Bayard, *Hill Country Tunes: Instrumental Folk Music of Southwestern Pennsylvania* (Philadelphia, 1944).

50. No topic of music scholarship has been more hotly contested than the question of how the African-derived five-string banjo and its styles moved into southern white folk culture. Robert Winans, for example, argues that professional white entertainers—the blackface minstrels—took the instrument and frailing techniques of performance into the southern hills. Robert Winans, "The Folk, the Stage, and the Five-String Banjo in the Nineteenth Century," *Journal of American Folklore* 79 (1976): 407–37. William Tallmadge and Cecelia Conway, on the other hand, believe that African Americans took the instrument and styles to the mountains. William Tallmadge, "The Folk Banjo and Clawhammer Performance Practice in the Upper South: A Study of Origins," in *The Appalachian Experience: Proceedings of the Sixth Annual Studies Conference*, ed. Barry M. Buxton (Boone, N.C., 1983); Cecelia Conway, *African Banjo Echoes in Appalachia: A Study of Folk Traditions* (Knoxville, Tenn., 1995). Three good studies of blackface minstrelsy, each of which assays the complicated questions concerning the origins of minstrel music, are Robert C. Toll, *Blacking Up: The Minstrel Show in Nineteenth Century America* (New York, 1974); Hans Nathan, *Dan Emmett and the Rise of the Early Negro Minstrelsy* (Norman, Okla., 1962); and Howard L. Sacks and Judith Rose Sacks, *Way Up North in Dixie: A Black Family's Claim to the Confederate Anthem* (Washington, D.C., 1993).

51. Gene Wiggins, "Popular Music and the Fiddler," *JEMF Quarterly* 15, no. 55 (1979): 144–52.

52. Folk dancing has become a favored topic and practice among people interested in old-time music, and discussions of it are carried in the *Old-Time Herald*, edited by Alice Gerrard in Durham, North Carolina. The journal regularly carries a column called "The Dance Beat."

53. Much of the interest in country dancing in the seventeenth century is ultimately traceable to John Playford's collection of 1651, *The English Dancing Master*. The book went through many editions and supplements. The best study of English rural dancing's transplantation in the United States is S. Foster Damon, "History of Square Dancing," *American Antiquarian Society Proceedings* (April 1952): 63–98. It can be usefully supplemented by Richard Nevell, *A Time to Dance: American Country Dancing from Hornpipes to Hot Hash* (New York, 1977). The best survey of the play party, the venerable tradition of children's game songs that often served as a substitute for dancing, is B. A. Botkin, *The American Play-Party Song* (1937; rpr. New York, 1963).

54. For discussions of the Old World origins of step dancing, see William Chappell, *Popular Music of the Olden Time*, 2 vols. (London, 1855), vol. 1; Vuillier Gaston, A History of Dancing (New York, 1898); and Charles Baskerville, *The Elizabethan Jig* (Chicago, 1929). There is as yet no comprehensive treatment of folk step-dance history in the United States, but see Marian Hannah Winter, "American Theatrical Dancing from 1750–1800," *Musical Quarterly* 24 (1938): 58–73; Alan S. Downer, ed., *The Memoir of John Durang* (Pittsburgh, Pa., 1966); the notes in Malone, *Singing Cowboys*; and various articles in the *Old-Time Herald*.

55. Lawrence Levine's arguments concerning slave culture are worth repeating here: "We have only gradually come to recognize not merely the sheer complexity or origins but also its irrelevancy for an understanding of consciousness. It is not necessary for a people to originate or invent all or even most of the elements of their own, embedded in their traditions, expressive of their world view and lifestyle." Lawrence W. Levine, *Black Culture and Black Consciousness* (New York, 1977), 24.

56. The widespread popularity in the late-nineteenth-century South of Montgomery Ward, Sears-Roebuck, and other mail-order catalogs is documented in Ayers, *Promise of the New South*, 87–89. The role played by merchandising in popularizing the autoharp is discussed in "The Autoharp: Its Origin and Development from a Popular to a Folk Instrument," in Harry Taussig, *Folk Style Autoharp* (New York, 1967), 10–20, originally published in *New York Folklore Quarterly* 19, no. 4 (December 1963).

57. The general outlines of that story can be found in Bill C. Malone and David Stricklin, *Southern Music, American Music* (rev. ed., 1997).

CHAPTER 3

BLACKS AND WHITES AND THE MUSIC OF THE OLD SOUTH

Mike Seeger, both a scholar and a musician, devoted a lifetime to our under-standing and appreciation of what he called "Music from the True Vine." By this, he meant the music created and shared by African Americans and whites in the American South, an interacting tradition that underlay and energized the music of the entire nation. This essay—which was originally presented to a conference at the University of Mississippi and then published in Ted Ownby's edited volume *Black and White Cultural Interaction in the Antebellum South* (1993)—covers only a small slice of that tradition. Although we are now generally aware of the influence exerted by African Americans on the field of commercial country music in the twentieth century, and that a much greater number of them than we have realized actually performed with whites on radio and recordings, we need more corroborative scholarship. Tony Russell pointed the way to a resolution of this topic back in 1970 with *Blacks, Whites, and Blues* (London: Stein and Day). This exemplary work has recently been joined by Diane Pecknold, ed., *Hidden in the Mix: The African American Presence in Country Music* (Durham, N.C.: Duke University Press, 2013). One of the essayists in the Pecknold volume, Charles L. Hughes, has more recently contributed a brilliant study of the subject called *Country Soul: Making Music and Making Race in the American South* (Chapel Hill: University of North Carolina Press, 2015).

THE SOUTH AND ITS PEOPLE, BLACK AND WHITE, HAVE MADE VITAL CONTRIBUTIONS TO THE MUSIC OF THE WORLD. Long before southern musicians won commercial or artistic acceptance, the South itself, as a region and an idea was an irresistible temptation to music makers.[1] It has never ceased to evoke that kind of fascination. From the blackface minstrels and Stephen Foster through the tunesmiths of Tin Pan Alley to our own day, the South has contributed greatly to the imagery of American music, while also spawning many of the nation's most creative musicians and its most dynamic commercial styles. The whole world knows the names of modern musicians like Louis Armstrong, Bessie Smith, Mahalia Jackson, Thelonius Monk, B. B. King, Allan Toussaint, Randy Newman, Jimmie Rodgers, Bob Wills, Bill Monroe, Earl Scruggs, Hank Williams, Willie Nelson, and Elvis Presley, but the musical roots from which they drew remain obscure. A rare professional musician from earlier times, like Joel Walker Sweeney, the white Virginia minstrel and alleged inventor of the five-string banjo, is known to us. But otherwise we perceive only the dim outlines of the musical culture of the antebellum South.

Although the blackface minstrels utilized southern musical materials, and even included an occasional southerner in what was essentially a northern white man's profession, the world did not really become aware of the South's musical wealth until the late nineteenth century when the Fisk Jubilee Singers and a talented array of ragtime pianists began to take their music north.[2] Spirituals and ragtime hardly constituted the whole of the region's music, but for an American public that had grown up on Stephen Foster and minstrel perceptions of the South, it was easy to believe that "Southern Music" was exclusively "Black Music." Until John Lomax, Cecil Sharp, and other collectors published their research on cowboy and mountain songs in the decade surrounding World War I, the musical landscape of southern whites was almost terra incognita to those enamored of American folk music.[3] Another fifteen years passed before George Pullen Jackson demonstrated, in *White Spirituals in the Southern Uplands*, that white people in the interior South were also capable of producing beautiful music.[4] It is beyond the scope of this essay to discuss why academicians, musicologists, and collectors ignored the music of the white plain folk, but such neglect obviously inhibits any attempt to discuss musical interchange in the South.

The most explicit tool for the documentation of music, sound recording, did not become available until the end of the nineteenth century and was not enlisted in the exploitation of southern folk or "grassroots" forms until after World War I. Commercial phonograph recordings promoted the widespread circulation of such styles. These—and the independent recordings made by the Library of Congress, academic institutions, and private collectors—also provide an enduring reminder of how such music sounded when performed by the folk themselves.[5]

Recording, however, came almost three hundred years after whites and blacks first came in contact with each other on the North American mainland, and about fifty years after the end of slavery. The utility of recordings for the understanding of antebellum black-white musical interaction is clearly limited. We can assume that some of the pioneer musicians who recorded in the 1920s had direct contact with singers and instrumentalists who predated the Civil War, and therefore that some of the vocal and instrumental styles heard on the early recordings had remained basically unaltered since the antebellum era. Furthermore, the recordings reaffirm what Mechal Sobel has stressed about black and white Southerners in general, that there was a "deep symbiotic relatedness that must be explored if we are to understand either or both of them."[6] Although black and white musicians inhabited very different worlds, they nevertheless shared a culture of songs, instruments, and stylistic performance. White folk musicians, generally described as "hillbilly," and black folk musicians who were usually subsumed in record catalogs under the rubric of "race," knew a common body of songs and instrumental pieces whose origins and "racial identities" cannot always be determined. Hillbilly performers exhibited a fascination with the blues and with black instrumental styles, and like their minstrel predecessors of the nineteenth century, they often exploited black resources, or public perceptions of black culture, for comic or risqué purposes.

Contrary to popular opinion, black entertainers did not confine themselves to the blues. As Paul Oliver has reminded us, early black recordings are repositories of a wide range of musical expression, including everything from sermons and gospel songs to ballads, minstrel songs, fiddle tunes, Tin Pan Alley pop songs, ragtime pieces and, of course, blues and jazz.[7] A few performers, who have been appropriately described as "songsters," possessed repertoires that virtually ran the gamut of these diverse styles. Above all, the early recordings reveal vigorous survivals of a black string-band tradition, as well as superb performances by black fiddlers, an art (and instrument) generally identified with their poor white neighbors.[8]

Odell and Joe Thompson from North Carolina—shown playing the five-string banjo and fiddle, respectively—were modern exemplars of the southern black string band tradition. They provided dramatic evidence of the interrelationship of black and white musical styles.
Photograph by Nancy Kalow, P4705 in the Tommy Thompson Collection (20359), Southern Folklife Collection, Louis Round Wilson Special Collections Library, University of North Carolina, Chapel Hill. Used by permission.

Although the recordings provide evidence of a common rural legacy of musical performance and an aural means of comparing style as well as repertoire, they can tell us nothing about the age or historical roots of this legacy or about the process of musical interchange. The story of music in the antebellum South must be constructed out of much more tenuous materials. It is difficult, but not impossible, to document the music and musical styles of antebellum black and white southerners. Most of the available information comes from the brief and scattered references made by contemporary and generally casual observers who had little or no knowl-edge of music or who viewed their subjects through the lens of western European musical experience. Although plantation tutors, journalists, politicians, abolitionists, humorists, local colorists, evangelists, and a host of travelers with widely ranging preconceptions and motivations generally left only incidental impressions of song and dance, their observations nonetheless provide tantalizing glimpses of the musical world inhabited by antebellum southerners.

The descriptions made by these observers can be augmented with information garnered from the people themselves, in memoirs and reminiscences, diaries, county histories, newspapers, or in the valuable but still largely unutilized WPA slave interviews.[9] Unfortunately, one finds nothing comparable to the slave interviews that deal with antebellum white culture, but some descriptions or recollections of military camp life and the social diversions available to Johnny Reb can be found in war journals, memoirs, or magazines such as *Confederate Veteran*.[10]

We should not be overly optimistic about what we will learn from these sources. After all, contemporary observers did not ask the questions that we might pose, and their observations tend to be broadly descriptive rather than analytical. However, we can learn a great deal about the social contexts in which the music was performed, about the roles it played in the lives of the people, and about the songs, dances, and instruments that comprised the core of the music.

The sources confirm the existence of spheres of performance in both black and white culture where independent stylistic traits, and possibly traces of Old World forms, were preserved. The scholar searching for "African survivals"—or, perhaps, even "Celtic" characteristics—will find them. One also encounters broad areas of similarity, as well as a common vocabulary of terms, such as "frolic" and "play party," to describe social affairs that included music and dance. Music lent a festive air to certain forms of communal labor, such as corn shucking and quilting. An informed observer at such gatherings might have seen traces of African or European dance steps, but he also would have seen rural American variants of English longways dances and the French quadrille, complete with the American innovation, the shouted call.[11]

Henry Jenkins recalled his days as a slave in South Carolina: "I can hear them fiddles and de pattin' now. Dis de way de dance was called. Balance all; sashay to your partners; swing her 'round and promenade all; forward on de head; ladies change, and all dat."[12] And Isaac Stier, from Mississippi, remembered that "when us had dances dey was real cotillions, lak de white folks had. . . . I use to call out de figgers: Ladies, sashay, gents to de lef', now all swing."[13] As the WPA interviews make clear, slave dancers were familiar with virtually every dance known to their white neighbors, from cotillions, polkas, schottisches, and quadrilles to jigs, clogs, "flat foots," and buck dances.

Similarly, dances were accompanied by a variety of instruments that probably reflected African, European, American, and home-contrived influences. If necessary, folk southerners could create accompaniment for dances without instruments by singing, clapping their hands, or stamping their feet. But they were also resourceful in their creation of homemade instruments and makeshift rhythm devices. Wash Wilson, who had been a slave in both Louisiana and Texas, provided a wealth of data about slave musical ingenuity: "Dere wasn't no music instruments. Us take pieces a sheep's rib or cow's jaw or a piece of iron, with a old kettle, or a hollow gourd and some horsehair to make de drum. Sometimes dey'd git a piece of tree trunk and hollow it out and stretch a goat's or sheep's skin over it for de drum. Dey'd take de buffalo horn and scrape it out to make de flute. Den dey'd take a mule's jawbone and rattle de stick 'cross its teeth."[14] One also finds references to instruments such as mouth bows, quills (flute-like instruments generally made out of reed), and banjos, which may have been of African origin, and a large retinue of instruments such as fifes, flutes, accordions, French horns, pianos, and fiddles that came out of the European experience. No instrument proved alien to the slaves (or free blacks) but none was more ubiquitous than the fiddle. Although all students of black music have commented on the prominence of fiddling among both slaves and free blacks, one is still staggered by the frequency with which the fiddler appears in accounts devoted to antebellum black life—from the newspaper ads dealing with runaway slaves to the WPA interviews.

The song repertoires of blacks and whites also tended to overlap. African songs or songs reminiscent of that tradition appear frequently in the sources dealing with slaves, but they are accompanied by repeated references to venerable hymns such as "Amazing Grace," "The Day Is Past and Gone," and "Hark from the Tomb," gospel songs, folk ballads, pop songs, fiddle breakdowns and play-party songs, and minstrel standards such as "Shoo Fly," "Old Dan Tucker," and "Old Black Joe."

While the sources present abundant evidence that music was a constant presence in the lives of antebellum blacks and whites, and that a shared tradition of songs, dances, and instruments characterized the lives of these peoples, we nevertheless receive little concrete or precise documentation about the styles in which the music was performed or the process by which the music moved back and forth between the races. Consequently, as in many areas of folk music scholarship, one finds a paucity of explicit data and an abundance of speculation, guesses, unwarranted inferences, and romantic leaps in the dark. Black singing attracted early recognition and, generally, praise. Thomas Jefferson was not the first white southerner to be impressed with the musical abilities of the blacks, describing them as "more generally gifted than the whites with accurate ears for tune and time," but his reservations about their potential for harmonic complexity were not generally shared by other observers.[15]

Most people who commented on black music in the antebellum period were quick to recognize the blacks' facility for improvisation, their habitual employment of the call-and-response technique, the polyrhythmic emphases of their music, the suppleness and power of their voices, and the emotional vibrancy of their singing. Black dancing attracted extensive comment as well, with observers assuming that the solo dances they saw, and the bodily actions that simulated the movements of animals and birds, were also African-derived. Except for descriptions of banjo playing that sometimes appeared in mid-nineteenth century minstrel instruction manuals, black instrumental styles, however, were almost never discussed or analyzed.

In contrast to the admiration that black music evoked in the nineteenth century, the music of the southern white plain folk was seldom praised or even described in any meaningful way. White folk music, however, was frequently mentioned during the antebellum period, if only for comic purposes, and if we are willing to undertake a thorough painstaking examination of the available sources—ranging from travel literature and reminiscences to local color fiction—we can obtain a reasonably adequate understanding of its scope and social utility. Antebellum literature and the reminiscences that followed the war often included references to camp meeting and church congregational music, singing schools, frolics and play parties, fiddle contests, Confederate army jam sessions, fife and drum groups, brass band concerts, parlor singings, and community serenades. As in black music, fiddlers appear constantly in descriptions of community work functions, social celebrations, holidays and weddings, and political campaigns.

While antebellum accounts vividly testify to the importance of music in the lives of the white folk, they tell us much less than we would like to know about the styles of musical presentation. Except for general references to the group singing heard at camp meetings or in other religious settings (and much of those references are condescending or derogatory), one finds virtually no discussion, and in fact few mentions, of vocal music. Consequently, we can only draw inferences from data collected long after the Civil War, and much of that devoted to the ballad singers of the southern Appalachians, or from nineteenth-century religious tunebooks, which at least instructed people how to sing.[16] Dances were mentioned frequently, but we generally come away from accounts of them with only a vague understanding of how the dancers moved. Describing his visit to a small settlement near Black Mountain, North Carolina, in the early 1850s, the Englishman Charles Lanman only whets the appetite when he says "We devoted two hours to a series of fantastic dances, and when we became tired of this portion of the frolic, we spent an hour or so in singing songs."[17] We are assured that the dances were lusty and vigorous, with participants adding much of their own spontaneity and originality, but we learn little about the actual steps and movements. Frederick Law Olmsted, for example, describes a scene where he took lodging, probably on the Louisiana side of the Sabine River: "All bade us good night, but, leaving the door open, commenced feats of prolonged dancing, or stamping upon the gallery, which were uproariously applauded."[18]

Olmsted takes us about as close to detailed observations of country dancing as we are ever likely to get when he quotes an informant from northern Mississippi in about 1853: "We dance cotillions and reels, and we dance on a plank; that's the kind of dancin' I like best. . . . You stand face to face with your partner on a plank and keep a dancin'. Put the plank up on two barrel heads, so it'll kind o' spring. At some of our parties—that's among common kind o' people, you know—it's great fun. They dance as fast as they can, and the folks all stand round and holler, 'Keep it up, John!' 'Go it, Nance!' 'Don't give it up so!' 'Old Virginny never tire!' 'Heel and toe, Ketch a-fire!' and such kind of observations, and clap and stomp 'em."[19]

We do find that both group and solo dancing were popular at country frolics, but while references to "heel and toe," "jigs," "pigeon wings," "double shuffles," "breakdowns," and what southwestern humorist A. B. Longstreet called "good old Republican six reels," provide some enlightenment, we cannot expect to learn much more than what the observers themselves saw and documented.[20] The vocabulary of description was imprecise, and "jig," for example, was used indiscriminately to describe almost any solo dance, whether performed by whites or blacks.[21] We can therefore only speculate about whether the dances were of commercial or folk origin, how they may have compared with those of the blacks, or indeed, whether they were anything more than the improvisations of the dancers. One suspects the latter. In a letter written in 1843 to the leading gentlemen's sporting magazine, *Spirit of the Times*, by an East Tennessee informant (probably George Washington Harris), a backwoods dance is described in the following revealing manner: "The music sounds high, and the wild woods ring; the feet of the company fly thick and fast; reels, cotillions, and waltzes, are all so mingled and blended together that it is a dance without a name."[22]

Students of folk instrumentation similarly can do little but imagine techniques of antebellum musicians. Guitars and dulcimers are almost never mentioned in antebellum sources, and banjos appear infrequently in accounts dealing with the plain white folk. Fiddles, of course, are omnipresent, but the fiddlers' alleged habits of heavy drinking and irresponsibility tend to receive as much attention as do their talents. A description of a country fiddler made in 1840 by a correspondent to the *Spirit of the Times* was not atypical. Described as "a rusty looking chap, with two large whiskers, and his right eye smashed out," the fiddler had been offered five dollars to play for a wedding frolic near Carrollton, Kentucky, "provided they did not get drunk."[23] Fiddling is invariably described as "sawing" or "scraping," and one generally searches in vain for any mention of tuning techniques, the way the fiddle was held, the way it was noted, and the way it was bowed. Above all, the sources seldom comment directly upon the processes by which folk musicians learned from each other. We are left to assume, perhaps rightly, that in a folk society musical technique was learned through observation, trial-and-error, and a minimum of formal instruction.

The transmission of song and style within a family, or within a cohesive folk community, can be easily understood. Cultural interchange between two racial communities is a more complex phenomenon. Songs and dances clearly were mutually exchanged. Were styles of instrumental and vocal performance also borrowed? The potential for interchange came at the first point of contact between European slave masters and African slaves. And, as Marshall Stearns has noted, European and African musical traditions were compatible enough to permit mutual learning. They blended easily, he argues, because "unlike other musics of the world they are very much alike."[24] Slaves mastered European instruments easily and early, and by the 1690s, as Dena Epstein points out, they were playing the violin well enough to earn extra money at white social functions.[25]

Religious interrelationship began as early as 1702 when the Society for the Propagation of the Gospel began its missionary work among the slaves. By the middle of the 1700s slaves were not only singing psalms and the hymns of Isaac Watts but were being praised for the soulfulness of their religious singing. The observations of Presbyterian minister Samuel Davies, who heard a group of blacks singing religious songs in Virginia in 1756, have been often quoted: "A torrent of sacred harmony poured into my chamber, and carried my mind away to Heaven." And he concluded that "the Negroes above all the human species that ever I knew, have an ear for music, and a kind of extatic [*sic*] delight in psalmody."[26]

The exposure to the music of white Protestantism continued throughout the antebellum era. Slaves apparently attended the camp meetings of the early nineteenth century in large numbers, and their participation in the singing and in the highly charged emotional atmosphere of the revivals often evoked comment. Although they frequently held their own praise meetings, most slaves also attended the churches of their masters. They worshiped in segregated sections but were never isolated from the music of the church. Folk spirituals, camp meeting songs, and even songs from

the Sacred Harp tradition, moved into the consciousness of black worship-
ers. The existence of a shared milieu of religious worship and a common
repertoire of religious songs can be easily documented. Religion provided
emotional release and the promise of a better future for both black slaves
and white plain folk. References to freedom and the soul's passage through
an unfriendly world abound in the songs of both groups. Lawrence Levine
argues that "similar images . . . served similar purposes," and that "many
of those whites who flocked to the camp meetings . . . were themselves
on the social and economic margins of their society and had psychic and
emotional needs which, qualitatively, may not have been vastly different
from those of black slaves."[27]

But did a shared environment and similar psychic needs also contribute to similar styles of worship and musical performance? Or did styles of
performance and behavior change discernibly under the influence of social
contact? Reverend Davies was certainly not alone in his admiration of the
power and emotional involvement of black singers, and impressionable
Christians, who were predisposed to see the hand of the Holy Spirit
behind every wondrous emotional manifestation around them, could easily
interpret the black emotionalism as Heaven sent. This emotionalism was
surely contagious, but did it somehow insinuate itself into the behavior of
some whites who were in its midst? Anthropologist F. W. Davenport in 1905
contrasted what he termed the "sensory automatism," such as trances and
visions, of the revivals of whites' British ancestors with the violent "motor
automatism" experienced by many whites at the Kentucky revivals of the
early 1800s. Both he and Melville Herskovits argued that the presence of
blacks at the Kentucky revivals generated the "motor automatisms" experienced by members of both races.[28] Neither of these scholars concentrated
on the music of the revivals but instead discussed such physical phenomena as the jerks, the "holy laugh," and other extreme examples of religious
possession. A formidable array of more recent scholars, including Dena
Epstein, Mechal Sobel, and Lawrence Levine, have strongly suggested that
the music of camp-meeting revivalism may have been forcefully influenced
by the presence of blacks.[29] Levine, for example, maintains that "insofar as
white evangelical music departed from traditional Protestant hymnology
and embodied or approached the complex rhythmic structure, the percus-

sive qualities, the polymeter, the syncopation, the emphasis on overlapping call and response patterns that characterized Negro music both in West Africa and the New World, the probability that it was influenced by the slaves who attended and joined in the singing at religious meetings is quite high."[30] One should be aware, however, that Levine's discussion concentrates on song structure or the style of "music" rather than on the style of "singing" heard in evangelical music. We still have little evidence, and only the faintest suggestions, that either black or white vocal styles were actually changed by the common religious experiences of the antebellum South. Vocal quality is a product of genetic and cultural conditioning and, as Alan Lomax has argued, singing styles are conservative traits that do not readily change or alter under the influence of external physical stimuli.[31]

If the potential for religious music interchange can easily be seen in the peculiar worship arrangements of the antebellum period, the opportunities for a similar pattern in secular music are not always so obvious. The most clearly documented examples of such exchange come from the upper-class white tradition, and they therefore hardly lend support to the idea of a more general and widespread interrelationship. Slave musicians played constantly for plantation balls, weddings, holidays, and other social functions. Slaves who demonstrated musical talent sometimes received formal instruction, and occasionally they were either loaned or hired out to neighboring plantations as musicians. William H. Harrison, for example, who was born a slave in 1832 in Richmond, Virginia, was one of these favored slave musicians: "This is how good my owner was to me. He sent me to Hendersonville, North Carolina, to learn to fiddle. I was so afraid of the old colored teacher I learned in a month about all he could play. I played for parties in eight states in slavery."[32]

Slave musicians, and the slaves who worked as servants at social affairs, had abundant opportunities to sample, and learn, European musical traditions and dances. It is impossible to know how much of the "African" style was overtly or covertly incorporated into the cotillions and other formal dances that the musicians were required to play, but we do have considerable evidence that plantation balls often included what Nicholas Cresswell saw in Alexandria, Virginia, in 1775 and described as "everlasting jigs": "Betwixt the country dances . . . a couple gets up and begin to dance a jig to some Negro tune. Others comes and cuts them out, and these dances always last as long as the fiddler can play."[33] The observations of Philip Fithian, who worked as a tutor on the Carter plantation in Virginia in 1773 and 1774, are often cited as evidence of the mixing of black and white cultural forms. While affirming the Virginia aristocracy's passion for music and dancing, saying "They will dance or die!" he also notes that jigs were danced along with minuets, reels, and country dances. Fithian complains that on at least two occasions the Carter boys and other young white men gathered in the schoolroom to listen and to dance to the music of slave musicians playing the fiddle and banjo.[34] Sobel and Epstein also cite the example of Thomas Jefferson's brother Randolph who sometimes took his fiddle to the slave quarters and joined in the general merriment.[35] His conduct was probably not exceptional. Whether motivated by the desire to taste an exotic or forbidden pleasure or by a genuine interest in the music, this kind of "slumming" very likely went on at most plantations in the South, and in those towns and cities where free black communities existed.

It should be emphasized that most of the conduct described above, and about which Fithian complained, was by its very nature largely an upper-class diversion. Nowhere in the secular world of the folk can one find the opportunity for the kind of sustained musical contact experienced by blacks and whites at religious gatherings, and only occasionally can one find documentation of mutual exposure in other settings. Plain whites were occasionally invited to plantation social functions—to a wedding, perhaps, or a political event where the master might announce his candidacy. Traveler Charles Lanman, for example, said that "all of the yeomanry of the immediate neighborhood were usually invited" to the Virginia barbecues of the early 1850s where feasting and dancing were common.[36] However, except as overseers or as patrolers on the lookout for slave violations of the curfew, non-slaveholders did not have the freedom to venture into the slave quarters where the music was probably dramatically different from that heard in formal plantation settings or at a planter-sponsored barbecue.

The opportunities for plain whites and blacks to share musical ideas, however, had never been entirely lacking in the pre–Civil War South. As T. H. Breen and Stephen Innes argue, non-slaveholding whites, slaves, and free blacks came into frequent contact during the late seventeenth century in the Chesapeake Bay region. Although explicit data describing common musical enjoyment or performance is rare, Breen and Innes note that such contact was marked by social as well as economic intercourse. Blacks and whites worked, hunted, fished, gambled, drank, fought, and made love together.[37] Are we free to assume that they also danced and made music with each other? The frequency of interracial socializing may have diminished as slavery matured, and as the rules restricting such relationships tightened, but social interaction among plain whites and blacks, both slave and free, never completely disappeared in the antebellum period. "Despite the dense wall of racial antagonism and the intense economic competition which divided whites and blacks," Ira Berlin writes, "close living conditions and the common pattern of their daily lives frequently pushed the races together." Berlin provides at least one example of a shared musical moment, in 1857, when an upcountry South Carolina patrol, drawn by "loud music and raucous laughter," discovered a group of free blacks, slaves, and white folks "fiddling and frolicking" in a free Negro settlement.[38] Plain whites continued to hear and observe black singers and musicians in a number of settings—as slaves sang and worked, or at plantation social affairs, at camp meetings and church services, at community gatherings such as county fairs, horse races, court days, or public hangings, on street corners, and in taverns.

Blacks also may have encountered occasional fiddlers, string bands, fife and drum players, brass bands, or ballad peddlers at these community social functions, and they most certainly would have heard the singing of whites at religious meetings. Apart from religious interaction, however, the incidence of such encounters is not easily documented, and the presence of both blacks and whites at the boisterous rural frolics and their common musical participation at these occasions are even harder to illustrate. The WPA interviews, for example, provide little proof of the existence of social interaction among plain whites and slaves. On the other hand, the interviews usually do not indicate the size of the plantation or farm on which the ex-slave lived, the number of slaves who lived there, the ratio between whites and blacks, or any number of other variables that might have affected the degree of social intimacy between the two races. Without such corroborative evidence, it is difficult to know the socioeconomic identities of the slaveowners who are mentioned in the interviews. The interview with Mollie Williams, born a slave near Utica, Mississippi, suggests that her fiddle-playing mistress was part of a rather substantial household: "Miss Margurite had a piany, a 'cordian, a flutena, and a fiddle. She could play a fiddle good as a man. I kin jes see her li'l old fair han's now, playin' jes as fast as lightnin' a tune."[39] We learn less about Guy Stewart's master in Mansfield Parish, Louisiana, who is described as a "good fiddler" who taught some of his slaves to play the fiddle and banjo.[40] Without supportive research in the census or local records, the WPA interviews alone can tell us little about the social standing or backgrounds of the masters and their families. The opportunities for musical interchange between slaves and plain white folk, it seems, may have been more available on the smaller plantations and on the farms owned by yeomen who owned a few slaves. One can envision slaves and yeoman whites trading licks on the fiddle or banjo; unfortunately, neither the WPA interviews nor other sources provide much hard evidence of such an interrelationship.

The search for a specific musical link between slaves and plain whites may be, in the final analysis, an irrelevant undertaking. They, and most other southerners, inhabited a rural landscape of shared folkways. Poor whites, yeoman farmers, drovers, herdsmen, and larger plantation owners as well shared with slaves and free blacks a social environment where certain types of music moved freely from group to group and from musician to musician. Social distinctions certainly existed and were preserved through custom and law, and musical preferences held in common with the lower classes in no way inhibited the plantation elite's exercise of power. Music, in fact, probably served as a vehicle of social control and a means by which powerful people ingratiated themselves with their social inferiors.[41]

But, above all, a common form of music touched the lives of a wide variety of people, black and white, in a society that did not yet make clear distinctions between folk, art, and popular music, nor between urban and rural music. Consequently, lawyers, judges, politicians, businessmen, preachers, planters, yeomen, poor whites, and slaves played fiddles, participated in dances that often included both cultivated and vernacular expression (or fusions of the two), attended rural revivals, and sang a common store of songs, including ballads that predated the settlement of the South.

With the passage of time, much of the old music and dances succumbed to social pretension, and the fiddle was abandoned—by many whites as a reminder of rural backwardness, and by blacks as an emblem of their slave past. The instrument, the dances for which it was played, and the total musical tradition of which it was a part, all endured however as the nucleus of country music.

The music of the South therefore was not simply a body of styles and songs preserved by the "folk" from their Old World traditions and adapted to the experiences of the American frontier. This music included also an amalgam of styles borrowed, consciously and unconsciously, from both the cultivated, or art, tradition and the world of popular entertainment. Of the latter, blackface minstrelsy had by far the most profound impact on the folk music of the South. Its presence in the music of the region complicates the task of understanding the process of cultural interchange, but it also makes the research much more intriguing. The minstrels popularized songs, instrumental pieces, dances, performance styles, humor, and instruments that entered the consciousness of the southern people, sometimes by indirect and circuitous routes, and often remained there long after they were forgotten elsewhere. Minstrel troupes maintained popularity in much of America as late as World War I, and material introduced or popularized by them endured even longer in vaudeville, burlesque, and medicine shows, on radio serials like "Amos and Andy," and in country music (one of the Grand Ole Opry's most popular tent-show attractions through the World War II period was a blackface duo known as Jamup and Honey). The music of minstrelsy, however, was already widely known before the Civil War. Antebellum accounts of backwoods frolics often refer to songs and dances that were of minstrel origin, and the WPA interviews reveal a familiarity with a large number of such songs. One finds, for example, a surprising frequency of references to the famous "Pateroller Song" ("Run Nigger Run"), a song that referred to the notorious slave patrols but is usually attributed to the minstrel stage.

The most challenging questions pertaining to minstrel music—that of its ultimate origins—bears directly upon the topic of black-white musical interchange. How authentic was the minstrel depiction of southern blacks, and how literal was the minstrel re-creation of black music? In addressing this problem we also need to ponder just how faithful American audiences wanted the minstrels to be. A central focus of minstrelsy, and a major factor in its remarkable hold on the American people, was the alluring web of fantasy that it spun around black life and culture. Nevertheless, at least in the early years of its history, its entertainers apparently did absorb and re-create a good deal of genuine black material. With a few dramatic exceptions, such as the Virginia-born Joel Walker Sweeney, the early minstrel performers were northern white men who often had toured widely through the South, and elsewhere, as song-and-dance men in circuses and other traveling shows. In a sense, they were "folk collectors" who absorbed musical ideas wherever they went—from blacks or from any other source whose music seemed commercially promising. Robert Toll argues that, "since cultural interaction between blacks and whites was common in southern frontier areas, minstrels probably unwittingly included elements of black culture in some of what they thought was white frontier lore."[42] Toll may be correct, but can we not also assume that white cultural elements circulated in the guise of black lore, and that much of the material that became part of the minstrel routines had in fact lost whatever "original" racial identity it once possessed?

The absorption of folk material and its consequent adaptation and dissemination as popular music do not exhaust the history or influence of that material. Whatever their origin or the intent behind their creation, popular songs and dances often take on a life of their own. Once they move into the possession of the people, they are sometimes reshaped and transformed in wondrous ways; and as they endure they once again assume "folk" identities—a "circular" process of transmission illustrated by the history of such famous minstrel pieces as "Listen to the Mockingbird." In 1855 Septimus Winner, a white Philadelphia composer, heard Richard Milburn, a black street musician, playing and whistling a tune with simulated birdcalls. Winner added sentimental love lyrics, published the song under the title "Listen to the Mockingbird," and then saw it circulated widely throughout the country by minstrel entertainers who performed it as a lyric piece, a series of bird imitations, and as an instrumental novelty.[43] The song enjoyed popularity in its genteel parlor form, but it eventually lost both its lyrics and its urban identification and became famous as it circulated among rural musicians as a virtuoso fiddle tune. In this latter guise, it once again assumed the status of "folk song" with neither Milburn's nor Winner's role in its making remembered.

The history of "Listen to the Mockingbird" is similar to that of scores of songs and dances in the nineteenth century, all of which illustrate the danger of glibly affixing racial or ethnic designations or origins to musical selections. The history of instruments and instrumental styles suggests a comparable problem of origin and development. One need not doubt the banjo's slave or African origins, but soon after it reached American soil, it began to change in shape, construction, function, and racial identity.[44] Minstrels adopted it in the 1830s, popularized it among a large audience, and thereby inspired a commercial production that manufacturers like S. S. Stewart were quick to exploit. The banjo survived in forms that were probably close to the "original"—fretless, homemade, percussive, and often of gourd construction—but manufactured models, complete with instruction manuals, became widely available.

Banjo performance presumably illustrated a similar diversity, with older styles enduring alongside those introduced on the stage. The early minstrels certainly copied black folk styles, but they soon popularized their own adaptations and innovations and these, in turn, were adopted by musicians. Is it now possible to know how early banjo styles sounded, and the degree to which either black or white southerners contributed to their shaping? Both vaudeville and rural banjo players, white and black, are heard on early commercial recordings, and at least one of these musicians, Uncle Dave Macon, a white "hillbilly" performer from middle Tennessee, is known to have learned some of his technique from minstrel entertainers sometime in the 1880s.[45] We might also assume that surviving banjo techniques in some of the more isolated regions of the United States, such as the southern Appalachians, are about as close to nineteenth-century styles as we are likely to find. But if that is true, then we are confronted with the question of how the instrument, and its styles, ventured into a region supposedly populated by few blacks, and where professional minstrel troupes presumably seldom performed. As in many areas of folk music inquiry, speculation on this question has been intense, while supportive documentation has been minimal. Black people, as a matter of fact, were

never totally absent from some areas of the mountains during the antebellum period, and their presence increased dramatically after the 1870s
when railroad building and coal mining lured thousands of black workers
to industrializing Appalachia.[46] But we need more information than that.
We also need to know if banjo pickers were within their midst, if their
residence in the mountains predated the Civil War, and if those musicians
played in styles similar to those associated with white mountaineers. Thus
far, such data has not been made available.

The intriguing research of Robert Winans, on the other hand, focuses
directly on the question of minstrel influence in the mountains. He has
reminded us that those hardy, intrepid blackface entertainers covered an
immense amount of territory, and that few areas were too remote or rugged for them to reach. Traveling by horse and buggy, by train, and by boat,
minstrel troupes visited little towns and villages all over the South. Showboats did not merely ply the Ohio and Mississippi Rivers, they also carried
minstrel entertainment down the Cumberland and Tennessee Rivers in
the 1850s, and down the tributaries of those streams. Showboats were still
visiting towns along the Big Sandy River, well back into the Kentucky hills,
as late as the 1890s. Winans notes also that medicine shows and circuses
exhibited their brands of blackface entertainment in communities not
visited by the minstrel troupes. Furthermore, his study of surviving banjo
instruction books from the late antebellum period, such as Briggs's *Banjo
Instructor* (1855) and Phil Rice's *Correct Method for the Banjo* (1858),
convinced Winans that the frailing and clawhammer styles associated with
rural and mountain banjo players are modifications of minstrel playing.[47]
Winans's conclusions are provocative, and they provide further evidence
of the intricate and complex interrelationship between folk and popular
culture in the United States, but they obviously do not tell us all we would
like to know. As Winans himself admits, early minstrel banjo players may
have copied black folk styles. One cannot know conclusively, therefore,
whether the techniques described in the instruction books of the 1850s
were survivals, adaptations, or departures from the original modes of banjo
performance.

The questions provoked by the banjo's history reaffirm the tentative-
ness of the hypotheses presented in this essay. We will probably never fully

understand the process of antebellum musical interchange, nor can we ever be confident of the styles used by singers, musicians, and dancers during that era. Our most reliable measurement of style comes from the twentieth century, but while audio recordings, like those made in the 1920s, do preserve intact the sounds of earlier years, we can never be certain of the age or derivation of what we are hearing. It is true that the older written sources and the later WPA interviews have been insufficiently utilized by scholars, but one suspects that additional research will do little to modify the general outlines of what we already know about the Old South's musical culture. As hazy and imprecise as the evidence generally tends to be, it nevertheless suggests a vigorous antebellum musical culture where music moved across social, economic, and racial barriers. Styles of performance probably mixed as well, through conscious imitation or through subtle and imperceptible borrowings. Although W. J. Cash was speaking of black-white relationships on the plantations, his comments may carry a special resonance for the understanding of musical interchange: "the relationship between the two groups was, by the second generation at least, nothing less than organic. Negro entered into white man as profoundly as white man entered into Negro—subtly influencing every gesture, every word, every emotion and idea, every attitude."[48]

Nevertheless, if styles mixed, they also preserved distinctiveness. Black and whites knew many of the same songs and dances, but a mutually cherished hymn like "Amazing Grace," or a commonly performed fiddle tune like "Old Zip Coon," assumed radically different forms when winnowed and shaped in the styles of black and white performers. Styles were influenced by the currents of popular and commercial music that moved across the South in the nineteenth century, but their distinguishing traits came from the historical backgrounds, racial heritages, and cultural imperatives of the performers themselves.

Music, however, is more than the expression of a people's history: it also authenticates, preserves, and communicates the uniqueness of a particular human experience to the rest of the world. Southern music, or images of it, began fueling the artistry and ambitions of American entertainers as early as the 1830s, but since the late nineteenth century, when the Fisk Jubilee Singers introduced their versions of the "sorrow songs" (in a form both Western and African), the musical styles of the southern folk have become both substance and soul of America's popular music. This New World fusion of sound has entered the consciousness of people everywhere as the dimension of American culture most valued around the world.

NOTES

1. I have discussed the South's music and its relationship to the nation's popular culture as a whole, in *Southern Music/American Music* (Lexington: University Press of Kentucky, 1979; rev. ed., with David Stricklin, 1997).

2. The best interpretation of blackface minstrelsy is Robert C. Toll, *Blacking Up: The Minstrel Show in Nineteenth Century America* (New York: Oxford University Press, 1974). Carl Wittke, *Tambo and Bones* (Durham, N.C.: Duke University Press, 1930) is a good factual survey of the phenomenon, while Edward LeRoy Rice, *Monarchs of Minstrelsy* (New York: Kenny, 1911), is a useful biographical compilation of minstrel entertainers.

3. John A. Lomax, *Cowboy Songs and Other Frontier Ballads* (New York: Sturgis and Walton, 1910); Cecil Sharp and Olive Dame Campbell, *English Folk Songs from the Southern Appalachians*, 2 vols. (1917; London: Oxford University Press, 1932).

4. George Pullen Jackson, *White Spirituals in the Southern Uplands* (Chapel Hill: University of North Carolina Press, 1933; Dover Edition, 1965).

5. I have written a general survey of the recording of southern white "grassroots" music in *Country Music, U.S.A.* (Austin: University of Texas Press, 1968; rev. ed., 1985; revised in 2010 with an additional chapter by Jocelyn Neal). Debra Kodish has provided an excellent account of the early efforts made by Robert Winslow Gordon and the Library of Congress to record American folk music in *Good Friends and Bad Enemies: Robert Winslow Gordon and the Study of American Folksong* (Urbana: University of Illinois Press, 1986).

6. Mechal Sobel, *The World They Made Together: Black and White Values in Eighteenth-Century Virginia* (Princeton, N.J.: Princeton University Press, 1987), 11.

7. Paul Oliver, *Songsters and Saints: Vocal Traditions on Race Records* (Cambridge: Cambridge University Press, 1984), esp. 20–27, 47, 49.

8. Available recordings that illustrate these traditions include "Altamont: Black Stringband Music from the Library of Congress" (Rounder 0238), and "String Bands, 1927–1929" (HK Records 4009). Exhilarating and infectious revivals and updatings of this music have been provided by the great North Carolina string band, The Carolina Chocolate Drops.

9. The interviews were originally published in nineteeen volumes, but additional discoveries of material have resulted in another twenty-two "supplements." See George P. Rawick, ed., *The American Slave: A Composite Autobiography* (Westport,

Conn.: Greenwood Press, 1972, 1979). The "narratives," with a few exceptions, were collected by WPA workers in the 1930s. I have begun a careful study of these collections but have thus far done research in only the first ten volumes, those dealing with South Carolina, Texas, Alabama, Indiana, Oklahoma, Mississippi, and Arkansas. A considerable amount of data on ex-slaves from other states, however, appears in the collections just mentioned. The musical material found in the narratives varies in quantity, quality, and reliability. Many interviewers asked no questions at all about music, and some ex-slaves had little memory of musical events, gave only minimal responses, or gave the kinds of answers they thought their questioners wanted. The interviewers almost never asked for elaboration or clarification. Some respondents clearly confused postbellum and antebellum experiences. Although the reservations often expressed about oral history certainly apply to the WPA interviews, these narratives nonetheless provide virtually the only available resources for getting close to the thinking of the ex-slaves themselves.

10. The *Confederate Veteran* devoted its major emphases to the annual reunions of ex-rebel soldiers and to the commemoration of the Lost Cause. However, it often included reminiscences, journal entries, or lengthy letters recalling the experience of the war. This material sometimes contained memories of music or musical happenings. Researchers of southern music should pay careful attention to the social history of the Civil War, for in the crucible of war, musical expressions tended to mix and gain a wider public exposure. For example, many soldiers may have heard minstrel material for the first time in their military bivouacs or in rest or recuperation settings.

11. The best introduction to the history of the "square dance" in the United States is a lengthy and impressively researched article by S. Foster Damon, "History of Square Dancing," *American Antiquarian Society, Proceedings* (April 1952): 63–98. "Calling" is discussed on pages 80–81.

12. Henry Jenkins, *South Carolina Narrative* (WPA), vol. 3, part 3, p. 25.

13. Isaac Stier, *Mississippi Narrative* (WPA), vol. 7, part 2, p. 146.

14. Wash Wilson, *Texas Narrative* (WPA), vol. 5, part 2, p. 198.

15. Thomas Jefferson, *Notes on the State of Virginia*, 135, available at http://www.thefederalistpapers.org/.

16. Shape-note books such as *The Southern Harmony* and *The Sacred Harp* generally included introductory sections where the "rudiments" of music and rules for proper singing were outlined. Modern performances of this music by rural southerners, who consciously try to preserve the styles of their ancestors, may very well constitute living museums of early nineteenth-century singing.

17. Charles Lanman, *Adventures in the Wilds of the United States and British American Provinces* (Philadelphia: John W. Moore, 1856), 1:441.

18. Frederick Law Olmsted, *A Journey Through Texas; or a Saddle-Trip on the Southwestern Frontier* (New York: Mason Brothers, 1861), 384.

19. Olmsted, *A Journey in the Back Country*, vol. 1 (1860; New York: G. P. Putnam's Sons, 1907), 160.

20. Augustus Baldwin Longstreet, *Georgia Scenes*, 2d ed. (1835; New York: Harper and Brothers, 1859), 15. This book contains one of the earliest and most

vivid descriptions of an omnipresent and enduring southern rural institution, the house party.

21. Charles Read Baskervill, *The Elizabethan Jig* (Chicago: University of Chicago Press, 1929), 12–13, describes a similar universality of usage in the British Isles in the seventeenth century.

22. *Spirit of the Times* (September 2, 1843), 313, quoted in George Washington Harris, *High Times and Hard Times*, ed. Thomas Inge (Nashville, Tenn.: Vanderbilt University Press, 1967).

23. *Spirit of the Times* (February 8, 1840).

24. Marshall Stearns, *The Story of Jazz* (New York: Oxford University Press, 1956), 19.

25. Dena Epstein, *Sinful Tunes and Spirituals: Black Folk Music to the Civil War* (Urbana: University of Illinois Press, 1977), 80.

26. Sobel, *The World They Made Together*, 187.

27. Lawrence Levine, *Black Culture and Black Consciousness: Afro-American Folk Thought from Slavery to Freedom* (New York: Oxford University Press, 1977), 22.

28. Melville Herskovits reviews the arguments of Davenport, and his own conclusions, in *The Myth of the Negro Past* (New York: Harper and Brothers, 1941), 229–32.

29. Epstein, *Sinful Tunes*, 217–19; Sobel, *The World They Made Together*, 184; Mechal Sobel, *Trabelin' On: The Slave Journey to an Afro-Baptist Faith* (Westport, Conn.: Greenwood Press, 1979), 153; Levine, *Black Culture*, 21.

30. Levine, *Black Culture*, 21.

31. Alan Lomax, "Folk Song Style," *American Anthropologist* 61 (December 1959): 927–55. See also Lomax's *Folk Songs of North America* (New York: Doubleday, 1960).

32. William H. Harrison, *Arkansas Narrative* (WPA), vol. 9, part 3, 188.

33. *The Journal of Nicholas Cresswell, 1774–1777* (London: Jonathan Cope, 1925), 53.

34. Hunter Dickinson Farish, ed., *Journal and Letters of Philip Vickers Fithian, 1773–1774: A Plantation Tutor of the Old Dominion* (Williamsburg, Va.: Colonial Williamsburg, 1943), 44, 82, 83, 232.

35. Sobel, *The World They Made Together*, 166; Epstein, *Sinful Tunes*, 122.

36. Lanman, *Adventures in the Wilds*, 2:256–59.

37. T. H. Breen and Stephen Innes, *"Myne Owne Ground": Race and Freedom on Virginia's Eastern Shore, 1640–1676* (New York: Oxford University Press, 1980), 35, 59, 104–107. One statement made by Breen and Innes is particularly pertinent for those who would explore black-white interrelationships in early America: "At any given time, the character of race relations in early America was a function of demography (how many persons of each race were present in the society), spatiality (how was the black and white population distributed over a region?), and wealth (how did economic standing affect racial attitudes?)," 23. An excellent summary of the relations between blacks and whites in the colonial Chesapeake society, and a discussion of the views of other historians on this subject, is Allan Kulikoff, *Tobacco and Slaves: The Development of Southern Cultures in the Chesapeake, 1680–1800* (Chapel Hill: University of North Carolina Press, 1986), esp. chapter 8.

38. Ira Berlin, *Slaves without Masters: The Free Negro in the Antebellum South* (New York: Oxford University Press, 1974), 260.

39. Mollie Williams, *Mississippi Narrative* (WPA), vol. 7, part 2, p. 159.

40. Guy Stewart, *Texas Narrative* (WPA), vol. 5, part 2, p. 62.

41. Rural southern history contains numerous examples of politicians and officeholders, from justices of the peace to governors and U.S. senators, who have played music or who have utilized the musical support of others in their campaigns for public office. The practice began during the colonial period; a fairly recent famous example was U.S. senator and old-time fiddler Robert Byrd, Democrat, from West Virginia.

42. Toll, *Blacking Up*, 42.

43. Historians of American popular music occasionally mention the birdcalls that accompanied the song, and a few note the role played by Milburn. However, they usually seem unaware of the song's widespread endurance as a fiddle tune. See, for example, Sigmund Spaeth, *Read 'Em and Weep: The Songs You Forgot to Remember* (Garden City, N.Y.: Doubleday, Page, 1927), 68–70; Douglas Gilbert, *Lost Chords: The Diverting Story of American Popular Songs* (Garden City, N.Y.: Doubleday, Doran, 1942), 43; Charles Hamm, *Yesterdays: Popular Song in America* (New York: W.W. Norton, 1979), 139, 260.

44. Dena Epstein, "The Folk Banjo: A Documentary History," *Ethnomusicology* 19 (September 1975): 347–371; Robert Winans, "Early Minstrel Show Music, 1843–1852," in *Musical Theatre in America*, Papers and Proceedings of the Conference on the Musical Theatre in America, ed. Glenn Loney, 71–97 (Westport, Conn.: Greenwood, 1981), 72.

45. Charles Wolfe, "Uncle Dave Macon," in *Stars of Country Music*, ed. Bill C. Malone and Judith McCulloh, 43–69 (Urbana: University of Illinois Press, 1976). An excellent source to Uncle Dave's repertory, as well as a compendium of songs borrowed from minstrelsy, is Ralph Rinzler and Norm Cohen, eds., *Uncle Dave Macon: A Bio-Discography*, JEMF Special Series, no. 3. The most complete recorded collection of Macon's music is found in a box set issued by the JSP label.

46. Ronald L. Lewis, "From Peasant to Proletarian: The Migration of Southern Blacks to the Central Appalachian Coalfields," *Journal of Southern History* 55, no. (February 1989): 77–102; William H. Turner and Edward J. Cabbell, *Blacks in Appalachia* (Lexington: University Press of Kentucky, 1985).

47. Robert Winans, "The Folk, the Stage, and the Five-String Banjo in the Nineteenth Century," *Journal of American Folklore* 89, no. 354 (October–December 1976): 407–37. Robert Cantwell has written a provocative discussion of the possible indebtedness of most professional banjo styles to African or Afro-American music, in *Bluegrass Breakdown: The Making of the Old Southern Sound* (Urbana: University of Illinois Press, 1984), ch. 4, esp. 100–103. The best study of this influence, as well as an exploration of the ways in which African Americans took the banjo to their white neighbors in the South, is Cecelia Conway, *African Banjo Echoes in Appalachia: A Study of Folk Traditions* (Knoxville: University of Tennessee Press, 1995).

48. W. J. Cash, *The Mind of the South* (New York: Alfred A. Knopf, 1941), 51.

CHAPTER 4

WILLIAM S. HAYS
The Bard of Kentucky

I have long been intrigued by the large number of popular songs from Tin Pan Alley or the late nineteenth century, and from even earlier, that made their way into the repertory of early country music. And I have been often bemused by the tendency of some people to view them as archaic remnants of Appalachian folk song or Elizabethan balladry. Most of these songs have composers (many of whom are easily identified) who originally wrote them for an urban middle-class audience, and who would have been surprised to learn they were preserved, often in greatly altered forms, by plain-folk Americans and by the commercial hillbillies. Thanks to the research of such scholars as Gus Meade, Richard Spottswood, Norm Cohen, and Henry Sapoznik, we now know the origins of many of these songs, as well as the names of the people who wrote them. In *Singing Cowboys and Musical Mountaineers* I tried to describe the interrelationship of the popular and folk music traditions in the United States and the ways in which they provided one of the major underpinnings of country music. In this essay—originally published in the *Register of the Kentucky Historical Society* (1995)—I have told the story of William S. Hays, one of the best of the late nineteenth-century pop music writers.

My bark of life was tossing down
The troubled stream of time,
When first I saw your smiling face,
And youth was in its prime.

I'll ne'er forget where e'er I roam,
Wherever you may be,
If ever I have had a friend,
You've been that friend to me.

ALTHOUGH THE LYRICS OF "YOU'VE BEEN A FRIEND TO ME" BETRAY THEIR ORIGINS in the Victorian climate of the late nineteenth century, most people now would probably assume that the song is a hillbilly piece. Real hillbilly fans, in fact, would describe it as a "Carter Family song" (named for the popular Virginia group who introduced the song and many others like it to country music) and would attribute its authorship to A. P. Carter. It actually was written by William S. Hays, the most popular American songwriter of the late nineteenth century.[1]

Hays did not become wealthy through his involvement in the music business, because sheet music merchandising was virtually the only available avenue through which a writer could make money from his compositions in the nineteenth century. Nevertheless, these sales do tell us something about popularity. It is now impossible to obtain the precise figures, but one contemporary estimate in 1873 declared that the John L. Peters Publishing Company had sold about 2,688,000 copies of seventy-one of Hays's songs.[2] While historians of popular music are generally aware of the commercial success that Hays enjoyed in his own time, most seem to assume that his songs enjoyed immediate popularity and then vanished forever after the ragtime revolution permanently changed the nature of American popular music. Hays's songs, then, are treated as period pieces when they occasionally resurface in nineteenth-century anthologies or when they are performed in recital by a properly costumed revivalist singer who attempts to re-create, with exaggerated diction and trilled "r's," the "quaintness" of the Victorian Age. The modern perceptions of Hays, both in and outside of the musical academy, were well summed up by a writer for the *Louisville Courier-Journal* who in 1987 assured his readers that "you've probably never heard of him" and "you've probably never heard of his songs, either."[3]

Although most of us today may never have heard of Will S. Hays, we probably have heard his songs. Old-time and bluegrass fiddlers sometimes play an instrumental version of one of his many "Irish" pieces, "Shamus O'Brien," while country singers still periodically revive such numbers as "We Parted by the River Side," "Jimmie Brown, the Newsboy," or "I'll Remember You, Love, in My Prayers." Those who have followed country music since long before it became chic will surely remember Eddy Arnold's popular recording of "Molly Darling." Hays's authorship of that song was properly acknowledged, but in most cases, contemporary musicians and fans have no clearer idea of the origin of these songs than do the historians. The songs have become the property of the people, or, to use a phrase once favored by folklorists, they have "entered folk tradition." Abundant evidence exists that, well before Cecil Sharp made his famous collecting expedition into the southern mountains in 1916, people there were already admitting some of Hays's songs into their hearts and repertoires.[4] A few of his religious dialect songs, like "Keep in de Middle ob de Road," circulated so sufficiently and anonymously that they were sometimes described as "Negro Spirituals."[5]

Hays's career reminds us of the thin line that has always separated folk and popular culture. His songs did not simply win widespread popularity in his own day; many of them quickly moved away from the song sheets and minstrel and vaudeville stages to become part of the musical repertoires of plain folk everywhere. By the time Hays died in 1907, he was generally aware that his songs had at one time attained widespread popularity, particularly among the plain people for whom he professed to write.[6] However, he may not have known that his songs and poems were also generating parody and imitation. "Keep in de Middle ob de Road," for example, experienced the fate of many popular and traditional songs; it was turned into a political parody in 1892 by a wing of the Populist Party that opposed fusion with the Democratic Party and remained faithful to the candidacy of James Weaver.[7] "Little Old Log Cabin in the Lane" may be one of the most parodied songs in history. It gave rise to numerous songs such as "Little Old Sod Shanty," "Little Joe the Wrangler," and "Little Red Caboose behind the Train." We do not know whether Hays was aware of these "tributes" nor whether he knew that one of his poems, "The Faithful Engineer" (1886), inspired the very popular and still enduring "Life's Railway to Heaven" (often known by its first line, "Life Is Like a Mountain Railroad") "composed" in 1891 by Charles Tillman and M. E. Abbey without attribution to Hays.[8] Certainly, Hays could not have known that very soon some of his songs would receive renewed life with the birth of the country music industry.

Regardless of the fate of his songs, Hays was not a "country" songwriter, because clear distinctions concerning "rural" and "urban" music had not yet appeared in a nation that remained basically rural, even as it moved to the city. On one hand, he was one of the many "poets" whose work often appeared in American newspapers, magazines, garlands, gift books, folios, or in private printed collections during the nineteenth century.[9] He was also a songwriter who, like most writers in mid nineteenth-century America, including Stephen Foster to whom he was often compared, had one foot in the "genteel tradition" of song composition and another in the thriving commercial business of blackface minstrelsy. Many of his songs, such as "Evangeline" and "I'll Remember You, Love, in My Prayers," clearly revealed the influence of the romantic school inspired by the Irish musician Thomas Moore, and they differed little from the large body of songs, in both England and the United States, designed for middle-class drawing rooms and piano-dominated family parlors. Blackface minstrelsy, on the other hand, made it possible for professional and semiprofessional songwriters to "thrive" in the United States.[10]

Whatever his pretensions for genteel acceptance might have been, Hays's songs won their widest circulation when performed by men in black-face who took their shows to cities, towns, and hamlets all over the United States.[11] "Darky" songs, replete with ham-hock sentiments and ham-fisted dialect, emerged often from Hays's facile pen. Minstrel entertainers knew very well, though, that their audiences loved to cry as well as laugh; consequently, blackface tenors such as D. S. Wambold also popularized Hays's genteel and sentimental love songs. Such songs then moved from the minstrel stages, via sheet music, into the middle-class parlors where Hays intended them to be.

While his songs eventually circulated around the world, Hays never strayed very far from his hometown, Louisville, Kentucky, where he was born on July 19, 1837, and died on July 23, 1907. The son of Martha Richardson and Hugh Hays, a prosperous manufacturer of wagons and agricultural implements, Will received a good private-school education and some private musical instruction before venturing off to Hanover, Indiana, and Georgetown, Kentucky, for a couple of years of college training. The musically precocious youth, who could play several instruments, did not earn a college degree, but he blossomed into a poet during that brief academic hiatus. Writing his first song at the age of fifteen—a tune called "The Little Ones at Home"—and easily turning out reams of doggerel and poetry, Hays inspired his classmates to refer to him as "Shakespeare," a moniker later falsely assumed to be his middle name.[12]

Hays wrote about 350 songs during his lifetime, but he never made music his full-time profession. We do not know why he was reluctant to commit his time fully to music, but his caution may have been motivated by the insecurity of the music business or by the grueling grind that defined the life of a minstrel or vaudeville performer. Hays supposedly had a good singing voice, and he made occasional appearances with professional groups who came to Louisville. In fact, he managed a minstrel troupe, Crème de la Crème of Minstrelsy, for a brief period. Anything more than this minor involvement with performance would have seriously strained the relationship he enjoyed with his wife, Rosa Bell McCullough, whom he married in 1865. Furthermore, Hays had considerable skills and interests outside of music that assured him and his family a comfortable living.

The three enterprises that forever dominated his life—newspaper reporting, riverboat piloting, and songwriting—engaged Hays's time when he returned home to Louisville in 1857. Profiting from his father's connections, he became a clerk on a riverboat and eventually worked his way up to the position of captain. Before and during the Civil War, he piloted boats on both the Ohio and Mississippi Rivers. He also became a secretary for George D. Prentice and a reporter for the *Louisville Daily Democrat*, and he served as a war correspondent for that paper for about a year during the Civil War, accompanying the Army of the Cumberland as it moved south. Hays also seems to have found time during this period (probably after the fall of Vicksburg) to pilot the *Grey Eagle*, a river transport, on the Mississippi between Vicksburg and New Orleans. During one of these trips he was arrested and placed in a New Orleans jail. His crime was authorship of "My Southern Sunny Home," a tune that angered the notorious General Benjamin "Beast" Butler, commander of Union troops who had occupied the Crescent City in 1862. It is difficult to understand why the song would have so infuriated the general:

> Oh! Mother dear, I have come home,
> The home I loved so true,
> But I'm unhappy, all is changed,
> Yet there's no change in you.
> Each flower lifts its blushing face,
> The birds are glad I've come,
> But nature seems to weep around
> My Southern, sunny home.[13]

Although the dates are unclear, Hays also worked for a period of time at the end of the 1850s for the D. P. Faulds Music Store in Louisville, a large merchandising store that also occasionally published the songs of local writers. For this firm Hays wrote his first successful song, "Evangeline" (based on Longfellow's poem about the Cajun exile). He then linked his name to the mythology of the South when, according to his later testimony, he wrote the first version of the great southern anthem, "Dixie." Hays claimed that he and a fellow worker, Charles Ward, obtained a piece of sheet music in 1857 that bore the title "Dixie." The melody was an old one that apparently had been floating around the South for many years (Hays said that it was a Scottish tune). He attached to it a couple of verses and a chorus describing the joys of life way down in Dixie's land.

> Dixie lan' am de lan' of cotton,
> Cinnamon seed and sandy bottom,
> Look away down South in Dixie.

> I wish I was in Dixie, hi ho, hi ho,
> In Dixie lan' I'll take my stan'
> To lib and die in Dixie,
> Hi ho, hi ho, I'll lib an' die in Dixie.

He eventually gave the song to a local militia group, the Buckner Guards, who took it South in early 1861 after the Civil War began. Hays never wavered in his claim to the song that is universally attributed to Dan Emmett. Unfortunately, no sheet music copy of his version survived since the files of the Faulds Company were consumed by fire, and only oral testimony provided any kind of corroboration.[14]

His brief employment with the D. P. Faulds Company was Hays's only full-time affiliation with any phase of the music business. His other all-consuming love, the Ohio River that ran near his birthplace at Hancock and Main Streets, competed successfully with his passion for music. Until retirement he worked off and on as a riverboat pilot, bought and sold steamboats, and served as the "river editor" for the *Louisville Courier* from about 1868 until 1898, writing about weather and stream conditions, sailing schedules, and river lore and gossip. He was greatly beloved by the men who plied their trade on the river, and at least two steamboats were named for him. Hays's intense and lifelong association with the Ohio River nevertheless remains strangely underrepresented in his music. He composed a few songs about railroads and other industrial ventures, but during his long career as a poet and songwriter he penned very few songs about the river and said virtually nothing about music in his newspaper columns. While many songwriters have exploited the romance of the river, Hays's failure to do so is intriguing. Consciously or unconsciously, he kept his vocations completely separate. River life—the rugged, dangerous experiences of rough men—seems to have dominated the masculine side of his nature, while music represented what may have been the feminine impulse in his personality.

During his long career as a songwriter, Hays wrote in virtually every idiom familiar to his American audiences. Many of these songs clearly embodied his personal predilections, but some of them also reflected current popular fashions and attitudes. Coming of age during the Civil War and living in a state with ardent and divided loyalties, Hays wrote a variety of songs that dealt with patriotism or otherwise commented on the war. His first successful war song, "The Drummer Boy of Shiloh," probably owed its popularity to the penchant for sentimentality that colored much of the literature of that era, as well as the religious symbolism that was universally employed by writers of all descriptions. Few people, North or South, could react with indifference to the fate of a young boy who knelt in prayer as he died. Like the soldiers who cried as they gathered around their youthful dying companion, wartime listeners may also have wept when they were reminded repeatedly in all five stanzas about the boy who "prayed before he died."[15]

Living in a politically sensitive border state, Hays was careful to cast most of his wartime patriotic songs in a cautious, nonpartisan vein. "My

Southern Sunny Home" suggests an affinity with that region, but the song makes no political allusions and actually is little different from the plethora of romantic songs about Dixie that poured from the minstrel stage both before and after the war.[16] Although he may have had some sentimental attachment to the South, Hays was an ardent Unionist, and he wrote songs like "The American Flag" and "The Union Forever" (both in 1861) that reflected this loyalty. He also composed a tribute to General Sherman's victories in Georgia, although the realization that the war would soon be over probably inspired "Sherman and His Gallant Boys in Blue" as much as did a surge of patriotism.[17]

Politically, though, Hays remained a staunch Democrat, and some of his songs embodied that loyalty. On at least three occasions, his songs endorsed Democratic candidates—George B. McClellan, Samuel Tilden, and Grover Cleveland. In a song that endorsed McClellan for president, "The Constitution as It Is. The Union as It Was," his conservatism and pro-southern attitudes also accompany Democratic Party loyalty:[18]

> The good old ship will brave the storm
> The pilot will be true.
> No danger while the Democrats
> Will constitute the crew.
> No North, no South, no East or West.
> They only know one cause,
> The Constitution as it is.
> The Union as it was.
> Let abolition find its grave,
> Secession sleep beside—
> And give "our little Mac" the helm
> And let the old ship glide.

While Hays's basic political affiliations emerge clearly in his songs, no distinct political philosophy can be discerned. On the whole, his lyrics endorse traditional relationships and divisions of roles among men and women; they support the racial hierarchies of his time and value sobriety, morality, and honest, productive toil as the keys to a successful life.[19] Some songs sympathize with the problems faced by farmers in the late nineteenth century, and these tend to endorse the pro-producer philosophy that claimed farmers as the true source of wealth in the United States. One finds no comparable songs about industrial workers, nor any recognition of the horrendous conditions found in the mills, mines, or railroads of the nation. While he could speak against monopolies and praise producers in a song like "Good as Wheat" (1873), Hays nevertheless admired the success-ful businessmen of his day, and he dedicated one of his nostalgic songs, "The Little Log Cabin's the Home After All" (1875), to General Basil W. Duke, the president of the powerful Louisville and Nashville Railroad.

Conversely, homeless and outcast people appear frequently in his songs, a preoccupation that carried him at least to the edge of the modern concern with social injustice. Songs like "No Name" about a poor girl found dead in the street (1869), "I Have No Home" (1873), and "Do Not Turn Me from Your Door" (1873) breathe with compassion but imply that the distress suffered by the poor is largely an individual failing that can be ameliorated only by private charity. Life in the cold, impersonal city reaffirms the age-old conviction that the poor will always be with us. The virtuous children of the poor, however—like "Jimmy Brown, the Paper Boy," or the unnamed orphan in "Nobody's Darling on Earth"—can die assured of a reconcilia-tion with Mother in Heaven.

> Nobody's darling on earth,
> Heaven will merciful be.
> There I'll be somebody's darling,
> Someone will care for me.[20]

Like other songwriters of his day, Hays often experimented with dialect. Old Hayseed, a character employed in both his poems and songs, dispensed homely wisdom and advice with a rustic dialect. Hays's German dialect pieces, on the other hand, express little subtlety and tend to be heavy handed in their depiction of ponderous and ludicrous characters. His darky songs come directly from the minstrel tradition and are similarly unsubtle in their exploitation of racial stereotypes. Both the humorous songs in this vein, like "Oh, Sam," about a good-for-nothing darky (1872), or the senti-mental pieces like "Aunt Jane and Uncle Jim," about faithful former slaves who live happily in the little cabin that old massa bequeathed them, paint

*"Mollie Darling" (1872) was probably Will S. Hays's most popular
and enduring song. Eddy Arnold called it "Molly Darling" when
he recorded it for RCA Victor in 1947. "Mollie Darling: Song
and Chorus," by Will S. Hays, composer; Snyder & Black, N.Y.,
lithographer; J. L Peters, N.Y., publisher (1871, 1872).*
Images courtesy of the Special Collections Research Center, Temple
University Libraries, Philadelphia, Pennsylvania.

portraits of childlike men and women clearly ill-equipped for freedom. A few
in this vein, such as "Huldy Hawkins Ball," even anticipate the later "coon
songs" with their heavy dialect, razor fights, and other alleged Negro traits.

Hays also participated actively in the popular musical fashion of
re-creating Scottish and Irish scenes along with appropriate dialect.[21] The
tremendous number of so-called Irish songs written by American writers in
the late nineteenth century might seem incredible unless one recalls the
massive immigration from Ireland to this country at mid-century. Many
consumers of American music could recall life in the old country or, like
Hays, could point to an immediate forebear who came from Ireland or Scotland. Some of his "Irish" songs dealt with comic situations, but the most
successful were such sentimental love songs as "Nora O'Neill," "Shamus

O'Brien," and "Mollie Darling." Hays wrote the latter song in 1871 while recuperating from a sudden bout of illness at the Monongahela Hotel in Pittsburgh, Pennsylvania, that delayed an intended trip to New York to visit his publisher, J. L. Peters. One evening he heard a conversation outside of his window between a young Irish couple, Mollie, a popular serving girl, and her earnest suitor. The young man pleaded with his sweetheart, "Do you love me, Mollie darling? Let your answer be a kiss." The astute songwriter could not let this moment pass. He immediately wrote the lyrics of what became his most popular song and later surprised and delighted the young Mollie with a rendition on thc hotcl piano.

> Won't you tell me, Mollie darling,
> That you love none else but me?
> For I love you, Mollie darling,
> You are all the world to me.
>
> O! Tell me darling that you love me
> Put your little hand in mine,
> Take my heart, sweet Mollie darling,
> Say that you will give me thine.
>
> Mollie, fairest, sweetest, dearest,
> Look up darling, tell me this.
> Do you love me, Mollie darling?
> Let your answer be a kiss.[22]

Sentimental songs like "Mollie Darling" far outnumbered other kinds of material in Hays's repertoire, and they have been the most enduring. In part, he responded to fashion—the sanctification of home and family, the deification of women, and the evocation of beloved but vanished scenes—that touched the lyrics of most writers in the Victorian age. American popular music was influenced strongly by the tradition embodied in "Home Sweet Home" and represented by Thomas Moore, whose songbook *Irish Melodies and National Airs* (1808) circulated widely in the United States during the antebellum period. Although Moore's songs extolled the domestic impulse (the glorification of home, family, and fireside), he often presented these themes through a veil of nostalgia that suggested their fragility or their remoteness in both time and space. Contemporary joys remained evanescent, and real security lay only in some distant or imagined past. And like Hays's great contemporary, Stephen Foster, and other writers who worked within the minstrel tradition, the mythical South often provided a context for songs that extolled home and family values.

Sentimental songs also reflected Hays's personal nature and demeanor. Intensely masculine in enjoying the company of working men and rugged outdoors activities, he was described as a man of "rough ways and profane language," but he was also known for his gentle disposition and strong sentimental streak.[23] In an age when songwriters were said to have "Mother on the brain," Hays's production of "Mother songs" is not surprising. On the other hand, when one recalls that his own mother died when he was ten years old, after leaving him a letter signed "your very affectionate and dying mother," one gains perhaps a better perception of why death and loss might have become such strong preoccupations with him.[24]

Hays loved women, but nothing in the scattered extant material about his life and career suggests that his affection was bestowed either illicitly or promiscuously. He sought female companionship, and most of his song sheets bear dedications to individual women with whom he was personally acquainted. And suitably flattered, they evidently basked in his attention. His lyrics, however, indicate that he reserved his love for old-fashioned women. Prostitutes occasionally appear in his songs, but only as objects of pity or subjects for reform. He saved his scorn for "modern women" like "The Parlor Pet," whom he ridiculed or lectured in both his songs and poems.

> She could play on the piano,
> She could sing and dance and flirt,
> But she couldn't sew a button
> On her poor old daddy's shirt.[25]

Hays treated most of his female song characters—little girls, young women, mothers—with great reverence and gentle affection. His bifurcated Victorian nature dictated that love be a powerful emotion in his songs, but with overt eroticism almost totally absent. Lovers generally conducted their relationships in scenes of pastoral innocence, with nature often serving as a benign backdrop for poignant tales of parting or heartbreak. In "We

Parted by the River Side," a placid natural scene serves as an effective counterpoint for a tale of broken love:

> We parted by the river side, the moon
> Shone down on you and me.
> The stars in Heaven brightly shone, the river
> Murmured to the sea.
> The dewdrops kissed the blushing rose,
> The gentle winds did sigh.
> One word broke nature's sweet repose,
> That sad word was "goodbye."[26]

And in "I'll Remember You, Love, in My Prayers" (often known as "The Curtains of Night"), one of Hays's most beautiful love songs, he once again evokes nature as a context for the narrator's memories of a loved one:

> When the curtains of night
> Are pinned back by the stars,
> And the beautiful moon sweeps the sky
> And the dewdrops from Heaven
> Are kissing the rose,
> It is then that my memory flies.
> As if on the wings of some beautiful dove,
> In haste with the message it bears,
> To give you a kiss of affection and say,
> I'll remember you, love, in my prayers.[27]

Survived by his wife, a daughter, and a son, Will S. Hays died in July 1907. After funeral services at the First Presbyterian Church in Louisville, he was interred in the Cave Hill Cemetery. Flags stood at half-mast on all the ships in the Louisville harbor. Musically, it seemed, more sophisticated audiences, particularly in the cities, had moved well beyond Hays in their musical tastes. Ragtime and other dance-related rhythms preoccupied them, but out in the hinterlands Hays's songs had never been forgotten. Southerners, above all, retained an affection for the songs of the man who had so often identified with their interests and whose lyrics seemed to echo their own self-image of family, home-centeredness, and religiosity. No one could have known that in less than twenty years a new form of commercial music, soon to be described as "hillbilly," would revive some of the songs, if not the name, of Will Hays.

When southern rural entertainers began appearing on radio stations and making phonograph records in the 1920s, they relied on a body of music that was widely known in communities all over the South—a body of music that drew upon British and African American folk resources, gospel songs, and melodies that had first appeared as pop songs in the nineteenth century. Columbia Records described its catalog of southern rural music as "old familiar songs."[28] The songs of Will Hays, Charles K. Harris, Gussie Davis, Paul Dresser, and lesser-known writers who had been active before and after the rise of Tin Pan Alley circulated widely among southern entertainers. These "old familiar" songs had sometimes changed dramatically in both lyric and melodic structure, and their writers' identities had been largely forgotten. In short, they had become folk songs. Their revival in the Jazz Age suggests that many Americans everywhere, north as well as south, still hungered for the songs and rhythms of a simpler and more rural society.[29]

In June 1923, Fiddlin' John Carson, a fiddler and singer from Atlanta, Georgia, made two recordings that ushered in the first phase of country music's commercial history.[30] One side of Fiddlin' John's Okeh record was a version of Hays's "The Little Old Log Cabin in the Lane." Hays's original version was almost ponderous in its use of heavy dialect:

> I am getting old and feeble now,
> I cannot work no more.
> I've laid de rusty-bladed hoe to rest.
> Ole massa an' old miss's am dead,
> Dey're sleeping side by side
> Deir spirits now are roaming wid de blest;
> De scene am changed about de place,
> De darkies am all gone,
> I'll nebber hear dem singing in de cane,
> And I'se de only one dat's left
> Wid dis ole dog ob mine,
> In de little old log cabin in de lane.

In Carson's version, the song had lost most of its original minstrel connotations and was now mercifully divested of its darky phraseology. It instead evoked images of a decaying and abandoned rural society. These nostalgic images resonated strongly with many Americans in the decade of the 1920s, when their own society seemed locked in an irreconcilable embrace with urban progress.[31]

In the years that have followed Fiddlin' John's initial recordings, other hillbilly and country musicians have dipped often into the songbag of Will Hays. Of course, we do not know whether such early hillbillies as Ernest Stoneman, Bradley Kincaid, Vernon Dalhart, the Carter Family, and others obtained their songs from old sheet music or songbooks or whether they learned this material from oral informants as they grew up. We do know that beginning with the next generation of country singers like Lulu Belle and Scotty, Karl and Harty, and the Blue Sky Boys, musicians have usually learned their versions of Hays's songs from the performances of earlier country entertainers or from friends and relatives who learned the songs from commercial sources. A new form of oral tradition generated by commercial entertainment had come into existence.

Country music always has been beset with warring impulses—its domestic side contesting with the penchant for rambling and rowdiness. With his songs of nostalgia, home and family, rural bliss, and tender affections, Hays helped to build country music's domestic repertoire while also serving as a model for other writers. John Lair, country music promoter and founder of the famous Renfro Valley Barn Dance in Kentucky, who made a career out of the commercial cultivation of nostalgia, contributed strongly to the perpetuation of Hays's songs among country entertainers. While working for WLS Radio and the National Barn Dance in Chicago, Lair encouraged the performers under his management—such as Linda Parker, Lily May Ledford, and Karl and Harty—to perform Hays's songs and other vintage sentimental material. While reprinting copies of "Mollie Darling" in 1936 (made available to fans through the station's magazine), Lair described Hays as that "grand old folk song writer."[32] Hays certainly would not have conceived of his music in such terms, nor would have any of the other pop music writers of the nineteenth century. They designed their songs for immediate consumption and seemed to have had little thought about the ultimate fate of their compositions. Hays might not recognize some of his songs today—they certainly do not flourish in the genteel environment so strongly favored by many of his songwriting contemporaries— but he could not be displeased to learn that his songs have moved into the permanent possession of plain folk throughout America.[33]

NOTES

1. Published by J. L. Peters, Cincinnati, 1867.

2. *Louisville Daily Leader,* 1873 (no other information available), from an undated clipping in the possession of Hays's grandniece Mary Frances Kaye (Mrs. Clarke Kaye), Louisville, Kentucky. Hays himself remembered in about 1898 that not one of his songs, which then totaled 348, had sold fewer than 10,000 copies. Dick Work, "Will S. Hays and His Songs," unidentified clipping, circa 1898, in the possession of Mary Frances Kaye, Louisville, Kentucky.

3. Alan Judd, "Fading Notes Hold Images of Claimant to 'Dixie' Fame," *Louisville Courier-Journal,* July 19, 1987.

4. Hays's songs appear, along with other items from popular sources, in the material collected by teachers from their Appalachian-born students at Berea College in 1915 and 1916. Berea College Archives, Berea, Kentucky.

5. *Southland Spirituals* (Chicago and Philadelphia, 1936), 31.

6. For the basic biographical information pertinent to Will S. Hays, I have relied on Mrs. Kaye; the Filson Club, Louisville, Kentucky; the Manuscripts Section in the Kentucky Library at Western Kentucky University, Bowling Green; and Martha Carol Chrisman, "Will S. Hays: A Biography" (Master's thesis, University of Minnesota, 1980).

7. Originally printed in the *Rocky Mountain News* and reprinted in John D. Hicks, *The Populist Revolt* (Minneapolis, 1931), 327.

8. Will S. Hays, *Songs and Poems* (Louisville, 1886); Will S. Hays, *Poems and Songs* (Louisville, 1895). I am indebted to Norm Cohen, who first unearthed the history of this poem/song in his *Long Steel Rail: The Railroad in American Folksong* (Urbana, Ill., 1981), 612–13.

9. In addition to the two collections cited in the previous note, Hays also compiled *Golden Leaves* (St. Louis, 1870), and *The Modern Meetin' House and Other Poems* (Louisville, 1874).

10. The best general history of minstrelsy is Robert C. Toll, *Blacking Up: The Minstrel Show in Nineteenth Century America* (New York, 1974). Nicholas Tawa is the best student of nineteenth-century American popular music. Most pertinent for an understanding of the musical climate in which Hays wrote is Tawa's *The Way to Tin Pan Alley: American Popular Song, 1866–1910* (New York, 1990). See also Martha Carol Chrisman, "Popular

Songs of the Genteel Tradition: Their Influence on Music Education in Public Schools of Louisville, Kentucky, from 1850 to 1880" (PhD diss., University of Minnesota, 1985).

11. In addition to the work of Robert Toll, other studies that illustrate the wide-ranging travels and influence of the minstrel shows and other forms of itinerant entertainment are Phillip Graham, *Show Boats: The History of an American Institution* (Austin, Tex., 1951), and Robert B. Winans, "The Folk, the Stage, and the Five-String Banjo in the Nineteenth Century," *Journal of American Folklore* 89 (1976): 407–37.

12. Hays apparently never used "Shakespeare" as his name. He always used as a signature, "Will S. Hays."

13. "My Southern Sunny Home" (New Orleans, 1864).

14. For a discussion of Hays's association with "Dixie," see G. E. Johnson, "Some Southern Writers: Will S. Hays," *Taylor-Trotwood Magazine* 6 (October 1907): 84–89. Given the free-and-easy way in which songs have circulated in the United States, Hays's claim of authorship is not altogether implausible. It should be noted, however, that the folk origin of "Dixie's" melody has always been universally recognized (even by Hays). A recent book challenges the claims made by both Hays and Emmett; see Howard L. Sacks and Judith Rose Sacks, *Way Up North in Dixie: A Black Family's Claim to the Confederate Anthem* (Washington, D.C., 1993). For Emmett's side of the story, see Hans Nathan, *Dan Emmett and the Rise of Early Negro Minstrelsy* (Norman, Okla., 1962).

15. "The Drummer Boy of Shiloh" (Louisville, Ky., 1863).

16. See Earl Bargainneer, "Tin Pan Alley: The South in Popular Song," *Mississippi Quarterly* 30 (1977): 527–65.

17. "Sherman and His Gallant Boys in Blue" (Louisville, Ky., 1865).

18. "The Constitution as It Is. The Union As It Was" (Louisville, Ky., 1863).

19. Unfortunately, no single definitive collection of Hays's songs exists, either on record or in print. The song sheets I have seen are located in the Filson Club, Louisville, Kentucky; the Manuscripts Section of the Kentucky Library, Western Kentucky University, Bowling Green; the Music Division of the Library of Congress, Washington, D.C.; and the W. R. Hogan Jazz Archives, Tulane University, New Orleans, Louisiana.

20. "Jimmy Brown, the Paper Boy" is now known as "Jimmy Brown, the Newsboy" because of a widely popular recording by Lester Flatt and Earl Scruggs (Columbia 20830, and on *Foggy Mountain Jamboree*, Columbia CL 1019). They learned their version from the Carter Family. It was originally published by J. L. Peters, New York, in 1875. "Nobody's Darling" was published by J. L. Peters, New York, in 1870.

21. Hays told one reporter, Dick Work, in about 1898 that two of his songs, "Nora O'Neill" and "Shamus O'Brien," were "heard from one end of Ireland to the other" and that "they are singing my songs in Scotland now." He noted further that he had written a collection of "Scotch songs under the name of Allen Percy and they had a great sale." Unidentified clipping in the possession of Mary Frances Kaye, Louisville, Kentucky. As far as I can determine, no attempts have been made in either Ireland or Scotland to verify or discount these intriguing statements.

22. Johnson, "Some Southern Writers," 84–89. The original title of the song was "Mollie Darling," published by J. L. Peters, New York, in 1871. Eddy Arnold's popular version of

the song, entitled "Molly Darling," was recorded on RCA Victor 20-2489.

23. Dick Work, "Will S. Hays and His Songs," unidentified clipping, circa 1898, in the collection of Mary Frances Kaye, Louisville, Kentucky.

24. A letter dated April 15, 1847, in manuscripts 28, box 1, folder 3a, Manuscripts Section, Kentucky Library, Western Kentucky University.

25. "The Parlor Pet," in Will S. Hays, *Poems and Songs* (Louisville, Ky., 1895). It may not have appeared as a song.

26. "We Parted by the River Side" (New York, 1866).

27. "I'll Remember You, Love, in My Prayers" (New York, 1869).

28. A variety of terms such as "old-time," "hill country," and "songs from Dixie" was used by record companies to describe rural-oriented music in the 1920s and 1930s. The "Old Familiar" designation described the rural records in Columbia's 15,000 series. The best account of the music business's groping for an appropriate label is Archie Green, "Hillbilly Music: Source and Symbol," *Journal of American Folklore 78* (1965): 204–28.

29. The pop origins of country music are discussed in Malone, *Singing Cowboys and Musical Mountaineers*, ch. 2, 43–68, and in Norm Cohen's extensive liner notes to *Minstrels and Tunesmiths: The Commercial Roots of Early Country Music* (JEMF recording 109).

30. The best account of the commercialization of early country music is the "Hillbilly Issue" of the *Journal of American Folklore* 78 (1965). See also chapter 1 in Bill C. Malone, *Country Music, U.S.A.*, rev. ed. (Austin, Tex., 1985).

31. Hays's version of the song, titled "The Little Old Cabin in the Lane," was published by J. L. Peters (New York, 1871). Carson's seminal recording in 1923 was Okeh 4890.

32. Ads for printed copies of "Mollie Darling" ran in successive issues of *Stand By*, November 14–28, 1936. Described as "one of the sweetest old songs ever written," it could be purchased for 25 cents from the Music Library at WLS in Chicago. Lair's quote comes from *Stand By*, November 21, 1936, 13.

33. The most recent adaptation of a Hays composition is the version of "I'll Remember You, Love, in My Prayers" done by the popular bluegrass band, The Seldom Scene, in *Like We Used to Be* (Sugar Hill SH CD-3822). The band preserves the lyrics of the song but performs it to a melody that neither Hays nor anyone else would recognize.

CHAPTER 5

STRANGER PASSING THROUGH YOUR TOWN
Jimmie Rodgers and the Rambler Tradition

This essay, first published in 2009 in a book called *Waiting for a Train: Jimmie Rodgers' America* (edited by Mary E. Davis and Warren Zanes), was inspired by my participation in a conference in Cleveland in 1997 when Jimmie Rodgers was admitted to the Rock-and-Roll Hall of Fame. Originally delivered as part of a panel discussion, my remarks were very different from the words found here. So when I was asked to contribute to a book of essays commemorating the conference, I decided to concentrate on a facet of Rodgers's career and style that has been endlessly popular to fans and students of country music. In many ways, Jimmie was the consummate Rambling Man.

For a fuller appreciation of Rodgers's music and life, one should consult the wonderful biography written by Nolan Porterfield, *Jimmie Rodgers: The Life and Times of America's Blue Yodeler* (Urbana: University of Illinois Press, 1979); as well as the interpretations contributed by Barry Mazor, *Meeting Jimmie Rodgers* (New York: Oxford University Press, 2009); Jocelyn R. Neal, *The Songs of Jimmie Rodgers* (Bloomington: Indiana University Press, 2009); and Tom Piazza, "Jimmie Rodgers," an essay found on his website, tompiazza .com. Barry Mazor has also written a perceptive book on the man who directed Rodgers's professional career and established many of the norms of country music's commercial development, *Ralph Peer and the Making of Popular Roots Music* (Chicago: Chicago Review Press, 2014).

FROM THE TIME JIMMIE RODGERS BEGAN HIS VICTOR RECORDING CAREER IN AUGUST 1927, his evocation of the rambler engaged many people. While such fascination cut across a wide spectrum of social and generational lines, this interest may have been particularly acute among people from cultures and backgrounds like my own, that is, people with constricted lives—socially, economically, religiously, geographically. Rodgers conveyed the image of a man who had been everywhere and done everything, and who had tasted many of the forbidden fruits of life. And, what's more, he had prospered! Rodgers also "ranged, roamed, and traveled" across many musical categories, sampling widely and exhibiting no apparent prejudice against any of them. This musical eclecticism paralleled a restlessness of spirit that contributed mightily to his appeal. His biographer, Nolan Porterfield, noted that "if the life of Jimmie Rodgers can be characterized by a single element, it would be impermanence. His early home life, continually subject to flux, was followed by a nomadic adolescence and the erratic rambles of an itinerant railroader; later, as a professional entertainer, he was forever on tour or simply going from here to there." The grim disease that killed him, tuberculosis, only added to the mythology already gathering around the singer, for it seemed to be an explanation of his decision to live out on the edge. His short life was and continues to be a romantic blur to most people, a compendium of rumors and half-truths about a man who seemed to live life to the fullest—drinking, carousing, gambling, loving and leaving women by the score, and living well. In this singing life, however, he managed masterfully to convey a sense of reality, not fantasy. Listeners heard and believed him and were introduced to the fullest panoply of ramblers who had ever passed through the lives, experiences, or imaginations of poor people. I use the term "rambler" in this essay as a metaphor for the man (he was invariably a man, even though many women shared his experiences) who defied social convention or responsibility—the gambler, badman, convict, rounder, drifter, hobo, rogue lover, and any number of other socially irresponsible characters—and survived to brag about it.

The original migrants who came to the South from the British Isles, Ireland, and Europe shared an almost symbiotic relationship with ramblers, either knowing them intimately through physical contact or waxing musingly romantic about them in stories and songs. Although the plain folk sometimes suffered from the exploits of pickpockets, brigands and highwaymen, con men, and gamblers, ramblers such as these nevertheless fascinated them. When the folk came to America, they transported remnants

Jimmie Rodgers exploited and profited from his listeners' desire for romantic escape. He is seen here in a cowboy costume, one of his several adopted professional guises.
Photograph courtesy the Bill C. Malone Collection, Madison, Wisconsin.

of songs about bold highwaymen and outlaws, convicts and condemned killers, and dashing but unfaithful lovers. "The Gypsy Davy" was known to most of them, as were Robin Hood, Sam Hall, various rakes and rambling boys, and doomed men who, allegedly, stood before the gallows and recited their farewell songs.

Although ramblers appeared often in British and British-derived folk culture, they also entered popular consciousness through the avenues of black folklore and popular entertainment. As early as the 1830s, touring blackface minstrels (white song-and-dance men who performed in blackface) began introducing to the rural and small-town South songs that described swaggering or ne'er-do-well black characters who seemed to have no visible means of support. Such songs evolved into the notorious "coon songs" of the 1890s, where irresponsible and probably oversexed "darkeys" such as "The Bully of the Town" were depicted as bad hombres who operated outside the pale of law and respectability. These characters were not always as mean as The Bully, and certainly not as vile as such black badmen as Stack-O-Lee, John Hardy, and Railroad Bill, who were commemorated in songs that swelled up from the black underworld of saloons, honky-tonks, and brothels, but they gave hints of the wild freedom and danger that supposedly resided in the forbidden zone of black culture. Then, as now, visions of black culture appealed to white youth who sought exotic and liberating alternatives outside of their own inherited and often repressed social milieu.

By the early 1920s, when Jimmie Rodgers began making his first tentative efforts at a singing career, a whole host of songs of both folk and popular origins that extolled ramblers of assorted types had gained public currency through the performances of minstrel, vaudeville, ragtime, and blues entertainers. Tin Pan Alley circulated its own watered-down versions of such songs, often in the infectious ragtime style. Rodgers certainly picked up songs from black workers during his childhood stint as a water boy and from assorted singers later during his jaunts as a railroad man, but many items in his repertoire came from phonograph records and vaudeville performances. Songs like "Frankie and Johnny" and "In the Jailhouse Now" were as familiar to Rodgers as were the popular love songs of the day.

Jimmie and his audience shared the experiences of living in a society, the rural South, that was being socially and economically transformed. The lives of southern men had been radically reshaped, first by the military defeat of 1865 and then by a succession of economic revolutions that whittled away at their sense of manly independence. Although the belief in freedom had been an illusion for many poor men in the nineteenth-century South, rich and poor alike fiercely defended the values of unfettered masculinity and patriarchal dominance. But in the final decades of the nineteenth century, the traditional avenues of opportunity for poor men gradually narrowed or disappeared. The closing of the open range; restrictions on hunting, fishing, and grazing rights; the expansion of tenantry and sharecropping; and campaigns to curb drinking and gambling and bring men into the moderating confines of the church all did their part to tame the older liberating and hedonistic impulses of southern rural masculine culture.

The era had also seen the emergence of new opportunities and temptations: the proliferation of towns and cities and city culture, an expanding market system, new employment opportunities (particularly railroading, textiles, coal, and petroleum), and the growing availability of popular culture and entertainment. During Jimmie Rodgers's childhood and adolescence, automobiles began to appear with considerable frequency in southern cities, and department stores, movie houses, and phonograph records increasingly brought to working-class eyes and ears the alluring world of cities and consumption that the Sears catalog offered only one-dimensionally.

Jimmie Rodgers cannot be understood as simply a brighter mirror image of the southern plain folk. While it is true that he emerged from and understood southern working people, he diverged from their culture in significant ways. He grew up in or near Meridian, Mississippi, a New South railroad city that lay in the heart of the region. There he had access or exposure to traveling entertainers, vaudeville houses, movie theaters, dance bands, and phonograph recordings. He succeeded as a popular entertainer because he brought to his working-class audiences reminders of the traditional rural society that was slipping away from them and glimpses of the exciting new world of the city that lay in their future. His audience probably included as many women as men, but the latter must have listened with greater approval as he sang, "I can find me more women than a passenger train can haul." But, then, we've been told by Lee Clayton and Waylon Jennings that "Ladies Love Outlaws," so many women may have listened and reacted to Rodgers's boastful songs with mixed emotions. Like the young ladies who centuries earlier had forsaken their husbands and babies to "lie on the cold, cold ground" with Black Jack David or to risk social disapproval and even death with the "demon lover" described in "The House Carpenter," some women may have found in such songs both excitement and cathartic release from hard lonely lives and unhappy marriages. How many of them had lost confidence in their own men as the burdens of poverty and social constriction arose and lingered in the defeated postwar South?

As railroad man and entertainer, Rodgers represented two alluring professions that were unavailable to most southern men. The railroad itself symbolized a distant and enchanting world of freedom and power, qualities that were absent from the lives of most of the region's rural people. In southern communities, railroad men were simultaneously apotheosized as successful and relatively affluent individuals and romanticized as intrepid ramblers who had seen another side of life and tasted its alluring freedom. Entertainers, similarly, lived exciting lives and were perceived ambivalently by the folk. In such communities the musician, almost by definition, was a rambler who provided a welcome service to people but who nevertheless was often viewed with suspicion as a ne'er-do-well who avoided work and responsibility (the classic stereotype of the musician as wastrel, of course, was the drunken fiddler—a figure who appears often in southern lore and narrative). Most touring entertainers in the late nineteenth and twentieth centuries lived hard lives filled with arduous travel, seedy hotels, broken contracts, and inadequate pay. They were often irresponsible in their relationships with family, community, and the law. But part of the illusion of professional entertainment—and every bit as important as the magic they spun on the stage—was the necessity for entertainers to convince the public that their lives were glamorous and exotic. Country singer Tom T. Hall was still insisting, as late as 1969, that "putting up a front" was a requirement in his profession.

Jimmie Rodgers's youth held neither glamour nor exoticism, but in many ways it shaped the rambling persona he later conveyed as an entertainer. Suffering the loss of his mother when he was about six years old, growing up in a succession of relatives' homes, running away repeatedly when he was very young, working on his dad's extra-gang railroad crew, and then traveling extensively as a railroad worker, he was introduced to people from all walks of life and to a multitude of experiences that most of his listeners had never shared. Workers, hoboes, traveling salesmen, policemen, bartenders, waitresses, prostitutes, gamblers, and bootleggers all contributed to a hard but useful education.

When Jimmie Rodgers walked on to a stage, often he was advertised and costumed, as the Singing Brakeman. As this persona, he carried a multitude of alluring and irresistible associations. And whether he wore the straw hat and informal attire of the city dude (which he tended to favor) or the rougher garb of the railroad worker, he exuded an aura of freedom and confidence that was especially attractive to humble Americans during the Depression years.

The urbane image implied by Rodgers's attire was accentuated by his voice, performing style, personality, and choice of songs. The spoken asides of his songs, the "hey hey heys" or "sing them blues, boy" addressed to accompanying musicians or to no one in particular, and the dialogue heard in the corny skits recorded with the Carter Family pulsated with a sense of brash self-confidence. In a preshow interview with a New Orleans reporter in 1929, he remarked that he had sung in Paris and London and before the king and queen in Buckingham palace (none of which was true). He posed for a variety of photographs during his career, in formal dress and as a cowboy or a brakeman, but a photograph that was later reprinted for the cover of one of his RCA Victor LPs captures the image that was probably most appealing to him: it shows him standing with one foot on the running board of a shiny new automobile, casually dressed, and brimming with the demeanor of a successful man-about-town. While his style of performance and affecting songs certainly inspired a host of would-be entertainers, the aura of affluence that clung to his persona probably did as much to convince them that music could be more than a momentary and psychological refuge from unrewarding labor. Professional music performance literally could provide a physical escape from cotton fields, textile mills, tobacco firms, oil fields, and coal mines.

Jimmie's repertoire was diverse, and it is not clear that he favored one type of song over another. His blues songs, however, were his initial ticket to fame, and critics have tended to stress that side of his repertoire most often. It's here that we find the first expression of his rambling catalog, and firm evidence of the fluid manner in which song material floated across the racial divide. The first royalty check he received after he recorded "Blue Yodel," the first of twelve similar items, probably convinced him and the Victor company that such material was highly marketable. In song after song—his blue yodels, and in songs similar to them—Jimmie boasted about his appeal to women ("Give me sweet Dallas, Texas, where the women think the world of me"), and about his refusal to be tied down to any stable relationship.

Rodgers was not the first white man to sing the blues, nor was he the first "hillbilly singer" to specialize in the form. Created by blacks as a medium of self-defense and expression, the blues nevertheless attained universal acceptance in the South. Southern whites had been intimately acquainted with the blues since the turn of the twentieth century when the style began to take shape, and they heard its mournful but liberating cadences on street corners, on work projects, in honky-tonks and saloons, and in traveling shows. White country singers exhibited a fondness for the blues almost from the time their music was first commercialized. They were fascinated with the word "blues" itself, and they attached it to all kinds of songs, some of which were depressing or despairing, but many of which—like "Florida Blues" or "Carroll County Blues"—had neither somber connotations nor any apparent relationship to the classic blues style crafted by blacks. Henry Whitter, however, not only introduced the style to country music with his 1923 recording of "Lonesome Road Blues," he also introduced a motif that has been enduringly appealing to both musicians and fans—the flight to the open road as an escape from responsibility or oppression.

Nor did Rodgers introduce the railroad song to the country music lexicon. Whitter can also claim credit for that innovation with "Wreck of the Old 97," which lay on the reverse side of his initial blues tune. Because of his long association with railroad work and because of his identification as "the Singing Brakeman," Rodgers became closely identified with railroad songs. His train songs generally extolled the idea of escape ("it's better on down the road," and "I'll eat my breakfast here, and my dinner in New Orleans"), but they also recognized the danger of railroad work and the loneliness that often accompanied life on the rails. Engineer Ben Dewberry encountered death with courage, but the hoboes in Jimmie's songs (much like the singer himself) yearned for the comfort of home and the tender care of Mother. Hobo Bill died without the consolation of either: "There was no mother's longing to soothe his weary soul; he was just a railroad bum who died out in the cold."

The "bad boys" in Rodgers's songs were usually young men who were just sowing wild oats, with a night or two in jail as the most extreme punishment that might be expected for their transgressions. A wild fling, however, could lead to death, as Johnny discovered when he two-timed Frankie one time too often. Genuine bad boys wound up with prison sentences, sometimes suffering because of someone else's crime (a fate often encountered by the heroes of country songs) and facing imprisonment for life. The rounders encountered in Rodgers's songs usually posed no real threat to anyone outside their own immediate households. They were good old boys who liked to drink and carouse, but who usually escaped penalty or punishment—except for the anger received from wives and sweethearts who felt neglected—and, presumably, they eventually settled down into a stable life with memories and advice that could be passed on to the next generation of willful young men.

When Rodgers ventured into the performance of cowboy songs, not only did he contribute to the making of a romantic genre that Hollywood exploited with immense commercial success but he also found a way of condoning the independent, wandering style of life that made it sound acceptable. As interpreted by Rodgers and most of the sagebrush poets who followed him, the cowboy was a rambler who apparently, and incongruously, had preserved the proprieties of middle-class society while cutting himself off from the cares and responsibilities of urban civilization. That is, he was a deeply moral person who drew his strengths from God and nature. And as country musicians have demonstrated ever since, with their depictions of rhinestone, Coca-Cola, urban, and cosmic cowboys, he was a character of infinite plasticity.

Rodgers's first utilization of the western myth came in "Waiting for a Train," probably his most commercially successful song, where the railroad bum refers to the wide-open spaces of Texas, "a state I dearly love." His infatuation with the Lone Star State—a love affair shared by many potential ramblers—appeared in still another song that opined "Take me out there where the cowboys sing in the campfire's gleam. Oh, let me rest out in Texas, it's the land of my boyhood dreams." Reinforced by his residence in the Texas hill country town of Kerrville, where he built a mansion called "Blue Yodeler's Paradise," Rodgers (and people like Billy Hill, who pitched songs to him) introduced a catalog of clichés that appeared often in the made-for-movies cowboy songs of the 1930s and 1940s. His cowboys lived carefree lives in the expansive West, surrounded by mild weather and freedom from home and responsibility. "The Yodeling Ranger," for example, while declaring that "My heart is light as I ride through the night," averred further that "I sing while I am in danger, trusting my trigger hand."

The devil-may-care attitude shown by the Yodeling Ranger also surfaced in songs that commented on Rodgers's battle with tuberculosis. He spoke of "whipping that old TB" in a song of the same name, but was more graphic and realistic in "TB Blues" where he noted that "my body rattles like a train on that old SP." His valiant, but losing, battle and his early death from the disease all added to the creation of his mystique. No story about Rodgers has been more often repeated than the tale of his last days in a New York recording studio. He sang his songs, rested between takes on a cot provided for him by the Victor recording crew, and died two days after the sessions were completed. Drawing upon the work of Susan Sontag, the writer and physician John P. Morgan notes that some nineteenth-century writers had seen tuberculosis as "a romantic sadness—a disease of the soul." Tuberculosis, it was believed, tended to "speed up life and to impart to the diseased a consuming passion." It was easy for fans to believe that in the face of impending doom Rodgers's creativity and his decision to live life fully and dangerously had been accentuated.

While Rodgers's early death contributed to his enduring mystique, the myth began well before he died—probably because most people only heard his disembodied voice on recordings and never saw him in person. Stories circulated during his lifetime about his drinking and womanizing, and about his wealth even though he and his family struggled to meet living and medical costs. The stories that allude to his visits to bootleggers may be true, but it seems impossible that he could have consumed so much liquor or caroused so extensively given the growing weakness that characterized his final years.

The fascination with rambling has never disappeared from country music in the years since Jimmie Rodgers's death. His personal imprint has not always been as strong as it was in the 1930s, when a multitude of singers, including Gene Autry, Jimmie Davis, Buddy Jones, and Cliff Carlisle, borrowed his yodel, stage demeanor, and blues idiom to strut and preen about their manly prowess. But the social imperatives that underlay and motivated such boasting persisted in the post-Depression decades. Both Rodgers and his disciples were heirs to a personal code and social system that were deeply rooted in the working-class culture of the South. The Good Old Boys of country music could not often resist the temptation to boast and swagger, or to push against the margins of respectability. Henry Whitter's lonesome road constantly beckoned. They clung to the comfortable fictions of machismo and patriarchal dominance, boasting of their mastery over women, while also seeking to escape them.

While the musical celebrations of the rambling man have drawn heavily on assumptions that would have been familiar in Shakespeare's England, they have often been couched in the cadences and rhythms of black culture. Black culture did not simply provide inspiration for change as well as a language of assertion, it also provided a safe zone for innovation. Black and white styles and idioms interacted so constantly, however, that it was impossible to define them in racial terms or to understand their ultimate origins. Singers continued to attach such words as "blues" and "boogie" to all kinds of songs that bore little or no resemblance to black culture. And they embraced musical styles that, while ultimately traceable to black musicians, nevertheless sometimes came more immediately from white entertainers.

The rambling spirit endured in country music in the lyrics of songs, in the experimentation with styles that reached across cultural borders, and

in the bad boy posturing that has often characterized the lives of entertainers. Lyrically, singers still pull out old warhorses like "Lonesome Road
Blues," "Freeborn Man," "Bumming Around," "Waiting for a Train," and "T
for Texas," or they adopt newly composed items like "On the Road Again,"
"Gentle on my Mind," and "Rambling Fever," to celebrate the flight from
responsibility or the hope for a better life somewhere else. Train songs have
become rare in country music, but truck-driving songs have emerged as
surrogate expressions of power and mobility. Cowboy songs have demonstrated a remarkable resilience and staying power, sometimes echoing the
pastoral fantasies of the Hollywood-generated style but also documenting
the loneliness and boredom that often accompanies the lives of both range
and rodeo cowboys. Political correctness and the lure of Top Forty respectability have warred against the continued acceptance of badman ballads
and rogue lover songs, but such items as "Folsom Prison Blues," "Cocaine
Blues," and "Black Jack David" still appear in bluegrass music or in the
repertoires of alternative country singers.

Stylistically, the excursions made by musicians across musical categories—usually into black music—have fueled country music's most exciting innovations. Whether judged by Charlie Poole's flirtation with ragtime,
Jimmie Rodgers's and Hank Williams's experiments with the blues, Bob
Wills's borrowing from jazz, or the Delmore Brothers' appropriation of
boogie rhythms, country music has profited vitally from the willingness
of certain entertainers to venture beyond the mainstream. Most of these
stylistic departures have been individualistic artists' statements and
should not necessarily be seen as comments about society. Poole, Rodgers,
Williams, and the other early country entertainers may have been restless
young men who sometimes sowed wild oats, but one finds no evidence that
they were ever in rebellion against the world of their parents.

The rockabillies of the late 1950s probably did not think of themselves
as rebels either, but they unleashed a full-scale revolution in American
popular music and contributed to the weakening of traditional racial,
generational, and gender relationships. Elvis Presley, Jerry Lee Lewis,
Carl Perkins, and their fellow rockabillies embraced and synthesized
white country music and black rhythm and blues, performed with a sexual energy that had not been present in earlier forms of white music, and

challenged older orthodoxies. These young ramblers strutted and preened like their country blues predecessors, but ironically, their musical fusions contributed to a sexual awakening among young women and a heightened awareness of their capacity for individual growth. In fact, a few young "wild women" participated aggressively as entertainers in the rockabilly movement, suggesting that a new day indeed was dawning in the lives of white working-class women in the South.

Boastful song lyrics and venturesome style bending were harmless expressions of the rambling spirit. More often than not—as in the case of Jimmie Rodgers—they did not equate with the actual character or personality of the performer. Singers could easily sing about shooting their women down or about coming off a week-long drunken binge and then go about a settled and normal life as husband and father. Wild or impulsive young men appeared in country music from the beginning of its history, and such hedonistic behavior generally added to their appeal. Charlie Poole, whose heyday came in the mid-1920s, was the prototype of the young musician whose "too-fast past" meant "a slow-down future." Poole was a textile worker from North Carolina, but music and good times often diverted him from the rigors and monotony of mill work. He was, according to writer Tom Piazza, "deeply allergic to routine." Before he burned himself out at the age of thirty-nine, this sometime textile worker, singer, and banjo player led a band called the North Carolina Ramblers, whose influence is still felt in the music of southeastern country entertainers.

Unlike Poole, most country music bad boys have managed to survive the experiences of youthful dissipation, and only a few have suffered the fate of his Texas contemporary, the fiddler Prince Albert Hunt, who died in 1931 outside a Dallas tavern, the gunshot victim of a jealous husband. Jimmie Rodgers's life pales in comparison with that of Poole or Hunt, or with any number of entertainers who have since appeared. But he nevertheless seems to have been the first country musician to sense that the hint of badness or irresponsibility could be commercially appealing. His early death encouraged still another romantic vision that had plenty of precedents in art and literature—that of the young doomed artist, cut down before his time by excesses that fed both creativity and destruction.

Bad boy role playing, which has been a common sport in American music, has usually been a benign fantasy in country music. Several of the music's early performers, such as Jimmie Tarlton, Harry McClintock, Harry McAuliffe, and Goebel Reeves, were merely wanderers—restless spirits who roamed the country searching for excitement and working at various jobs (as cowboys, miners, seamen, or common laborers) before they took up the profession of full-time entertainer. In a few cases, the wandering spirit brought a complete separation or estrangement from home and family. Harry McAuliffe, who built a long career on WWVA in West Virginia as "Big Slim, the Lone Cowboy," was orphaned at age eight and on the road by the time he was eleven. Referring poignantly to his sisters and brother, he said, "I have seen and talked to them very few times in these years gone by, always on the roam I go." But if McAuliffe was cut adrift by misfortune, Goebel Reeves consciously abandoned a settled and respectable life in order to follow a rambling existence. This self-styled "Texas Drifter," who roamed widely in the 1930s as a migrant laborer and radio hillbilly singer, was the son of a prominent Texas businessman and state legislator. Not only did he break ties with his family, he concocted an autobiography that made no mention of his true roots. His most famous song, "Hobo's Lullaby," described the personality that Reeves had assumed.

Thirty years after Reeves's career, Lecil Travis Martin revealed that visions of the solitary migrant life could still pique the curiosity of music fans. His travels through the world had been no less expansive than those taken by Reeves, but his journeys were undertaken as a professional airline pilot. When he retired from that job, Martin assumed the professional stage moniker of "Boxcar Willie" and embarked on a new career as a country singer and yodeler, winning acclaim in England and the United States. Martin was an avid partisan of "traditional" country music at a time when pop styles seemed to be overwhelming it. His embrace of the hobo mystique, then, was more than a tribute to the rambling tradition; it was also a reminder that this venerable impulse was central to the music's identity. But unlike Reeves, Martin never let the fantasy consume his life. Boxcar Willie ruled the stage, but Lecil Travis Martin preserved his ties to family, home, and middle-class life.

One can point to the working-class roots of the rambling impulse and see its close relationship to the transformation of southern manhood, but it is clear that the idea would not have endured as an inspiration for song had it not found resonance in the larger American popular culture. The rambler, in the final analysis, is the projection of our hopes, dreams, and fantasies. Rambling itself has always been a defining American option, a way of coping with life—an escape from responsibility or a promise of new opportunities somewhere else—"I ain't gonna be treated this away," and "It's better on down the road." Increasingly bound to conventional middle-class life and to jobs that offer little excitement, we turn to foot-loose characters who either defy the system or work outside of its confines. More accurately, we romanticize those who seem to fulfill our expectations or who are skillful enough to play the roles that we desire. Country music has had more than its share of rebels or star-crossed personalities who have catered to public fantasies.

One thinks, for example, of "the man in black," Johnny Cash, a basically conservative and religious individual, who nevertheless built up a public profile as an anti-authoritarian battler against both the music establishment and social injustice. No country singer has had a larger or more avid following among rock-weaned youth than Cash. His popularity with the readers of *Rolling Stone* gives testament to his reputation as a rebel and an individualist. Widely believed to be an ex-convict, Cash's outlawry instead was confined largely to pill addiction and a youthful habit of trashing hotel rooms. His contemporaries Merle Haggard and David Allen Coe had genuine prison records. Haggard traded on his convict past with hit songs like "Branded Man" and "Mama Tried," while Coe came before his fans with profane language, a scowling face, tattooed arms, and the moniker of "the Mysterious Rhinestone Cowboy." He spent much of his time in the early 1970s arguing vociferously that he had indeed killed a fellow inmate in the Ohio State Prison.

Jerry Lee Lewis and Hank Williams Jr. claimed neither convict pasts nor lives of lawlessness, but they paraded through country music as swaggering hedonists, inordinately fond of whisky, women, good times, and making music. Williams added an historical touch of rebellion to his persona with the use of Confederate symbols and songs that glorified Dixie, but sometimes sounded more like a modern survivalist with belligerent songs like "A Country Boy Can Survive."

Except for their reputed (and trumpeted) close association with drugs, Willie Nelson, Waylon Jennings, Billy Joe Shaver, and their circle of friends were generally law-abiding musicians who nevertheless bore the description of "outlaws" during the early 1970s. Sporting beards, black hats, and cowboy paraphernalia, these musicians fused a variety of musical and cultural elements—rock, country, counterculture, antihero, and western desperado—and won the largest audience among young people that country music had ever enjoyed. Their receptivity to the sound and energy of rock music and their predilection for marijuana and cocaine set them apart from earlier country musicians and allied them with other young entertainers who were conducting similar experiments. southern rock musicians such as Charlie Daniels, the Marshall Tucker Band, and the Allman Brothers, along with Gram Parsons and his country rock cohorts in California, borrowed heavily from older musical styles and projected the fantasy that they were in rebellion against middle-class norms of behavior.

Musicians such as the Austin Outlaws did not simply strive to satisfy the longings of their fans. They also had their own fantasies with which to contend. They and other musicians who had come of age in the 1950s often displayed the temptation to borrow more than the songs and styles of their musical heroes. Jimmie Rodgers's music apparently had little impact on their lives, but that of another star-crossed singer—Hank Williams—figured prominently in their thinking. Put in its crudest form, it meant that they got drunk because Hank Williams got drunk. They flirted with an early death because their hero had presumably done so. Making cutting-edge music and living life on the edge seemed synonymous to them. Waylon Jennings described this propensity as the "Hank Williams Syndrome." When he declared that "Hank, it's no thanks to you that I'm still living today," Jennings recognized not only the appeal of the rambler legend but its destructiveness as well.

Like Jimmie Rodgers in an earlier era, Hank Williams attracted musicians and fans with both his music and presumed lifestyle. Since both men died early, at the peak of their professional careers, they were easy to mythologize. Hank has been exploited by those who hope to justify or rationalize their own behavior. Hank Jr., for example, sang "If I get stoned, I'm just carrying on a family tradition." Today's rebels in country music see Hank as a parent figure, the music's first outlaw who resisted authority and lived life recklessly. In short, they take the materials of a pathetic and tragic life—the unconquerable habits of a dissipated young man—and use them to lend legitimacy to their own rebellion. Hank has been described also as a musical rule breaker. Citing a couple of up-tempoed songs like "Rootie Tootie" and "Move It On Over"—a brief snippet of video footage that shows him bobbing and weaving as he sings "Hey, Good Looking," a few observers have seen him as an early rockabilly. One historian, with even less evidence, declared that Hank's "frequent reliance on a heavy beat and physical gestures and gyrations on stage clearly made him controversial in more conventional circles and foreshadowed the style of Elvis Presley."

It is easy to see why some musicians, fans, and commentators today gravitate toward the presumed rule breakers or bad boys of country music's past. Many of country music's most exciting innovations were fueled by such musicians and by fantasies about Rodgers, Williams, Woody Guthrie, Bob Wills, Johnny Cash, Merle Haggard, and other free spirits who continue to inspire the work of creative artists. Above all, though, the search for rebel path breakers or outlaws should be seen as a reaction against the corporate mentality of Nashville, its reluctance to experiment, and the blandness and sameness of its sanitized musical product. This tendency to search for and emphasize the alleged blood-and-guts history of country music had been particularly noticeable among those singers variously described as "Alternative," "No Depression," or "Insurgent." Singers with widely differing styles of performance, but all of them sharing a refusal or inability to compromise with the Top Forty compulsions of Nashville, have all been placed under the alternative rubric. Few, however, have expressed their disgust as graphically as Robbie Fulks, who vented his feelings about Nashville in a tune called "Fuck This Town."

When Fulks made that recording in 1997, he was performing his fusion of country and rock for a little storefront recording label in Chicago called Bloodshot. Describing its musical product as "insurgent," Bloodshot featured artists who performed country music with an edge or attitude. One of these performers, the Scottish-born artist and musician Jon Langford—the central force in the Waco Brothers—spoke first of hearing country music back home in Leeds, England. His comments provide insight about the way in which perceptions of the older styles of country music have given voice to a pent-up rebellion in many young fans like himself. Hard country music, he said, "was a total eye opener; confirmation of something dark, sinewy, and beer-drenched that lurked beneath. These stripped down tales of lust and loneliness, sex and death, struck a chord . . . and connected our alienated drunk, commie souls to a strident tradition we barely knew existed."

Although neither Jimmie Rodgers nor Hank Williams would have described their music the way Langford heard it, they nevertheless constitute part of the pantheon of heroes that inspire many of today's young musicians. Most of us, of course, neither make music professionally nor do we harbor any deep-seated desire for rebellion. But sometimes we do seek momentary escape in the rhythms of a song or in contemplation of an entertainer who seems unfettered by rules and regulations. When we face frustration in this increasingly complex world or confront injustice at the workplace, we generally respond as Merle Haggard did in the great song written by Sonny Throckmorton: "I just dream and keep on being the way I am." But when we dream, our thoughts sometimes turn to the gestures, exploits, or songs made by those who hew an independent course or who stand against the norm. We love our ramblers, whether they pass through our imaginations in the lyrics of a song or appear to us in the flesh-and-blood guise of a performer. They seem to take the risks and seize the thrills that we are afraid to venture. Above all, we love the passion that they bring to life and the visceral resistance that they bring to the complexities that dog our day-to-day existences. Admittedly, we do romanticize these entertainers, and sometimes see heroism where only weakness is present. After all, most country music singers—such as Merle Haggard, George Jones, Johnny Cash, Townes Van Zandt, and Steve Earle—achieved greatness in spite of their blemishes or only after they had overcome them. Nevertheless, it is hard to resist believing that the same restless energy and desire for personal freedom that often lured them into temptation also fueled their artistic creativity. Consequently, we're not always sure about how much we want our heroes to "reform." Country music's most recent bad boy, Steve Earle, brought a personal turbulence to professional entertainment that eventually landed him in jail while also making him one of the most respected musicians in the last few decades. The arrogance, passion, and resistance to authority that have defined his life, for good or ill, have also shaped his music, endowing it with pulsing vitality, experimentation, and creativity, attributes that have been in short supply in recent country music. The untamable quality that clings to Earle's life and music simultaneously repels and attracts, suggesting both the perils that lie outside the prescribed boundaries of our culture and the possibilities of renewed strength and excitement that lie hidden in these forbidden zones. With his freely offered four-letter words and air of angry defiance, Steve Earle seems far removed from the gentle Jimmie Rodgers. But we need to remember that fathers can't always control the direction taken by their progeny.

CHAPTER 6

THE BLUE SKY BOYS
The Sunny Side of Life

I'm sure that I had heard occasional records by the Blue Sky Boys on disk jockey shows, or perhaps on Shreveport's Louisiana Hayride, but I did not really pay much attention to them until the mid-1950s when I found copies of a few of their RCA Victor 78 rpm records in an old furniture and antique store in Oak Cliff, Texas. My life was changed when I heard their precise, plaintive harmonies on songs like "The Sweetest Gift," "You've Branded Your Name on My Heart," and "Kentucky." I thought then—and still think—that they made the prettiest sound ever fashioned in country music. I was also impressed by the Bolick Brothers' choice of songs, and by their commitment to traditional sounds and styles. When Richard Weize, proprietor of Germany's Bear Family record label, offered me the chance to write the liner notes to the CD box collection of the Blue Sky Boys' complete array of RCA Victor recordings—*The Sunny Side of Life*—I eagerly accepted the opportunity. The results are offered here in this essay. Bill Bolick died in Hickory, North Carolina, on March 14, 2008, but he did live long enough to see the issuance of the Bear Collection and my accompanying notes.

IT'S HARD TO BELIEVE THAT THE BOLICK BROTHERS WERE ONLY SIXTEEN AND EIGHTEEN YEARS OLD when they made their first records in 1936. We hear their boyish, and seemingly innocent voices singing with a wisdom and maturity far beyond their years, songs about tragic love, murder, suicide, and spiritual passion. They went on to fashion a sound and style of harmony unlike any ever heard before in country music, qualities that have remained unmatched. Over a career that, except for four years of military service during World War II, extended from 1935 until 1951,

*The Blue Sky Boys, Bill Bolick with mandolin and Earl Bolick with
guitar, in California for an appearance at the UCLA Folk Festival, 1965.*
Photograph courtesy the Collection of Peter Feldmann,
Bluegrass West, Los Olivos, California.

Bill and Earl Bolick bequeathed a legacy of such songs as "The Sunny Side
of Life," "Why Not Confess," "Kentucky," and "Behind These Prison Walls
of Love" that are still sung by bluegrass and old-time country musicians
today. A wonderful achievement for a duet that went into professional
music essentially because the $10 a week they received for their first gig
was better than the $3.50 or less that was available for menial jobs back
home!

Originally named Bolch, the Bolicks were heirs to the German migration that came down out of Pennsylvania over the Great Wagon Road into
the Piedmont South in the late eighteenth century. Descendants of those
migrants still live in the southern Piedmont, which extends from western
Maryland to northwestern Georgia. Bill and Earl's ancestors settled in
Catawba County, a region of heavy German concentration, and Bill now
lives very near to the place where he was born. Serious, disciplined, and
often austere in conduct, these people were mostly Lutherans, but Men-
nonites and various pietistic groups also thrived among the migrants who

ventured south. Most became farmers, and evidence of their efficient husbandry can still be seen in the region. Over time, however, many people in the area around Hickory became workers in the furniture or cotton mills. Hickory in fact still prides itself in being the furniture capital of America.

The Piedmont, that broad geographical expanse that lies between the coastal plain and the mountains, was a region of social, economic, and ethnic diversity. A medley of people, mostly English, Welsh, Scots-Irish, and Huguenot French came in from the east and north where they met and intermarried with the Germans. Lutherans, Presbyterians, Baptists, Methodists, dissenting sects, and Holiness people established churches and set out to convert the region, but they found more often than not that believers moved very easily from one group to another. Although the mountains can be seen looming in the West and have always exerted a romantic fascination for people everywhere, the Piedmont has had its own special history. Comprising about 35 percent of the state, the North Carolina Piedmont long remained rural, but in the late nineteenth century the area became a diversified region of farming, milling, lumbering, and railroad activity. It was a meeting ground for agricultural and industrial enterprises and for rural and urban folkways. In short, it was the region where the Old South confronted the New, a crossroads or intersection of change. Railroads came; towns and cities appeared along the "fall line," that imaginary line that marked the place where water from the western rivers rushed over the falls on the way to the coast. Rural people, mostly from agricultural backgrounds, came into the emerging cities from nearby hinterlands and from the mountains to work in the tobacco, cotton, and furniture mills.

These newcomers came in contact with, and usually embraced, town ways—ready-made clothes, new fashions, labor-saving commodities, department stores, vaudeville and movie houses, and innovations in technology. Automobiles became increasingly available after World War I, and radio stations began to appear in such towns as Danville, Roanoke, Charlotte, Raleigh, Durham, Chapel Hill, Greenville, and Columbia, booming their signals through the surrounding countryside, down along the Atlantic Coast, and sometimes well into the mountains (musicians also went to nearby stations in Atlanta, Asheville, Bristol, and other towns that were contiguous to the Piedmont). Fledgling musicians flocked to the stations from all over the rural Southeast during the 1920s and Depression years, sharing their songs and styles with each other and building networks of personal appearances through their broadcasts. The Piedmont, in short, was one of the historic but often overlooked birthplaces of American country music.

Bill Bolick was born in West Hickory, North Carolina, on October 29, 1917, and Earl was born on November 16, 1919, to Garland and Annie Elizabeth Hallman Bolick. Bill and Earl were the fourth and fifth children in a family of four boys and two girls. Mom Hallman came from a farm "out in the sticks" in the adjoining county of Caldwell, but went to work in a cotton mill when she was about nine years old. She met her future husband, Garland, in the Ivey Mill where he was working at the age of twelve or thirteen. She once told her son Bill that conditions in the mill and mill village were no worse than they had been out in the country, and that she had worked in the fields as a small girl. Garland Bolick, who grew up in Catawba County, left the mills much earlier than his wife did, and he worked for a short time in the furniture industry, largely in the pay of Hickory's most prominent industrial proprietor, George Ivey. Almost everyone in West Hickory worked for Mr. Ivey, who was the owner of an iron foundry, the Southern Desk Company, maker of school and church furniture, and the cotton textile mill where Garland and Annie Elizabeth had met. By the time Bill and Earl were born, Garland had found employment in the local post office, a position that carried greater respectability and a measure of economic security than would have been possible for a mill worker. The Bolicks in fact were one of the few families in their area of North Carolina who owned a telephone, a radio, and an automobile.

Religion was a defining component of the Bolick Brothers' lives. The family's forebears were Lutheran, but Garland and Elizabeth were converted to the teachings of a holiness denomination, the Church of God (Anderson, Indiana, branch), early in the twentieth century. This version of the Church of God (which should not be confused with the Pentecostal denomination headquartered in Cleveland, Tennessee, and which is noted for its belief in "speaking in tongues") sent evangelists into the South and Midwest and held its first meetings in people's homes. On its Internet website, the church describes itself as a "conservative, Bible-believing church in the holiness tradition," that is, it believes in scriptural inerrancy and the necessity of striving for a sinless life.

Bill recalls that his parents were "religious to the extreme." He and his brothers and sisters lived a "very guarded life" and were required to attend church faithfully. Forbidden to go to the movies, or to say bad words (even "darn" was proscribed), or to consume liquor or cigarettes, Bill and Earl suffered the ridicule of other kids who sometimes called them "old saints." This early religious indoctrination definitely shaped the Bolick Brothers' character and outlook on life, contributing a seriousness, moral purpose, and social conservatism that also appear in their music. Religion also contributed mightily to the songs they chose to perform. Throughout their radio career, gospel songs constituted more than half of their repertoire. Many of those hymns were learned from their father, who in turn obtained them directly from hymnals, such as *Reformation Glory*, used in Church of God services and even sometimes written by such church patriarchs as D. S. Warner and B. E. Warren. The boys almost inevitably recoiled against the strictness required in their homes and eventually rebelled against the institutional side of religion.

When Bill and Earl were born, the country music industry had not yet emerged. People made music at home, in church, or at religious-related meetings, or in some community setting, but professional outlets for such talents were limited. Although the Bolicks did not exhibit exceptional musical talent, music was nevertheless loved and cherished in the home. Mom Bolick had played the autoharp and parlor organ when she was a girl, but it seems she did not play after her children grew up. The Bolicks did enjoy singing around the house, with secular songs almost as common as hymns in the family's repertoire. As was probably true in most rural homes, they generally remembered songs in fragments. Mrs. Bolick, for example, knew portions of such songs as "Single Girl," "Bonnie Blue Eyes," "Cripple Creek," and "I'm Troubled." Garland Bolick knew a few old ballads, such as "Lord Thomas" and "The Butcher's Boy," which he tried to teach to his sons, but his chief preference was religious material. As a young man he had attended singing schools, bought the paperback hymnals that were promoted there, and could read shape notes. Some of his favorites, augmented by versions that the Bolick Brothers learned from published hymnals, can be heard in the box collection produced by Bear records.

Radios were scarce in Catawba County when Bill was growing up, but in 1924 Dad Bolick obtained a battery-powered receiving set, one of only four that were owned in West Hickory. The Bolicks began listening to Chicago's WLS Barn Dance virtually from the time the show went on the air, receiving an introduction to the music of such people as Chubby Parker, Lester McFarland and Robert Gardner (Mac and Bob), Doc Hopkins, Bradley Kincaid, and Arkie the Woodchopper (Luther Ossenbrink). Dad Bolick particularly liked Chubby Parker and ordered the sheet music of such songs as "Nickety Nackety Now Now Now." The Bolicks also bought copies of Bradley Kincaid's famous songbooks, along with the 1932 edition of *Mac and Bob's Book of Songs*, a publication that became an indispensable source of several of the Blue Sky Boys' songs.

Bill Bolick became fascinated with music as a small child. He collected old songs and copied them down in a school tablet. He was never an antiquarian, however, and instead looked upon songs as items that were to be sung. He genuinely loved and revered the old songs, but he never hesitated, either as a child or as a performing professional, to alter the lyrics or the melodies in order to make them coherent and singable. Garland Bolick also supported the musical interests of his sons, and he bought instruments and instruction books for them. Probably reflecting his interest in Chubby Parker, he first bought a five-string banjo for Bill for $4.95, and later an orange-colored guitar with a sprung neck for $6.00. In about 1930 or 1931 a neighbor named Hugh Rinehardt taught Bill a few guitar chords and a thumb and three-finger style of playing. Bill then bought a chord book and began chording the songs that he learned at home and over the radio. He soon began playing with Richard "Red" Hicks, a newspaper delivery boy who sometimes stopped by the house to pick and sing. This was the same Red Hicks who sang and played with the Blue Sky Boys on the radio in the late 1930s.

Armed with a few chords and a growing storehouse of songs, Bill became a mentor to his younger brother Earl who, in about 1932, had begun making tentative steps toward learning the mandolin that their dad had bought for him. Earl never warmed up to the mandolin, however, and instead began playing the guitar, utilizing the few chords that Bill taught him. Earl developed a rock-solid sense of rhythm, using only his thumb and employing only a few basic bass runs. Bill's first tentative steps toward public entertainment came in about 1934 or early 1935 when he began playing music with Lute Isenhour, a very talented musician from Taylorsville, about twenty-five miles from Hickory. Lute had a huge repertoire of songs and had mastered several instruments, including the five-string banjo, which he played with thumb and two fingers, a style reminiscent of Charlie Poole. Singing with Lute could be difficult, because their two voices did not blend smoothly, but Bill nevertheless began to pick up invaluable experience as a harmony singer. He also began to make personal connections that provided an entrée into the professional performance of country music in North Carolina.

Lute had already played with Homer Sherrill, a fiddler, in the East Hickory String Band and had made a few appearances on the Crazy Barn Dance on WBT in Charlotte. The Barn Dance was the brainchild of J. W. Fincher, the Atlanta representative for Crazy Water Crystals, a Dallas-based concern that marketed a product that though little more than a laxative was touted nevertheless as a cure for numerous bodily ailments. Crazy Water Crystals sponsored country music on radio stations throughout the Midwest and South and often required bands to use "Crazy" in their titles. Hoping to use the East Hickory String Band more frequently on his radio shows, Fincher asked Homer Sherrill to find a singer for the group. On the recommendation of Lute Isenhour, Bill Bolick joined the band and traveled with them in March 1935 to WWNC in Asheville. Bill had been earning $3.50 a week in the stock room at Woolworth's in Hickory. He found the $10 a week offered by Fincher too tempting to turn down. Sponsored by Crazy Water Crystals, the band now became known as the Crazy Hickory Nuts.

Still playing guitar, Bill stayed with the band from March to June 1935. Despite their presence on the powerful broadcasts of WWNC, and despite an occasional appearance on the Crazy Barn Dance in Charlotte, the Hickory Nuts received few requests for personal appearances, the lifeblood of country bands during the Depression years. Bill left the group and went back home to Hickory. During his absence, Earl, who was only fifteen years old, had run away from home with two local boys, ostensibly "looking for gold" but probably more anxious to find some relief from the stern discipline exacted by his parents. After experiencing the exotic charms of Oklahoma, Texas, New Mexico, Wyoming, and Colorado, he returned home, determined not to go back to school (even telling his parents that he would run away again if school was required). He and Bill began making music together, this time with Earl on guitar and Bill, more and more, on mandolin. In October 1935, WWNC once again asked the boys to return to Asheville. Lute, however, chose not to make the trip. He was married with two children and believed that his position as a straw boss at the Hickory Overalls Company was more secure than a radio hillbilly gig. With Earl as their new musical sidekick, Bill and Homer won the sponsorship of a Knoxville concern, JFG Coffee, and began playing as John, Frank, and George, the Good Coffee Boys.

The Good Coffee Boys became one of the most popular acts that WWNC had ever hosted. With a repertoire of gospel and old-time songs similar to that later used by the Blue Sky Boys, the trio earned ten dollars a week each. More important for their tenure at the station and for the future of their careers, they also pulled an extensive amount of fan mail. Since they had no car, they could not at first respond to requests for personal appearances. Homer, however, had accumulated a little money while working at a hosiery mill and was able to make a down payment on a 1929 Whippet automobile. Their bookings picked up. They were in Asheville until March 1936, playing in the WWNC studio atop the Flatiron Building, when J. W. Fincher asked them to relocate to Atlanta on WGST. His offer of a weekly salary of twenty dollars apiece, and a four-hundred-dollar automobile purchased with no down payment and five dollars a week subtracted from each musician's pay, was too good for young country boys to refuse.

Bill's vivid memories of the make, color, and style of the vehicles used in those years amply illustrate the importance of the automobile as a status symbol, and as an indispensable means of promoting the careers of itinerant country entertainers. They chose one of the two company cars that were offered, a "pretty and sporty" black 1934 Ford with red wheels and silver rims. The fascination with new automobiles—the most visible sign of urban allure and a powerful material symbol of some status—contrasted strongly, though, with the hillbilly image that Fincher fastened on the boys. During this first Atlanta stint, they were required to perform at their radio sessions dressed in overalls and straw hats, posed in such attire for a photograph that was widely circulated, and were described as the Blue Ridge Hillbillies.

The trio arrived at WGST the day after the Monroe Brothers played their last show on the station. The Monroes presented their final show at 12:15 P.M. on March 3, and the Blue Ridge Hillbillies gave their first program the following morning at 7:00. Even though they were bucking up against powerful WSB, a local fifty-thousand-watt station, and had to build their audience slowly, listener by listener, Bill Bolick maintains that they "were an immediate hit." Mrs. Hingle, who ran Crazy Water Crystals' Atlanta office and was Fincher's fiancée, became their booking agent and actually accompanied the boys on many of their concert trips. She received a fourth of the money that was made, but no one was dissatisfied as long as bookings remained constant. Playing almost exclusively in schoolhouses in northern Georgia, eastern Alabama, and western North Carolina, the Blue Ridge Entertainers played to consistently large crowds and added to their gate receipts with the hawking of a small songbook that Fincher financed. Mrs. Hingle also received a fourth of the book's profits, mainly because some of her poems and her photograph were included.

Bill Bolick was still alternating between guitar and mandolin when the group went to Atlanta, but increasingly he turned exclusively toward the mandolin. His adoption of the instrument came partly in response to listeners' requests but also because the Monroe Brothers were making people conscious of the mandolin. Bill Bolick, though, was never seduced by the hard-driving style of Bill Monroe and, instead, drew his stylistic model from Lester McFarland, the WLS Barn Dance performer whose tasteful, melodic mandolin tremolo had distinguished the performances of Mac and Bob. Bill particularly liked McFarland's occasional habit of playing a third part while he and his partner, Robert Gardner, were singing duets.

Bill and Earl became the Blue Sky Boys in June 1936 shortly after their first recording session for RCA Victor in Charlotte. J. W. Fincher had arranged an audition for the Blue Ridge Hillbillies after consultation with Van Sills, a Victor talent scout. Before the trip to Charlotte took place, however, the Bolicks had a dispute with Fincher who accused the brothers of trying to exclude Homer Sherrill from the forthcoming record session. As Bill remembers it, he and Earl had made it clear to Homer, whose background fiddling was incompatible with their singing style, that they would sing their duets alone with mandolin and guitar. Homer agreed with the arrangement, and they mutually decided that he would be included on other cuts playing breakdown fiddle tunes. When "old man Fincher," as they described him, told them that they were getting too big for their britches, Bill and Earl quit the station and went their way thinking that the Charlotte session was still scheduled.

Fincher organized another version of the Blue Ridge Entertainers, featuring Homer Sherrill and, unknown to the Bolicks, canceled the Charlotte sessions. Bill and Earl went back to West Hickory and on the appointed day rode to Charlotte with their parents. When they arrived at the site of the proposed audition (the second floor of the Southern Radio Corporation Building), another North Carolina duo, the Dixon Brothers (Howard and Dorsey) were recording. Bill and Earl waited in a room nearby, and Earl began reading some material that was there. The veteran Eli Oberstein, who was directing the recording session, spoke sharply to them: "What do you think this is, a reading room?" Earl Bolick responded just as testily and said he didn't give a damn what it was. After learning who they were and expressing surprise that they had shown up for a session that had supposedly been canceled, Oberstein said, "So you're the fellows that imitate the Monroe Brothers?"

Replying that they didn't imitate anyone, Bill and Earl then prepared to leave the building. But Oberstein apologized and permitted the audition to proceed. After one verse and a chorus of "The Sunny Side of Life," with its enchanting syncopated harmony response, Oberstein stopped them, and said "That'll do. That's good. That's different."

Despite this rather tense beginning, the relationship between Oberstein and the Blue Sky Boys seems to have been warm and friendly in the years that followed. He even contributed to the coining of their stage name. Feeling that too many country acts had "brothers" in their title, Oberstein suggested that they come up with some alternative name that could be used on their recordings. Together, they devised the name "Blue Sky Boys," a fusion of two colorful images that described the landscape of western North Carolina, "Blue Ridge," and "Land of the Sky."

The ten songs recorded at this first session were representative of their prewar repertoire—gospel, traditional ballads, old parlor pop tunes, and one recently composed song (by Karl Davis) that had an old-time feel, "I'm Just Here to Get My Baby out of Jail." Sales figures for these early recordings are unavailable, but they apparently sold well enough to warrant a second session on October 13, 1936 (also in Charlotte), and the release of a Victor flyer that described them as "the new hillbilly kings." Bill and Earl's youthfulness come across strongly on these early records, but so does their trademark facility for harmony and tasteful selection of songs. Although as brothers they shared a variety of traits that contributed to a close vocal blend (similar phrasing, a common pronunciation of words, and an intimate awareness of each other's mannerisms), the Blue Sky Boys' harmony was not a spontaneous product of smooth and similar sibling interaction.

The two brothers were actually quite different in temperament and style. Bill was intense, something of a worrier, and cautious; Earl was low-key, lackadaisical, and a risk taker. But no two people in country music have ever achieved such a close vocal blending. They chose their songs carefully, strived to find lyrics that told a sensible and complete story, but did not hesitate to alter them if greater coherence was necessary. Vocally, they chose keys that permitted easy phrasing and harmony, and they tried earnestly to avoid singing in unison on any line or phrase. Bill and Earl were equally responsible for the signature Blue Sky Boys sound. Earl sang the lead in a nasally resonant, and almost reedy, tone that blended seamlessly with Bill's smooth tenor harmony. Although their contemporaries the Delmore Brothers (Alton and Rabon) also sang with a sweet harmonious blend, neither they nor any other "brother duet" ever achieved the kind of close and poignant tone fashioned by the Bolick brothers.

Recordings like these lent prestige to performers' names and did bring in a little bit of money, but a successful career could not be sustained on the strength of the one-cent-per-record royalties that performers received. Victor's Bluebird records sold for thirty-five cents, and artists could purchase bulk orders of them for twenty-two cents apiece. The company also subtracted a breakage fee from the meager royalties that were accumulated. Consequently, early country music entertainers depended on radio broadcasts and the personal appearances that they generated. The typical country entertainers of the 1930s were itinerants who moved from one radio station to another, building a string of concert appearances in the listening range of the station, and hawking their picture-songbooks and commercial sponsors (if they had any) until the territory was "played out." Then they moved on to another more potentially lucrative radio deal. The Bolicks were no exception.

Although radio was central to the Blue Sky Boys' career, at least a couple of years passed before they achieved any kind of stability in that format. It is clear that people often exploited them because of their youth and inexperience, and in those years, the Blue Sky Boys seldom got the respect that they deserved. They actually went back home two or three times during the early years of their career, not certain that they would return to full-time entertainment. Illness sidetracked the brothers on at least two occasions, first in the summer of 1936 immediately after the initial Charlotte session. Prior to the session Bill had been afflicted with acute sinus blockage and was able to sing only through the extensive use of a Benzedrine inhaler that his father provided. A doctor informed him that one nasal passage was blocked, probably through a broken nose that had gone undetected. For about six or eight weeks their career was put on hold while Bill recovered from both nasal surgery and a tonsillectomy.

In September 1936, they joined with the veteran old-time fiddler and bandleader, J. E. Mainer, for a short stint on WSOC in Charlotte sponsored by Crazy Water Crystals. Although Mainer denied the assertion, Bill and Earl always believed that J. W. Fincher had covertly engineered the association. In any case, they left the station within three weeks feeling that their independent identity as performers was being ignored. Despite prior assurances by Mainer that they would be introduced on shows as the Blue Sky Boys, the station's announcers called them Bill and Earl and treated them as if they were simply part of Mainer's cast.

After a short sojourn in Hickory, they returned to Atlanta and WGST in February 1937, accompanied again by the fiddling of Homer Sherrill, who came in and out of their career and did not hesitate to leave if he got wind of a better deal. In late July of that year, Homer left abruptly to take a job in Raleigh with Wiley and Zeke Morris. The old-time fiddler Charlie Bowman joined the Bolicks on personal appearances for a short time, but an automobile accident near Conyers, Georgia, soon brought their career to a halt. No one was seriously injured, but the loss of the car, which was absolutely necessary for personal appearances, coupled with Homer's departure thoroughly demoralized Bill. He and Earl went back home to Hickory again in August, convinced that fate had never intended for them to have a successful career as musicians. They did complete a scheduled recording session in Charlotte on August 2, but Bill had resolved to quit the music business. Back in Hickory, he and Earl worked for ten cents an hour doing odd jobs for an uncle and cut wood on an older brother's farm for four dollars a cord. Happily for all of us, an old friend encouraged them to make one more try at a successful musical career.

In late December a childhood friend, Carroll Hollar, offered to accompany them back to Atlanta, said they could use his car on personal appearances, and declared his willingness to be their booking agent. The Bolicks knew that they would find a friendly reception at WGST but were decidedly skeptical about Hollar's ability to book shows in the small schoolhouses in Georgia. Largely through the insistence of their parents (who among other reasons wanted to divert Earl's professed intention to join the navy), Bill and Earl returned to Atlanta. They were accompanied by Carroll and by another childhood friend, Richard "Red" Hicks, who had agreed to become a member of the Blue Sky Boys. Hicks played the guitar, learned to sing lead on their trio pieces, and sang an occasional solo. This stint on WGST lasted for two years, from early January 1938 to December 1939.

Bill was right in his estimation of Hollar's booking abilities. Hollar was gone within two months, along with the automobile that supported their tours. Dad Bolick, though, came to the rescue and supplied them with his 1936 Ford. For at least six months or so, the Blue Sky Boys barely survived, living mostly on boardinghouse food and the cheap hamburgers they bought on the road. Their circle of listeners, however, rapidly expanded, despite the fact that WGST had to contend with the powerful competition of another Atlanta station, WSB. No act on WGST had ever attracted the fan mail that the Blue Sky Boys received.

One of the best recollections of their career, and a poignant example of the faithfulness shown by loyal fans, survives in a hand-inscribed journal written in ink in an 8x10 school tablet, by Ruth Walker of Greensboro, Georgia, and maintained from May 9, 1939, to May 9, 1940. Covering both the last seven months of their stint on WGST and the first five months of a new tenure on WPTF in Raleigh, North Carolina, Walker wrote down each day the titles of the songs and comedy skits performed by the Blue Sky Boys. She then sent the booklet (emblazoned with a self-illustrated cover) to the boys. From this valuable journal, we learn that a typical Blue Sky Boys radio show was much more varied than the sound heard on their recordings. Bill and Earl, of course, sang their famous and usually mournful duets, but they also joined with Red to sing trio pieces, usually vintage gospel songs. Red generally sang a cowboy or contemporary country song, or even a pop tune like "Red Sails in the Sunset," and Bill, accompanied by his thumb-and-fingers style of guitar playing, occasionally sang old parlor songs like "After the Ball" or "Just Tell Them That You Saw Me."

Realizing that Depression audiences expected a complete entertainment package, Bill and Earl made humor an essential element of their radio programs and personal appearances. The boys actually did blackface comedy on some of their early stage shows, but their most enduring comic creation was the character of Uncle Josh. While Bill sang one of his solos, or did some sort of routine with Red, Earl would leave the stage and return in the guise of an old rustic gentleman, sporting a goatee and bedecked in floppy hat, baggy pants held together with suspenders and a big safety pen, with wire-rimmed glasses sitting on the end of his nose. Probably inspired by an earlier stage character with the same name, who had been played by the vaudeville humorist Cal Stewart, Uncle Josh was a know-it-all who bragged about his conquests with the women, ribbed his fellow musicians, and drawled corny jokes: "What did one heel say to the other heel? We're being toed (towed) in!"

Hillbilly entertainers ultimately judged radio station affiliations by the number of personal appearances that they generated. For this reason, then, the Blue Sky Boys' association with WPTF in Raleigh, North Carolina, which ran from December 1939 to May 1941, was one of the most successful of their career. This five-thousand-watt station reached up into Virginia and down the coast into South Carolina. Owned by the Durham Insurance Company (the call letters meant "We Protect the Family"), the station profited from the prosperity generated by the region's tobacco economy. The boys each earned salaries of twenty dollars a week, but they prospered more from the rash of personal appearances made within the listening range of the station. They had no booking agent but, instead, gauged the size and location of potential audiences through the fan mail that came to the station. Most of their shows were held in schoolhouses and were generally sponsored by churches, women's clubs, and other civic organizations. The personal appearances generated by their shows on WPTF kept them on the road almost every day of the week. One concert in Roanoke Rapids, North Carolina, netted them $266, a sum that seemed impressive to the boys during those often-bleak Depression days. The boys received 65 percent of the gate and were free to peddle their songbooks and other products. One item, a little paperback songbook called *Your Favorite Songs*, printed in 1940, sold over five thousand copies.

When the Bolicks began their professional radio career, this network of schoolhouses and theaters was still being described as the "Kerosene Circuit," because the venues often had no electrical power and were instead illuminated by oil lamps. In the absence of sound amplification, audiences had to be very quiet and attentive in order to hear the programs. Government-sponsored rural electrification, though, gradually brought power to all but the most remote areas, and sometime in 1940 the Blue Sky Boys bought their first sound system (one microphone and two speakers).

When the Blue Sky Boys moved to WFBC in Greenville, South Carolina, in May 1941, war was already raging around the world. The conflict, however, probably seemed far away and irrelevant to the lives of most Americans, including the Bolicks. The Blue Sky Boys were on top of the world. Their radio sound had improved greatly, they believed, through the presence of Samuel "Curley" Parker from Gilmer County, Georgia, who had joined them in October 1940. Parker's voice blended well with theirs when he sang lead in their trio numbers, and he could play both backup fiddle for their duets as well as occasional breakdowns. They owned two automobiles, had money in the bank, owed no bills, and enjoyed great popularity throughout the Atlantic South.

WFBC promised to be as economically rewarding as WPTF. They first had a show at 6:30 in the morning and later added another one at 12:45. The shows inspired more mail than any act had ever garnered on the station—from three hundred to four hundred cards and letters per day—and requests for personal appearances that were too numerous to fill. Hoping to use them as bargaining power for increased compensation, Bill gathered up a few bags of mail and took them to program director Jim Reid's office. Reid responded a few days later with a generous offer of eighty-seven dollars per week and the promise of a sustaining sponsor. By that time, however, their prospects had changed dramatically. Bill reached in his pocket and pulled out the military draft notice he had just received. On August 11, 1941, both brothers were inducted into the army. They did not return to civilian life and their interrupted music career until more than four years later.

Bill saw service in the Pacific Theater, including the initial landings on Leyte in the Philippines and Okinawa. Earl went to the European Theater as a member of the 507th Parachute Infantry Regiment, was wounded, and won a Purple Heart and Silver Star for his participation in the invasion of Normandy and the Battle of the Bulge. Apparently, except on casual and informal occasions, neither Bill nor Earl made music during their military service.

Earl was discharged on September 22, 1945, and Bill on Christmas Day of the same year. When they got back home, they did what most Americans did in the immediate aftermath of the war: they tried to return to what was familiar. They invited Curley Parker to meet them at their parents' house in Hickory and began practicing for a resumption of their music career. During these postwar years they received overtures from other radio stations, including the powerhouses in Richmond and Wheeling, West Virginia, WRVA and WWVA, and from the queen of country radio barn dances, the Grand Ole Opry. But on March 25, 1946, they returned to reliable WGST and the friendly folks who had befriended them there. For several months the transcriptions of their Atlanta shows were also played on stations in Macon and Savannah. Their fans had not forgotten them. In April 1947, for example, WGST received 1,443 letters and cards addressed to the Blue Sky Boys from 175 towns in Georgia, Alabama, and

North and South Carolina. Bolstered by this outpouring of fan support, the boys very easily resumed the busy schedule of personal appearances that had prevailed before the war.

Other record labels, including Bullet, King, Columbia, and Decca, also courted the Blue Sky Boys, but they returned instead to the familiar territory of RCA Victor. In the months that followed, they often had reason to doubt the wisdom of the Victor affiliation, correctly sensing that the company was pouring most of its resources into the careers of budding superstars like Eddy Arnold. They returned to the recording studio on September 30, 1946, working under the direction of A&R man Stephen Sholes, but they never felt as comfortable with him as they had with earlier directors Eli Oberstein and Frank Walker. For the first time another musician, fiddler Curley Parker, joined them on their recordings. They recorded only four songs, but if RCA Victor was testing the waters to see how well they would do in the postwar era, the label must have been satisfied with the success of a song borrowed from the Bailes Brothers, "Dust on the Bible," which sold two hundred thousand copies. The next session, held in New York City in May 1947, yielded eight recordings and the biggest hit of their career, "Kentucky," a beautiful performance marked by Bill and Earl's sweet soulful vocal harmony and a stunning interchange between mandolin and fiddle. The recordings and radio transcriptions from these years inform us that, while the war years had cost the Bolicks dearly in time and money, the brothers had lost nothing in vocal or instrumental quality. Their voices were stronger; their harmonies were more precise and nuanced, and Bill's mandolin playing was exquisite.

The chief difference heard in the music of the Blue Sky Boys after the war was in the increase of newly written songs, several of which commented directly on the recent military conflict and its consequences. In their eyes, though, there was little difference in the prewar and postwar repertories. The new material was "traditional" in that it embodied the mood, the seriousness, and moral purpose they had always sought and valued. In the preface to a little booklet called *Favorite Hymns and Folk Songs* prepared in 1947, the Bolicks reaffirmed, in language similar to that used by Bradley Kincaid in his songbooks back in the 1920s, their affection for "traditional" music as the possession of decent and down-to-earth people. Like Kincaid, they rejected the term "hillbilly" and said that the word was properly associated with songs of the hobo and honky-tonk nature.

The Bolicks played on four different radio stations between March 1948 and February 1951 when they retired: twice at WNAO in Raleigh, WCYB in Bristol, Virginia, WROM in Rome, Georgia, and KWKH in Shreveport, Louisiana. As before the war, they stayed on a station until they played out the territory, or until they found what seemed like a better deal. Recognizing that such a schedule would keep them constantly on the road, Bill bought a twenty-nine-foot trailer in Raleigh and lived in it for the rest of the Blue Sky Boys' career. Their association with WNAO was one of mutual respect. Remembering the good days in Raleigh before the war, when they were associated with WPTF, they decided to test that market one more time. They were present when WNAO opened its doors in March 1948, and during their stay on the station, they enjoyed an extensive and enthusiastic fan response. Bill Bolick recalls that the Blue Sky Boys were "the big attraction at the station." Bookings for personal appearances, however, were not as good as expected in Raleigh (some venues, for instance, were canceled because of a local polio scare). When they left the station in January 1949, the station's general manager, Dudley Tichenor, wrote an unsolicited and glowing letter of recommendation for them, noting that during their stay the Blue Sky Boys had received over half of the mail sent to the station.

After a possible deal with WNOX in Knoxville fell through, the Bolicks transferred in March 1949 to WCYB in Bristol, Virginia. It is not surprising that they thought of Bristol as a viable option. Bill and Earl felt that WCYB must be a "Mecca" for musicians because its popular hour and a half noontime show, Farm and Fun Time, had attracted such legendary musicians as Charlie Monroe, Flatt & Scruggs, and the Stanley Brothers. Even though the station paid no salary and demanded 5 percent of any proceeds made from personal appearances, the Bolicks believed that a good income could be earned through an affiliation with the station. Although this arrangement was not unusual in the radio business, bookings were sparser than expected and were held too often in very small schoolhouses. Consequently, revenues were smaller than anticipated. A series of strikes in the southern Appalachian coal fields also reduced the amount of money that was available for entertainment.

The Bristol association may have been economically disappointing for the Blue Sky Boys, but it did mark the beginning of their partnership with the famous fiddler Leslie Keith, the "composer" of "Black Mountain Rag" and probably the most versatile musician with whom they were ever associated. He joined them in November 1949 and stayed with them for the remainder of their career. His fiddling style did not complement the Bolicks' vocal sound as well as Parker's did, but he was a consummate showman and helped them to put on an entertaining show. He played such tunes as "The Fox Chase" and "Pan American Blues" on the harmonica, flailed the banjo in the old-time style, and was a bullwhip artist, a talent that he sometimes displayed in conjunction with Uncle Josh's comedy routine.

The Blue Sky Boys moved again in December 1949 to WROM, a five-thousand-watt station in Rome, Georgia. They felt that they were treated well at this station and were back in the territory that had been good to them during their WGST days. More and more radio stations were beginning to appear, however, and Rome itself had three. Consequently, the competition for broadcasting space and revenue made it difficult to obtain a sufficient number of bookings.

In early 1950, Mel Foree, a representative of Acuff-Rose Publishing House, advised the Bolicks to contact KWKH in Shreveport, reminding them that a similar act, the Bailes Brothers, had done quite well in the market served by that powerful station. KWKH's broadcasts reached out into surrounding states and sometimes could be heard as far west as Arizona. The station's reputation had thrived because of the earlier tenure there of Hank Williams. The Blue Sky Boys moved to Shreveport in April 1950 and became part of the famous Louisiana Hayride, the Saturday night radio show that was often described as "the Cradle of the Stars." The station's general manager, Henry Clay, promised them a sponsored program and a good salary but insisted that, in line with station policy, they must have five members in their band. The promise was never fulfilled, and the insistence on additional band members was never fully enforced. On the whole, the time spent in Shreveport was disappointing. Bill recalls the Hayride as "one place where we were never received well," and he notes that the show's flamboyant announcers never went out of their way to encourage encores after the Blue Sky Boys finished their sets.

In August 1950, the Blue Sky Boys returned to WNAO in Raleigh, hoping to profit from the onset of the tobacco harvest season, when money would become more plentiful among the small farmers and workers who heard their music. It was there about six months later that they made the fateful decision to retire from the music business. In February 1951, Earl announced he had decided to quit. Bill, who very much wanted to continue the act, was disappointed, saddened, and embittered, but Earl's announcement could not have come as a complete surprise. Since Earl's marriage to Geraldine "Gerry" Bennett back in 1946 and the birth of his sons, William Steven and Joseph Alan, it had become increasingly difficult for him to commit his time fully to a music career and at the same time maintain a viable private life. Gerry refused to follow her husband in his successive relocations and, except for occasional visits, insisted on staying in her hometown of Tucker, Georgia. By February 1951 their relationship had deteriorated to the point where Earl had to choose between his marriage and his musical career.

The relationship between the brothers had also become severely strained over the years, and Bill virtually issued an ultimatum to Earl in early 1951 that he must commit himself fully to the Blue Sky Boys. Earl loved the music, but he had never been as wedded to it as Bill was. Bill had always chosen or written most of the songs they performed and had made most of the decisions concerning their business affairs, itinerary, and performance venues. Earl took up permanent residence with his family in Tucker, a suburb of Atlanta, and after attending a trades school in a local community college he became a machinist at Lockheed Aircraft. Although he had dropped out of school in the ninth grade, Earl's mechanical aptitude was so strong he eventually rose from machinist to a supervisory position at Lockheed.

Bill, who was not yet married and very depressed, sadly went back to his parents' home in Hickory. He had wanted neither to disband the group nor to leave the music. After anguishing over whether he should try to organize a new band, he finally decided that nothing could replace his association with Earl. Utilizing the G.I. Bill, he enrolled at Lenoir-Rhyne, a Lutheran liberal arts college in Hickory and began working on a degree in business administration. He accumulated 114 hours out of a required 120 but never finished his degree. Meanwhile, his father had been encouraging Bill to take an exam for the railway mail services, thinking that it would be an easy job with good benefits. Faced with mounting debts, the ending of G.I. Bill benefits, and the uncertain prospects of life after graduation, Bill passed the examination and in 1954 accepted a position with the railway service in Washington, D.C. He remained in Washington for three years, and in February 1957 married Doris Wallace, an Ohio girl with whom he had corresponded during the war. Never one to rush into an arrangement, Bill married Doris eleven years after meeting her, and three years after she had moved to Washington. In 1957 Bill was transferred to Greensboro, North Carolina, and was working there for a railway mail service when a renewed interest in the music of the Blue Sky Boys set in.

Some writers have maintained that the Blue Sky Boys retired in 1951 because they could not sustain a viable career as traditional artists in a fast-paced music business that no longer had an interest in or an audience for old-time musical values. The Blue Sky Boys retired, it is argued, because they refused to compromise with modernity. Bill counters that it was family pressures—not aesthetic values or economic concerns—that motivated the choices made in 1951, and he insists that an audience for their music still existed. While he was correct in arguing that the old fan base remained, he may not have sufficiently understood that the country music industry had changed dramatically. With its preoccupation with grooming superstars such as Eddy Arnold, it was becoming increasingly difficult for old-time acts to survive in mainstream country music unless they adopted electric instruments or the high-powered trappings of blue-grass—compromises that the Blue Sky Boys *did* indeed resist. Less than ten years after the Blue Sky Boys retired, though, new audiences for their style of music emerged.

At the beginning of the decade of the 1960s, in the wake of the Kingston Trio's hit version of "Tom Dooley," a folk revival erupted in the United States, when young fans in urban centers and on college campuses around the nation became fascinated with folk music, both ersatz and real. Fortunately, Bill had carefully collected and preserved as much of his musical memorabilia as was possible, among them an extensive array of radio transcriptions made by the Blue Sky Boys at WGST and WCYB in the late

1940s. These shows contributed directly to the first rediscovery of the Blue Sky Boys in the early 1960s. A former fan, Hugh Chapman of Bessemer, Alabama, contacted Jimmie Skinner, the proprietor of a country mail order business in Cincinnati, and inquired about the availability of Blue Sky Boys' records. Skinner contacted Don Pierce, owner of Starday Records, who was filling a niche in the record world by recording bluegrass and old-time country musicians. Hoping that the Blue Sky Boys might be coaxed out of retirement, Pierce contacted Bill Bolick in December 1961 and learned that radio transcriptions were available. In 1962 Starday issued an LP sampling of songs taken from transcriptions made in about 1946 of their WGST radio shows. It was called *A Treasury of Rare Song Gems*. One year later, Bill and Earl took some vacation time from their respective jobs, met in Greensboro, found during their rehearsing that they could still produce the old harmony magic, and then journeyed to Nashville to make two LPs for Starday. One LP, *Together Again*, consisted of secular songs and, at the insistence of Starday engineer Tommy Hill, included Nashville session musicians playing electric lead and pedal steel guitars, piano, bass, fiddle, and drums. The other collection, *Precious Moments*, adhered closely to the traditional Blue Sky Boys format. It was an all-gospel collection and featured Bill and Earl on mandolin and guitar and other musicians playing fiddle and bass.

The three Starday issues brought pleasure to the Bolicks' older fans but also introduced a new generation of listeners to the brothers. Coming in the midst of the folk revival, the Blue Sky Boys found themselves valued not only for their close harmony but also for their storehouse of traditional songs. In 1964 folklorist Archie Green annotated for RCA's Camden label an album of reissued Blue Sky boys material that contained ballads and folk songs recorded before World War II. In October of that year Bill and Earl gave their first concert in thirteen years, a program at the University of Illinois in Urbana that had been organized by Archie Green and the campus folk music club. John Schmidt, an animal science researcher in Urbana, taped the concert, and after circulating in various forms for many years among fans and collectors, a version of the show appeared in 1989 as an LP on the Rounder label. It must have been surprising, but particularly gratifying for the Bolicks, to encounter a polite audience of young people who took their music seriously. The next year they gave a similar program at UCLA in Los Angeles and recorded a new album of songs for the Capitol label. Co-produced by Ken Nelson and folklorist Ed Kahn, this was a superb album consisting of traditional songs that they had never recorded before. The album, however, was poorly promoted and soon became unavailable. In 1974 it was reissued by the John Edwards Memorial Foundation with notes by David Whisnant but also suffered the fate of quickly going out of print.

The Bolicks gave a few more concerts in the mid-1960s, including programs at Carnegie Hall (a variety show headlined by Johnny Cash) and New York University, but then went back to their regular lives. Bill resolved again to quit the music business forever and declared to David Whisnant, who had requested that the Blue Sky Boys do a concert at Duke University, that nothing could ever again get him back on stage. He did not reckon, though, with the persuasive powers of Carlton Haney, the North Carolina bluegrass promoter who was already becoming famous for his "reunion concerts," sentimental affairs that brought musicians back on stage with people with whom they had once played. As a native North Carolinian, Haney would have been very familiar with the Blue Sky Boys, and as the former manager of bluegrass great Don Reno, he may have been aware of Reno's affection for their music. Bill declared it was hard to turn Haney down. The Blue Sky Boys played at five Haney-sponsored bluegrass festivals in 1974: twice at Camp Springs in May and August–September; at Berryville, Virginia, in July; Gettysburg, Pennsylvania, in August; and Lake Norman, near Hickory, North Carolina, in September. The Bolicks were never very comfortable with the easy-going and often rowdy ambience of the festivals and found it disconcerting to play for crowds that were often noisy and restless. The Blue Sky Boys' style, too, contrasted dramatically with that of the musicians who played at the festivals, but their songs would have been familiar to them. Bluegrass musicians in fact had been playing such songs as "The Sunny Side of Life," "The Banks of the Ohio," "Little Bessie," "Midnight on the Stormy Deep," "The Knoxville Girl," and "Behind These Prison Walls of Love," long before the Blue Sky Boys made their temporary return to performance.

After having agreed to perform at Haney's affairs, Bill Bolick then felt obliged to honor a request made earlier by David Whisnant to play at a festival at Duke University. Whisnant had fallen in love with the music of the Blue Sky Boys when he first heard them at the University of Illinois in 1964. Not only did the Bolicks present a well-received program at Duke in 1974, but they also gave another one there in April 1975, the last one of their career. The flurry of activity in 1974 and 1975 probably inspired the decision by RCA to release a double album of their re-released songs in 1976. Produced and annotated by Douglas B. Green, this was the first reissue that featured their postwar songs as well as their earlier ones.

Recording companies since 1976 have shown only sporadic interest in the Blue Sky Boys. Rounder has issued both older and newly made recordings of the Blue Sky Boys, one consisting of songs recorded on a home tape recorder during their 1963 practice session in Greensboro. But thank Heavens for the transcriptions that Bill saved! Gary Reid produced and wrote the notes for a series of CDs taken from shows given at WGST in Atlanta in 1947 and 1948 and at WCYB in Bristol in 1949. These transcriptions, released in the early 1990s, provide examples of Blue Sky Boys' music when the brothers were at the peak of their performing abilities and provide a glimpse of the total context in which they performed: the hawking of Willys-Jeeps and other products, the humor of Uncle Josh, and a fast-paced variety of vocal and instrumental music. And they give us a bit of the larger country music story in those immediate postwar years when country music still had one foot in its rural past and another in the urban future.

Earl died on April 19, 1998, apparently of a heart attack and is buried in Suwannee, Georgia, where he had moved after his retirement from Lockheed. He is survived by two sons, William Steven and Allan. Bill and Doris now live in a little house in West Hickory on property once owned by Bill's father, and a little over a mile from where he was born. He suffers from a degenerative nerve disease, familial spastic paresis, and walks with great difficulty. His mind, though, is as sharp as ever, and he can instantly recollect every detail of the Blue Sky Boys' career. He still holds a tinge of bitterness about the professional disappointments they endured, and about the four lost years of World War II. Often self-deprecating and dismissive of his own abilities, he nevertheless takes great pride in the sound that the Blue Sky Boys achieved, and he recognizes their unique contributions within the realm of American music.

If Bill Bolick ever ponders the question posed by the old gospel song—"What Will I Leave Behind?"—or wonders if the grueling and often disappointing years of hillbilly radio were worth all the effort, he can find the answer in the devotion to the Blue Sky Boys' music displayed by countless fans and musicians. The Blue Sky Boys' influence did not cease with the dissolution of their professional career; it yet lives in the songs and styles of performers who either learned directly from the Bolicks or from people who had absorbed their music. Naomi and Wynonna Judd, for example, learned their version of "The Sweetest Gift (A Mother's Smile)" from Hazel Dickens and Alice Gerrard, not knowing that Hazel and Alice had learned the song from a Blue Sky Boys' recording. In 1958 the Everly Brothers recorded an album of old-time songs and named it *Songs Our Daddy Taught Us.* Daddy very likely learned his versions of "Kentucky," "I'm Just Here to Get My Baby out of Jail," and "Lightning Express" from the Bolick Brothers.

The Blue Sky Boys' legacy lived, and still lives, in the music of numerous other musicians who have been quick to acknowledge their indebtedness. These include Ray and Ina Patterson, Johnnie, Homer, and Walter Bailes, Don Reno, Jim and Jesse McReynolds, Ira and Charlie Louvin, Everett and Mitchell Lilly, the Country Gentlemen, Seldom Scene, Hazel Dickens and Alice Gerrard, Bill Clifton, and Charlie Moore. This boxed collection will not only reawaken pleasant memories among those people who have already heard the Blue Sky Boys, it will help to extend their musical legacy to a new generation of listeners who can thrill to the compelling songs and wondrous vocal blend produced by the Bolick Brothers.

CHAPTER 7

ALBERT E. BRUMLEY
Folk Composer

As a fan of gospel quartet music, and as a person who collected shape-note paperback hymnals, I had always been aware of the songs of Albert Brumley, but I only slowly came to realize that his music was also a vital part of the country and bluegrass traditions. Marshall Louis "Grandpa" Jones, the veteran country music comedian and musician who also recorded with the gospel quartet Brown's Ferry Four, spoke of the repertoire favored by the group: "Most of the songs came from Albert Brumley." When the musical soundtrack of the movie "O Brother Where Art Thou?" became a widely popular CD, I also learned that at least a few of his songs, such as "I'll Fly Away," had become known around the world. In getting this essay published in *Bluegrass Unlimited* magazine, I felt that I could make a contribution to a general understanding of Brumley's importance in the realm of American music while also paying homage to a man whose music had enriched my life. While I have interviewed or chatted with a large number of country and gospel musicians, I have been most honored by having had the privilege to interview Brumley and Thomas Dorsey, two of the greatest composers of southern religious music.

Much work is still needed in telling the story of southern white gospel music, but James Goff, in *Close Harmony: The Story of Southern Gospel* (Chapel Hill: University of North Carolina Press, 2002), has made an excellent beginning.

ALBERT E. BRUMLEY, COMPOSER OF "I'LL FLY AWAY" AND OTHER POPULAR GOSPEL SONGS, lies buried in a remote country cemetery near the hamlet of Powell, in McDonald County, Missouri. Brumley came to Powell in 1931 as a singing school teacher and met and married Goldie Edith Schell, and there he remained in the peaceful spot he called Memory Valley until called away by death on November 15, 1977. Powell is in the Ozark mountains, not far from Oklahoma where Brumley was born nor from Arkansas where he began his musical career. Brumley's comfortable home was not the "little log cabin" he spoke of in "By the Side of the Road," nor did "the pilgrimage of man go passing by," but it was a safe retreat tucked away from the hustle and bustle of contemporary civilization. Brumley settled down in this quiet, picture postcard–like pastoral haven, with little thought of wealth or fame, while his songs circulated around the world.[1]

Brumley was born near Spiro, LeFlore County, Oklahoma, on October 29, 1905, into a tenant farm family that he was to commemorate often in songs like "Dreaming of a Little Cabin" and "There's a Little Pine Log Cabin." The young Albert Brumley, born two years before Oklahoma received statehood, grew up in a region still marked by its frontier origins and culturally indebted to pioneer migrations from both the Midwest and the South.[2] His parents, William Sherman Brumley, who came to Oklahoma from Mis-

Albert E. Brumley, America's greatest gospel composer,
poses in front of a river near his home in Powell, Missouri.
Photograph courtesy the Brumley Music Company, Powell, Missouri.

souri in the land run of 1889, and Sarah Isabelle Williams Brumley, who migrated from Illinois, bequeathed to him their strong Protestant religious commitment (they were Campbellites, a name bestowed upon the Church of Christ adherents of the theology of Thomas Campbell) and a love of and a facility for music. Their religious beliefs may have encouraged a rather rigid demarcation of the world into unalterably opposed value schemes of good and evil, but secular and religious musical forms flowed freely across the arbitrary boundaries. The Brumley family drew sustenance from both the ballad and the hymn, the play party and the camp meeting, and Albert's mother sang the sentimental parlor songs such as "Little Rosewood Casket," while his father was a popular old-time fiddler.

The security gained from family gatherings and church functions was particularly cherished in a society that had little to offer economically. The promise of the Oklahoma frontier remained unfulfilled for most farmers, and many of them—like an increasing number of farmers throughout the South and Southwest in the early years of the twentieth century—became part of the system of tenantry, where they farmed land that belonged to someone else. Brumley's father was a sharecropper during most of these early formative years, and Albert recalled moving several times during his youth, but never more than twenty miles from the place of his birth. These recollections of poverty and chronic dislocation, as well as the family love that helped to make such conditions bearable, did much to shape the lyrics of his songs, reinforcing both his Protestant sense of human fragility in a crumbling world and the hope for the Heavenly future awaiting those who remained faithful.

Albert's future life and subsequent musical career were determined in about 1922 when, through the encouragement of one of his father's hired hands, he attended the sessions of a shape-note singing "normal school" (a three-week session with day and night classes) at the Rock Island community where he spent most of his teen years. Brumley was intrigued that so many tunes could be made out of the scale, and he began almost immediately to tinker with the idea of song composition. His first published song, "I Can Hear Them Singing over There," appeared in a 1927 convention book, *Gates of Glory*, published by the Hartford Music Company of Hartford, Arkansas. Although Brumley paid for the printing plates, this association with the Hartford Company proved the beginning of an almost lifelong relationship (Brumley did not always write exclusively for the company, but he was its owner from 1948 to his death in 1977).

The Hartford Music Company evolved out of the Central Music Company of Little Rock, Arkansas, but had relocated in Hartford by 1918 where Eugene M. Bartlett became associated with it. Hartford was a fairly prosperous coal-mining town, and its strategic location virtually on the Oklahoma line, and about one hundred miles south of the Missouri border, enabled the Hartford Company to exploit successfully the strong gospel market in that three-state area. Specializing in the seven-note do-re-mi style, the company's teachers and quartets roamed widely throughout the region, teaching singing schools and normals, holding singing conventions (the famous all-day singings with dinners-on-the-ground), and selling hordes of paperback songbooks. Along with the Dallas-based Stamps-Baxter Company, with whom it shared the southwestern market, and the J. D. Vaughan Company of Lawrenceburg, Tennessee, the Hartford Company was one of the dominant forces in the gospel shape-note music business.

The dominating presence in the Hartford Company, and the man whom Brumley would always acknowledge as his mentor and guide, was Eugene M. Bartlett. Born in Waynesville, Missouri, on December 24, 1884, Eugene Monroe Bartlett grew up in Hackett, Arkansas, south of Fort Smith. Like Brumley, he entered gospel music through the singing school route, but he also received a thorough grounding in bible education at William Jewell College in Missouri where he received one of the four bachelor's degrees he eventually earned in his academic career. Bartlett was an effective lay Baptist minister, a popular and beloved teacher, an accomplished singer, a successful publisher, and a skillful writer of such enduring songs as "Everybody Will Be Happy over There," "I Heard My Mother Call My Name in Prayer," and "Victory in Jesus." Bartlett also gained a niche in country music history as the composer of the Jimmie Dickens hit "Take an Old Cold Tater and Wait," originally written as a novelty number for the "comic quartet" segments that often came at the end of gospel concerts. His varied talents certainly must have made him appealing to the young Brumley, but his warmth and compassion contributed more directly to winning Brumley's lifelong respect and affection. As owner of the Hartford Music Company, Bartlett gave Brumley his first job in the gospel music business, and as a songwriter, he remained Brumley's principal source of inspiration.

Rock Island was just a short distance from Hartford, but Brumley had only $2.50 when he went there in 1926 to attend the Hartford Musical Institute. Bartlett took the young farmboy into his home, fed him, and encouraged his natural inclinations toward songwriting. During his tenure at the Institute from 1926 to 1931, Brumley came in contact with some of the most famous names in gospel music, men who came there either as visiting lecturers or as teachers. A few, like J. H. and W. H. Ruebush, descendants of Jacob Funk of Singers Glen, Virginia, were direct links to the shape-note tradition of the early nineteenth century. Homer Rodeheaver, former trombonist and song leader for evangelist Billy Sunday, came out of the urban revival movement, which in the late nineteenth century had done so much to fuel new departures in gospel music. James Rowe, the Englishman who had written literally thousands of religious poems, such as "If I Could Hear My Mother Pray Again," was a living testament of the potentialities of gospel composing. Thomas Benton, pianist and composer, was a pioneer in the use of after-beat rhythms, a stylistic innovation featuring syncopated notation that enabled Brumley and his composer contemporaries to break new ground and win new audiences. And, in Virgil O. Stamps, Brumley encountered the man whose quartets ultimately would do most to popularize his songs around the nation.

Until he married in 1931 and settled down in Powell, Brumley was intimately associated with the Hartford Company in several capacities. In addition to being a staff writer, he taught fifty-one singing schools and normals in Arkansas, Oklahoma, and Missouri and was, for a short period after 1928, a bass singer and occasional pianist in the traveling Hartford Quartets. The gospel quartets were apparently introduced before World War I by J. D. Vaughan in Lawrenceburg, Tennessee. They worked as agents for selling his songbooks and became virtually synonymous with the developing gospel music business.

They and their publishing house sponsors perceived their role as a spiritual one: the evangelizing of America through song. But they were never immune to, nor isolated from, the popular musical currents that swirled around them, and since they were designed to make money for their sponsors, that is, to market and sell songbooks, they inevitably seized upon any innovation that seemed potentially appealing to a mass market. As quartets competed with each other, they stressed catchy tunes and novel rhythms and tried to obtain the highest tenors, the lowest basses, and the flashiest pianists.

Although gospel songwriters had flourished in the late nineteenth and early twentieth centuries, none was more intimately associated with the quartet business than Albert Brumley. In a career that lasted over fifty years, Brumley composed more than six hundred songs, of both the gospel and the sentimental secular variety. Most of the songs have faded from the public view, but ten or twelve have endured as all-time favorites among gospel music partisans, and several have become part of the staple repertory of country and bluegrass music.[3]

Brumley's most famous song, "I'll Fly Away," was published by the Hartford Company in the convention book, *Wonderful Message*, in January 1932. To Brumley, the song was just a "little ditty" and was never one of his favorites; however, it was his entrée to success and fame as a gospel composer. When he wrote the song he was working in his father-in-law's general store for a dollar a day and was also employed by Hartford as a $12.50 a month staff writer. "I'll Fly Away" did not make him rich, even though it eventually earned him a considerable amount of money. Hartford owned the rights to his songs, and typically, he received fifty or one hundred copies of the book in which a new song was published. If he sold the copies, he made some extra money. "I'll Fly Away" has been recorded in virtually every field of music, by performers as varied as Roy Acuff, Ralph Stanley, Arthur Fiedler, Carolyn Hester, Ray Stevens, the Ray Charles Singers, Gillian Welch, and Alison Krauss.[4] Few people can sing the song in its entirety, but it is one of those songs like "Farther Along" or "Will The Circle Be Unbroken" that is known at least in fragmentary form by almost everyone. With its spirited melody and simple, repetitive lyric structure, the song demonstrates Brumley's debt to the camp meeting tradition, a socioreligious phenomenon that was well-known to him in his youthful Oklahoma experience:

> Some glad morning when this life is o'er,
> I'll fly away.
> To a home on God's celestial shore,
> I'll fly away.

After the publication of "I'll Fly Away," Brumley's songs began appearing frequently at the singing conventions, in the performances of the gospel quartets, and in rural homes all over the South. "Jesus, Hold My Hand" came in 1933, and Brumley's own personal favorite, "I'll Meet You in the Morning," appeared in 1936. Despite his own experience as a bass singer, the latter song was distinguished by its use of a tenor lead in the chorus, a trait that he used again and again. In 1937 he collaborated with his mentor, Eugene Bartlett, in writing another popular song, "Camping in Canaan's Land," whose melody, Brumley himself later pointed out, was unconsciously taken from "The Easter Parade." These songs have endured long past the decade of their birth, but they were particularly compelling for Depression-era Americans who needed the comfort of a caring, personal savior:

> Jesus, hold my hand;
> I need thee every hour.
> Through this pilgrim land
> Protect me by thy power.

Or the reassurance of a bountiful reconciliation beyond the grave:

> I will meet you in the morning
> By the bright riverside,
> When all sorrow has drifted away.
> I'll be standing at the portals
> When the gates open wide,
> At the end of life's long dreary day.

Along with the songs of his African American contemporary Thomas Dorsey ("Peace in the Valley," "Precious Lord, Take My Hand"), and those of the earlier black composer Charles Tindley, whose songs were still cherished by whites and blacks alike in the thirties ("Stand By Me," "We'll

Understand It Better By and By," "Leave It There"), Brumley's songs acutely fit and countered the mood of hard times, and they have endured as part of the treasury of our greatest songs.

While the gospel songs may have been particularly meaningful for Americans in the early thirties, the gospel music business suffered during the economic crisis. Few commercial outlets existed for the quartets; consequently, neither singers nor songwriters made much money during the decade. The churches and the singing conventions remained the most important arenas for the quartets, but financial rewards were slim here too, and often only a modest collection could be raised, even though the hospitality of a sumptuous dinners-on-the-ground could preserve the singers' morale.

Actually, the churches were far from universally receptive to the gospel songs. The mainline denominations were, in fact, hostile to the music, and Eugene Bartlett was always troubled by the fact that his own Southern Baptist denomination was resistant to his songs. However, both he and Brumley testified to the warm support given to their music, and to the quartets, by the Holiness and Pentecostal denominations. These churches over the years have provided enthusiastic forums for the gospel groups while also contributing a long line of the greatest professional gospel singers, such as James Blackwood, the Happy Goodman Family, and Dotty Rambo.

The Pentecostal congregations, in particular, had little concern for decorum, and they sought in the confines of the church a safe and respectable emotional release that was not always realizable in the world at large. As they strived to enforce the biblical precept "to make a joyful noise unto the Lord," the otherworldly Pentecostal groups demonstrated a remarkable receptivity to the styles, melodies, and instruments of the world. No musical instrument was taboo in their church services, and secular musical styles were successfully adapted to religious purposes. Holiness-Pentecostal people stressed a religion of the heart in a Protestant culture that was becoming increasingly lukewarm to the value of emotional commitment. The quartets, and other professional religious singers, were welcomed through their doors, and Brumley songs flourished in their joyous congregational singing.

Brumley's music was obviously indebted to older Protestant religious music, especially to the camp meeting and shape-note traditions, but it drew strength and received its currency from the communications revolution of the twentieth century, particularly that inspired by the phonograph and radio. Brumley's popularity, and that of the quartets, was directly linked to the radio, the medium that came of age in the thirties. All of the quartets used Brumley material, and some of the most historically important groups made his songs the nuclei of their early repertories. The Chuck Wagon Gang, for instance (composed of D. P. Carter, and his three children Anna, Rose, and Jim) sang his songs often on their noontime WBAP (Dallas, Texas) broadcasts and eventually devoted an entire album (*God's Gentle People*) to his songs. The Blackwood Brothers sang one of his songs, "They Will Welcome Me Back Home," as their opening song when they began their tenure on KWKH (Shreveport) in 1938. In the years that followed, James Blackwood generally used "I'll Meet You in the Morning" as his personal testimony, typically moving into the audience and shaking hands as he sang the song.

Brumley was particularly fortunate in being associated with the Stamps-Baxter Company as a staff writer after 1937, where such popular songs as "I Found a Hiding Place" were published, and with the Stamps Quartet Publishing Company after 1945. All of the quartets who bore the Stamps name popularized the Brumley songs in their personal appearances and in the songbooks they hawked, while Frank Stamps's parent quartet featured them on their daily broadcasts on KRLD in Dallas. It was therefore fitting that when Brumley wrote his tribute to the radio, the enduringly popular "Turn Your Radio On," he should dedicate it to the Stamps Quartet. As the southern folk have persistently done in their association with the "machine," Brumley both chronicled the story of an innovation and employed it as a means to illustrate eternal truths. Like the earlier composers of "The Royal Telephone" and "Life's Railway to Heaven," Brumley used "Turn Your Radio On" to symbolize man's communication with God:

> Turn your radio on,
> And listen to the music in the air.
> Turn your radio on,
> Heaven's glory share.
> Turn the lights down low and
> Listen to the master's radio.
> Get in touch with God;
> Turn your radio on.

Brumley's production of popular material declined during World War II, as did the activities of all the quartets. His songs of the previous decade, however, still circulated widely. But in 1945 he did write one of his most appealing songs, and one whose popularity contributed mightily to the success of Frank Stamps's new publishing house, the Dallas-based Stamps Quartet Publishing Company. This was "If We Never Meet Again," designed by Brumley as a closing song for singing conventions and printed in Stamps's first convention book *Divine Praise.* The song gained immediate popularity in the Southwest through the noontime programs of the Stamps Quartet over KRLD in Dallas. For thousands of listeners the song will always be identified with the clear, sweet tones of Walter Rippetoe who sang the tenor lead on the chorus:

> If we never meet again
> This side of Heaven,
> As we struggle through this
> World and its strife,
> There's another meeting place
> Somewhere in Heaven,
> By the side of the river of life.
> Where the charming roses bloom
> Forever,
> And where separations come no more,
> If we never meet again this side
> Of Heaven,
> I will meet you on that beautiful
> Shore.

There is no way of knowing how many people were touched by the song. On his gospel LP *The Land of Many Churches*, Merle Haggard says that the song was his father's favorite.[5] It was sung at Elvis Presley's mother's funeral and is alleged to have been her favorite song. My own family's response to the song was probably not untypical; our yellowed copy of *Divine Praise* opens almost automatically to song number 115, testifying to the frequency with which the Malone family turned to this much-cherished song.

Brumley continued to write songs into the sixties, but his peak period of production was over by the end of the forties. Gospel music, it is true, was on the threshold of becoming a big business—but it was a business and a way of life that were increasingly alien to the gentle and low-keyed Brumley. The postwar period saw the emergence of high-powered quartets who were divorced from the publishing business and often only remotely related to religion.

Brumley settled more securely into his Ozark retreat, ran unsuccessfully for the post of circuit clerk and recorder, and devoted most of his attention to publishing and to the rearing of his five sons and daughter (Bill, Albert Jr., Tom, Bob, Jack, and Betty). In 1948 he purchased the Hartford Publishing Company for only twelve hundred dollars and in so doing finally gained full control of his early compositions, including "I'll Fly Away," which earned him many thousands of dollars during the next thirty years before his death. He also owned Albert Brumley and Sons, founded in 1944, and was the co-promoter along with his sons of two music festivals, both inaugurated in 1969, the Sunup to Sundown Sing (devoted to gospel music), held in Springdale, Arkansas, and the Hill and Hollow Folk Festival, held in Powell. While Bill and Bob Brumley assumed direction of the family's music business ventures, the other sons moved into varied aspects of the music profession, Al as a singer in Nashville, Jack as a promoter, and Tom as a steel guitarist (first for Buck Owens and later for Rick Nelson).

By the time Albert Brumley retired in January 1976, his contributions to both country and gospel music had been recognized by his elections to the Gospel Music Hall of Fame and to the Nashville Song Writers Hall of Fame. At his funeral in 1977, James Blackwood and E. M. Bartlett Jr. led a choir in the a cappella singing of his hymns. It was a fitting tribute to the composer's memory, and a ritual highly reflective of the austere tradition of the Church of Christ.

Although Brumley was a member of the Church of Christ, his songs are nondenominational, at least within the larger evangelical, fundamentalist framework, a fact that, in part, accounts for their universal popularity. The Brumley songs have been appealing because, like the compositions of most popular songwriters, they depict universal themes that are couched in simple lyrics and pretty, singable melodies. The Brumley "theology" is fundamentalist, but it affirms a conception of a benevolent God at great variance from that of the stern unyielding God of the Calvinists. God, as described in the Brumley lyrics, is a loving, merciful Father who waits to gather in His children in a reunion marked by pastoral beauty and simplicity. Brumley's evocation of pastoral imagery is reminiscent of that of the nineteenth-century popular songwriter Will S. Hays, who employed the device to paint affecting pictures of domestic contentment or unrequited love. Brumley sometimes invested the scenes of his childhood with a romantic placidity that only a child could have felt during those bleak, tenant-farm days:

> Did you ever go sailin'
>   Down the river of memories
> To a little log cabin that is
>   Nestled among the sycamore trees.
> Where the sunshine is cheery,
>   And nothing in the world goes dreary,
> That's my cabin at the end of my river
>   Of memories.

But his most bucolic references are generally reserved for Heaven. A persistent Brumley image of Heaven is of a quiet, rural land traversed by flowing rivers, a "land of endless spring" with "rolling green meadows" and "where the charming roses bloom forever."

Although their specific denominational affiliation may be nebulous, the Brumley songs easily demonstrate their roots in the rural South. Two major themes predominate within the Brumley repertory: the disintegration of rural society and the consequent nostalgia for the way of life associated with such a society, and the belief in a reunion in Heaven where the family circle will be restored and old friends will be reunited in a state of permanent and pastoral security. Brumley demonstrates his thorough indoctrination in southern Protestant tradition when he speaks, as he often did, of the Christian as a "wayworn pilgrim" traveling through a "vale of sorrow," but he is more acutely attuned to the preoccupations of Depression-era southerners when he tells in his songs of a disrupted rural society and of a world of shifting and ephemeral values (in other words, God is benevolent, but the world is not). In a world of ceaseless and unsettling change, Brumley and his listeners put their faith in an unchanging God and His unchanging truths, values that were now deemed "old-fashioned." But, as Brumley asserted, "I may be a little old-fashioned, but my savior was old-fashioned too." Mankind at large might lose its soul in its pursuit of wealth, but Brumley opined that he would rather "be an old-time Christian" and live in "a little log cabin by the side of the road."

Several Brumley songs—those he described as his sentimental songs—such as "Rank Strangers to Me," "Nobody Answered Me," "Dreaming of a Little Cabin," and "Did You Ever Go Sailin'"—may have been inspired by his recollections of youth on the Oklahoma frontier, but they are more concerned with the disappearance of rural society and of the security symbols (home, family, mother, the old country church) associated with it. The songs evoke images of deserted and decaying farmhouses and the alienation of the individual in the land of his birth where:

> Everybody I met seemed to be a
> Rank stranger.
> No mother or dad, not a friend
> Could I see.
> They knew not my name, and I
> Knew not their faces.
> I found they were all rank
> Strangers to me.

Only in memory can one recapture the sense of security that the old homestead once conveyed:

> In dreams of yesterday I wandered
> Back to my little cabin door.
> I strolled beside an old rock garden
> And saw familiar scenes once more.
> I heard the organ softly playing;
> Its music came so sweet and low.
> And I heard my mother sweetly singing
> As oft I did so long ago.

If the old scenes of rural life cannot be temporally recaptured, the righteous individual can at least hope for revitalization beyond the grave. Reconciliation with friends and relatives in Heaven is a persistent theme of the Brumley songs. In "God's Gentle People," he asks, "will I see the same faces that I knew down by the side of the road?" and he answers the question affirmatively in several songs, including "Rank Strangers to Me" where he says "some beautiful day I'll meet them in Heaven where no one will be a stranger to me"; in "I'll Meet You in the Morning," which he dedicated to his family; and in "If We Never Meet Again," which reassures the Christian whose earthly existence is perpetually saddened by the severing of familial and social ties that "there's another meeting place somewhere in Heaven by the side of the river of life."

While Brumley continued to write songs almost to the end of his life, never again did his songs so effectively mirror the thinking of an audience as they did during the bleak thirties or the socially disruptive forties. His evocation of little cabins and other idyllic images meshed closely with the feelings of millions of southerners who had shared similar experiences of being rural, poor, and migrant. Brumley, by choice, remained isolated in the rural tranquility of Powell, while the majority of white southerners faced a traumatic transition: the coming of World War II and the associated move to the cities and into industrial work.

The Brumley songs did not immediately lose their currency in such a context. If anything, their descriptions of an idyllic, but vanishing, rural past assumed an even greater importance to uprooted people whose ambivalent feelings about this abandoned world were given a nostalgic focus through his lyrics. Nevertheless, except for "I'll Fly Away," which has shown a remarkable durability, his songs now appear with much less frequency in the repertoires of gospel singers. The Brumley songs, in fact, now find their most enthusiastic reception in country music, and above all in bluegrass, country music's most tradition-based form, where visions of mother and dad, the family fireside, and the old country church still strike vibrant heart strings. Singers like Mac Wiseman, the Sullivan Family, and the Stanley Brothers have repeatedly demonstrated a fondness for Brumley's music. Indeed, Wiseman's version of "Dreaming of a Little Cabin" and the Stanley's haunting rendition of "Rank Strangers to Me" are two of the most powerful performances in all of country music. "Rank Strangers" has become a standard of bluegrass music and is done by virtually every bluegrass group in a version that is directly traceable to the Stanley performance.

Brumley gratefully acknowledged the patronage of the country music world, but he averred that he had never consciously written a country song. His songs, instead, reflected the total worldview of the man: his view of life as he remembered it or wished it to be and his hopes for the rewards that awaited the faithful Christian. If his songs were country, it was because they reflected the profound rural emphasis of their creator, and the tendency of his listeners to equate rural virtues with godliness. The Missouri Ozarks held as much of Heaven-on-Earth as he desired, or thought realizable, and when he dreamed and wrote of Heaven, he invested it with the scenes and gentle people whom he had cherished in his earthly domicile. As a writer, Brumley drew upon the folk resources, religious and secular, of his past, as well as upon the popular music currents of his own day—a debt that he has more than repaid. Whenever the whole story of folksong making in this country is compiled, one name that will surely prevail is that of Albert Brumley, whose songs have moved through the realms of religious, country, and popular music to become the possession of the American people.

NOTES

1. The bulk of my information on Albert Brumley came from interviews with him in Powell, Missouri, on April 5, 1972; with Eugene M. Bartlett Jr. in Ardmore, Oklahoma, on July 12, 1978; and with Bill Brumley in Powell on July 13, 1978. Additional information came from a telephone conversation with Bill Brumley on July 30, 1979 (between New Orleans and Powell). Eugene Bartlett Jr. also provided me with a copy of a taped interview with Albert Brumley, conducted by J. M. Gaskin, in Powell, Missouri, on October 12, 1976. Published accounts of Brumley are rare. But some good summaries of his career include Kay Hively and Albert E. Brumley Jr., *I'll Fly Away: The Life Story of Albert E. Brumley* (Branson, Mo.: Mountaineer Books, 1990), and Kevin D. Kehrberg, "Albert Edward Brumley (1905–1977)," in *The Encyclopedia of Arkansas History and Culture.* See also David Charles Deller, "'Sing Me Home to Gloryland': Arkansas Songbook Gospel Music in the Twentieth Century" (PhD diss., University of Arkansas, 1999).

2. Oklahoma, as a composite of folk cultures, deserves the special attention of folklorists and cultural historians. A state that could produce Woody Guthrie and Albert Brumley, two great song makers with radically different political perspectives, while providing a spawning ground for that dynamic fusion of folk music styles called western swing should be treated as a valuable and illustrative laboratory of social change.

3. I have examined numerous gospel paperback songbooks, but the best one-volume collection of Brumley songs is *The Best of Albert E. Brumley* (Powell, Mo.: Albert E. Brumley and Sons, 1966), which contains one hundred songs and numerous useful tidbits about his life and career. Many of his sentimental songs can be found in a book entitled *Lamplitin' Songs* (Wesson, Miss.: M. Lynwood Smith Publications and Albert E. Brumley and Sons, 1966), a volume that contains many "classic" nineteenth-century parlor songs.

4. According to Bill Brumley, the song "I'll Fly Away" was not recorded at all until 1949 when the Chuck Wagon Gang did their version for Columbia. The song's widespread circulation before that date, then, is all the more remarkable and is a testament to the pervasiveness and power of the radio and of the singing conventions. The song's prominent inclusion in the soundtrack of the popular movie *O Brother Where Art Thou?* has introduced it to a new and large audience.

5. Merle Haggard's version of "If We Never Meet Again," his spoken tribute to Brumley, and two other Brumley songs are on *The Land of Many Churches* (Capitol SWBO-803). A live performance of James Blackwood's rendition of "I'll Meet You in the Morning" and his "testimony" is on the *Blackwood Brothers, Live from Nashville* (Skylite SLP 6173). Mac Wiseman's great recording of "Dreaming of a Little Cabin" (along with "By the Side of the Road") is on *This Is Mac Wiseman* (Dot DLP 3697), and on the massive Bear CD collection *Tis Sweet to Be Remembered.* The Stanley Brothers recorded "Rank Stranger to Me," which they call "Rank Stranger," on *Sacred Songs from the Hills* (Starday SLP 122), now also available on *The Starday Sessions* (County CCS-106/7). Ralph Stanley has since recorded it on *I Want to Preach the Gospel* (Rebel SLP 1522).

CREDITS FOR QUOTED SONGS

"Did You Ever Go Sailin'?" Copyright 1938, in *Gospel Tide*, The Stamps-Baxter Music Co.

"Dreaming of a Little Cabin." Copyright 1940, in *Pearly Gates*, The Stamps-Baxter Music Co.

"If We Never Meet Again." Copyright 1945, in *Divine Praise*, Stamps Quartet Music Co.

"I'll Fly Away." Copyright 1932, in *Wonderful Message*, Hartford Music Co.

"I'll Meet You in the Morning." Copyright 1936, in *Lights of Life*, Hartford Music Co.

"Jesus, Hold My Hand." Copyright 1933, in *Gems of Gladness*, Hartford Music Co.

"Rank Strangers to Me." Copyright 1942, in *Super Specials No. 5*, The Stamps-Baxter Music Co.

CHAPTER 8

THE CHUCK WAGON GANG
God's Gentle People

The Chuck Wagon Gang was one of the first groups of country musicians that I ever heard on radio. This was in 1939, after Daddy bought our first radio, a Philco battery-powered device. This essay was first published in the *Journal of Country Music* (no longer in existence) and was later revised substantially and reprinted as the liner notes for a Bear Family box set, a comprehensive collection of all the records made for Columbia by the Gang between 1936 and 1955.

AMONG THE PLEASANT MEMORIES ASSOCIATED WITH GROWING UP IN RURAL EAST TEXAS in the seven years or so before World War II was the joyful experience of listening each day to the Chuck Wagon Gang radio show on WBAP in Fort Worth. One of my few remaining artifacts of those days is a yellowed, slightly-frayed picture postcard of Dad Carter, his three children, and their announcer, Dwight Butcher, all standing beside or leaning out of a little covered wagon. The postcard had been solicited by my mother, an ardent radio listener and faithful fan of the family singers whose likenesses were captured there. Life was hard for most rural women in those bleak Depression years, and there on our isolated tenant farm on the western edge of Smith County, even the presence of an organized church was a rare privilege. The comforting songs of the Chuck Wagon Gang, with their visions of a caring savior and a heavenly reward, brought both immediate solace and a promise of ultimate redemption.

My mother was an alto singer who, like most people hearing the Chuck Wagon Gang, was captivated by the warm, liquid-smooth alto singing of Anna (born Effie) Carter. Years later, upon meeting Anna Carter Davis for the first time, my thoughts went back to my mother who had given me my introduction to music many years before. Anna seemed genuinely moved, and even surprised, when I told her of the affection that my mother had held for her and her family's music. Even after more than four decades of public performing, neither Anna nor the other members of the Church Wagon Gang really seemed aware of the myriad ways in which their music had touched the lives of other people.

For almost eighty years, and through a multitude of personnel changes, the Chuck Wagon Gang still retains a dependable, reassuring, and vital presence in American religious music. Despite the cowboy aura suggested by the professional title they inherited, the Chuck Wagon Gang is more properly an heir to the singing school and brush arbor traditions of rural America. Originally established in New England as a device to stimulate and improve congregational singing, the singing school insinuated itself into the backcountry South in the years following 1800. Itinerant teachers moved down the Great Valley of Virginia and into the hinterlands of the trans-Appalachian South, traveling all the way to Texas. They held ten-day schools to impart the rudiments of musical theory and sight-reading of shape notes to rural community members in churches or schoolhouses before moving on to another location. The term "brush arbor" refers to the practice of fabricating a protective canopy of brush coverings against the sun or rain so that people could meet informally out of doors, perhaps with a picnic supper, but primarily to hear the preaching and singing.

These traditions have appealed to successive generations of people who either recall those actual experiences or who savor the basic wholesomeness and decency associated with them. Even more important, the quartet known as the Chuck Wagon Gang embodies the venerable tradition of family singing, in this case that of David P. "Dad" Carter and his children. Despite the personnel changes (and there have been many since Dad's last recording session in 1955), the group still sounds much like the original quartet (Dad, Anna, Rose, and Jim) did when they inaugurated the quartet's career back in 1935. In fact, neither time, personnel changes, nor the commercial revolution that gospel music has undergone since World War II have really altered the overall mood or sound conveyed by these family singers and the people who have followed in their wake.

*The "classic" Chuck Wagon Gang: Dad Carter, with mandolin;
Anna; Rose; and Jim, with guitar.*
Photograph courtesy the Collection of Shaye Smith, Hertford, North Carolina.

The Chuck Wagon Gang owe their enduring and widespread popularity in large part to the fact that their style has successfully wedded both country and gospel singing traditions. Like such groups as the Stamps Quartet and the Blackwood Brothers, the Chuck Wagon Gang chose the quartet format, sang in a style drawn from the singing schools, and performed songs taken from the paperback shape-note hymnals (songbooks that indicated the pitch of a note by its shape rather than simply its placement on the staff). But their voices conveyed an unmistakable rural flavor, they used a guitar long after most quartets had adopted pianos for accompaniment, and they were never affiliated with any specific religious denomination or publishing house. They were part of that large, often neglected body of grassroots religious music that has long existed as an omnipresent and, in fact, defining component of southern rural culture.

While drawing its impulse from evangelical Protestantism and deriving much of its repertory and style from the shape-note hymnals, this folk religious tradition nevertheless developed and continues to evolve apart from the churches and even from the formal quartets. This genre was a string-band-accompanied style of music analogous to, and except for its lyric content virtually indistinguishable from, secular "hillbilly" music. Such music has embodied the essence of the rural and small-town South: intensely fundamentalist and evangelical, often tinged with a holiness energy, rendered with unmistakable southern accents, part secular, part religious, and permeated with a highly moralistic view of life.

Southern audiences had certainly been aware of such music for generations, having heard it performed by blind street singers, or by ballad hawkers at public gatherings, or by holiness evangelists. But it was commercially introduced to the larger American public in the 1920s through the recordings and radio performances of such people as Smith's Sacred Singers, Rev. Andrew (Blind Andy) Jenkins and his family, Rev. Alfred Karnes, and the Phipps Holiness Singers. Since that time the tradition has been well represented in commercial country music by such musicians as the Blue Sky Boys, the Bailes Brothers, the Louvin Brothers, Mac O'Dell, Martha Carson, the Johnson Family Singers, the Masters Family, and the Lewis Family. While their approach has differed in many particulars from the groups just mentioned, the Chuck Wagon Gang remains America's most important representative of folk gospel music, and a valuable link between the world of the formal quartets and country music.

When the Chuck Wagon Gang launched their career in 1935, the distance between the society of which they sang and the one in which they actually lived was not yet an overwhelming one. Theirs was a Texas that was still basically rural, with an economy dominated by cotton farm tenantry, a state with a population little more than one generation removed from residence in the older southern states. The oil boom presaged Texas's future; it did not yet dominate its present. Roman Catholicism was a powerful presence in the southern part of the state, particularly among Mexican Americans, but for the great majority of other Texans, both black and white, church preference inclined toward the evangelical and fundamentalist groups: Baptists, Methodists, Campbellites, and Holiness. For such people the brush arbor revival and the singing convention, with its dinners-on-the-ground—an all-day music convocation held in a church or county courthouse and marked by a sumptuous picnic to which all contrib-uted their special dishes—were not quaint remnants of a frontier society but, instead, vital and cherished aspects of community life.

The worst days of the Great Depression had subsided, but hard times still prevailed. Many Texas families had seen husbands, fathers, or sons (and sometimes daughters) hitting the road to find employment, and more than a few had become part of that large stream of California-bound migrants, the Okies, who journeyed west on Route 66. Nevertheless, most people stayed at home, clinging more tightly than ever to its familiar security. Inexpen-sive entertainment such as radio, therefore, experienced a golden age, and Texans were second to none in their reliance on the medium. Devotees of homespun music (black and white, secular and gospel) could hear live entertainment throughout the day, especially early in the morning and at noon, on Saturday nights from the radio barn dances, and late at night over the Mexican border stations. Radio performers hoped for wider exposure and an opportunity to move beyond regional identification. Some managed to sign recording contracts. For most, the road to stardom presented hard and frustrating challenges with goals that were seldom reached. Enter-tainers supplemented or relied heavily upon personal appearances made in movie theaters, schoolhouses, churches, or at store openings, root beer stands, or in honky-tonks and dance halls—generally without benefit of sound amplification.

The Chuck Wagon Gang wedded the singing traditions of two farm families who had migrated to Texas from Kentucky and Arkansas. David Parker Carter—born on September 25, 1889, and always known simply in the quartet as "Dad"—came to Texas as a small boy with his parents from Milltown, near Columbia, Kentucky. In 1909 he married Carrie Brooks (born on February 7, 1891), an emigrant from Arkansas, whom he had met, appropriately, at a singing school. They settled briefly near Tioga, in north-east Texas, the area where Gene Autry had been born in 1907, but then found themselves often on the move, looking for steady work and a settled home life. To support the family, Dad farmed and did railroad work for the Rock Island Line in Texas and Oklahoma. Dad's railroad career—chiefly as a brakeman in Missouri and Oklahoma—ended suddenly in 1927 when he was seriously injured in a crash near El Reno, Oklahoma. The right side of his face was crushed, and he lost most of his teeth on that side of his face. After the railroad refused payment, he filed suit but never received proper compensation. To support his growing family, he picked cotton (as did his children) on a succession of farms in the Southwest, worked in grain harvests in Kansas, but sometimes quite reluctantly had to depend on government relief programs. Many a day, the family was forced to rely on government handouts of molded cheese, or on the meat of jackrabbits, antelopes, prairie chickens, and blue quail (Eddie, one of the Carter sons, told his great niece, Shaye, that he sometimes shot quail with his sling shot in order to help feed the family).

While the Carters often suffered from a lack of sufficient material possessions, they did possess one treasured resource: their ability to make music. At home and at church, Dad, Mom, Lee Brooks (her brother), and Nan Carter Brooks (Dad's sister and Lee's wife) sang as a quartet from approximately 1909 to 1914, in the northern Texas area running roughly from Grayson to Clay County. Dad came out of a strong Baptist background, and Mom was a Nazarene, so they leaned rather naturally toward religious music. Their vocal style reflected the Carters' training in the shape-note singing schools, which emphasized four-part harmony and clearly served as the model for the style of the Chuck Wagon Gang. Mom played the organ, and Lee, a singing-school teacher, bought all the new paperback songbooks from the Hartford, Trio, Vaughan, and Stamps-Baxter gospel publishing houses. The group often sat up all night, learning and singing the new songs.

Mom and Dad bequeathed their love of music to their nine children (Clellon, Ernest, Roy, Lola Rose, Effie, Anna, Ruth Ellen, Eddie, and Betty). All of the children sang and played various instruments, and each of them, except for Clellon, sang at one time or another as members of the Chuck Wagon Gang. Clellon, in fact, took vocal lessons at the Stamps-Baxter School of Music in Dallas, preparing as a possible replacement for Ernest, but never became a member of the group. Dad and the children sang constantly at home for their own and for their neighbors' pleasure. These casual, ad hoc performances exemplified the essence of parlor singing and probably typified the home entertainment that southwestern farm families enjoyed during the World War I era and on into the twenties. They sang old songs learned in church or from neighbors, from the paperback hymnals, from sheet music or songsters, or from radio broadcasts accompanied by a guitar or parlor organ or perhaps, if one were more affluent, to the chords of a piano. Old songs circulated freely in rural Texas via the "young people's page" of the *Dallas Semi-Weekly Farm News* where readers exchanged song lyrics. Whatever the source, the Carter children literally learned their songs, and how to sing, at their parents' knees. Rose and Anna remembered as small children taking turns sitting on Dad's lap, listening to him sing their favorite songs. As long as Dad lived, he remained the principal arbiter of the Chuck Wagon Gang style, often choosing their songs and insisting that they adhere to the vocal instructions found in the songbooks.

Ernest, born on August 10, 1910, in Sherman, Texas, but who became known professionally as Jim, played the guitar and sang bass; Dad played the mandolin and sang baritone or low tenor; Rose, born on December 31, 1914, in Altus, Oklahoma, sang soprano; and Anna, born on February 17, 1917, in Shannon, Texas, sang alto. Together they achieved a serious, but unaffected and uncluttered, style that endured throughout their professional careers. While living near Lubbock, in a little community called Bledsoe where the family had drifted as farmworkers, the Carters would rush home after a long day of picking cotton and begin singing as soon as supper was finished. Sitting outside in the gathering darkness they would soon see cigarettes lighting up as the neighbors gathered to hear them sing. Before long they received the encouragement that talented amateurs have often heard: "You folks ought to be on the radio!"

Their singing remained informal and home-centered, though, until mid-1935 when Dad decided that they were indeed good enough to be on the radio. Country music had proved itself commercially, with radio as its chief medium of exposure. Jimmie Rodgers, an adopted Texan, had shown that it was possible to get rich singing country music, and the Carter Family of Virginia became known for the family singing style that would long be inspiring to other similar groups. The famous western band The Sons of the Pioneers had begun their recording career the previous year and in 1936 appeared at the Texas Centennial in Dallas. The Pioneers' repertory, and their style of close four-part harmony (done originally by Bob Nolan, Tim Spencer, Roy Rogers, and Hugh Farr), affected the styles of many groups who came after them and doubtless fueled the dreams of other would-be professionals. The Carters also were most certainly aware of the famous gospel singers the Stamps Quartet who, also galvanized by appearances at the Centennial, soon began their daily noon broadcasts on KRLD in Dallas.

No one knows how far Dad's expectations or dreams extended, when he approached the directors of the local Lubbock radio station, the 250-watt KFYO, to discuss the possibilities of a radio show. He had rented a little tourist court called North Canyon Camp, just outside Lubbock. His immediate inspiration was the need to buy medicine for Effie, who had contracted pneumonia. They were given a fifteen-minute show and an advance of $12.50, the weekly salary they would receive during their almost one year of performance on the station. During Effie's convalescence, Dad, Ernest, and Lola sang as a trio, and then as a quartet when Effie fully recovered. Sponsored by Martin's Bakery, and later by Conoco Oil, the group performed as the Carter Quartet and did a variety of songs that were reminiscent of that other group of Carter singers from Virginia, but which were actually a bit more broad-ranging. When performing for Martin's Bakery, the Carter Quartet's theme song was the sponsor's favorite, "Red River Valley"; for Conoco, it was "Highways Are Happy Ways." Otherwise, their shows were filled with the folk and sentimental favorites they had learned in their family parlor gatherings. While their song choices may not have been identical to those of the other Carter Family, their performing image was very much like that of the Virginia singers: here was a decent family clan conveying the virtues of home, parents, and God. Like the Virginia group, they could easily describe their shows as "morally good."

The Carter Quartet built a faithful audience for their KFYO radio shows and made occasional appearances in schoolhouses and at store openings, but they sought no broader horizons until the following year when they moved to Fort Worth and began their long-standing tenure on WBAP. Dad approached several radio stations in the area, until WBAP granted the family an audition. WBAP (Fort Worth) and KGKO (Dallas) were jointly owned enterprises that together played major roles in the dissemination of grassroots music in the Southwest. Owned by the famous publisher Amon G. Carter, WBAP had hosted, on January 1, 1923, one of the earliest radio barn dances in the United States and, from 1970 to 1993, maintained an all-country music format. In 1936 WBAP moved to the forefront of those southwestern radio stations (such as KWKH in Shreveport, KVOO in Tulsa, and WOAI in San Antonio) that programmed all kinds of rural folk music. Its fifty-thousand-watt, clear-channel coverage gave it access to much of the South and the Middle West, and membership in the Texas Quality Network provided an additional means of exposure for the folk entertainers who frequented its studios.

Financially for the Carters, the WBAP connection marked a significant step up from their Lubbock radio engagement. They received sixty dollars a week for five fifteen-minute weekday shows. For the first three months of their tenure on WBAP, the Carter Quartet were sponsored by Morton's Salt, but thereafter they performed under the auspices of Bewley Mills, a Fort Worth flour company. Before World War II, the Carters were one of at least three important acts in Fort Worth that were associated with a popular brand of flour: the Light Crust Doughboys (from Burrus Mills); Ernest Tubb, the Gold Chain Troubador; and Bewley's Chuck Wagon Gang. Farm families and small-town listeners valued home-cooked meals and the comfort of early morning biscuits before they ventured off to work. When the Carters moved into a Saturday morning time slot called "The Roundup," they inherited the performing title of the western string band, the Chuck Wagon Gang, that had previously hosted the show. The western band continued to go out on the road selling Bewley's products, and at least one of the Carter children, Eddie, sometimes went with the group's Traveling Kitchen to grocery stores in the Fort Worth area making biscuits for Bewley Mills. The Carters, though, remained attached to the station with their weekly program of music. After 1936 they were never again known as the Carter Quartet; instead, they became permanently identified with the name affixed to them by Bewley Mills, a name that strangely encapsulated neither their style nor their repertory. Performing for fifteen minutes each day at 12:15 P.M., they did occasionally sing a cowboy song, such as "Cowboy Jack" or "The New Frontier," but such songs made up only a tiny minority of their total offerings. They seem to have dressed in cowboy attire only once—at Bewley's request—donning silk shirts and western hats at a store opening in Fort Worth, and the ensuing photograph eventually appeared on the cover of their long-out-of-print Columbia LP, *Chuck Wagon Gang* (Columbia Historic Edition FRC 40152). Although their radio shows always featured spiels for Bewley's Best Flour, or for other Bewley-made products like Anchor Feed, they were seldom permitted to make personal appearances with the Bewley chuck wagon, a little covered wagon from which sample biscuits and cakes were dispensed. (Bewley Mills, however, did send out a picture of the group with the chuck wagon upon receipt of a coupon). Groomed exclusively as a radio group, the Gang's public profile was kept as low as possible, and they were even discouraged from singing at funerals.

The Chuck Wagon Gang's radio shows remained consistent through the years: no comedy, no frills, and few announcements or song introductions. At the insistence of announcer Cy Leland, a former track and football star at Texas Christian University (TCU) in Fort Worth, they adopted new names that somehow seemed more broadcast-worthy. That's when David became known as Dad, Ernest became Jim, Effie became Anna (although she already had a sister named Anna), and Lola became simply Rose. Leland, who also worked as their agent, hawked the Bewley products and the Chuck Wagon Gang sang—as many as six numbers in a fifteen-minute show. They also performed the Bewley theme song, which thousands of their former listeners can still sing from memory, but which the Carters recalled only with some embarrassment (the current group is still asked to sing the song):

> Bewley Mills is here again,
> Singing a song of growing men.
> Full of pep as we can be,
> And this is the reason that you see.
> We eat the bread that mother bakes;
> Biscuit, pastry, pie, and cake;
> This is the flour that makes it best,
> From the East to the West,
> It's ahead of the rest,
> It'll stand any test; it's Bewley's Best,
> . . . and Anchor Feed

The only significant departure from their usual routine came in about 1941 when veteran radio performer Dwight Butcher, born in Oakdale, Tennessee, joined them briefly as a singing master of ceremonies. At 6:30 A.M. Butcher hosted his own show with the Cedar Ridge Boys, but he appeared with the Chuck Wagon Gang at 10 A.M. for five days a week and again at noon on Sundays. He had attained some fame as the writer of "Old Love Letters," a song recorded by Jimmie Rodgers in his last recording session on May 24, 1933, and as the writer of the tribute song "When Jimmie Rodgers Said Goodbye." Butcher typically announced the group's selections, read an inspirational poem, and about three times a week sang a song. Like most of the hillbilly performers of the prewar era, Butcher was an itinerant entertainer, and he soon left for another radio job in California.

The Chuck Wagon Gang's early WBAP repertory remained much like that of the Lubbock period. It included examples of all the song types learned at family gatherings: sentimental parlor songs, cowboy songs, folk tunes, an occasional barbershop quartet piece, Stephen Foster songs, and religious material. The style they had developed never deviated and would forever distinguish them. Dad sang tenor, and Jim a pleasing not-too-low bass; together they provided a framework around which Rose and Anna worked the vocal magic that gave the group its distinctive sound. No two voices could be more dissimilar: Rose's soprano voice had a powerful penetrating edge to it, while Anna's alto had a low, resonant, and caressing timbre. In order for the voices to dominate, musical accompaniment remained spare and incidental. On secular songs the quartet featured Dad playing mandolin and Jim on guitar, while the sacred numbers had only guitar backing. The singing arrangements, however, were far from simple. They followed the printed scores and could be quite intricate. Above all, they revealed hours of careful and conscientious practice. Rose usually sang the lead parts (at least on the verses) while her dad and siblings created a close, dependable, and multi-layered harmony with their tenor, alto, and bass and their own respective solo passages.

The Chuck Wagon Gang already had a large and faithful radio audience when the family first ventured into a recording session in November 1936. Although it cannot now be verified, some reports (such as one printed in *Billboard* on December 4, 1965) suggest that the Carters had driven to Dallas from Lubbock in 1935 to ask Don Law, the regional talent scout for the American Record Company (soon purchased by Columbia), for an opportunity to record. Although he liked their music, he felt that the girls' voices had not yet matured sufficiently. Law turned them down and asked them to "come back in a year or two." Whether the story is true or not, Law seems to have heard the Chuck Wagon Gang broadcasts the following year and became convinced that they were now prime candidates for recording.

Don Law, born in London, worked first for Brunswick Records but then moved to Columbia where he became the protégé of another Englishman, Arthur "Uncle Art" Satherley, who played a profound role—as a longtime A and R man for Columbia—in promoting the careers of a large retinue of American country entertainers such as Roy Acuff and Gene Autry. His brilliant student, Don Law, became Columbia's face of country music in the Southwest. Working out of an office in Dallas, Law played major roles in the careers of such seminal southwestern performers as Lefty Frizzell, Ray Price, and Marty Robbins, as well as the legendary Mississippi bluesman Robert Johnson. Johnson, in fact, made his first recordings for Law in San Antonio on November 23, 26, and 27, 1936, during the same time span when the Carters made their initial recordings. While the Carters and Johnson may very well have been aware of each other's presence in the Alamo City, there is no documented evidence that they made any contact with one another. On November 25 and 26, 1936, a nervous Carter clan gathered in room 414 at the Gunter Hotel at 205 East Houston Street in San Antonio to sing for Law's mobile recording crew.

Recording ledger accounts provide no evidence of what Law personally thought about the music made by the Carters, but he was clearly impressed by their potential as recording artists for Columbia or one of its affiliates such as Vocalion. He and Satherley cared nothing about satisfying their own personal tastes but, instead, insisted on producing material that record buyers wanted to hear. The Carters needed no preparation, for they chose songs that seemed most popular on their radio shows. The Carters began their session with a venerable gospel song, "The Son Hath Set Me Free" (co-written by Miriam E. Oatman, a political scientist who taught at American University, over thirteen hundred miles away in Washington, D.C.), but given their modern reputation as premiere gospel singers, it may come as a revelation to modern enthusiasts that not only did secular songs such as "Put My Little Shoes Away," "I'll Be All Smiles Tonight," and "Where the River Shannon Flows" outnumber the gospel songs in their initial recording session, but they completely dominated the second session in Dallas in 1937.

We do not know how or why they chose their songs, but their choices reflect the kind of material that was heard often on radio broadcasts during the thirties. For example, "Carry Me Back to the Mountains," composed by Carson Robison, and "Take Me Back to Renfro Valley," written by radio entrepreneur and song collector John Lair, typified the sentimental and nostalgic songs that appeared frequently on broadcasts of the National Barn Dance in Chicago or on early morning hillbilly shows throughout the nation. Their 1937 song choices demonstrate the fascination with cowboys and cowboy songs that touched the repertories of almost all country entertainers during the Depression years. Worried and anxious Americans sought reassurance that their values were still intact. They longed for the individualistic heroes that the cowboys seemed to be. It is not surprising, then, to hear the Chuck Wagon Gang do songs like "The New Frontier" (from the Sons of the Pioneers) or "Cowboy Blues" (from Gene Autry) but also to hear Rose do a creditable job of yodeling. After all, everyone else in that decade was doing it. The sessions in 1936 and 1937 were their sole recordings made in that decade. By the time they recorded again, in April 1940, they had become exclusively a gospel group.

The Chuck Wagon Gang's evolution as gospel singers reflected not so much a conscious choice by the group to demonstrate their religiosity but, rather, a calculated response to the demands of their audience. The Carters usually included at least one religious song on their broadcasts but gradually increased the number as requests poured in from their listeners asking for sacred songs. They began to set aside their Wednesday shows for gospel music (coinciding with evening mid-week prayer services commonly held those nights in evangelical Protestant churches) and then added a Sunday show also devoted to sacred material.

Bewley Mills, of course, quickly recognized the appeal and marketing potential of religious material. Ironically, Dad and his children were not ardently religious, and one does not hear the passion or revivalistic fervor heard in the music of, say, the Bailes Brothers or the Louvin Brothers. Nevertheless, by 1936 the Carters were already skillful gospel singers. They had learned their lessons well, and some of the religious songs recorded at the 1936 sessions quickly became some of their most enduringly popular numbers: "Kneel at the Cross," "A Beautiful Life," "The Church in the Wildwood," "I'd Rather Have Jesus," and "Standing Outside." As late as 2016, the modern incarnation of the Chuck Wagon Gang is still asked to perform songs like "The Church in the Wildwood."

With the coming of World War II, the first phase of the Chuck Wagon Gang's professional career came to an end. By this time, they had become household words in Texas, and their radio shows were among the most-listened-to programs in the Lone Star State. Honky-tonk country stalwart Johnny Bush (who wrote and first recorded "Whiskey River"), for example, told Eddie Stubbs that the Chuck Wagon Gang provided the "sound track" of his youth. He and people like Ray Price are fond of recalling that one could walk down the street of just about any Texas town at noontime and hear the sounds of Chuck Wagon Gang songs coming from radios in every house. Their Columbia recordings were also introducing their names and music to an ever-growing national audience.

In their third recording session, on April 23, 1940, in the Fort Worth suburb of Saginaw, Texas, they recorded twelve songs (all gospel), including their superb performance of "We Are Climbing," as well as their first venture into the repertory of the great songwriter Albert Brumley, "I've Found a Hiding Place." In this first extensive foray into gospel music, the Carters set patterns of song choice and styling that remained with them for the rest of their career. Beginning with "After the Sunrise," where they note that "all will be glory, singing the story," all twelve of these recorded items paint positive and comforting pictures of the soul's relationship with a loving savior, describe the Christian's passage through an unfriendly world ("pilgrims in a lowland of sin," as described in "Sunset Is Coming, but the Sunrise We'll See"), and hold out the promise of a reunion with friends and loved ones in a heaven that is free of earth's travails and imperfections. Indeed believers are promised more than a simple reunion free from care; they are assured of "An Empty Mansion" in Heaven that is awaiting their occupancy.

Their performance styles were also firmly fixed by the time this session was held. Jim introduced each song with a simple strum of his guitar. The vocal arrangements came from the songbooks and were skillfully executed. While Rose usually led the verses of the songs with her high soprano, Anna and Jim took repeated solos on the choruses and sometimes exchanged vocal lines in a highly affecting manner. Dad, on the other hand, seldom did more than a line or two of solo singing but nevertheless played a central role in building the landmark Chuck Wagon Gang vocal blend.

Like all of the gospel quartets of the prewar years, the Chuck Wagon Gang frequently featured a syncopated vocal response known as the "afterbeat." One hears an early example of their employment of this style in Lonnie B. Combs's "I Love to Tell of His Love." This antiphonal style seems to have been borrowed from the world of instrumental jazz and was brought into gospel music by pioneering piano players like Dwight Brock who accompanied the Stamps Quartet. In 1927 the Stamps Quartet had recorded a song called "Give the World a Smile"—which was extremely popular in the Southwest—that featured a bass vocal lead followed by an antiphonal, syncopated response made by the other three singers. By the end of the thirties, songs employing the style were appearing often in songbooks and in the performances of virtually every gospel quartet.

Despite the vocal strength shown on the 1940 recordings, the next Chuck Wagon Gang recording sessions, of March 8 and 9, 1941, were destined to be their last until December 1948. A variety of factors, mostly beyond their control, contributed to their absence from the recording field. On August 1, 1942, the Chuck Wagon Gang fell victim to a two-year recording ban imposed by James C. Petrillo, president of the American Federation of Musicians, against the recording companies, whose "canned music," Petrillo believed, was making it difficult for musicians to find work. Seeking royalty payments from the companies, Petrillo and the AFM in 1948 instigated still another eleven months" ban. The Chuck Wagon Gang recordings of December 16, 1948, are said to have been the first recordings made by any Columbia artists after the ban.

More serious restrictions, however, arose from problems imposed by the war. With three Carter boys and four Carter sons-in-law in military service and travel curtailed by the rationing of gas and tires, the family virtually withdrew from public performance. Anna, in fact, moved to Florida to be with her husband, Howard Gordon, whom she had married on May 26, 1939.

In 1942, the remaining members relocated briefly to Tulsa, Oklahoma, for the summer only, where they performed on KVOO. They then moved back to Fort Worth, where Rose became a riveter in a bomber plant. As expected, Rose received considerable ribbing from her siblings because of her similarity to the heroine of the popular song "Rosie the Riveter." Their radio shows on WBAP continued on an irregular basis. Rose and Anna joined their soldier-husbands on their respective military bases and therefore often missed programs.

Other sisters sometimes filled their positions, and their fans did not forget the Chuck Wagon Gang. Their records and Sellers radio transcriptions (made in 1940) could still be heard on radio throughout this relatively inactive period. The group had already built an extensive popularity in the Southwest, and their sound, in fact, had been transmitted to other parts of the United States by means of the powerful outreach of WBAP and the Mexican border stations. But most crucial to their future fame were the efforts of Rev. J. Bazzel Mull. In the far off southeastern states he had begun collecting scarce Chuck Wagon Gang 78s and playing them on his evangelistic radio shows. When the Carters returned to professional performance in the late 1940s, a large nucleus of support awaited them among their old faithful fans in both the Southeast and the Southwest.

American music, however, like American society, changed drastically during the war and in the years that followed. The ability to maintain commercial viability, without the alteration of styles, would be a severe test for simple homespun acts such as the Blue Sky Boys or the Chuck Wagon Gang. The audience for commercial music was larger, more affluent, more urban, and more youthful than ever. This new audience could be won, at least temporarily, to acoustic-based, simple folk sounds (as evidenced by the emergence of the urban folk music revival in the late fifties), but music entrepreneurs and recording executives correctly perceived that the permanent big money lay in the uptempo electrified sounds that seemed to mirror the aggressive life of the quickly growing urban centers. Old-time country music could demonstrate commercial strength only in its electrified manifestations, or in the accelerated, supercharged guise of bluegrass. Gospel music similarly adopted the electric sounds of secular pop and country music or, if the impulse for tradition was strong, attached itself to bluegrass music. Solo guitar or piano backing was almost universally abandoned.

Perhaps more significant, mainstream gospel music radically "de-theologized" in the years following World War II, a trend that had, in fact, set in long before the outbreak of military hostilities. The music remained Christian, and perhaps even Protestant, but references to the fear of hell and the aura of a blood-stained cross and redemptive suffering gradually disappeared, along with the themes of fatalism and world-rejection that once figured so prominently in southern Protestant music. Led by such pacesetters as Marion Snider and the Imperial Quartet of Dallas, the gospel groups began emulating the crooning styles and mannerisms of the pop quartets. The new gospel music was designed to soothe and sell, not to frighten, offend, or evangelize.

Given these modernizing trends that swept across southern Gospel music in the postwar years—along with the increasing emphasis on youth that affected the physical appearances, performing styles, and repertories of all performers—it is remarkable that the Chuck Wagon Gang thrived as well as they did. Even more amazing, they were on the threshold of attaining the largest national audience they had ever had. Part-country and part-gospel, they acutely felt the modernizing pressures of the period but nevertheless made a better adjustment to them than did most groups. By the time of their 1948 recording sessions, they had come to rely pretty heavily on songs written by the team of writers such as Luther G. Presley, James B. Coats, Marion W. Easterling, and Albert E. Brumley who worked for the Stamps-Baxter Music and Printing Company.

The Stamps-Baxter company emerged in 1926 when Virgil O. Stamps and Jesse Randall Baxter Jr. fused their independent companies and established branch operations in Dallas, Chattanooga, and Pangburn, Arkansas. Two or three times a year Stamps-Baxter published "convention" songbooks, bearing names like *Pearly Gates* and *Heavenly Highway Hymns*, containing well over one hundred songs in the seven-note style that were designed for all-day singings and church services. Although these books usually contained a few traditional hymns, the majority of the selections came from the company's staff of writers who tried to come up with something original for each new edition. The company sent out quartets (about thirty-five by the end of World War II) to popularize and sell the books and held singing schools in various locations including churches. Usually at the end of the June school held in Dallas, the company sponsored an all-night singing convention that featured scores of quartets and other gospel singers. The Stamps-Baxter company became the most influential business in the gospel quartet field and would have been well-known to the members of the Chuck Wagon Gang.

Unlike other acts in the religious field, the Chuck Wagon Gang continued to rely solely on the use of one guitar for accompaniment. Each song was introduced by a guitar strum, after which the instrument provided only rhythm chords for the singing. Jeremy Stephens, who is a first-rate guitarist and student of the instrument, argues (from visual and audio observation) that, on the 1930s sessions, Jim played a Kay Kraft Venetian body-style archtop guitar, but through the rest of his career he played a Gibson L-Century flattop guitar. Using a flat pick, Jim played mostly closed bass-note chords, with a vamp-sounding rhythm. After Jim retired from the road in 1951 (while continuing to record with the group through 1953), the Chuck Wagon Gang made a significant change by replacing his acoustic sound with an electric guitar played by Anna's husband, Howard Gordon (born May 30, 1916, in Krum in Denton County, Texas), who joined the group in the early fifties with his tasteful and unobtrusive style. Howard's first recordings with the group came in 1954. Although he played a variety of guitars, he is most closely identified with his Gibson ES-5 Switchmaster. Like Jim, Howard also played with a flat pick, using closed chords quite often but also interjecting a complex rolling strum.

In spite of the augmented instrumental sound and the addition of newly composed songs to their repertory, the Chuck Wagon Gang approach remained blessedly familiar: a soft cushion of sound provided by the male tenor and bass voices, overlain with the melodic interplay of Rose's soprano and Anna's alto. A much more dramatic change came after 1955 when Dad chose to retire. The group, however, always managed to find excellent replacements who could preserve the distinctive Chuck Wagon Gang sound. Dad, in fact, was replaced as tenor for one year by another son, Eddie. Substitutes, though, now more often came from outside the family—including the great bass singers Haskell "Hi-Pockets" Mitchell and

Jim Waits who in 1952 replaced Jim for short periods of time. On the other hand, musical talent was spread so widely throughout the Carter family that all of the sisters and brothers except one ("spare tires," as Dad had called them) sang with the Chuck Wagon Gang at one time or another. The sibling with the longest duration in the group, aside from the original four, was Roy (born March 1, 1926, in Calumet, Oklahoma) who first became their bass singer from 1952 until 1957 and then served off and on in that capacity until 1995.

The Carters' postwar career exposed them to a larger number of listeners than had ever heard them before. After severing their relationship with WBAP in 1951, they no longer had the benefit of live radio programming but they reached new audiences through the widespread playing of their old 78 rpm recordings, occasional television coverage, and an increased level of personal appearances. The Chuck Wagon Gang did receive some jukebox exposure, but most of their popularity came from radio programming. Radio disk jockeys like Randy Blake in Chicago and Nelson King in Cincinnati often played their songs as the "Hymn of the Day" or otherwise included them in Sunday morning gospel shows. Many older listeners can still fondly recall stations playing fifteen minutes of Chuck Wagon Gang recordings around the noon hour. The *Billboard Disk Jockey Supplement* of October 7, 1950, reported that the Chuck Wagon Gang had ranked number 18 on a list of the "Top Small Singing Groups of the Year." The poll was headed by such pop acts as the Andrews Sisters and the Mills Brothers. Among country acts, only the Sons of the Pioneers polled higher, at number 15. This kind of exposure became increasingly possible through the multitude of long-playing albums that Columbia began producing in 1950. (Only the best-selling acts on the label received this kind of early treatment from Columbia). The first ten-inch LP of Chuck Wagon Gang material, released in June 1950, consisted exclusively of previously recorded material, some of which dated back to that first session in 1936: "A Beautiful Life," "Kneel at the Cross," "The Church in the Wildwood," "I'd Rather Have Jesus," "Looking for a City," "I've Found a Hiding Place," "If We Never Meet Again," and "I'll Fly Away."

The last three songs came from the pen of Albert E. Brumley, the composer whose creations had appeared repeatedly on Chuck Wagon Gang broadcasts since the mid-thirties and on their recordings since April 1940. Brumley was born near Spiro, Oklahoma, on October 29, 1905, and was educated in the shape-note sound in Hartford, Arkansas, at the Hartford Music Company (which his family now owns). He and the Chuck Wagon Gang seem to have formed a mutual admiration society. Brumley had been listening to the group's records on stations in Arkansas, Missouri, and Kansas since the late thirties. He often sent them copies of his latest songs, hoping they would record them. The Chuck Wagon Gang was more than ready to comply. In 1948 they recorded "I'll Fly Away" and helped to put that song on its way to international popularity. Inspired in part by Vernon Dalhart's "Prisoner's Song," which contained the lines "If I had the wings of an angel, over these prison walls I would fly," the song was written in 1929, and first published in 1932 in a Hartford songbook, *Wonderful Message*. It was recorded as early as 1940 by the Rex Humbard Family, and by the Selah Jubilee Singers in 1941, but the Chuck Wagon Gang's version proved to be the most influential and commercially viable of the various recordings (or at least until the year 2000 when the song appeared in the soundtrack of the immensely popular movie *O Brother, Where Art Thou?*). This informal alliance between the Oklahoma-born Brumley and the Chuck Wagon Gang seems to have been a perfect fit. Their gentle, rural sound and nostalgic evocation of old-fashioned values and way of life resonated with millions of American listeners. On December 5, 1960, the Chuck Wagon Gang paid tribute to their old friend in an album called *God's Gentle People: The Chuck Wagon Gang Sings the Songs of Albert E. Brumley* (Columbia CL 1899), which contained twelve of his songs.

The most significant innovation in the Chuck Wagon Gang's postwar career, the public concert, came through the efforts of John Wallace "Wally" Fowler. Before the war they had made only occasional appearances in schools, churches, and at store openings, but almost always within easy driving distance of Fort Worth. They had consequently remained primarily a southwestern group. After the late forties, though, they became personally known to Americans living far beyond the borders of their Texas homes. Their entry into big-time show business came through two kinds of productions: the "package show," a concert that featured several entertainers, and the all-night gospel singings that flourished in the 1950s.

The all-night singings apparently had begun in 1938 when the Stamps-Baxter company began holding the events in Dallas at the conclusion of their annual singing schools. Probably the principal continuing exponent of the tradition, Wally Fowler (born in Adairsville, Georgia, in 1917), was a jovial singer, songwriter, and entrepreneur who had tried his hand at country and western music before settling into his gospel role and had written such songs as "Mother's Prayer" and "That's How Much I Love You" for Eddy Arnold and others. By 1948 he had organized the Oak Ridge Quartet—an ironic name for a group headquartered in Knoxville, but named for the nearby city where a crucial element of the atomic bomb was constructed.

The events that dramatically changed the lives and direction of the Chuck Wagon Gang occurred on November 25 and 26, 1950, when Fowler lured them to Georgia to participate in some of his promotions. Coincidentally, these shows in Atlanta and Augusta came fourteen years to the day(s) after their first 1936 sessions. It had taken them a long time to hit the road! At the time, Fowler was still a member of the Grand Ole Opry cast but was venturing into the realm of music promotion and had held his first all-night singing two years earlier at the Ryman Auditorium in Nashville. He had been aware of and had loved the music of the Chuck Wagon Gang since at least 1938. At their 1948 session, the Gang had recorded the first of three songs that Fowler submitted to them, "The Sunshine Special," followed in 1949 by "The Signs by the Side of the Road" and "Perfect Joy." Fowler had begun corresponding with Jim Carter, urging the group to come to Georgia. The Chuck Wagon Gang accepted the invitation with considerable trepidation, dreading the long drive of approximately 825 miles over two-lane roads, fearful of the bitter winter weather that had beset the Southeast, and wondering if their music would be accepted in that part of the world. Although they all piled into Rose's Pontiac and headed out on the trip, they phoned Fowler at one point along the route to express their intention to abandon the venture and return home. The highly anxious Fowler had to employ all of his persuasive skills to coax the Carters on into Atlanta, and the show occurred as advertised and scheduled.

This version of the Chuck Wagon Gang included Dad, Rose, Jim, and Ruth Ellen, who was substituting for Anna—back home in Fort Worth with her third child, Greg, who had been born earlier in the week. Held at the City Auditorium, the Atlanta show was an all-night singing, from 8 P.M. to 2 A.M., that featured at least seven gospel groups. When the Carters walked on stage with their songbooks, many in the large audience chuckled, conveying the impression that they believed they were watching some country yokels who had not yet learned the words of their songs. Although singing from songbooks had been a common practice for the Chuck Wagon Gang when they did their radio shows, they probably used the books in Atlanta as a favor for sister Ruth Ellen who was not completely familiar with the songs. But as Rose later testified, "Why, we didn't need them anyway. We knew all the songs by heart." To his credit, Wally Fowler tried to make the Carters feel comfortable by suggesting to the audience that he had asked them to hold the songbooks as a tribute to and re-creation of their radio broadcasts.

The next afternoon, November 26, 1950, the Chuck Wagon Gang appeared in Augusta, Georgia, as part of a country package show, sponsored by Local 603 of the Augusta Fire Department as a fund-raising function for its welfare bureau. The show took place in the Municipal Auditorium (soon renamed the Bell Auditorium) following a dangerous winter storm, but it still attracted several thousand people. The Chuck Wagon Gang was received warmly during the three-hour show, which included Little Jimmy Dickens and the Country Boys, Wally Fowler and the Oak Ridge Quartet, and the Log Cabin Boys, a local gospel quartet.

The Chuck Wagon Gang's "new" career took them far from Fort Worth and into the competitive realm of commercial gospel entertainment. From Augusta, they soon ventured to Winston-Salem, North Carolina, for an outdoor concert at a ball park and then back to Atlanta for another auditorium show. Periodically, Wally Fowler began booking them on grueling ten-day tours. These Fowler-sponsored tours seem to have lasted at least through 1955, although Ron Crittenden (a later bass singing member of the Chuck Wagon Gang) recalls them working dates for Fowler during his 1958–1961 tenure in the group. Ron recalls one package show in Atlanta where they performed before 10,400 paid attendees. Described as the Original Wally Fowler and Spiritual All-Night Singing Concert, one tour in October 1954, which included the Oak Ridge Quartet and Stuart Hamblen, saw the Chuck

Wagon Gang move in successive nights to Detroit, Akron, Ohio, Huntington, West Virginia, Cincinnati, and Indianapolis. That kind of schedule was too much for Jim to take, and although he appeared with his family on their 1953 recording session, he withdrew from active road performances and was replaced by his brother Roy.

Recognizing their appeal in the southeastern states, the Carters began to explore the possibility of relocating to that region. Largely through the encouragement of Rev. J. Bazzel Mull, they moved to Knoxville, Tennessee, in 1956, not only singing to an older audience already familiar with their name and sound but also building a new following among people delighted to find singers who projected an old-timey ambience. Knoxville had been an important market for country music with live programming on stations WROL and WNOX. Grocery magnate Cas Walker was also an important promoter of talent in that city. Ron Crittenden recalls hearing that the Gang worked some shows for Walker and also did some radio programs while they were based in Knoxville.

Mull, though, had contributed mightily to the popularization of the Chuck Wagon Gang in the Southeast during the war years and afterward and deserves much of the credit for keeping the name and sound of the group alive. Mull was a blind Baptist minister, born in Valdese, North Carolina, who grew up in an atmosphere permeated with old-time religion and gospel music. His grandfather was a singing evangelist and singing-school teacher, and his father was a music teacher who organized a family band, the Valdese Sacred Band, which included J. Bazzel as five-string banjoist. When he was twenty-four, Mull entered the ministry, conducting tent revivals throughout the North Carolina piedmont, and finally settling down in Knoxville where, in 1944, he married Anna Elizabeth Brown.

Mull began his radio ministry on WGNC in Gastonia, North Carolina, in 1939. Soon thereafter he began playing religious records as companion pieces for his sermons. His brother Romulus, an appliance dealer in Kannapolis, North Carolina, collected used 78 rpm records on his business trips throughout the South and passed them on to J. Bazzel to play on his shows. By 1942 Mull was playing Chuck Wagon Gang records on such stations as WJHG in Johnson City, Tennessee, and WNOX in Knoxville. After 1950, when the first Chuck Wagon Gang LP appeared, Mull became even more deeply involved in the merchandising of their records. He and his wife established the "Mull Singing Convention," selling gospel albums, songbooks, and bibles on several clear-channel radio stations. Of the three hundred thousand or more records sold per year on the Singing Convention, those of the Chuck Wagon Gang greatly predominated, and Mull claims that he sold so many of their records that Columbia asked him to advertise and sell other religious records for the company. Mull typically bought about eighty thousand records at a time (entire truck trailer loads), which he then sold in packages of four at $6.35 a package. Right on through the seventies, late night radio listeners could hear—most notably on WWL in New Orleans—the gravelly but amiable voice of Rev. Mull introducing the songs of the Chuck Wagon Gang while Mrs. Mull read the list of songs that could be heard on the albums being hawked. The thirty-minute programs contained minimal sermonizing and were devoted almost exclusively to music. The Mulls made a compelling team, and their Singing Convention was a wonderful piece of Americana that preserved the flavor of old-time radio.

While the fifties marked the beginning of national exposure for the Chuck Wagon Gang, the decade also witnessed significant changes in the composition of the group. Except for Jim who remained in Fort Worth and Dad who continued to live in Springtown, twenty-seven miles northwest of Fort Worth, the Carters stayed in Knoxville for about two years (in 1956 and 1957), playing frequent concerts in the Southeast. Brother Eddie now sang Dad's tenor part. These loyal native Texans, however, never really adjusted to their new home. It was in this period that the combination of television and rock and roll initiated the eventual demise of Knoxville's once-vibrant tradition-based country music hotbed. When the Gang returned to Fort Worth in 1957, the rock and roll boom had begun, temporarily eclipsing all forms of traditional music. Roy left the quartet and became a manufacturer's representative for a school supplies firm in Nashville and did not return as bass singer until 1963. Dad's retirement from professional music, however, had greater symbolic importance than Roy's temporary departure.

The last recording session in which the Carter clan's patriarch participated, on September 5, 1955, was also ironically the Chuck Wagon Gang's last one in Texas. Their last eight recording sessions—from September 22, 1950, through September, 1955—were held in the famous

Jim Beck Studios at 1101 Ross Avenue and 1914 Forest Avenue in Dallas, the same venues that hosted early sessions made by Marty Robbins, Ray Price, Lefty Frizzell, Billy Walker, and a host of other country and rockabilly artists. Beck worked with several recording companies and producers but had a particularly close relationship with Don Law, who brought many of his Columbia artists to the Beck Studio. It was an easy decision for Law to integrate the Chuck Wagon Gang into this setting. Law loved the relaxed, easy-going environment and the cadre of musicians who played there and was impressed with Beck's mastery of magnetic tape recording technology that was introduced in 1949. According to country music historian Charles Wolfe, the sessions at Beck's studio contributed to the "birth of the great Texas honky-tonk style in the early 50s" and might have made Dallas a major competitor of Nashville if they had continued. However, Jim Beck's accidental death on May 3, 1956, from exposure to carbon tetrachloride fumes used to clean recording equipment in his studio lent further force to the fact that the historic Texas phase of Chuck Wagon Gang history had come to an end.

Dad's departure marked the end of the era that is documented and celebrated in this collection. Still, the Chuck Wagon Gang was destined to live on beyond this period. Beginning with a session at the Bradley Studio on October 8, 1956, all of the remaining Chuck Wagon Gang's Columbia recordings were to be made in Nashville. In the immediate years following Dad's retirement, the Chuck Wagon Gang remained a family group, with a sound that remained markedly similar to that of the past. But after Eddie's one-year tenure replacing his dad as tenor singer, the slot was generally held by non-family members such as Pat McKeehan, Howard Welborn, Jim Wesson, and Ronnie Page. Roy took over as bass singer in 1953 and held that position until 1995, except for occasional periods of retirement, such as the period from 1958 to 1961when Ron Crittenden replaced him. Rose and Anna now remained as the only representatives of the original group, and while Howard Gordon continued to be their sole musical accompanist on personal appearances, he was often joined on recordings by some of Nashville's finest studio musicians, such as guitarists Hank Garland (who received equal billing with them on one LP) and Harold Bradley and bass players Bob Moore and Joe Zinkan.

The Chuck Wagon Gang actually entered their most commercially successful phase in the years following Dad's and Jim's departures. By the early sixties the first iteration of the rock and roll revolution had subsided, allowing other mainstream and traditional forms of music to revive. With Nashville now a major music center, the burgeoning gospel music industry followed the lead of country music and made its headquarters in Music City. The Chuck Wagon Gang began venturing into areas in the North and West where they had never previously traveled and found to their surprised delight that their southern harmonies were favored in those areas, too. Crowds everywhere were large and enthusiastic, especially in Detroit and Chicago. On June 22, 1963, the Chuck Wagon Gang appeared at the Hollywood Bowl in Los Angeles, as part of a package show that included country superstars such as Johnny Cash, George Jones, Faron Young, Lester Flatt and Earl Scruggs, and the television and movie actor Walter Brennan. The show drew an estimated crowd of eighteen thousand. On June 7, 1966, the Chuck Wagon Gang became part of the first gospel concert ever presented at New York's famed Carnegie Hall. The Don Light Agency in Nashville actively booked them in places ranging from the Gator Bowl in Jacksonville, Florida, to the Daytona International Speedway to the Grand Ole Opry. In fact, they soon began making appearances in Canada and the Bahamas.

In contrast to the $300 fees that they had typically received back in the early to mid-fifties, their fees for a show now ranged from $1,500 to $1,800 in the sixties and early seventies, and from $2,000 to $2,500 in the following decade. It is tempting to explain their expanded appeal in terms of an audience of transplanted southerners, but Chuck Wagon Gang popularity was more likely the product of their widely circulated LPs, a generation of Mexican border broadcasts, domestic airplay on country radio, J. Bazzel Mull promotions, the cravings of many Middle Americans for a wholesome sound and image, and possibly, the resurgence in America of evangelical Protestantism. More immediately, the Chuck Wagon Gang gained exposure through syndicated television broadcasts. In September 1965, for example, they joined the Rangers Trio as featured performers on a show taped and syndicated in Nashville called "Gospel Roundup." Because the quartet was now recording in Nashville, in June 1966 they decided to relocate there officially.

Since then the Chuck Wagon Gang has sometimes undergone various periods of inactivity, from time to time giving the impression that the quartet's future was in jeopardy. Long tired of the road and yearning for the stability of her country home in Azle near Fort Worth, Rose chose to leave the group in 1966. Initially, Louise Clark replaced her, leaving Anna as the only active member of the original four. On August 27, 1967, Roy went back to his high school teaching job in Fort Worth, and about a month later, on October 3, 1967, Anna's husband and the group's longtime guitarist Howard Gordon suffered a fatal heart attack while taping the Wilburn Brothers TV show in Nashville. Anna reconstituted the group for a short time in late 1967, singing with her daughter Vicki, son Greg, and bass singer Jim Black. When Anna married former Louisiana governor and popular country and gospel singer Jimmie Davis on December 9, 1969, she moved to his home in Baton Rouge and began performing with him as part of the Jimmie Davis Trio. While she occasionally returned for special performances, this new personal and professional relationship obviously removed her from full-time participation in the Chuck Wagon Gang. With all of its original members gone, the quartet faded—temporarily—from the active arena of professional gospel music.

The Chuck Wagon Gang, though, never officially disbanded as a recording unit; they still made albums for Columbia including Anna and Rose and other family members. In the mid-seventies a newly constituted version composed of tenor Ronnie Page (and sometimes Pat McKeehan) and three of the Carter siblings—Roy, Ruth Ellen, and Betty—resumed a reduced schedule of concerts held mostly during the summer, or when vacation time permitted lengthy absences from their jobs. Their records still circulated widely, but the Carters now correctly perceived that Columbia had lost interest in promoting their music with any dedication or zeal; the company spent little time, for example, in making their records available to country or gospel radio stations, and airplay had virtually come to an end. In fact, the label hadn't released a single by the group since 1965.

The industry was changing and radio was changing as well. With music directors and more formalized playlists dominating the radio scene, non-charting acts like the Chuck Wagon Gang now received little focus from their labels. Consequently, they severed their relationship with

Columbia soon after their last recording session on September 23, 1975. The thirty-nine-year relationship, which had yielded 408 known masters and over twenty LPs, was one of the longest of any group's affiliation with a single record label in American music.

By 1979 the Chuck Wagon Gang had begun recording for the Copperfield label in Nashville, and Roy and Ruth Ellen had made a renewed determination to, as they phrased it, "rebuild what Daddy started"—that is, take their music to as many people as possible and with little thought of the money that might be made. In the stepped-up activity that came in the 1980s, Roy and Ruth Ellen (bass and alto) provided the consistent core of the Chuck Wagon Gang, and they were joined by a variety of other singers such as Patricia Neighbors, Debby Trusty, and Pat McKeehan. The most significant innovation in the total Chuck Wagon Gang sound occurred between 1985 and 1994 when Harold Timmons added his piano stylings to the group's performances. A native of Winston-Salem, North Carolina, who as a child had been introduced to the Chuck Wagon Gang's music by his parents, Timmons came to the group as a veteran performer of professional gospel music. During his long association with the Chuck Wagon Gang, which has remained constant since 1994, as a historian, discographer, publicist, and marketing specialist Timmons became the most ardent champion of the group's legacy and music.

The contemporary version of the Chuck Wagon Gang began to take shape in 1993 when Roy Carter asked his great niece Shaye to join the group shortly after her graduation from college. Shaye brought many positive qualities to the Chuck Wagon Gang. She had previously paid little attention to the historic meaning of the quartet, but as Vicki's daughter and Anna and Howard Gordon's granddaughter, she was eager to learn. Already an exceptional singer, she had acquired two bachelor's degrees, one from Southeastern Louisiana in Hammond in vocal performance and the other from the University of Texas in Arlington in Choral Conducting. Although she was a natural alto, she first joined the Gang as the soprano singer in a group that included Roy, Ruth Ellen, and Jim Wesson. Except for a couple of absences, she has been the central presence in the Chuck Wagon Gang since the year 2010, when she returned as owner, manager, and alto singer. Now married to Andy Smith, she embarked on a campaign

Carrying the tradition today are Shaye Smith, Stan Hill,
Melissa Kemper, Jeremy Stephens.
Photograph courtesy the Collection of Shaye Smith, Hertford, North Carolina.

to revive the Chuck Wagon Gang, to honor the legacy established by the original four, and to reassert the quartet's identity as the tradition bearer of the country gospel tradition.

As of 2014, the Chuck Wagon Gang was composed of Shaye Smith (alto), Julie Hudson (soprano), Stan Hill (tenor), and Jeremy Stephens (bass and guitar). Stephens brings to the quartet a master musician with a strong experience in bluegrass music, a champion of the "original" Chuck Wagon Gang and collector of their records, and a student of the Howard Gordon style of guitar playing (he insists on accompanying their songs with either Howard's or Jim Carter's styles). He therefore brings an additional sense of history and commitment to authenticity. He and his colleagues average around two hundred shows per year. While traveling extensively through the southern, mid-Atlantic, and midwestern states, they appear in a variety of venues, including churches, the Grand Ole Opry, the Marty Stuart Show on RFD Television, the annual CMA Music Festival, and periodic visits to WSM radio.

As they approach eighty years of almost continuous existence as gospel singers, the Chuck Wagon Gang still clings closely to the vision promoted by Dad Carter way back in 1935: "Sing the old songs, and sing them the way I taught you." While the group does not adhere solely to old songs, many still remain in their repertory—like "Church in the Wildwood," "We Are Climbing," "Echoes from the Burning Bush," "Looking for a City," "I'll Meet You in the Morning," and "I'll Fly Away"—that have thrilled Chuck Wagon Gang fans for generations. The current Gang is fond of telling audiences that these old favorites were once new songs. In 2013 they recorded an album called *Meeting in Heaven—The Chuck Wagon Gang Sings the Songs of Marty Stuart*. The well-known country music renaissance man wrote all of these religious songs, most of which sound like they were composed over a half a century ago.

Whenever a final assessment of the Chuck Wagon Gang is made, their importance to gospel music will not be measured in terms of originality. They made few innovations in gospel music. Their style of four-part harmony came from the singing schools, and their arrangements followed closely the dictates of the printed scores. If the bass, alto, or tenor voices assumed lead passages at various times in songs, it was because the original music had been written that way. Even their most distinctive feature, the female soprano lead, was rooted in the shape-note singing schools. The Chuck Wagon Gang's retention of such traditional performing patterns, however, made them *seem* unusual because very few commercial quartets in the thirties and forties featured women singers. Unlike many of the white gospel groups who competed with them, the Chuck Wagon Gang exhibited little discernible African American influence (except, perhaps, for the afterbeat rhythm that probably reached them, though, through white innovations) and virtually none of the free-wheeling holiness influence that has touched the styles of so many other gospel singers. (There was a world of difference, for example, between the styles of the Chuck Wagon Gang and the effervescent Happy Goodman Family.) Singing on the beat, and with a dignified and almost gentle restraint, the Chuck Wagon Gang nevertheless invested their music with an appealing warmth and depth of feeling that few groups have matched and a sense of harmony that no quartet has surpassed.

Through years of societal and musical change, when most gospel singers made stylistic concessions to the dominant commercial trends of their day, the Chuck Wagon Gang remained faithful to the socioreligious tradition that had spawned them. While newly composed songs freely moved into their repertory, they never abandoned the old favorites, and they gave both new and old similar treatment. Nashville musicians joined them on recordings, but the distinctive Chuck Wagon sound remained unimpaired. Audiences have cherished their music, not because they were a pioneering group but because the Chuck Wagon Gang has represented and preserved a valued and hallowed tradition. To their listeners, both young and old, the Chuck Wagon Gang sound has been both comfortable and comforting, a rock of certainty in a world of ceaseless change, and a source of reassurance in a time of trouble.

ACKNOWLEDGMENTS

This essay was built around the nucleus of an article I wrote, "The Chuck Wagon Gang: God's Gentle People," published in the *Journal of Country Music* 10, no. 1 (1985). I was fortunate in being able to interview three of the members of the Chuck Wagon Gang: Rose Carter Karnes in Azle, Texas; Anna Carter Gordon Davis in Baton Rouge, Louisiana; and Roy Carter, by telephone from Fort Worth, Texas. I also interviewed Dwight Butcher and Reverend J. Bazzel Mull. Issues of the *Music City News* were also helpful in gathering pertinent performing data concerning the Chuck Wagon Gang. Charles Wolfe provided me a copy of a Chuck Wagon Gang "discography" garnered from Don Law's notebooks, along with a tape of a telephone interview that Wolfe had with Harold Timmons.

Since that time I have profited greatly from Bob Terrell's biography and history, *The Chuck Wagon Gang: A Legend Lives On* (Goodlettsville, Tenn.: privately printed, 1990). John Rumble, archivist at the Country Music Foundation in Nashville, made available the pertinent material on the Chuck Wagon Gang held by that institution and provided me a copy of Charles Wolfe's essay on Jim Beck and his famous studios: "Honky Tonk Starts Here: The Jim Beck Dallas Studio," *Journal of Country Music* 11, no. 1 (1986), 25–30.

Above all, I wish to acknowledge the generous and unselfish assistance of Shaye Smith, who provided information on her famous singing forebears; Harold Timmons, who was able to recall invaluable details about his memories of and relationship with the Chuck Wagon Gang; Jeremy Stephens, who is a fount of knowledge concerning the music and history of the group; and, of course, Eddie Stubbs, whose passion, commitment to detail, seemingly inexhaustible energy, and unflagging love for the Chuck Wagon Gang's music kept us all close to the task. Eddie enriched the essay through his research in the *Augusta Herald*, and through his interviews with Bob Brumley, Ron Crittenden, and Ronnie Page. The Chuck Wagon Gang website has been a highly useful source for both history and information concerning the group's current activities.

Richard Weize, of course, through his encyclopedic knowledge of all kinds of American music and through his meticulous, state-of-the-art recording projects made it possible for this essay to reach an international audience. For a broader overview of the larger field of white gospel music, one should consult Don Cusic, *The Sound of Light: A History of Gospel Music* (Bowling Green State University: Popular Press, 1990) and James Goff Jr., *Close Harmony: A History of Southern Gospel* (Chapel Hill: University of North Carolina Press, 2002).

CHAPTER 9

HONKY-TONK
The Music of the Southern Working Class

As I re-read this essay in May 2016, I see a few assertions and judgments that really should be changed. But I will let them stand as an indication of where my thinking was over thirty years ago. I still think that the honky-tonk style has been one of the most vital musical expressions of working-class culture, and it has been less susceptible to romance and myth-making than other country music styles. Regrettably, it has almost disappeared from mainstream country music.

One of its most enduring practitioners, Dale Watson, has even begun to call his brand of music Ameripolitan. This descriptor is his personal protest against the current group of pop performers who have lately appropriated the word "country." It is satisfying to know that Watson is still on the road presenting his honest and uncompromising style of music. Let him call it what he will. To his faithful fans, his music is good old honky-tonk country. Otherwise, anyone who would like to hear this infectious barroom sound would have to go to the small clubs in, say, California or Texas—to a place like the Cheatham Street Warehouse in San Marcos, Texas, where George Strait honed his skills back in the mid-1970s. The shuffling beat pioneered by Ray Price still holds sway in the music of people like Justin Trevino, Darrell McCall, Joe Paul Nichols, Amber Digby, and James Hand, wonderful entertainers who preserve the sound that their mentor long ago abandoned. Thankfully, a few small record labels—such as the Heart of the Country label in Brady, Texas—make this music available everywhere.

While reviewing the subject of this essay—which first appeared in *Folk Music and Modern Sound* (1982), edited by William Ferris and Mary L. Hart—I can't help but recall the influence of my good friend Tom Crouch, a fellow history graduate student at the University of Texas in Austin and one of "my first guitar players," at a time when I was singing at parties and knew only a few chords. Tom was the first person I ever heard use the term "honky-tonk" to describe a style or sound of country music. He made me aware of the role played by beer joints, particularly in Texas, in the making of a style of music we both loved. I tried to describe the origins and evolution of the style in my doctoral dissertation of 1965 and then saw this discussion repeated—with my consent—in Robert Shelton's *The Story of Country Music* in 1966. Honky-tonk music's central role in the history of country music is now universally acknowledged. Nevertheless, we still need a major comprehensive study of the phenomenon, and one that will explore the roles played by musicians in other parts of the South and in California (birthplace of the Bakersfield Sound).

Although "honky-tonk" and its association with African American culture have been traced back to at least the 1890s, we still do not know the term's precise origins or what it meant when it was introduced. Oscar Brand theorized that the term came from the clubs where cheap pianos manufactured by the Tonk Brothers were universally found. Explicit confirmation of this assertion, however, has not been found. Some good written accounts, which evoke the grit and ambience of honky-tonk life, include Johnny Bush with Rick Mitchell, *Whiskey River* (Austin: University of Texas Press, 2007); Daniel Cooper, *Lefty Frizzell: The Honky-Tonk Life of Country Music's Greatest Singer* (Boston: Little, Brown, 1995); and Ronnie Pugh, *Ernest Tubb: Texas Troubadour* (Durham, N.C.: Duke University Press, 1996).

One would also profit greatly from the music heard on some of Dale Watson's CDs, such as *Cheatin' Heart Attack* (Hightone HCD 8061) and *Blessed or Damned* (Hightone HCD 8070).

> I left my home down on a rural route
> And told my mom I'm going stepping out,
> To get the honky tonk blues.[1]

THE COUNTRY CHURCH, THE COUNTRY SCHOOLHOUSE, THE VILLAGE BARN DANCE, AND THE FAMILY PARLOR all occupy honored places in the history of country music as shaping forces in the evolution of the genre. All of them mirror the pastoral origins of country music, just as their continued emphasis in written accounts reflects a rural bias on the part of scholars. The honky-tonk, on the other hand, which Hank Williams described in the above song, has been anything but pastoral, but it may have been the most powerful influence yet. Since antiquity a powerful interrelationship has existed between drinking and musical entertainment, and the tavern or its equivalent has always played an important role in the dissemination of music. But as a force for musical change in country music, its history properly begins in the 1930s. It was then that the combined forces of prohibition repeal and increased commercialization and professionalization in the still new hillbilly music field led to the movement of musicians into the taverns and beer joints where their music was welcomed. When country music entered the honky-tonks, its performing styles and its thematic content changed significantly. Much of that story I have told elsewhere.[2] My chief focus in this paper, however, will be on the years since World War II when the music of the honky-tonk became, at least for a time, virtually *the* sound of country music, as well as the most valid expression in song of the worldview of the southern working class.

If the thirties were important as years of nourishment, the war years were absolutely indispensable in both the maturation and popularization of honky-tonk music. Like no other phenomenon before it, the war contributed to the weakening of the agricultural nexus and the subsequent migration of people into towns and industrial cities of the South, as well as into cities in the Midwest and on the West Coast. While rural civilians changed their locales and their occupations, their military sons and daughters moved to training camps both in and out of the South and to combat theaters around the world. For a people in transition, who were now urban in residence but yet rural in style and outlook, the adjustment was often fraught with frustration and pain: housing was both inadequate and scarce; work was plentiful but fraught with an unfamiliar regimentation; and family solidarity was weakened by a whole host of complex urban problems, not the least of which was the growing entry of women into the workforce and the increased availability of alternative role models for youth. In that time of stress people tended to seek security in that which was familiar. Women, for example, often sought the solace of religion (probably to a greater extent than men), and radio evangelists and charismatic tent revivalists found a large and enthusiastic audience among southerners in the late 1940s. For men the pressures and frustrations of city life could be especially traumatic, and the threats to masculine supremacy, already strongly present in rural life, were made even more glaring in the newly adopted urban milieu. Many men, and their sons (but, it is hoped, not their daughters), sought to reaffirm their identities in a sympathetic setting: over a bottle of beer in a honky-tonk.

The honky-tonk was a man's world.[3] Although women were sought there, it was not considered their domain, and those who entered were not respected. Men might accompany their wives or girlfriends to a dance, but the unattached "honky-tonk angel" was both a lure and a threat. While she tempted, she also reminded one of that potential in all women and was a premonition of the liberation that was soon to come. Men went to honky-tonks for the widest variety of reasons, and as both casual and serious drinkers. Many who frequented honky-tonks during the war years, whether industrial laborer or serviceman, were gripped by a sense of isolation—the loneliness that came from social displacement or from the physical separation from loved ones. The lonely drinker sought communion with the bottle, his companion on the nearby barstool, and the music of the jukebox. The music of the honky-tonks, whether live or on jukeboxes, reflected increasingly the preoccupation of these displaced ruralites. Furthermore, a body of songs about the honky-tonk world itself and about the experience of entertainers who appeared there began to comprise a significant portion of the country music repertory. Rustic sounds still thrived in country music during the forties—the decade, after all, marked the heyday of "mountain singer" Roy Acuff. But styles born in the honky-tonks of Texas predominated, and names like Bob Wills, Ted Daffan, Floyd Tillman, Moon Mullican, Cliff Bruner, and Al Dexter dominated the jukeboxes. Al Dexter's "Pistol Packin' Mama," a giant hit of 1943, and an example of the rollicking side of honky-tonk, was inspired by its singer-composer's experiences in the oil-town honky-tonk atmosphere of Texas in the thirties (the story grew out of an incident witnessed by Dexter in a Longview dance hall). Voicing the cry-in-your-beer side of honky-tonk, almost to the point of suicidal impulse, were such songs as Rex Griffin's "The Last Letter," Ted Daffan's "Born to Lose," and Floyd Tillman's "It Makes No Difference Now," which poured forth from a thousand jukeboxes and were carried around the world by lonely and homesick southern servicemen. When Ernest Tubb moved to the Grand Ole Opry in 1943, his Texas-born and beer-joint-nourished

Two of the stalwarts of the Texas honky-tonk tradition,
probably in Houston during the early 1950s: Harry Choates and
Floyd Tillman with two unidentified women companions.
Photograph courtesy the Bill C. Malone Collection, Madison, Wisconsin.

style gained a national forum. As he won disciples with songs like "I Ain't Going Honky Tonking Any More" and "Walking the Floor over You," the style he embodied insinuated itself into the music of country entertainers everywhere, from West Virginia to California.

The immediate years following World War II witnessed country music's first great commercial boom. Postwar prosperity created an audience that was eager for and receptive to commercial music diversion. The number of musicians and the establishments receptive to their music proliferated. Not all singers went willingly to the honky-tonks. The honky-tonk's reputation for violence comes more from this period than from any other. The threat to life and limb was as real for the entertainer as it was for the customer, as drunken oil field roughnecks or industrial workers playing cowboy worked out their fantasies or tested their macho impulses in the competitive arena of the barroom. For many young men a violent barroom encounter was ritualized expression of manhood. For others it was a way of coping with the frustrations of boring, generally low-paying jobs. The stories may be apocryphal, but musicians still tell of playing on stages that were protected from flying beer bottles by chicken wire. Few entertainers have very pleasant memories about what Glen Campbell would later call the "fightin'-and-dancin'" clubs. The honky-tonk circuit was a hard apprenticeship for country entertainers, but the styles developed there moved into the recording studios and the concert halls where they altered the whole sound and tone of American country music.

Honky-tonk performance worked hand in hand with technological progress to encourage sophisticated innovations in instrumentation. Electric guitars, both standard and steel, became common in most country bands, and by 1954 the pedal steel guitar, a basic ingredient of honky-tonk instrumentation, and probably the closest thing yet to an approximation of the vocal honky-tonk whine, had been introduced (first on Webb Pierce's recording of "Slowly"). The honky-tonk style never exercised a complete monopoly (Eddy Arnold's successful sound of the mid-forties embodied a composite of influences), but for all practical purposes, it had become the all-pervasive sound of mainstream country music. The typical band was small and featured a fiddle, a steel guitar and "takeoff" guitar (both electrified), a string bass, a rhythm guitar played in "sock," or percussive, style, occasionally a piano, but almost never any drums. The musicians were capable of performing the hot instrumental licks pioneered by the western swing bands of the thirties, but instrumentation was usually subordinated to the needs of a vocalist. A new generation of honky-tonk singers had emerged, and some of them, like Hank Thompson, Webb Pierce, Lefty Frizzell, and Floyd Tillman, were among the most distinctive stylists that the country music field has seen.[4]

Surpassing them all, however, was the immensely talented singer from Alabama called Hank Williams, whose style reflected the tensions that had produced the honky-tonk genre and whose career marked the greatest commercial flowering yet of the honky-tonk sound. Hank sang to an audience who, for better or worse, was having to come to terms with life in an industrial-urban environment. Adults might dream of the abandoned rural life, but few had thoughts about returning to it. Their children had no illusions about rural life, and they made up the bulk of country music's burgeoning audience in the early fifties. Very soon, the youngest of them would be lured away by the rollicking, and sensual, sounds of rock and roll, a style that would render honky-tonk a strong, almost devastating blow. Hank Williams's career and style certainly do not totally embody the whole of country music history, but they epitomize a large slice of it. Reared in a fundamentalist, but violently unstable, religious atmosphere, Williams was never able to rid himself of the influences learned there, both musical and doctrinal, and he took them into the honky-tonks of south Alabama where he began singing by the time he was fourteen years old.[5] Stylistically, his music represented a fusion of that of his two heroes, the Texan Ernest Tubb and the Tennesseean Roy Acuff (an example of similar amalgamations in the larger field of country music), and thematically, his songs embodied the ambivalence that lay at the heart of southern working-class culture: hedonism and puritanism, machismo and sentimentality, sin and guilt. Williams and his audience interrelated with an intimacy that had hardly been equaled in country music's previous history, because culturally they were one.

When Hank Williams died in 1953, few could have anticipated that very soon the honky-tonk style would be driven from recordings, and that the whole country music genre, which had thrived so mightily after the war, would be in shambles. The rock and roll phenomenon, which ironically derived much of its energy and stylistic traits from the country music tradition (a fascination with boogie and "hot" rhythms often exhibited by earlier country musicians), was also a product of the urbanization process. The rock and roll wave inundated American music, and all forms of traditional country music were driven underground as promoters and recording men began their frantic searches for young and vigorous stylists who could re-create what Elvis had done and who could permanently hold that youthful audience that now dominated American music. The Nashville music industry responded to these challenges in a variety of ways, one of which was the production of a pop style of country music, known by such designations as "the Nashville Sound," "country pop," or "countrypolitan," which would allegedly preserve the ambience of older country music while building a new audience of listeners who preferred their music to be served up in less raw forms. For a brief period in the mid-fifties, fiddles and steel guitars almost disappeared from country recordings and from jukeboxes.

Honky-tonk music, like bluegrass, did not vanish, however. Both forms went "underground," and honky-tonk continued to thrive, especially in the clubs of Texas and southern California where veterans like Ernest Tubb and newcomers like Willie Nelson, George Jones, Charlie Walker, Buck Owens, and Wynn Stewart remained faithful to the beer-drinking style. One singer resisted both the rock and roll and the country-pop tides and not only prospered with his version of the honky-tonk genre but introduced dynamic innovations that have influenced the field ever since. This was Ray Price, whose recording of "Crazy Arms" in 1956 successfully competed on the charts with country-pop tunes and ushered in a new and vital phase of honky-tonk history. Price's band, the Cherokee Cowboys, were almost totally electrified (fiddles included); the electric bass had replaced the older standup instrument; and drums had become an integral aspect of this dance-hall-oriented music. While the wailing pedal steel guitar and the heavily bowed single-string-style fiddle took their lead passages, the drums and rhythm guitar set down a hard rhythm as the electric bass surrounded it all with walking bass patterns. This was the "Texas Shuffle Beat," an infectious dance style, and some of the best country music ever made.

Like his mentor Hank Williams before him, Price inspired a host of disciples. The Cherokee Cowboys' roster reads like a who's who of country music. At one time or another, the band included Johnny Bush, Roger Miller, Johnny Paycheck, Willie Nelson, Darrell McCall, Buddy Emmons, Tommy Jackson, and Buddy Spicher. By the beginning of the sixties, these men had gone on to pursue their own careers, and many others, both within and outside the pale of Ray Price influence, had contributed to a honky-tonk revival. George Jones, building on a long tenure in the southeast Texas dance halls of Beaumont, Port Arthur, Orange, and Houston, produced hit after hit as he became one of the supreme stylists of country music. Buck Owens, Texas-born but a product of California's country ballroom scene, topped the charts in the early sixties with a supercharged instrumental style (part honky-tonk, and part rockabilly) dominated by the sound of the pedal steel guitar. Later in the decade another California-based singer, Merle Haggard—a rare breed, indeed, because he was born in the state— took the honky-tonk style to even greater commercial heights with songs like "The Bottle Let Me Down" and "Swinging Doors." He and Loretta Lynn demonstrated in the late sixties and early seventies that it was possible to be both "hard country" and successful at the same time. It was a lesson readily absorbed by many young performers, but one from which the country music industry as a whole has profited little.

Honky-tonk music, therefore, revived with new strength from its doldrums of the mid-fifties. The style has never since predominated as it did in the early fifties, though, and probably never will do so again. The country music industry has prospered to an extent never thought possible back during the rock and roll period, and the Nashville facet of the industry, absorbed with self-image, has attempted to be "all things to all people." Country music has simultaneously identified with Middle America, the working man, and progressive youth, while also reaching out for that affluent middle-class audience that is apparently presumed to be different from the other three categories. In an industry obsessed with "crossovers," the hard honky-tonk sound is unwelcomed; indeed, it is embarrassing.

Furthermore, the temptation among performers to cross over to the more lucrative and respectable pop-country field is almost irresistible. Singers experiment with the honky-tonk field, as in the case of Johnny Rodriguez with his initial recording of "Pass Me By" but soon move into other stylistic categories. A few, like Ronnie Milsap, Jerry Lee Lewis, and Hank Williams Jr. demonstrate a mastery of the honky-tonk style, when they choose to do so; but that choice is made infrequently. For a singer to perform consistently in the honky-tonk vein is rare; for one to prosper doing so is even more unusual. As of this writing, Ernest Tubb still makes from two to three hundred personal appearances a year. His audience is large and loyal, but it has also been with him for probably thirty years. Other singers like Norman Wade, Vernon Oxford, and Boxcar Willie project sounds and often songs that come directly out of the fifties. And there are probably a thousand others much like them in a thousand honky-tonks throughout America, unnoticed and unknown anywhere outside their own locales, who still remain true to visions cast long ago by Ernest, Lefty, Hank, or Ray.

The singers who have done most to preserve the honky-tonk style, while at the same time creating identities apart from earlier models, are

Gene Watson, John Anderson, and above all, Moe Bandy (born in Meridian, Mississippi, but reared, biologically and musically, in San Antonio, Texas). Bandy probably does not deserve to be called "the Jesus Christ of country music," as Nick Tosches has termed him, but his clean, crisp articulation of lyrics dealing with drinking, cheating, and heartbreak, performed with a backdrop of fiddle and pedal guitar, cuts like a breath of fresh air through the fetid morass of country pop.

This essay began with the argument that honky-tonk was once the sound of mainstream country music. It concludes by arguing that, while it no longer predominates, it now represents the best in a music that is losing its soul. Honky-tonk music, unlike other country styles, has been hampered less by artificiality. It has not consciously tried to preserve or re-create (as has bluegrass), nor has it reached out to build a new audience. Of all country music styles it has been the closest organic reflection of southern working-class culture, and the one that most closely marks the evolution of the southern folk from rural to urban-industrial life. Although intimately tied to the urban adjustment of southern plain folk, it has been ignored by folklorists because it is not pastoral, and because it does not protest. It is scorned by the country music industry because it is too country. And it is dismissed by many of us, I am convinced, because it is too real.

Honky-tonk instrumentation both attracts and repels: to many of us, the whine of the pedal steel guitar and bounce of the shuffle beat evoke elemental, and often cathartic, impulses and emotions. To others, they undoubtedly conjure up distasteful images both seamy and seedy. The lyrics and instrumentation of honky-tonk music combine to evoke a side of human nature that we do not always like to see, or at least do not like to recognize: a vision of emotional pain and isolation and human weakness that we have all shared. The lyrics may be too revealing emotionally to accept intellectually. At their worst, the songs can be so full of trite self-pity as to drown us in their bathos. But at their best, songs like "Borrowed Angel," "Who'll Turn Out the Lights," or George Jones's marvelously per-formed "The Grand Tour" speak to the loneliness and the need for human empathy in each of us.

NOTES

1. Hank Williams, "Honky Tonk Blues." This essay was originally a paper, delivered orally, and illustrated with relevant recordings. These included Floyd Tillman, "Slipping Around"; Ernest Tubb, "Walking the Floor over You"; Ray Price, "Crazy Arms"; Stoney Edwards, "Old Hank and Lefty Raised My Country Soul"; Moe Bandy, "It Was Always So Easy (to Find an Unhappy Woman)"; and George Jones, "The Grand Tour."

2. The first history and analysis of honky-tonk as a subgenre of country music appeared in my doctoral dissertation, "A History of Commercial Country Music in the United States, 1920–1964" (University of Texas, Austin, 1964), and in my subsequent book, *Country Music, U.S.A.* (Austin: University of Texas Press, for the American Folklore Society, 1968). Another analysis of the phenomenon, along with recorded examples, is found in *The Smithsonian Collection of Classic Country Music* (organized and edited by Bill C. Malone, 1981).

3. The term "honky-tonk" probably has urban black origins, but by the thirties it had come to be identified with roadhouses generally frequented by southern whites. Honky-tonks were usually located on the outskirts of town, partly because of the quest for reduced legal surveillance and for low tax rates but also because of the county option policy favored by such states as Texas. Honky-tonks often operated near the county lines in order to draw clientele from both wet and dry counties. With the passage of time, "honky-tonk" became virtually a generic term for any establishment that sold beer, permitted dancing, and featured country music.

4. Floyd Tillman had been an active participant in the Texas honky-tonk scene since about 1935, as both singer and sideman, but he did not become known as a solo singing star until after 1949.

5. The best account of Williams's early life and influences is Chet Flippo, *Your Cheatin' Heart* (New York: Simon and Schuster, 1981).

CHAPTER 10

JOHNNY GIMBLE
The Music Came Up from His Soul

This essay was first solicited by the editors of *No Depression* magazine and appeared in issue number 42 (May–June, 2002). It was later published in an anthology, *The Best of* No Depression: *Writing about American Music* and can now be found on the journal's online site. I do not know whether the editors were aware that Gimble and I have the same hometown—Tyler, Texas—but I was pleased to have the opportunity to say something about him and about the strong fiddling tradition of my native area of East Texas, while also acknowledging the vital role he played in the shaping of both western swing and modern country music. Gimble died on May 9, 2015, in Dripping Springs, Texas.

THE TITLE OF ONE OF JOHNNY GIMBLE'S CDs, *JUST FOR FUN*, goes a long way toward explaining the man and his music. It would be naïve to say that the money wasn't important to him; he had, after all, been an extraordinarily commercial musician. But his sheer passion for music and his compulsion to share it with others did the most to sustain him through his long and varied career.

Gimble made consistently good music for over sixty years. Mention his name, and many people immediately remember him as the award-winning session musician who, along with Buddy Spicher and a few others, brought the fiddle back into prominence in Nashville in the 1970s, after it had been virtually abandoned by mainstream artists. But that was over forty years ago. Others will think of his tenure as a Texas Playboy with Bob Wills. That was back in the first half of the twentieth century.

When he joined Wills in California in 1949, Gimble had already been making music in Texas and Louisiana for more than a decade. He never stopped.

A stroke on Christmas Eve in 1999 slowed the master fiddler a little bit, but he continued to play an occasional gig, making records, and teaching fiddling workshops in Texas and New Mexico. The satisfaction of seeing, as Gimble termed it, "the light bulb go off" when a young musician masters a difficult chord or, better yet, puts an original spin on a tune was more than enough to keep Gimble busy teaching the apprentices who made the trek to Taos.

When Gimble entered the world on May 30, 1926, in the Chapel Hill community near Tyler, Texas, he could scarcely have avoided the sound of the fiddle. In many ways, East Texas remained a cultural outpost of the Old South. Confederate statues still guarded courthouses in virtually every county seat, and a biracial population, Democratic political leanings (with a strong populist flavor), and evangelical Protestant religious preferences provided evidence of the region's kinship with Dixie.

Although young men in this part of Texas typically wear cowboy hats, boots, and jeans, their society is a product of the mid-nineteenth-century migration that brought the Gimbles and people like them from Georgia and other southeastern states. Marked by heavily wooded rolling hills and red dirt (except for the sandy lands where Tyler's famous rose fields flourish), the region still knelt before the throne of King Cotton.

Fiddle contests, such as the yet-thriving affairs held in Athens and Crockett, convened regularly in East Texas, as expressions of civic spirit or as celebrations of old-time traditions. When Gimble was born, a few veteran fiddlers such as James Knox Polk Harris, from nearby Longview, could still speak of their experiences in the Confederate army. People still met frequently in their neighbors' homes to dance to "Tennessee Wagoner," "Hell among the Yearlings," and other lively fiddle tunes that were already old before they were transported from Tennessee, Alabama, and other southern climes.

The domino game "42" was all the rage at that time, and often families would invite their neighbors in for a series of matches that might be going on simultaneously at four or five tables. Fiddlers were frequently invited to provide relief between contests or to play for the dances that sometimes concluded the evening.

It wasn't hard for budding young musicians to find role models, and Gimble found his in the performances of his paternal uncles John and Paul who played fiddle, "tater bug" mandolin, and guitar at the house parties or simply on the back porch. They played many of the old hoedowns; but occasionally a tune like "Washington and Lee March," probably learned from a Milton Brown recording, or a pop number like "Redwing," from the turn of the century, would creep into their repertoire.

Most Texas fiddlers, in fact, probably did not "swing" their tunes the way Gimble did, but they were always receptive to a broad range of musical styles, from ragtime to pop. Gimble didn't have to go very far—only a scant fifteen miles to Lindale—to find an example of these eclectic inclinations and a link to the early-radio string bands. This was Huggins "Lefty" Williams, at one time the mainstay of the famous East Texas Serenaders, who was then living with his invalid mother, not far from where Uncle John Gimble lived.

Like many of the fiddlers and string bands in Texas, Williams and the Serenaders had been receptive to new tunes and styles and had shown a particular fondness for ragtime melodies. Gimble remembered learning "Beaumont Rag" from Williams and being fascinated by the infectious bow shuffle with which the old fiddler invested the tune. He sat enthralled as he watched Williams play, but it wasn't easy to learn from a left-handed fiddler.

Intriguing as Williams's playing style may have been, the evidence of his show-business experience may have been more thrilling to young Gimble and his brothers. He recalled that "we saw a stack of records, and that really impressed me." These were the recordings the Serenaders had made for Brunswick, Columbia, and Decca in the late twenties and early thirties, evidence of the seemingly glamorous world that beckoned professional musicians. Lefty Williams lived long enough to learn of Gimble's awesome fiddling talent, and as an old man, he was once quoted as saying of his protégé, "Johnny can beat me playing hot fiddle."

Music was a constant diversion in the Gimble household. Johnny's father, James Frank Gimble, had a small farm but made his living as a telegrapher for the Cotton Belt Railroad. He worked at his job all night long and then slept only a few hours before managing a few hours of farmwork alongside his sons. He played no instrument, but he encouraged the music preferences of his six sons and three daughters, mainly by bringing fiddles, guitars, and mandolins into the household. All of the Gimbles played or sang, and soon the Gimble boys were in business as a family band. Johnny was about ten years old when he developed a love for both the mandolin and the fiddle and discovered they were tuned the same way.

Johnny's first professional experience came in about 1937, when he and his brothers Jack, Gene, and Jerry went to work for a flour salesman named Big Boy Green, who enrolled them into a group known as the Peacemaker Boys, named for a local flour brand. Big Boy installed a speaker on his car and advertised their appearances with a recording of Bob Wills's "Black and Blue Rag." Performing on flatbed trucks, the boys played music and sold flour in towns all over East Texas.

Big Boy was a promoter from the old school. He drummed up interest in his product by holding concerts and using corny gimmicks that seemed straight out of blackface minstrelsy or vaudeville. Sometimes, a little African American boy would tap dance and play tunes by rapping on his teeth. Occasionally, after a layer of flour was spread on the makeshift stage, local boys were encouraged to root for hidden coins with their hands tied behind their backs.

About two years later, in 1939, Jack having departed for the navy (he volunteered prior to the bombing of Pearl Harbor and was there when the Japanese made their attack), the three youngest Gimble boys (Gene, Johnny, and Jerry) and good friend James Ivy attained sponsorship from Howard Dodd Grocers and became the Rose City Swingsters (inspired by Tyler's claim to be the "Rose Capital of America"). Clearly profiting from the influence of the seminal Fort Worth band, the Light Crust Doughboys, the Swingsters played a mixture of pop, hillbilly, and cowboy tunes while advertising their sponsor's product, Rose Queen Flour, all over East Texas.

The Swingsters often performed from flatbed trucks, but they also appeared on radio broadcasts in Tyler and Kilgore, and in the dance halls and honky-tonks that had emerged in the wake of Prohibition's repeal. Gimble and his brothers knew the hoedowns and folk ballads inherited from the Old South, but they and their audiences were also increasingly receptive to the current dance tunes that marked the repertory of early western swing.

Cotton and its folkways may have dominated the lives of most East Texans as the thirties drew to a close, but the booming oil fields of nearby

Van, Kilgore, Gladewater, and Longview forecast the region's future. Few people got rich from the oil discoveries, but they put a little bit of money in circulation, inspired a quest for diversion and recreation, and made it possible for "fighting-and-dancing" joints to thrive, such as Tyler's Ambassador Club, Longview's Mattie's Ballroom, and a dive in Lufkin remembered only as "the hammer and hatchet" club. The Gimble boys recalled these clubs with amusement but little affection, noting, for example, that people went to the Ambassador Club mainly to fight.

Gimble didn't hear much big-band jazz in those days. Nor did he recall having heard the music of the great gypsy musicians Django Reinhart and Stephane Grappelli. Sometime in 1938, though, he heard the recorded music of Cliff Bruner and the Texas Wanderers, a discovery that changed his life.

Bruner had joined Milton Brown's Musical Brownies as a fiddler in 1935, when he was only twenty, and after Brown's death in April 1936, he embarked on his own influential career as a fiddler and bandleader. His name became known and revered throughout southeast Texas and southwest Louisiana. Working mainly out of Beaumont, Bruner virtually inaugurated a revolution in nearby Cajun country, where fiddlers such as Harry Choates and Leo Soileau added songs and styles learned from the Texas musician to their traditional French mix. Gimble declared, for example, "You can hear Cliff when you hear Harry Choates play 'Dragging the Bow.'"

Gimble was fascinated not only by the hot, improvisatory fiddling of Bruner but also by the jazz licks laid down by steel guitarist Bob Dunn (probably the first country musician to electrify an instrument) and mandolin player Leo Raley. Gimble described Raley's style as "rinky tinky ragtime," but he was impressed by his early attempts at electrification. Hearing these examples of "hillbilly jazz" (which Bruner described as "hokum"), Gimble realized that, as talented as he already was with his fiddle, many musical worlds remained unexplored, and the fiddle was capable of seemingly limitless possibilities. He remained fond of quoting Cliff Bruner, who told him that "if you can hum it, you can play it, if you'll practice until your fingers do what your mind thinks."

Gimble's career apart from his brothers began in about 1943, right after his graduation from high school, when he joined the locally famous Shelton

Johnny Gimble with his family band, the Rose City Swingsters, and a few close friends, probably during the early 1940s near Tyler, Texas. (Left to right) Jerry Gimble, Tom Mallory, C. E. Mallory (almost concealed behind Tom), Gene Gimble, Johnny Gimble (with fiddle), Elbert Ingram, an unidentified person, and Huggins "Lefty" Williams, the legendary fiddler who was one of Johnny's teachers.
Photograph courtesy the Collection of Randy Mallory, Tyler, Texas.

Brothers (Bob and Joe, whose real name was Attlesey) with their Sunshine Boys. The Sheltons presented an odd mixture of old-fashioned "brother duet" singing and progressive western swing instrumentation. Gimble was hired to play tenor banjo and fiddle but was permitted to play only one or two tunes on the latter instrument during their schoolhouse shows, the venues where most prewar hillbilly bands played.

After Gimble expressed his frustration one day when another fiddler was employed to play at one of their gigs in a Texarkana nightclub, Joe Shelton clumsily tried to console the teenager by saying his banjo was indispensable for the rhythm the band was trying to achieve. Shelton also tried to console Gimble by telling him, "I don't think you'll ever be a fiddle player"—a prediction that fortunately went unfulfilled.

Working out of Shreveport, Gimble continued to play the tenor banjo as he toured with the Sheltons in Texas and Louisiana, and through their influence he became part of the band that accompanied Jimmie Davis in

1944 in his successful campaign for the Louisiana governorship. The stage experience gained through his involvement with the Sheltons was invaluable, but Gimble's most cherished memory was the tutelage received from fiddler Jimmy Thomasson, who became a lifelong friend and "taught me how to hold a fiddle," Gimble claimed.

The Gimble boys certainly contributed more than their share to the campaign against fascism in World War II. Three of them served in the navy, and Johnny did a stint with the army. His induction into military service came toward the end of 1945, but he arrived in Germany too late for combat. He therefore spent much of his time playing music in the officers' clubs and absorbing the big-band jazz heard on the Armed Forces Network. Listening to Benny Goodman and bass player Slam Stewart, Gimble was introduced to a host of jazz and blues improvisations and received further confirmation of the wisdom imparted earlier by his mentor, Bruner. Gimble argued that he learned as much from Goodman's swinging clarinet style as from any other source, and he always spoke with wonderment at the antics of Stewart, who bowed his bass while he hummed the notes.

In the immediate postwar years, during country music's first great commercial boom, Gimble began putting these ideas to use in a succession of Texas bands, beginning in 1947 with Jesse James and his Gang in Austin (where he first electrified his mandolin). Next, he joined his brothers in a band called the Blues Rustlers in Kilgore and Goose Creek. Then he moved on to Buck Roberts's Rhythmairs in Corpus Christi. The Corpus Christi stint was particularly fortuitous because one night when Bob Wills and the Texas Playboys played a gig in the city, the Playboys mandolinist Tiny Moore heard the Rhythmairs play and was impressed by Gimble's scat singing, fiddling, and electric-mandolin playing. Moore quickly mentioned Gimble's name to Wills, who was looking for a replacement for fiddler Jesse Ashlock. Gimble didn't hesitate when the invitation was made to join the Texas Playboys, even though the affiliation promised a grueling life on the road. Gimble was fond of saying, "Would a sandlot baseball player turn down the opportunity to play for the New York Yankees?"

The three years spent with Bob Wills, from 1949 to 1951, were the most exciting in Gimble's career. He exulted in the freedom he found with the Texas Playboys, eagerly accepting Wills's challenge to "play everything you know." Executing the swinging improvisations that Wills heard but could not play, and sometimes joining Tiny Moore on scorching mandolin duet pieces, Gimble set a standard that other swing musicians could hope to emulate but would never surpass. He participated in three recordings sessions for MGM that included such classics as "Warm Red Wine," "Remington Ride," "Boot Heel Drag," and "Faded Love."

Recalling those exciting days and the exhilarating music that issued from them, Gimble said, "Playing a swing chorus is like being a surfer. You just ride the wave if you have a good rhythm section. You don't have to think. Turn on and it comes out." Life as a Texas Playboy was exhilarating and challenging. Gimble insisted that, despite the rigors of a demanding schedule, he and the other Playboys "couldn't wait to get on the bandstand." This life, however, soon proved exhausting for a man who loved his home and family. By 1951 he had "settled down" in Dallas, playing music there with the bands of Al Dexter and Dewey Groom and working for producer Don Law, a talent scout for Columbia Records who was recording many of that label's acts at Jim Beck's local studio.

Gimble, therefore, had the distinction of having been part of western swing in its waning days and of being an active participant in the burgeoning honky-tonk scene that edged Wills-style music aside in the early 1950s. He never felt comfortable playing in honky-tonks (even though he did so quite frequently), but he contributed directly to the shaping of the honky-tonk sound, chiefly through his performances in Beck's studio.

This experience marked Gimble's first stint as a session musician, and he became a sideman for a remarkable group of singers, including Ray Price, Marty Robbins, and Lefty Frizzell who, in the early 1950s, made their first important recordings in Dallas. The Dallas–Fort Worth area was rife with musicians who found eager and loyal audiences among the local aircraft and automobile-industry employees and other blue-collar workers who sought relief and diversion in the local clubs or at weekend variety radio shows such as Fort Worth's *Saturday Night Shindig* or Dallas's *Big D Jamboree*. Nevertheless, most country musicians still had to supplement their musical habits with outside employment.

Gimble was no exception. He worked a host of jobs to support both his musical passion and his family's needs. At one point he was employed as a carpenter during the day while playing music four nights a week at Rosa's Ballroom and appearing frequently on KRLD's *Big D Jamboree*. Gimble brought a measure of security into his life, however, when he obtained a license at a local barber college—a route followed, not by coincidence, by several of his musical colleagues (Bob Wills had also been a barber). Three of his old buddies from the Rhythmairs had already decided to go to school there, and they received good deals because one of the owners was a brother of club proprietor Rosa (who was married to singer and bandleader Al Dexter). Until Gimble moved to Nashville in 1968, his professional life revolved around cutting hair and making music.

In 1955 Gimble moved to Waco and became the host of a noon television show on KWTX, *Home Folks*, inherited from his old friend and mentor Jimmy Thomasson. Playing music mostly on weekends, he supported his family as a barber, including a stint at the VA hospital from 1961 to 1968. Except for a brief period when he and his family lived in Alaska (1959–1960), Gimble spent most of these years playing music in his off-hours or on weekends, and generally using Waco as his home base. He sometimes ventured to Dallas to play for square dances and occasionally provided entertainment for rodeos when someone like cowboy actor and singer Rex Allen passed through the area.

Gimble's participation in the 1964–1965 tour of the Aunt Jemima Band Wagon was one of his most significant musical adventures of these years, primarily because it marked the beginning of his talented bass-playing son's professional career. Along with fifteen-year-old Dick Gimble, Johnny joined a group headed by longtime Dallas musician Jim Boyd (a former Light Crust Doughboy) that advertised flour and pancake mix at grocery stores throughout East Texas. This interlude could not help but bring back memories of the Rose City Swingsters.

Gimble made his first foray into the world of big-time commercial country music in 1968 when he moved to Nashville and entered, arguably, the most productive—certainly the busiest—period of his life. Averaging about eight sessions a week, each stint running about three hours, he recorded with most of the city's leading musical lights, from Porter Wagoner and Dolly Parton early on to George Strait and Keith Whitley a couple of decades later, and just about everyone in between. An undoubtedly incomplete discography on the All Music Guide website notes Gimble appearances on 225 albums. Since recording sessions were built around the individual needs of singers and writers, Nashville's producers were reluctant to let Gimble "play everything he knew." But he soon became one of the most valued members of the industry's A-Team of session musicians, a distinction few fiddlers had known since the days of Tommy Jackson in the mid-fifties. "The thing I enjoyed most was the camaraderie," he explained, and he marveled at the ease with which the local producers and musicians adjusted to the widely differing styles of singers. Gimble credited producer Bob Ferguson and singer Connie Smith with the recognition he received throughout the industry. On Smith's 1972 recording of "If It Ain't Love (Let's Leave It Alone)," Ferguson told him to play what he wanted to, telling him, "Just jump in there and play me some Johnny Gimble." Smith was so impressed with his contributions that she sent out a handwritten note to DJs all over the country to let them know that Gimble was the man who executed all those heart-stopping improvisations.

Despite the crucial role he played in shaping the sound of the recordings made in Nashville, Gimble never felt comfortable with the mass-produced artifacts of Top 40 country music. He simply wanted to play swing, the music closest to his heart. Thus he was more than eager and willing when Merle Haggard asked him into the studio in 1970 to be part of the Capitol album *A Tribute to the Best Damn Fiddle Player in the World (Or, My Salute to Bob Wills)*. Gimble's presence on that album, and on a collection in 1972 devoted to a reunion of the Texas Playboys, *For the Last Time*, made his name known and revered among a new generation of young fans and musicians who were discovering western swing for the first time. He participated only briefly in Leon McAuliffe's revival of the Texas Playboys but otherwise made vital contributions to the renewed popularity of the music he loved.

The most satisfying moments of his venture into western swing revivalism were not only his frequent collaborations with such veterans as Herb Remington but also the opportunities to play with and tutor such young and influential enthusiasts as Alvin Crow and Asleep at the Wheel. Such exposure contributed to his being selected in 1975 as the Country Music Association's Instrumentalist of the Year. He eventually won four more of these awards, as well as nine awards from the Academy of Country Music (between 1978 and 1987) for Best Fiddler of the Year.

Gimble also was a ubiquitous presence during the mid-seventies' "outlaw country" breakthrough, appearing on dozens of records by Willie Nelson, Waylon Jennings, Jerry Jeff Walker, Guy Clark, Jessi Colter, and countless others. In addition, he branched into pop realms far from the reaches of the country charts. His name, for example, can be found on the Manhattan Transfer's *Pastiche* and Paul McCartney's *Wings at the Speed of Sound*, to cite just two examples from 1976.

Nashville was good to Gimble, but the insistent and regimented routine of session playing became "work," and he longed to go back to Texas to do "his kind of music." His own sense of nostalgia dovetailed perfectly with the realization that the longing for the good old days sells a lot of records in country music, and probably explains why he wrote the popular tune "Under the X in Texas" (best known through the performances of Red Steagall).

Bolstered by a good pension supported by money invested in the musicians' union fund, Gimble moved back to Texas in July 1978. In an environment that was much more accepting of his free-spirited style of music, he immediately became one of the kingpins of the state's thriving music scene. He had already achieved almost iconic status in his native state as the virtual embodiment of western swing, largely through his association with Willie Nelson since 1975, and because of a series of albums with groups such as Asleep at the Wheel.

Increasingly, however, solo performances gave free reign to his virtuosity. Gimble's first solo album, *Fiddling Around*, recorded in Nashville for Capitol in 1974, had been co-produced by Haggard. In 1975, chiefly through the influence of Nelson, he issued the widely circulated *Texas Dance Party* (for Columbia), which received extensive exposure from the "progressive" programming of Austin's KOKE and other Texas radio stations. These early solo recording projects were popular, but quickly went out of print.

Consequently, Gimble decided to issue his own recordings or to work with smaller labels such as Delta in Nacogdoches, Texas. Around 1978 he produced his first independent recording, *My Kind of Music*. The next year he was part of a particularly satisfying project, released by CMH Records in Los Angeles, called *The Swing Pioneers*. On the latter record he played alongside some of the founding fathers of western swing, including his hero Cliff Bruner, Fred "Papa" Calhoun (piano player for the legendary Musical Brownies), Deacon Anderson (the lap steel guitarist who had played with Bruner), Muryel "Zeke" Campbell (the hot guitarist for the Light Crust Doughboys), and J. R. Chatwell (the legendary fiddler, who sang on the LP but could not play because of an incapacitating stroke).

Gimble's identification with western swing became so strong that he even played the role of Bob Wills in the 1982 Clint Eastwood movie *Honky-tonk Man*. He had previously appeared in Willie Nelson's 1980 film *Honeysuckle Rose*. Gimble never stopped making music, but he had attained the kind of legendary status that now allowed him to do it on his own terms. Residing first in the Austin suburb of Round Rock, Gimble and his wife, Barbara, lived in a succession of homes but by 1991 had settled down in Dripping Springs, just west of Austin.

From this convenient vantage point, Gimble could make frequent trips into the capital city to play with and lend encouragement to the young musicians there who idolized him. He toured with Willie Nelson for about a year. He also occasionally teamed with steel guitarist Herb Remington, his old friend and fellow Texas Playboy from their West Coast days, to pay homage to vintage western swing in a group called Playboys II.

In the midst of Gimble's reunion with his Texas roots, national attention beckoned once again, courtesy of an innocently made home recording that produced unforeseen but fortuitous results. One early morning he had stepped out on his front porch to record the singing of a mockingbird and had playfully "mocked" the bird with his fiddle. The bird then saucily imitated the fiddle licks. Gimble sent the recording of this spirited interchange between bird and fiddle to his friend Chet Atkins, who in turn gave the tape to Garrison Keillor, longtime host of NPR's *Prairie Home Companion*. Keillor declared, "I've gotta get that guy on my show." Playing his music and sometimes appearing in humorous skits, Gimble found a new audience through the show. He says that when he mentions Garrison Keillor or *A Prairie Home Companion* in his concerts, audiences invariably break into applause. Keillor in turn paid tribute to Gimble in a short poem:

He smiled as he played
Some old serenade
And the music came up from his soul
You could hear the stars falling
Whenever he picked up his bow.
And the shuffling and sliding
Of ghost dancers gliding
On kitchen floors long ago.

Since the early nineties, awards came frequently. In August 2001 Gimble was the featured act at the new Country Music Hall of Fame's first special exhibit, Nashville Salutes Texas! Country from the Lone Star State. Texas Folklife Resources, located in Austin, often invited him to appear in Texas classrooms as part of its campaign to present "master folk musicians" to the state's schoolchildren. In 1994 he received his most prestigious honor when the National Endowment for the Arts presented him with a National Heritage Fellowship.

As special as these acts of recognition may have been, the experience of making music with his bass-playing son, Dick, was probably the most gratifying. Since at least 1964 he often played alongside Dick in a band that was first called Home Folks and later, Texas Swing. His granddaughter Emily, an ardent disciple of Ella Fitzgerald and Peggy Lee, appeared on one of Gimble's CDs, and a nephew, Jason Roberts, played the Gimble style as a current member of Asleep at the Wheel. Johnny could be assured that the Gimble name and heritage would remain prominent in Texas music for a long time to come.

The key to understanding Gimble's musical productivity, apart from his remarkable creativity, is simply his passionate love for music. Gimble could just as easily have been referring to himself when he recalled an oft-told story about one of his mentors, J. R. Chatwell: "J. R. didn't seem to go where the money was; he went where the rhythm was good." When Gimble was in the army, and brothers Jack, Bill, and Gene were in the navy, they typically carbon-copied their letters to one another. Looking back on some of that surviving correspondence, Gimble noted that "all we ever talked about was music." His brothers told me that during the peak of Gimble's Nashville days, when he occasionally came back home for a visit after a series of grueling sessions, the first thing he wanted to do was play music.

The stroke of 1999 made some of his fretwork more difficult, since it attacked the right frontal lobe of his brain, which controlled the left side of his body. But it impaired neither his sense of humor nor his enthusiasm for making music. When informed by an MRI scan that a black hole had appeared in his brain, he said, "I hope that 'Orange Blossom Special' falls through it. I get requests to play the damned thing and have to play it."

Jim Baker, a fiddle-playing friend in Dallas, put a different twist on Gimble's impairment when he asked him how the stroke had affected his playing. Gimble replied that, in a recent concert with pianist Floyd Domino, he had tried to reach the notes on one of his tours de force, "Fiddlin' Around," and "couldn't play the son of a gun." Baker ruefully replied, "Now you know how the rest of us feel."

Gimble strived mightily to pass his heritage on to contemporary generations, through workshops, seminars, and summer camps given under the auspices of Texas Folklife Resources in Austin, and through his annual Swing Week workshop held each July at the Fort Burgwin campus of Southern Methodist University near Taos, New Mexico. (A brochure described the event as "hot music in the cool mountains.") Recalling a workshop in July 2002, Dick Gimble remembered that his dad was always the first person up each morning and was already playing his fiddle on the porch of the dining hall as the students gathered for breakfast.

These opportunities to transmit his gifts and preserve his legacy undoubtedly awakened memories of the little boy who thrilled to the discovery of Cliff Bruner's music and who once sat at Lefty Williams's feet in Lindale. "It was all passed on to me," Gimble declared, "and if I can get people to enjoy the music as much as I do, I'll be satisfied."

CHAPTER 11

TEXAS MYTH/TEXAS MUSIC

Growing up in Texas, it was easy to get caught up in the belief that the state was a special and superior place. After all, there has been much in this huge and abundant state for which one can be proud. Texas musicians of every stripe, from Van Cliburn and Scott Joplin to Willie Nelson, have made vital contributions to the culture of America and the world. By and large, the Texas Myth has been a benign and harmless perception, and, with the strains of Ernest Tubb's "Waltz across Texas" floating through one's head, it has even been easy for outsiders to accept the assumption. But at times the myth can become pernicious: one recalls, for example, the then-Texas governor Rick Perry's hubristic statement that the state should secede from the Union. While a variety of myths have clouded our understanding of country music, this essay concentrates on the ways in which the Texas Myth has intersected with and shaped perceptions of the state's music.

This essay was first published in the initial issue of the *Journal of Texas Music History* (Spring 2001). The editor of the journal, Gary Hartman, has written a fine survey of the subject, *The History of Texas Music* (College Station: Texas A&M University Press, 2008).

MUSIC HAS ALWAYS PLAYED A VITAL AND SUSTAINING ROLE IN THE LIFE OF THE PEOPLE OF TEXAS and has contributed mightily to the mystique of the Lone Star State. Indeed, in many important ways, the music has also been a by-product of the Texas Myth—the deeply held belief that the state has a unique and special history and destiny, and that its frontier heritage has encouraged freedom, individualism, experimentation, and flamboyance. Hearing the infectious dance tunes of Bob Wills, the irresistible accordion riffs of Flaco Jimenez, the anguished moans of Janis Joplin, or the unorthodox vocal phrasing of Willie Nelson, it is hard to resist the feeling, if not belief, that this music ushered from the soil in the same way that oil spontaneously erupted in Spindletop back in 1901.

At least since the emergence of Austin as a southwestern musical mecca in the 1970s, Texas musicians have invested in and promoted this image, professing to believe that their music embodies a liberated spirit and anti-commercial impulse that cannot be found in Nashville or other music centers. Growing multitudes of fans have responded fervently to the idea that "when you cross the old Red River" into Texas one enters a unique musical domain that follows its own impulses and rules. At least for the duration of the song, many fans who have never visited little Luckenbach, Texas, have identified with the village and have been ready to move there with "Willie, Waylon, and the boys."

Texas's musical heritage predates the birth of the Republic, with roots in the music of the Mexicans already living there and in the cultural baggage brought across the Sabine by whites and blacks moving from the older South. Music, we are told, played a central role at Texas's first great historical event, the Battle of the Alamo. Two musical performances that occurred shortly before the battle seemed to define the cultural conflict that helped generate the war between Anglos and Mexicans. Accompanied by bagpipe player John McGregor, Davy Crockett fiddled lively hoedowns to bolster the spirit of his compatriots in the Alamo. The Mexican commander Santa Anna, on the other hand, instructed his military band to play "Deguello," the no quarter anthem designed to strike terror in the hearts of the Alamo defenders. Although these examples suggest a scenario of warring cultures in Texas, Anglos, Mexicans, and other ethnic groups actually began learning songs, dances, and musical styles from each other at the point of first contact. Stylistic diversity and the interchange of ideas, not division or conflict, have always distinguished the music of Texas.

Texas's two most important folk music traditions, the Anglo and the African American, had already interacted in vital ways even before they were transported to the region. Whites and blacks came as masters and slaves, but their geographical proximities, shared experiences as rural and agricultural people, and common exposure to evangelical Protestantism contributed to the making of a body of music that shared many traits. The fiddle was the dominant instrument in both cultures, and banjos were much more common than guitars in nineteenth-century Texas. Despite the opposition voiced by many church leaders, dancing was widely popular in both racial groups. Community dances, generally called frolics or house parties, prevailed among whites and slaves alike, and a common body of songs and dance tunes moved freely across racial lines. Styles of performance, of course, often differed dramatically, with black Texans tending to improvise more freely than whites and to sing with expressive, open-throated voices. White people generally admired the emotional abandon and sensuous expressiveness of black singers, but their performance styles more often reflected the inhibitions fostered by Calvinistic Protestantism and its suspicions of physical display.

Both blacks and whites valued religious music highly, and the context of church or church-related activities provided the inspiration or training ground for many of the state's best singers. Shape-note singing schools, camp meetings, and revivals flourished in the state, and street-corner evangelists could be heard in virtually every community expounding the word of God and singing the gospel with the backing of guitars, mandolins, and fiddles. At the turn of the century, Pentecostal preachers (both black and white) came to Texas, dispensing their fiery brand of religion and popularizing their variety of spirited, emotional music. Partly through their presence, white singing styles changed, becoming more emotion-laden and sometimes closely akin to the loose-throated sound associated with black music.

Black Texans' most crucial contribution, of course, was the blues. The blues had moved west from Mississippi, but Texas singers became famous for their fluid, supple styles of singing and for their inventive and free-flowing instrumentation. Created by African Americans, the blues nevertheless was familiar to most white Texans (and to southerners in general). This lonesome but liberating music came from field workers, road crews, stevedores, prisoners, barrelhouse piano players, brothel and honky-tonk musicians, and street-corner buskers. Some of the best of them, such as Blind Lemon Jefferson, Texas Alexander, and Henry Thomas, were more than ready when the nation's recording companies began looking for such performers in the 1920s.

Anglo and African Americans were certainly not alone in making Texas's music. Long before either group migrated into the Texas region Mexican Americans, or "Tejanos," had built a vibrant musical culture of love songs, *corridos* (ballads), *bailes*, and fandangos. Fiddles were also present in Mexican culture, as was the guitar and various kinds of wind instruments. By the middle of the nineteenth century, Tejano musicians had acquired the accordion and a taste for polka rhythms, possibly from south of the border, but more likely from their German neighbors in South Texas. Conjunto music, played usually with the accordion, bajo sexto (a twelve-string guitar), and drums, along with other "Latin" styles, insinuated themselves into the hearts of all Texans with, as Bob Wills confessed in "San Antonio Rose," an "enchantment strange as the blue up above."

In various parts of the state, other ethnic and racial populations contributed to the general musical mix. In the late nineteenth century, French-speaking Cajuns from Louisiana began bringing their patois, love of life, and fiddle- and accordion-based musical styles to Orange, Beaumont, Port Arthur, and Houston. Cajun styles, however, did not reach Texas in unalloyed forms. The presence of African Americans in southwest Louisiana, the central locus of Cajun culture, along with oil discoveries there in the early twentieth century, added new sounds and songs to the traditional French mélange. French-speaking blacks in Houston added their own unique spice to Texas's and America's musical gumbo with the making of the now popular style known as Zydeco, which melded Louisiana French forms with rhythm and blues. Czechs and Germans in the communities of Central and South Texas absorbed musical ideas from the people who lived around them but also preserved their love for drink, dance, and community celebration. They bequeathed a legacy of polkas, schottisches, and waltzes to the state's musical culture. Like their counterparts elsewhere in the United States, German Americans made lasting contributions to music at all levels—as teachers, composers, publishers, businessmen, and musicians.

Cultural diversity and musical interaction may define the reality of Texas music, but all styles evolved in a context dominated by the Cowboy Myth. In the American popular mind, cowboys and Texas have been practically synonymous (that helps to explain why President George W.

Bush and his entourage felt the necessity to wear custom-made cowboy boots at his inaugural balls). Of course, some "reality" does undergird the myth: the cattle kingdom of the late nineteenth century did originate in South Texas and was exported to the upper plains through the famous long drives of the era. The "real" cowboy was a composite of the cultures discussed earlier—Anglo, African, Mexican. Nevertheless, the cowboys that populate the landscape of America's music were sons, not of the sweat, toil, and grime of the frontier but of popular culture.

Well before his music was discovered and introduced to the world, through the famous collections produced by Nathan Howard Thorp and John Lomax (in 1908 and 1910), the cowboy had been mythicized and romanticized through dime novels, silent films, and Wild West shows. It now seems inevitable that music would be touched by the same kind of idealization. From the beginning of commercialization in the 1920s, Texas grassroots musicians exhibited the appeal of the cowboy myth. Fiddler Alexander Campbell "Eck" Robertson wore cowboy clothes to his first recording session in New York for the Victor Talking Machine Company, a session in 1922 that marked the beginning of commercial country music. In 1925 Carl Sprague, born in Alvin, Texas, and a proud owner of the Lomax book, recorded for Victor a popular version of "When the Work's All Done This Fall." A few years later Jimmie Rodgers, the ex–railroad brakeman from Mississippi who had taken up residence in Kerrville, Texas, intro- duced romantic cowboy songs into his repertoire, and such songs have remained part of country music ever since. Beginning in 1934 Gene Autry, a native of Tioga, Texas, did most to create and popularize the version of the singing cowboy that we all remember, through his motion pictures, popular Columbia recordings, and weekly radio shows. Largely because of Autry, an industry of "made-for-movies" cowboy songs came into existence, along with a wardrobe of colorful simulated cowboy attire that attracted generations of country singers.

It is easy to see why the cowboy image would prevail. No entertainer really believed that dressing like a farmer or oil driller, or any other eco- nomic type then prevalent in Texas, would win the admiration of the audi- ence. The cowboy, on the other hand, demanded respect. In most popular guises, he tended to be Anglo—fearless, individualistic, moral, and free. It

*Bob Wills on stage with his favorite horse, Punkin. This son of cotton
farmers loved the music of New Orleans and embraced the image
of the cowboy. He became an enduring symbol of the myth of Texas.*
Photograph courtesy of Carolyn Wills, the Estate of Bob Wills,
and the Oklahoma Museum of Popular Culture, Tulsa, Oklahoma.

was easy to believe that he, and the expansive environment that nourished
him, had produced a body of music that, in contrast to the tradition-bound
music produced back east, was bold and liberated. The Cowboy Myth has
touched virtually all of the various manifestations of country music, but its
most explicit identification with freedom, spontaneity, and experimentation came with its association with the style now known as western swing.

In 1940 Bob Wills and the Texas Playboys appeared in their first
movie, *Take Me back to Oklahoma,* playing the part of dapper cowboys
but performing an infectious blend of urban and country music that had
been born in the dance halls and radio stations of the southwest. Clearly
recoiling against the hillbilly persona that tainted much of country music
at the time, and profiting from their association with the cowboy movies in
which they often appeared, Wills and his Playboys seized upon a romantic
image that has been endlessly appealing to the popular mind. Since that
time the cowboy periodically has been resurrected to fuel various kinds of

country music revivals, usually those that oppose Nashville and its hegemony. Whether presented in the persona of a Willie Nelson–style "outlaw" allegedly defying both social and musical convention, or as an urban cowboy seeking momentary release from work stress on a mechanical bull, simply in the joyous guise of a Bob Wills tune, or more recently as a "hat act" in mainstream country music, the cowboy has endured as a figure of almost infinite plasticity and as an inspiration for music that values freedom over restraint and fun-making over money.

The stress upon western symbolism and on the state's ethnic and racial diversity (all of which suggests a body of music and music-making rooted in the soil and in rural and frontier sensibilities) should not obscure the role played by technology, commercial entrepreneurship, and urban culture in the making of Texas music. The source of Bob Wills's innovations lay neither in the ranch country of West Texas nor in the cotton fields of the Lone Star State. Inspiration for musical experimentation came instead from the cities and from the radio stations, recording companies, and commercial forms of entertainment that were located there.

From the very beginning of Texas history, town culture had in fact played a profound role in the shaping or transformation of the state's music. Towns and cities extended their influence out into the hinterlands long before they were transformed by the migrations of rural people. Traveling salesmen, tent repertoire shows, and medicine shows brought songs and new musical ideas. The mail-order catalogs of Sears-Roebuck, Montgomery Ward, and other national department stores made available the newest editions of sheet music, phonograph records, guitars and other string instruments, parlor organs, and pianos. Even a locally based periodical such as the *Dallas Semi-Weekly Farm News*, which reached thousands of rural Texas homes prior to World War II, brought exciting hints of the comforts and diversions that could be found in the city. On its "young people's page" the paper responded to readers' requests by printing the lyrics to old songs, many of which had been published as sheet music originally in New York's Tin Pan Alley.

Cities like Dallas, Houston, and San Antonio acted as magnets for restless rural youth long before the abolition of slavery, the emergence of sharecropping and tenantry, and the collapse of agriculture fatally weakened the older institutions of rural life. Those people who went to town on a Saturday night for an evening of fun, perhaps to one of the notorious "sin streets" like Deep "Ellum" (Elm) in Dallas or Fannin Street in Shreveport, probably heard a street-corner blues musician or a barrelhouse piano player. Itinerant musicians may have learned their art and polished their repertoires in rural settings, but they moved to cities to find audiences for their music. Scott Joplin, from Texarkana, seems to have been the first Texan to take his music to the North. Absorbing songs and musical riffs wherever he went, from Sedalia, Missouri, to New York, Joplin reshaped them into a body of musical suites, such as "Maple Leaf Rag," that fueled the ragtime revolution of the early twentieth century. Blind Lemon Jefferson, from Wortham, came along a few years later with his wailing vocals and fluid guitar style. He moved first to Dallas and then to Chicago, making listeners conscious of the emerging Texas blues style. Since that time, an unending stream of Texas musicians, such as Aaron "T-Bone" Walker, Gene Autry, Bob Wills, Jack Teagarden, Harry James, Eddie Durham, and the Stamps Quartet, have taken their styles of music to cities all over the United States.

While we are well aware of the contributions made by Scott Joplin, we cannot be sure of how many Texas musicians, prior to the 1920s, physically participated in such urban entertainment forms as blackface minstrelsy and vaudeville. We do know that the music of these phenomena insinuated itself into the consciousness of both fans and musicians in the state. Phonograph records and radio broadcasts, on the other hand, permitted grassroots musicians to popularize their music on a broader scale and to learn more readily from other sources. Indeed, most of the commercial vernacular forms that have dominated American music in this century—country, blues, gospel (black and white), cowboy, Tex-Mex, and Cajun—were products of the communications revolution launched in the 1920s by radio and recording. Eck Robertson's fiddling licks, for example, were largely confined to contests and house parties until he made his first records in 1922 for Victor. Blind Lemon Jefferson and the great gospel singer and bottle-neck guitarist Blind Willie Johnson had built passionate clienteles in the saloons, brothels, and church conventions of their home state, but phonograph recordings made after 1926 introduced them to audiences throughout the nation and ensured their enduring fame. Playing with her family band, La Familia Mendoza, Lydia Mendoza had already become known as "the Lark of the Border" when the Victor Company recorded her in 1934. But these recordings ultimately made her name and music known around the world. The Stamps Quartet had been pillars of the shape-note singing conventions, those beloved all-day-singings with dinners-on-the-ground, but their Victor recordings after 1927 made them regional favorites. The list could go on and on.

Texas musicians found even larger audiences through broadcasts on such powerful fifty-thousand-watt radio stations as Fort Worth's WBAP (the first station in the nation to feature a Saturday night barn dance), Dallas's KRLD, San Antonio's WOAI, Tulsa's KVOO, Houston's KTRH, and Shreveport's KWKH. Gene Autry's radio broadcasts as the Oklahoma Singing Cowboy, first on KVOO and later on the WLS Barn Dance in Chicago, made his name known to the Hollywood entrepreneurs who in 1934 invited him to make movies. Bob Wills and the Texas Playboys also used KVOO broadcasts to popularize their danceable blend of jazz and country throughout the Southwest. The Chuck Wagon Gang, on WBAP in Fort Worth, and the Stamps Quartet, on KRLD in Dallas, made their varying brands of southern gospel music available to regional audiences.

The territory covered by these stations, however, was small compared to the reach of the powerful Mexican border stations. With power that sometimes extended well beyond one hundred thousand watts, stations such as XERA, XEG, and XEPN blanketed North American with spiels for spurious products, religious evangelism, populist politics, and vernacular music programming. Well into the 1940s insomniacs, truck drivers, cross-country travelers, and fans would have heard either live or transcribed music by such entertainers as Cowboy Slim Rinehart, Mainer's Mountaineers, and the Carter Family.

Since the 1930s, Texas grassroots entertainers have demonstrated that their music could be put to a multiplicity of social purposes, including the selling of laxatives, the saving of souls, and the election of politicians. With Jimmie Rodgers, Gene Autry, Bob Wills, Lydia Mendoza, and T-Bone Walker pointing the way, Texas entertainers had suggested that music could liberate people from cotton fields, oil patches, and barrios while also building within them a sense of identity and cultural pride. During the Depression years, musicians exhibited the healing and restorative powers of music through the religious consolation provided by gospel singers, the social release promoted by the dance bands, and through the fantasy evoked by the singing cowboys who could be heard on radio and recording and seen in Hollywood movies. In 1938 Wilbert Lee "Pappy" O'Daniel campaigned for and won the governorship of Texas with the support of his radio band, the Hillbilly Boys, the first political exploitation or utilization of a commercial country music group. Woody Guthrie's radicalism would have prevented the Okie balladeer from winning any political office, but his social conscience and conviction that music could speak on behalf of the downtrodden had already begun to take shape during his residence in Pampa during the early 1930s.

With their vision of an unsullied land and unsullied people, the cowboy songs and movies provided heroes for an economically deprived populace craving reassurance. Dance halls and honky-tonks, on the other hand, provided a different kind of fantasy and diversion: the release provided by dance and the escape contained in a bottle. It was through this union of drink, dance, and music that Texas performers made one of their most unique and enduring contributions to American music. Dancing had never abated even during the days of Prohibition, and the German and Czech dance halls of central and southwest Texas had remained popular as family-oriented gathering places. The repeal of prohibition in 1933, though, encouraged the establishment of large dance halls, such as Cain's Ballroom in Tulsa and Mattie's Ballroom in Longview, where big dance bands often performed. Literally hundreds of beer joints and small establishments appeared as well where music might be provided only by a coin-operated jukebox. Legal alcohol inspired the creation of clubs everywhere, but those that emerged in East Texas oil towns, catering to the needs and desires of the oil workers, contributed directly to a new style of country music. The oil boom brought money to communities ravaged by hard times, and fostered the growth of clubs offering drink, dancing, and easy women to receptive men looking for escape. Generally described as honky-tonks and often located on county lines in order to attract patrons from "dry" areas, these clubs encouraged a style of music with a strong danceable beat and lyrics that addressed the temptations, desires, and anxieties of blue-collar workers. The result was an electrified body of musical performances that spoke of cheating, drinking, and the sins of the flesh.

Although born in the 1930s, the honky-tonks flourished during the war years when rural folk moved to Houston, Beaumont, Texas City, Velasco, Dallas, Fort Worth, and other industrial areas to become part of the nation's defense production. The clubs and the music heard there did not simply function as social diversion; for many people, the honky-tonk also helped to ease their transition from rural to urban life and from agriculture to blue-collar or industrial work. Musicians like Al Dexter, Floyd Tillman, Ted Daffan, Cliff Bruner, Moon Mullican, and Ernest Tubb, all of whom served apprenticeships in the "fighting and dancing" clubs, dominated the country jukeboxes throughout America during the 1940s and early 1950s. Ernest Tubb took his Texas honky-tonk style to the Grand Ole Opry in 1942. Before long, singers everywhere in the United States were trying to emulate the sounds heard on Tubb's records and radio shows. Country music, in short, had taken on a decided Texas cast and tone. By the time the war ended in 1945, the music of Texas was becoming the music of America.

Since World War II, Texas musicians have played vital and transformative roles in American music. A steady procession of singers, musicians, and songwriters, representing virtually every kind of vernacular music, have won national acclaim. These musicians have demonstrated the influence of the performers and styles discussed earlier in this essay, either consciously or unconsciously, but none has been a slavish imitator striving to preserve some ideal of purity (in jazz music such purists have been described as "moldy figs"). The most important performers have been those who created something new and vital out of older materials, and who, like Janis Joplin, have successfully fused individual persona and art. Joplin adored the music of Bessie Smith, but she meshed that blues style with elements borrowed from the folk revival and, above all, from the 1960s' rock culture. Stevie Ray Vaughan, who grew up in the Oak Cliff section of Dallas worshiping the music of the classic blues singers, went on to create his own widely admired style. Before her early and tragic death, Selena became an almost iconic heroine in the world of Tejano music. With a stage persona clearly inspired by the rock singer Madonna, Selena combined her barrios-derived style with components borrowed from pop, soul, and salsa music. Willie Nelson never lost his appeal to the honky-tonk community that had nourished his music, but he exhibited an affinity for and an ability to perform virtually every kind of pop music. Steve Earle, who grew up near San Antonio, has been similarly eclectic in his musical tastes, on one hand exhibiting the instincts of a folk revival singer-songwriter with his songs of social protest and on the other hand displaying the aggressive, almost nihilistic, energy of a rock entertainer.

Some singers, including Steve Earle, have been described as neo-traditionalists (a description often given to young country singers whose styles seem grounded in older forms). But, like Earle, these entertainers usually display styles that their predecessors and heroes would scarcely recognize. George Strait, for example, did not become a country superstar because he merely re-created the sounds of Bob Wills and Merle Haggard. His neo-traditionalism instead embodied elements of western swing and the honky-tonk sound combined with Strait's smooth pop vocals and cowboy good looks. The Austin band Asleep at the Wheel has become famous for its homage to Bob Wills, but their version of western swing is spiced with enough elements of rock and roll to make them palatable to a broad constituency. Only the cowboy singers of today exhibit a tendency to cling to styles and repertoires rooted in the past. But even the Texas singers Don Edwards, Red Steagall, and Michael Martin Murphey—while wearing cowboy costumes and paying tribute to Gene Autry, Roy Rogers, and the Sons of the Pioneers—mix their western songs with other kinds of material (Murphey, for example, typically includes in his stage act such hit pop songs as "Wildfire" and "Carolina in the Pines" from his earlier career). Like their predecessors from the Hollywood silver screen, however, the modern cowboy singers perform with smooth harmonies, dexterous yodeling, and jazz-like instrumental riffs that were never heard in the cattle country.

Although the evidence may not be quite as clear as it is among the cowboy singers, the Texas Myth has touched virtually all Texas musicians. It is clear that the Texas that is celebrated in their mythology (and press agentry) is a rural or frontier region still untouched by oil derricks, skyscrapers, or computer technology. We find the Texas musical landscape populated, then, by an assemblage of musicians who ply their trade with technological tools crafted in the city, but who pay at least symbolic tribute to a mythical land of free-spirited cowboys. For example, ZZ Top, a trio of long-haired musicians from Houston, play some of the most thoroughly urban music heard in America, a high-decibel blues-based style of rock, but they surround themselves with the trappings of frontier nationalism complete with a Texas-shaped stage and a longhorn steer and black buffalo. Richard "Kinky" Friedman, the self-styled "Texas Jewboy," who pursued a country music career before becoming a best-selling writer of detective stories, is similarly urbane in his irreverence and worldly-wise sophistication, but he wears cowboy boots and hat and a belt buckle emblazoned with the Star of David. Kinky facetiously argues that Jews and cowboys are similar because they both wear their hats in the house!

In Austin in the 1970s, the young musicians there displayed a well-publicized brand of Texas nationalism, or what folklorist Nicholas Spitzer described as "romantic regionalism," popularizing a body of styles that drew upon both rock and country elements. Striving to create identities that illustrated both their Texas frontier heritage and their celebration of freedom (in both lifestyle and music), these musicians embraced a cluster of symbols such as longhorn steers, longneck beers, armadillos, and cowboy costumes and used them often as logos and illustrations. The bustling and fast-growing city of Austin had become the urban locus of what writer Jan Reid called "the rise of redneck rock." This was the community that Willie Nelson joined in 1972, when he fled Nashville and the stultifying conservatism that he felt hampered his artistic creativity.

Texans still play decisive roles in American music, and our music would be much poorer without their contributions. As this essay is being written, a trio of dynamic musicians from Texas known as the Dixie Chicks (Natalie Maines from Lubbock, and two sisters from Dallas, Martie and Emily Erwin) has asserted a dominance in American popular music that few people have equaled. The Erwin sisters can play anything with strings on it, while lead singer Natalie Maines fashions compelling vocals that draw on rock, blues, and country sources. Eclectic in both style and repertoire, the Dixie Chicks project a blend of tradition and modernity that defines the best in Texas music. Hordes of young fans respond enthusiastically to the group, including many young girls truly thrilled and emboldened by the spectacle of fun-loving, good-looking women expertly playing instruments and taking control of their own destinies.

The world continues to be turned on by Texas music. The word "Austin" still has a magic and commercial ring, and a host of young musicians of varying stylistic persuasions proudly claim an identification with the city. *Austin City Limits*, the nationally syndicated public television show, has reached millions of Americans each week since 1976. Thousands descend upon the city each spring to attend a huge cultural convention known as South by Southwest (SXSW), a showcase for innovative films and music. Still others throng to the Texas Hill Country each Memorial and Labor Day weekend to attend Rod Kennedy's Kerrville Folk Festival, a haven for refugees from the folk revival and a onetime showcase for such singer-songwriters as Nanci Griffith, Tish Hinojosa, and Lyle Lovett. One can even receive instruction in the performance of bluegrass music at South Plains College in Levelland, Texas, a rather unlikely site for this style of music until 1986 when banjo wizard Alan Munde joined the faculty. Honky-tonks, of course, still thrive in the Lone Star State, providing escape and diversion for dancers and passive listeners and venues for performers.

Fortunately, the commercial health of the wide variety of Texas musicals styles is clearly in good hands. Since 1990 the Texas Music Office (in the governor's office) has acted as a clearinghouse for information concerning the state's music industry. Its publication, *Texas Music Industry Director*, serves as a vehicle for the promotion of all kinds of commercial music ventures. Although such business-oriented efforts are necessary to keep musicians in front of the public, we also need to document, preserve, and commemorate the music they make. Celebrating the Texas musical legacy, however, should not include blurring the lines between fact and fiction. While we can enjoy the cowboy persona and other self-styled Texana that have been attached to the music, we must not permit such romantic musings to blind us to the relationship between symbol and song. We should neither ignore nor discard the myths that have surrounded the music and other forms of culture that have issued forth from the state. They are part of being a Texan, and they are played out in our lives in a multitude of ways. The Texas Myth is basically harmless and mostly good fun (except when it is put to politically destructive uses). Myths have shaped public perceptions of Texas music around the world, and a refrain such as "I want to go home to the Armadillo" (heard in the theme song of "Austin City Limits") becomes an anthem of inclusiveness and pride. Yet, it's important to remember that the central reality is that fantasies of cowboy and frontier life have been played out in urban settings and most often by musicians who have fled the very life they sing about or portray in costume and publicity.

Certain assumptions about Texas music cannot be denied. The love of dancing is the central focus of Texas music culture, and a phenomenon that cuts across class and ethnic lines. But while the love of frolic and joie de vivre are salient attributes of Texas music styles, they are far from being the only themes that one finds there. For example, one hears almost no evidence of western swing in the music of Waylon Jennings, even though this great Texas singer declared in 1975, in a song purportedly performed before a cheering Austin crowd, that "Bob Wills Is Still the King." Not only does Jennings's song of tribute contain little or no element of style that seems attributable to Wills, his revealing autobiography makes no reference to the great western swing pioneer. When Jennings made that particular recording, he was not acknowledging a musical debt; he was paying tribute to a myth. At the date of the recording, Wills in fact had only recently been rescued from undeserved neglect by Merle Haggard and other admirers.

One does no disservice to Wills to note that he was only one of several musicians, representing widely disparate styles of performance, who won the hearts of Texas music fans. Wills's famous and strutting stage shout, "ah ha," expresses the joy Texans have often found in music, but Jennings's somber country-blues tunes and George Jones's anguished and clenched-teeth laments remind us of the loneliness and sorrow that have also been our lot. The country music band Alabama spoke volumes about the nature of Texas music when they sang "if you want to play in Texas, you gotta have a fiddle in the band." But legions of fans have also found comfort in the music of such Texas gospel groups as the Chuck Wagon Gang and the Stamps Quartet, neither of whom ever found it necessary to have a fiddle in their band. With a simple style of vocal harmony and the accompaniment of only a chorded guitar, the Chuck Wagon Gang has endured for over seventy years, while winning devoted fans all over the country. First recorded in

1927, the Stamps Quartet similarly extended their influence throughout the nation with the backing of only a piano. The original members of the group have long since passed on, but the Stamps Quartet trademark has remained as the identifying name of similar gospel singers to our own time, evidence of the potent appeal of the name and of this kind of music.

I hope it is understood that I am not suggesting that the Stamps Quartet was the driving force of Texas music (even if the style they fashioned was central to the sound made by Elvis Presley in the 1960s). Nor are my remarks designed to disparage or repudiate the legacy of dancing in Texas culture. Dancing is the central animating impulse that touches and colors the music made by every ethnic and racial group in the state. But it is not the only musical passion that has won the hearts of Texans, nor is it the only style that they have bequeathed to the world. Those of us who document, commemorate, and explain Texas music have the obligation to cast our nets broadly and to tell the stories of all of the styles that have found favor in this state. I have attended too many conferences on Texas music that do little more than celebrate the good-time spirit and anti-commercial impulse that allegedly characterizes the music.

Of course, as these remarks are written I am aware that my own observations may seem narrow in scope. My perspectives are admittedly shaped by what I know best, the music of white working-class Texans. When I listen to that music, I am conscious of the paradoxes and contradictions that have shaped its content and style and that have influenced its perception throughout the world. I cannot pretend to speak with much authority about the music of Tejanos, Cajuns, African Americans, and other groups that have shaped the music of Texas. But I suspect that the plethora of styles created by those Texans have also been colored in various ways by the myth of Texas. Judging from the list of fine critics and scholars who have contributed to the first issue of this journal, I feel that not only is the telling of the complete story of Texas music in capable hands but also that a constructive dialogue free of chauvinism, cant, and hyperbolae is about to begin.

CHAPTER 12

THE ROMANCE
THAT WILL NOT DIE
Appalachian Music and
American Popular Culture

This essay was written for *High Mountains Rising: Appalachia in Time and Place, an Anthology on Appalachian Culture and History* (2004), edited by Richard Straw and H. Tyler Blethen. I have always appreciated—and have in fact been an ardent fan—of many musicians such as Roy Acuff, Buell Kazee, Molly O'Day, Wilma Lee Cooper, the Stanley Brothers, Jean Ritchie, Dock Boggs, Doc Watson, Ricky Skaggs, Patty Loveless and Dolly Parton who hail from the Appalachian region. The list of such musicians is almost staggering. But I have always insisted that their music is neither uniform nor predictable and that it does not spring from an environment of arcadian simplicity. There is no such thing as Appalachian Music. There is, instead, a large and vital body of diverse musical strains made by people of Appalachian origin. Furthermore, many of the songs attributed to Appalachian origins have in fact been the products of Tin Pan Alley, minstrel, vaudeville, and Nashville composers. We need to love and appreciate this music without oversimplifying it and without exaggerating its contributions to the larger American musical culture. Country music, in short, did not originate in some remote and isolated mountain glen.

"CARRY ME BACK TO THE MOUNTAINS, BACK TO MY HOME SWEET HOME." Roy Acuff, "the Smoky Mountain Boy," sang those lines often as his theme song on the Grand Ole Opry. Like many of the songs about the southern mountains, this one was written by a northerner, Carson Robison (from Chetopa, Kansas), one of the pioneers of commercial hillbilly music. Acuff used the song as an affectionate recollection of his home in the Tennessee hills near Knoxville. For Robison and the rest of us, "Carry Me Back to the

Mountains" conjures up an almost mythical place and a special kind of music.

No concept in American life has had a more magic or enduring appeal than Appalachian music. For a hundred years and more Americans have exhibited a romantic fascination with a body of music that seems to evoke a cluster of values and a way of life that stand in stark relief to the dominant culture of our urban-industrial nation. The values evoked may be negative (feuding, moonshining, violence), or they may be positive (family solidarity, religious faith, or a simple life lived close to the soil), but they are appealing because they seem to stand in short supply today or because they provide dramatic relief from the boredom that many find in our society and in the homogenized sounds of popular music. Appalachian music simultaneously suggests the roots from which our culture evolved and stands as an alternative to other presumably soulless musical styles that have become dominant in our popular culture.

The discovery of English and Scottish ballads in the southern hills, at the end of the nineteenth and beginning of the twentieth centuries, was both cause and product of a larger preoccupation with the southern mountains and the belief that the Appalachians were an unchanging repository of traditional British lore. In our own time, we mercifully have abandoned many of the stereotypical assumptions of that era, but we still respond enthusiastically to the *idea*, if not the reality, of Appalachian music. The recent success of the movie *O Brother, Where Art Thou?* and the phenomenal sales of its soundtrack were accompanied by declarations that Americans were turning once again to "mountain music."[1] A musical tour that featured songs and singers from the soundtrack was billed as the Down from the Mountain concert. The resulting vogue for bluegrass music was widely interpreted as a reaction against the suburbanized sound of Top 40 country music and as an effort to take the music back to its true roots in the mountains.

The assertion of mountain identity was indeed strange, however, because the movie's plot was set in the Depression-era Mississippi Delta, and the music heard there, with one singular exception—the award-winning "Man of Constant Sorrow"—was generically southern rural and not mountain at all. Of all the singers on the soundtrack, only Ralph Stanley, from Dickenson County, Virginia, was genuinely Appalachian. His lonesome tenor voice seemed to summon up the strains of Old Regular Baptist singing and to evoke visions of isolated glens and village churchyards. However, none of the songs he sang, including "Conversation with Death," was uniquely indigenous to the mountains. The *O Brother* phenomenon is best understood as an example of the lingering romantic appeal of Appalachia and the lazy inclination to describe anything that seems old, rural, acoustic, and out-of-the-mainstream as "Appalachian."

There is no such thing as "Appalachian music." There is instead a wide variety of instrumental and vocal styles made by Appalachian musicians, many of which have exerted great influence in the larger realm of American music and all of which have exhibited the eclectic and steadily evolving nature of life in the mountains. The music is diverse because the culture in which it evolved is diverse. It exhibits the influence of many ethnic and racial groups and, above all, the interaction of city and rural forms and the changing economic patterns of the southern mountains.

That kind of diversity existed in the mountains long before its music was introduced to the outside world.[2] Although one finds scattered evidence of musical performance in travel accounts, local color stories, diaries and memoirs, newspapers, and county histories, hard evidence for the years before the 1920s is hard to come by. But it is clear that the music made by Appalachian musicians bore the marks of an intensely rural society and of the technological forces that were transforming life in the region: the railroads, textile industry, coalmining, lumbering, and urban growth. Ancient ballads, gospel songs, ragtime pieces, and Tin Pan Alley ditties coexisted in the repertoires of mountain musicians, with no apparent sense of contradiction. Jean Ritchie became famous singing the British songs bequeathed to her by her family in the remote Cumberland Mountains of eastern Kentucky, but she has also testified that her father brought a Sears-Roebuck "talking machine," along with such ragtime records as "Whistling Rufus," into their home as early as 1905.[3] Ballad singing was common among young and old, but women seem to have been the premier conservators of tradition. The writer Emma Bell Miles knew only her small section of Appalachia in southeastern Tennessee, but her comments about ballad singing in that area probably have resonance for the region as a whole: "It is over the loom and the knitting that old ballads are dreamily, endless crooned."[4]

Except for the performance of old ballads encouraged by the settlement schoolteachers among their students, ballad singing was largely a private act, intended for personal or family consumption. Dancing, in contrast, was a community enterprise. Described often as "frolics," dances accompanied all kinds of community events, both work and social: house raisings, corn shucking, bean stringings, quilting parties, syrup making, fish fries, weddings, Christmas, or for no reason at all. People cleared a room of furniture, invited the neighbors in for a Saturday night dance, and stepped to the music of a fiddler or banjo player. Music enlivened church meetings of all kinds, brush arbor revivals, camp meetings, singing conventions, and shape-note singing schools. Some religious groups, such as the Old Regular Baptists and Primitive Baptists, resisted as unscriptural any instrumental accompaniment, but the newer Pentecostal or "Holiness" sects enthusiastically accepted every kind of instrument. Fiercely conservative and otherworldly in doctrine, the Pentecostal people nevertheless were modern in their acceptance of new tunes and instruments or of anything, in short, that would enliven their worship. Their accepting spirit tells us much about the receptivity to modern forms of music in the mountains and of their presence alongside the venerable ballads and love songs.

We need only recall that Cecil Sharp, the English collector who came to the mountains in 1916, went about his ventures, as did other academic folklorists with a sense of urgency. They realized that the old ballads were being engulfed by more modern forms of music. Sharp noted sadly but wisely that the traditional ballads he sought tended to be rare in the region's railroad towns.[5]

To many people, the defining core of Appalachian music will always be the ballads and folksongs collected by Sharp and Olive Dame Campbell from 1916 to 1918. Their great contribution was to show not only that this material existed in greater profusion than it did in England but that it was cherished and sung in the mountains by young and old alike. Ballad singing in the Appalachians was not the static possession of a few elderly people, as it was back in England (or in New England, for that matter). Sharp remarked, "I discovered that I could get what I wanted from pretty nearly every one I met, young and old," and he commented further about the mountaineer habit of mating modern lyrics to traditional modal tunes.[6]

Tin Pan Alley songs, ragtime pieces, gospel hymns, or any other example of modern musical innovation did not interest Sharp. Much influenced by Francis James Child, the Harvard professor who had collected 305 English and Scottish ballads and their variants (all from manuscripts), Sharp labored to find living examples of these songs among the peasantry of the southern hills.[7] Accompanied by Campbell and the woman who copied down the lyrics, Sharp spent about twelve months winning the confidence of the people and noting the tunes of the songs they contributed. That justly celebrated expedition has endured as a benchmark in the discovery of indigenous American culture and has since shaped the vision of what Appalachian music is.[8] Sharp knew what he was looking for, he found it, and we are all the richer for his discoveries. But he knew that other forms of music were available in the mountains, and he sometimes referred to them and in a few cases noted down their tunes.[9]

We cannot fault Sharp for his preferences but can only conclude that in ignoring the products of the pocket songsters, sheet music, paperback gospel hymnals, minstrel shows, vaudeville acts, and phonograph records, all of which were present in the mountains, Sharp was not simply ignoring much music that was beloved by local people but was also rejecting the economic and social processes that had been transforming mountain life since at least the Civil War. The riverboats that followed the tributaries of the Ohio River far back into the Appalachians, the railroads that ended mountain isolation, and the coal mines, textile mills, and lumber camps that fostered economic growth also lured new people with new songs, instruments, and styles. Consequent town growth made available department stores, movie and vaudeville houses, sheet music, instruments, piano rolls, and phonograph records.

Only five years after Sharp left the mountains, a textile worker from Fries, Virginia, armed with a guitar and a French harp attached to a rack around his neck, journeyed to New York and recorded two songs for the Okeh label, "Lonesome Road Blues" and "Wreck on the Southern Old 97" (Okeh 40015). Henry Whitter was only the first of many mountain-born musicians who made commercial recordings in the years after 1923 or who appeared on the radio stations emerging in Asheville, Wheeling, Knoxville, and other mountain cities. Samantha Bumgarner, Eva Davis, Ernest Stoneman, Kelly Harrell, Buell Kazee, G. B. Grayson, Al Hopkins, Clarence "Tom" Ashley, Alfred Karnes, B. F. Shelton, Frank Hutchison, Dick Justice, and the Carter Family were only a few of the Appalachian-born musicians who emerged in those early years.[10]

The discovery made by the commercial record companies that money might be made from the music of mountain and other rural musicians inspired field trips into the southern hills, not totally unlike the expeditions made a few years earlier by Cecil Sharp. The most historic of these ventures came in late July 1927, when producer Ralph Peer took a Victor recording crew to Bristol, a city astride the boundary of Tennessee and Virginia. Peer already knew that one mountain musician, Ernest Stoneman, had made money from his recording of "The Sinking of the Titanic" and other traditional tunes. Peer contracted to record Stoneman again and, announcing his visit in local newspapers, lured other musicians to the makeshift studio on the Tennessee side of State Street. The resulting Bristol Sessions did not mark "the birth of country music," as some observers like to argue, but they did preserve the music of nineteen different acts on seventy-six recordings, and they introduced to the world the music of country music's two most enduring seminal acts: Jimmie Rodgers and the Carter Family.[11] An ex–railroad worker from Meridian, Mississippi, Rodgers had temporarily relocated in Asheville in an attempt to find relief from tuberculosis, the disease that took his life only six years later. With his fusion of blues, pop tunes, and traditional material, bolstered by his unique style of yodeling, Rodgers enjoyed a brief but influential career that eventually won for him the title of the Father of Country Music.

The trio of musicians now remembered as the Carter Family (A.P., his wife, Sara, and their sister-in-law Maybelle) came down from Maces Spring, Virginia, where they had gained a local reputation singing at house parties and church socials. They eventually recorded about three hundred sides for various companies and introduced both a vocal sound and an instrumental pattern (distinguished by Maybelle's guitar playing) that captivated hosts of rural and urban musicians in the decades that followed. They bequeathed to the world a body of songs now remembered as "Carter

Family Songs." A.P. had picked up most of these songs from a variety of sources, often from friends and other informants in the mountains, but, like their two most famous songs—"Wildwood Flower" and "Keep on the Sunny Side"—the Carter Family songs emerged generally from a large reservoir of musical material known to rural southerners everywhere. Drawing on nineteenth-century pop tunes, gospel resources, African American items, and some British folk fragments, the Carter Family recorded a body of music that breathed with the essence of the rural South.[12]

A substantial body of material came from the British Isles and Ireland. The Carter Family's "The Storms Are on the Ocean," Tom Ashley's "House Carpenter," Buell Kazee's "Lady Gay," Bradley Kincaid's "Barbara Allen," and songs similar to them appeared on early country broadcasts and recordings. But such songs were heavily outnumbered by material that derived, ultimately, from the popular culture resources of urban America or from the presses aligned with religious revivalism in the nation.

Mountain musicians, like rural entertainers everywhere, were fascinated with the blues, and elements of the form showed up on the earliest recordings. Henry Whitter recorded "Lonesome Road Blues," also known as "Going down the Road Feeling Bad," as his initial effort in 1923. The word "blues" itself turns up repeatedly in the title of tunes, even on fiddle pieces that evoke no melancholy at all, and in songs whose themes or moods seemed far removed from the classic African American pattern. But some mountain musicians exhibited a familiarity with the country blues and faithfully re-created what they had heard. As early as 1926 Frank Hutchison covered tunes such as "Worried Blues" that he had learned directly from black musicians back home in Logan County, West Virginia. His recordings featured some of the earliest examples in country music of slide or bottleneck guitar accompaniment. Hutchison's fellow West Virginian Dick Justice made a famous recording of a British ballad, "Loving Henry Lee," but at the same session he also recorded a creditable performance of "Cocaine" (probably learned from bluesman Luke Jordan's earlier recording), complete with a finger-picking style of guitar that is also traceable to African American sources.[13]

Tom Ashley and Dock Boggs were similarly eclectic in their song tastes, and their performances of blues tunes with five-string banjo accom-

Bradley Kincaid, "the Kentucky Mountain Boy," popularized
the idea of mountain music through his performances on
northern radio stations.
Photograph courtesy of Loyal Jones, Berea, Kentucky.

paniment provided capsule examples of the ways in which the British
and African American traditions meshed in mountain music. The Carter
Family had a large storehouse of Victorian parlor songs, but with songs
such as "Worried Man Blues" and "Bear Creek Blues" they also demonstrated a fondness for the blues and other African American tunes. A black
musician named Lesley Riddles sometimes accompanied A. P. Carter on

his song-hunting expeditions in the southern hills. These performances, and others like them, point to a significant African American influence in mountain culture, either through the physical presence of black people as workers or as itinerant musicians or through the music found on phonograph records that were sold in the region's towns and cities.[14]

By the end of the 1920s Americans had been presented with two contending visions of Appalachian music. There was the one fashioned by the commercial hillbillies on radio broadcasts, phonograph recordings, and stage shows and the one conveyed by the apostles of Cecil Sharp in books, concerts, and recitals and, in the 1930s, at folk festivals. Although songs and styles from the two traditions often overlapped, the musicians basically played to two different audiences—the hillbilly workers and farmers of the South, and the urban, middle-class audiences of the North.

Although many mountain-born musicians performed in the first two decades of the country music business, they could not have presented an "Appalachian" image even if they had wanted to do so. Mountain and other varieties of rural scenes, or representations of them, easily meshed in the public mind. Consequently, it was hard to play mountain roles without resorting to caricature or stereotype, the result being a depiction drawn from vaudeville or popular culture of the feuding, moonshining, jug-toting hillbilly. On the other hand, if musicians chose to depict a wholesome picture of mountain life, that of down-to-earth simplicity and virtue, they wound up portraying placid and thoroughly romantic scenes that conformed to the Currier and Ives vision of rural America. When attempting to don appropriate costumes that portrayed mountain life, entertainers had to face the troubling question of what mountaineers wore that might set them apart from other rural people. People in Appalachia donned overalls, work pants, brogans, bonnets, and gingham dresses, but no more so than in other regions of the rural South. Stage entertainers faced equally difficult choices when pondering what kind of speech to use and what kind of values to embody. Are mountaineers simpler and more old-fashioned than other rural people?[15]

As a matter of fact, the early entertainers exhibited a remarkable diversity in style and song. Most of them chose to go on stage or pose for publicity pictures wearing their best Sunday go-to-meeting clothes or, after the

Hollywood film industry popularized the image in the 1930s, in the garb of a cowboy. Few of the entertainers explicitly chose to wrap themselves in rural or mountain symbolism.

On the other hand, they were aware of the allure of Appalachian imagery, whether positive or negative. They knew that many Americans hungered for old songs. And they knew that the words "Appalachian" and "mountain" carried romantic, almost mystical connotations for most people. Consequently, bands gave themselves regional or local mountain names, as in the case of Ernest Stoneman's Dixie Mountaineers, Mainer's Mountaineers, Smoky Mountain Boys, Blue Ridge Entertainers, Cumberland Mountain Folk, and Clinch Mountain Clan, or in the case of an individual singer such as Bradley Kincaid who marketed himself as the Kentucky Mountain Boy.[16] They sang songs that referred to mountain life, nostalgically, humorously, or stereotypically. Although occasional songs such as A. P. Carter's "Foggy Mountain Top" and "Clinch Mountain Home" came from the pens of local entertainers, more often than not many famous "mountain songs" such as "Blue Ridge Mountain Blues," "Zeb Turney's Gal," "The Martins and the Coys," "I Like Mountain Music," and "Carry Me Back to the Mountains" were written by outsiders—by the tunesmiths of New York's Tin Pan Alley or by people such as the Kansas-born Carson Robison, who in the mid-1920s "converted" to hillbilly music.

The efforts made by radio barn dance entrepreneurs to evoke a mountain feeling were similarly shrouded in ambiguity. John Lair began cultivating the image of going home to the warmth and security of the mountains when he was working in the mid-1930s as an announcer for WLS on Chicago's National Barn Dance.[17] Inspired by his memories of the old home place in southeastern Kentucky, he wrote a popular song called "Take Me Back to Renfro Valley" that was performed often by the Barn Dance's entertainers. Though designed as a tribute to mountain pastoralism, the song presented mixed messages and images with its references to both "the old plantation" and "springtime in the mountains." In Chicago and later in Kentucky, where he created the Renfro Valley Barn Dance, Lair organized and cultivated musicians who were encouraged to portray mountain characters. He gave them names that conjured up mountain origins, such as the Cumberland Mountain Folk and Coon Creek Girls, supplied them with old-fashioned songs, and required them to dress in homespun costumes.

One of these entertainers, the North Carolina–born Myrtle Eleanor Cooper, performing under the name of Lulu Belle, became one of the most popular radio personalities of the 1930s. Lulu Belle played the role of an innocent but sometimes saucy mountain girl who often upstaged the male entertainers with whom she was paired. With her husband, Scott Wiseman (as the team of Lulu Belle and Scotty), she contributed vitally to the cultivation of the Mother and Home mystique that has always been central to country music's self-proclaimed image. Scott Wiseman's "Homecoming Time in Happy Valley" beckoned listeners to return, at least symbolically, to a land of rural innocence and family security.[18]

Although immensely influential, the tradition inaugurated by Sharp and other collectors of British material long remained the province of a small elite. Enshrined in books and scholarly articles, taught in English literature and music appreciation courses, or performed in concerts and recitals, this essentially art music approach to the ballads was narrowly focused and largely disembodied because it stressed the music rather than the people and culture that had produced it. Pianist Howard Brockway and singer Loraine Wyman had been presenting their versions of Kentucky mountain ballads to sophisticated audiences for at least a couple of years before Cecil Sharp entered the field. They and other musicians such as Grace Wood Jess, Edna Thomas, and John Jacob Niles tended to be classically trained graduates of Juilliard and other music schools. They romanticized, and even venerated, the culture from which the music came, but they treated it as a static phenomenon. On the other hand, they were not averse to changing the songs to fit their personal artistic preferences. For example, Niles changed the melody of "Black Is the Color" because his father did not like the original. Niles's melody is the one that most people remember.

This first generation of "urban folk singers" valued the oldest representations of British folk music. They were contemptuous if not hostile to hillbilly and other commercial manifestations. From Brockway and Wyman to Aaron Copland's "Appalachian Spring," the concert performers and arrangers of Appalachian music strived to create a body of music that would appeal to an elite audience of educated and articulate listeners.

Did listeners ever wonder, though, about how *real* mountain musicians sounded?

The folk festivals became the chief vehicles for preserving the oldest musical material of the mountains and venues where mountain people themselves could be featured. Somewhat analogous to fiddle contests, held in the South since 1737, the festivals served as both preservators of tradition and promoters of economic growth. They were sometimes adjuncts of chambers of commerce. The first festival convened in 1928 when Bascom Lamar Lunsford organized a series of musical events as part of the Rhododendron Festival in Asheville, North Carolina—a musical venture that has thrived ever since as the Mountain Dance and Folk Festival. A lawyer and businessman, musician (five-string banjo and fiddle), and amateur folklorist, Lunsford straddled the worlds of commercial country and folk music. He had recorded a few songs for the Brunswick label in 1928 and hundreds of items by 1949 for the Library of Congress and other collectors. He valued and tried to preserve the oldest ballads, instrumental pieces, and dances. Group clog dancing may have been the most enduring legacy of Lunsford's festivals and—as a composite of folk, stage, minstrel, and native American dancing—the most vibrant evidence of mountain music's diverse sources.[19]

The festivals that came after Lunsford's forays were openly hostile to commercial adaptations of folk music. Not only did they strive to preserve old musical traditions but they also combated hillbilly and pop styles. Annabel Morris Buchanan, cofounder in 1931 with John Powell of the White Top Mountain Folk Festival in southwestern Virginia, announced that the "products of the streets, penitentiaries, and the gutter," or songs from the paperback gospel hymnals, would never gain admittance to the festival.[20]

Jean Thomas, the self-styled Traipsing Woman and founder of the American Folk Festival in Ashland, Kentucky, sought Elizabethan survivals in mountain culture and, like the mountain settlement schools and some of the other festival entrepreneurs, sometimes introduced archaic forms such as Morris dancing into the festival setting. Powell and Buchanan rigorously restricted participation at the White Top Festival and sought to censor the kinds of songs that were performed, striving to preserve the "Anglo Saxon" cast of the music that was presented and prohibiting the performance of African American entertainers.[21]

Although much was excluded, the festivals showcased the performances of such fine mountain musicians as Horton Barker, Maud Long (daughter of Jane Gentry, Cecil Sharp's most important informant), Hobart Smith, and Texas Gladden. Profiting from the renewed appreciation of America's folk roots inspired by the Great Depression, some of these singers were invited to perform in venues outside the South and were asked to record for the Archive of Folk Song at the Library of Congress.[22] Eleanor Roosevelt attended the White Top Festival in 1933, suggesting White House endorsement for the venerable arts of the Appalachians. In 1939 an array of mountain musicians that included Bascom Lamar Lunsford, the Coon Creek Girls, and the Soco Gap clogging team performed for the king and queen of England at a White House soiree, which added still more luster to the performance of Appalachian songs and dances.[23]

The Great Depression years did not simply inspire a search for roots. They also provoked an outcry for social justice and an awakening of southern labor. Labor's rise in turn was accompanied by an outpouring of protest music and a new suggestion of what Appalachian music might be. Americans began to be aware of working-class unrest in the rural south after 1929 when a wave of strikes, at first spontaneous, spread through the textile mill towns of the Piedmont. A similar fusion of radical ideology and local populist anger occurred in 1932 in the coal-mining counties of Bell and Harlan, Kentucky, when the National Miners Union (NMU) moved in to take advantage of a vacuum left by the immobility of the conservative American Federation of Labor. In each labor context, the ancient art of traditional ballad making was put to the service of the struggling workers. Folklorist Archie Green declared that "from this setting came a group of topical songs using old melodies to set off intensely stark and militant texts."[24]

The most famous textile strike of that era, in Gastonia, North Carolina, found its balladeer in the music of Ella May Wiggins, a native of Sevierville, Tennessee, who had followed her husband into itinerant cotton mill work. Her death in 1929, from shots fired by scabs, gave labor radicalism its first southern martyr. Her name, and at least one song, "A Mill Mother's Lament," became widely known among radicals throughout the North. The most famous song to emerge from the Kentucky coalfields was Florence

Reece's "Which Side Are You On?" written in angry response to the deputy sheriffs and company "gun thugs" who had ransacked her house looking for union material. Northern radicals and labor organizers took many of the songs back home and introduced them to local singers. Radical activists also encouraged Aunt Molly Jackson, Jim Garland, and Sarah Ogan to relocate in the North, where, along with Woody Guthrie and Huddie Ledbetter (Leadbelly), they became the center of an emerging urban folk music scene that has ever since carried a pro-labor and left-wing edge.[25]

The protest songs popularized by Aunt Molly and her brethren were only a small slice of the "mountain music" that reached out to Americans in the 1930s. Folk festivals had strived to keep the oldest music alive. The Carter Family and Mainer's Mountaineers, to cite only two examples of a larger throng, found exposure for their music through the powerful broadcasts of XERF and XEG and other radio stations on the Mexican border. The Smoky Mountain Boy, Roy Acuff, won a new title as the "King of Country Music" during the war with his broadcasts over WSM, the fifty-thousand-watt clear channel station in Nashville, Tennessee. By no means was his popularity confined to the southeastern United States. He took his road shows all over the United States and played to such an enormous crowd in Venice Pier, California, that promoters were fearing the pier might sink under the weight. Transplanted southerners certainly contributed to the popularity of "mountain music" in cities throughout the industrial North, in places such as Chicago, Detroit, Cincinnati, Dayton, Akron, Baltimore, and Washington, D.C.

Southern migrants adjusted to city industrial life in a variety of ways. Some people welcomed the new way of life they had found and never looked back with nostalgic yearning at the old home place. However, many working people sought refuge in storefront churches, neighborhood social clubs, hillbilly bars, and "Dixie cafes" or searched their radio dials looking for familiar voices and stories. Hillbilly and gospel songs proliferated on music machines (jukeboxes) in Detroit, Chicago, and other industrial cities. Mountaineers communed easily with southern rural flatlanders, all of whom often bore the stigma of "hillbillies" when judged by their "Yankee" neighbors. Local differences vanished in the quest for something familiar and comfortable.

Musicians were among the migrants who moved to Baltimore, Cincinnati, Detroit, and other industrial areas. Once "hillbilly enclaves" emerged in these cities, professional country musicians began to make them part of their touring schedules. Singers or bands did not have to be from Appalachia to find acceptance, because such musicians as the Texan Ernest Tubb or the Alabamian Hank Williams spoke and sang in cadences and styles that were appealing to southern working-class people everywhere.

Although writers and historians have found southern migrations to the West Coast or the industrial Midwest dramatically appealing, the population dispersions *within* the South, from rural hinterlands to the towns and cities, have been more dynamic forces in the creation, evolution, and dissemination of various forms of music. In the 1930s and 1940s many rural southerners, from mountains and flatlands alike, gravitated toward the Piedmont South in order to work in the cotton mills, furniture plants, tobacco factories, and other industrial settings. Not only did they constitute an audience for country music, they also contributed musicians to the field, such as J. E. and Wade Mainer, Roy Hall, and Dewitt "Snuffy" Jenkins, who found radio homes in Raleigh, Durham, Winston-Salem, Columbia, Spartanburg, and other cities. In these Piedmont towns they found mill audiences eager to hear their music and radio stations that could circulate their names and songs to broad swaths of territory throughout the South.[26] Once they made their reputations through radio broadcasts, musicians could then enlarge their audiences through public appearances in country schoolhouses and movie theaters. Mountain musicians joined with rural entertainers from the Piedmont and other parts of the South to craft a body of music that fused traditional and modern elements. Charlie and Bill Monroe, for example, relocated from Western Kentucky (after short stints in the industrial Midwest) to the Carolinas in the mid-1930s and became popular sensations throughout the Piedmont region.[27] The Piedmont was crucial in the development of country music in the 1940s, where the Old South confronted the New, and where rural and industrial values met and mixed. It was, in short, the birthplace of bluegrass music.

Bluegrass is neither Appalachian nor very old. Bluegrass received its name from the music made by Bill Monroe's string band, the Blue Grass Boys, between 1944 and 1948.[28] No one in that seminal band came from the heart of Appalachia. Earl Scruggs, who perfected the sensational three-finger style of five-string banjo playing, grew up in the Piedmont town of Flint Hill, North Carolina. The band's bluesy fiddler, Chubby Wise, came from Florida. Bill Monroe, the dynamic mandolin player and bandleader, hailed from western Kentucky, and his high tenor singing, the basis for bluegrass music's vaunted "high lonesome sound," came not from the mountains but from Monroe's fascination with the blues and the music of Mississippi-born Jimmie Rodgers.

Bluegrass, however, found a receptive audience among mountain people, especially those who had relocated to the working-class sectors of Detroit, Cincinnati and other southern Ohio industrial towns, Baltimore, and Washington, D.C. The pioneer hillbilly performer Ernest Stoneman had moved with his family from Galax, Virginia, to Washington as early as 1932.[29] His talented children easily made the transition to bluegrass in the early 1950s. The bluegrass phenomenon remained largely unknown—or confined to southern working-class people—until "outsiders" heard it on the big radio stations such as WSM in Nashville or WWVA in Wheeling, West Virginia, which sometimes boomed into New England. Touring blue-grass bands took the music beyond the Upper South, and some musicians such as the Osborne Brothers and the Lilly Brothers spent long periods playing in northern cities such as Detroit, Dayton, and Boston. The music clearly had been winning new adherents throughout the 1940s and early 1950s, but the urban folk revival after 1958 did most to introduce the style to new audiences and to assert the genre's alleged Appalachian identity.

The folk revival of the late 1950s and early 1960s was only one of many flirtations that Americans have had with roots music.[30] The revival was linked almost seamlessly to the Great Depression experimentation with old-time music and to the left-wing or populist heritage bequeathed by such Appalachian performers as Aunt Molly Jackson, Sara Ogan, and Jim Garland. Folk music moved to a new dimension of popular acceptance in 1958, when the Kingston Trio recorded an old Appalachian murder ballad, "Tom Dooley." The recording's spectacular success triggered a national craze for folk and folk-like music. The Trio had learned the song from a version collected by Frank Warner from the North Carolina ballad singer Frank Proffitt, whose version probably came from the 1930 recording of

G. B. Grayson and Henry Whitter, a duo that hailed from the mountain regions of eastern Tennessee and western North Carolina. The Kingston Trio and their youthful cohorts turned a multitude of people on to folk music and acoustic instruments.

The quest for roots music gave exposure to many Appalachian performers. Jean Ritchie, from Viper, Kentucky, deep in the heart of the Cumberland Mountains, had already built an avid following in New York, singing old ballads and love songs learned back home in Perry County. She impressed her friends and students with her sweet soprano singing and velvet touch on the dulcimer, an instrument that had been quite common in her part of the Appalachians.[31] Through Alan Lomax she secured a recording contract with the Prestige label. At first she sang very rare versions of traditional ballads learned mostly from her family, but during the folk revival she began to add other kinds of material to her repertoire. Admitting that she had once made fun of hillbilly songs, she nevertheless recorded a fine album of such material, performed with Doc Watson, and discovered that she could also write her own material. Such Ritchie songs as "Dear Companion," "The L and N Don't Stop Here Anymore," and "Black Waters" (a lyrical but angry complaint against the ravages wrought by strip-mining) have since entered the repertoires of many country and folk singers.[32]

Just as Ritchie was popularizing her versions of Appalachian ballads and love songs, a new generation of urban folk fans were learning about early commercial hillbilly musicians through the Folkways record collection the *Anthology of American Folk Music*, compiled from the private collection of Harry Smith.[33] Issued in 1952, these six records contained eighty-four recordings of blues, hillbilly, cowboy, Cajun, and gospel music taken from 78-rpm records made between 1927 and 1934. The "folk" designation lent to the music both respectability and a sense of exoticism that "hillbilly" or other early labels could not have given. The collection contained a host of important Appalachian performers, including the Carter Family, Grayson and Whitter, Ernest Stoneman, Buell Kazee, Tom Ashley, Frank Hutchison, Dick Justice, Bascom Lamar Lunsford, Kelly Harrell, and Dock Boggs. During the revival Bob Dylan and Joan Baez were only two of the young urban musicians who sang songs learned from the collection.[34]

Inspired in part by the Harry Smith collection and by the music heard on other 78-rpm records, a trio of young northerners (Mike Seeger, Tom Paley, and John Cohen) formed a band called the New Lost City Ramblers and set out to re-create the sound of the early hillbilly string bands. Through a series of Folkways albums and innumerable concerts at festivals and college campuses, the Ramblers won an enthusiastic audience for their music, introduced hosts of people to early hillbilly styles, and inspired a passion for the performance of old-time string band music that still endures.[35] The songs performed by the Ramblers reflected the broad spectrum of rural southern music, but in the introduction to their influential songbook Mike Seeger declared, misleadingly, that "most of the songs that we sing and play were originally recorded by commercial companies and the Library of Congress in the southeastern mountains between 1925 and 1935."[36]

Seeger, Cohen, and other northern folk music enthusiasts began searching to see whether any of the people heard on the Harry Smith collection were still alive and whether any other living musicians reflected the old-time traditions or were making valuable departures from them. One can imagine their delight in finding that not only were such people as Maybelle Carter, Tom Ashley, Dock Boggs, and Buell Kazee still living, but that they could sing and play as well as ever. Maybelle Carter was easy to find. She performed with her daughters almost every Saturday night on the Grand Ole Opry.[37] These hillbilly pioneers must have felt immense gratification at the resumption of their careers, after long years of being unknown or forgotten. But they were often bemused if not troubled by the radical politics and lifestyles of the folkies with whom they came in contact, particularly when the Vietnam conflict threatened to polarize the nation.

The most important by-product of the search for pioneer hillbilly musicians was the "discovery" of Arthel "Doc" Watson. Watson was making his living playing electric guitar in a country swing band at his home in Deep Gap, North Carolina. Watson went to New York with Ashley and soon swept away fans and critics with his immense repertoire, smooth and supple voice, and virtuoso style of guitar flat picking (marked by the use of a flat pick rather than finger picks). He could present to audiences the entire range of music available in the mountains: everything from a cappella performances of ballads and gospel songs to dazzling renditions of hillbilly, country and western, blues, jazz, and rock tunes. He designed MerleFest, held each April in Wilkesboro, North Carolina, as a memorial to his deceased son, but it stands now as a showcase and tribute to the acoustic music phenomenon that flowed largely from Watson's singular achievements as a guitarist.[38]

Watson has been only one of many mentors for the musicians who have set out to learn what they perceive as Appalachian styles of musical performance. Much could be learned from concerts or repeated playings of a record until a desired sound was re-created, but the best form of apprenticeship was to stand or sit alongside a fiddler, banjo player, balladeer, or other musician and painstakingly observe the way a note was played or voiced. Trips to the mountains and immersion in the family and community life that surrounded the music became almost mandatory rituals for young musicians who had been converted to what they perceived as Appalachian music. Like John Cohen, who filmed important documentaries of mountain musicians, some fans sat at the feet of Roscoe Holcomb in eastern Kentucky.[39] Or some journeyed to one of America's citadels of traditional music, Madison County, North Carolina, to learn from banjoist Obray Ramsey or balladeers Berzilla Wallin, Dellie Norton, Doug Wallin, or Dillard Chandler. Still others traveled to Surry County, North Carolina, to revel in the stories and tunes of Tommy Jarrell, the gifted fiddler who could demonstrate fiddle licks and tunings that he had learned from musicians who lived in Civil War days. The future director of the Archive of American Folk Song, Alan Jabbour, began his apprenticeship in American folk music by immersing himself in the fiddle music of Burl Hammons and Henry Reed, from West Virginia and Virginia, respectively. Nashville music personality John Hartford, best remembered for his composition of the hit song "Gentle on My Mind," was a passionate student of American fiddle styles, and his most significant research involved the music and life of one of Appalachia's most influential musicians, the West Virginian Ed Haley.[40]

The reawakening of interest in traditional Appalachian music that was inspired by the folk revival occurred also in the context of President Lyndon B. Johnson's War on Poverty and still another national discovery of Appalachia. Volunteers in Service to America (VISTA) personnel and music collectors alike recognized that music was a vehicle for popular and regional pride and a medium of protest. Institutions that stressed Appalachian identity and culture—such as Berea College's Appalachian Center in Kentucky, and Appalshop in Whitesburg, Kentucky—invariably promoted both regional betterment and musical enrichment. Such northern musicians and social activists as Si Kahn and John McCutcheon relocated in or near the mountains. The memory and legacy of people such as Florence Reece, Aunt Molly Jackson, Jim Garland, Sara Ogan Gunning, and Don West were resurrected, and newer balladeers and social activists such as Nimrod Workman and Hazel Dickens were encouraged.

Dickens, from Montcalm in Mercer County, West Virginia, was comfortable performing in most of the styles of country music. While living in Baltimore in the late 1950s, working in a factory and trying to come to terms with the loneliness and alienation of life as an exile in a big city, she began singing and playing bass in local bluegrass bands. Eventually, through her mentor Mike Seeger she met Alice Gerrard, a graduate of Antioch College who had fallen in love with traditional music, and their searing, soulful harmonies inspired other women to perform in what had been perceived as a good old boys' genre of music. Although she loved and could perform all styles of traditional country music, from the Carter Family to George Jones, Dickens may be more widely known as a singer of protest and socially conscious music. She sang often at union rallies, and her voice filled the soundtrack of the movie documentary *Harlan County, U.S.A.*, the gripping story of a protracted coal strike in eastern Kentucky. Although her stark, passion-filled style of singing is widely admired, her songs—such as "Black Lung," "They'll Never Keep Us Down," "Working Girl Blues," "Will Jesus Wash the Blood Stains from Their Hands," "West Virginia, My Home," and "Mama's Hand"—will ultimately be her most enduring contributions to American music and the struggle for social justice.[41]

Once the folk revivalists discovered hillbilly music, it was almost inevitable that an upsurge of interest in bluegrass would follow. This southeastern-based style, it seemed, was the logical modern extension of old-time string band music. In an influential article in *Esquire* magazine in 1959, folklorist Alan Lomax described bluegrass as "folk music with overdrive."[42] Mike Seeger and Ralph Rinzler, young folk enthusiasts who were making the transition from Library of Congress discs to commercial recordings, heard and taped the music of people such as Ola Belle Reed at the country music parks in Maryland and Pennsylvania. Seeger in 1959 produced a recording of rural musicians in Baltimore for the Folkways label called *Mountain Music Bluegrass Style*, the first explicit linking of the two terms.[43]

Mountain-born musicians made vital contributions to the popularization of bluegrass in the North and to the popular identification of the style with mountain culture.[44] In Boston, the West Virginia–born Lilly Brothers dispensed their appealing blend of old-time brother duet singing and bluegrass music seven nights a week at a seedy and dangerous bar called Hillbilly Ranch in the Combat Zone, where prostitutes were more frequently seen than banjos were heard. The mixed metaphors conveyed by the club's name were echoed by the name used for the Lilly Brothers' band, the Confederate Mountaineers. The Osborne Brothers (Bobby and Sonny) from Hyden, Kentucky, had also moved north early, playing in the mid-1950s to transplanted southerners and curious Yankees in the honky-tonks of Detroit and Dayton, Ohio. In March 1960 the Osbornes gave the first bluegrass concert at a college, at Antioch in Ohio.

Two of the most popular bluegrass acts in the folk revival, Jim and Jesse McReynolds and Ralph and Carter Stanley, grew up within a few miles of each other in southwestern Virginia. They had strongly contrasting styles and repertoires, however. Jim and Jesse (as they were usually called) sang with smooth, clear, high harmonies and were famous for Jesse's syncopated style of mandolin crosspicking. The Stanley Brothers, on the other hand, conveyed a more strident, backwoods sound that carried the flavor of such earlier hillbilly groups as Mainer's Mountaineers. More than any other band, including that led by bluegrass's founding father, Bill Monroe, Carter and Ralph Stanley and their Clinch Mountain Boys fit the public perception of how a mountain band should sound. Noted for their high, lonesome harmonies, hard-driving rhythms, and storehouse of old-time songs, the Stanley Brothers conjured up visions and sounds of deep rolling hills, isolated mountain glens, lonesome rivers, little country churchyards, broken family circles, and the undying love of Mama and Daddy. In the decades since Carter's death in December 1966, Ralph Stanley has remained a pillar of tradition, singing in his high, clench-throated style with vocal mannerisms learned in Primitive Baptist church services. Relying increasingly on old-time songs and harmonies, Stanley has impressed growing numbers of listeners—most of whom heard his voice for the first time in the soundtrack of *O Brother, Where Art Thou?*—with his rugged integrity and uncompromising commitment to tradition. For many people, Ralph Stanley is the embodiment of mountain music.[45]

Appalachian music today bears the major characteristics that it possessed in the days of Cecil Sharp. It is a vigorous composite of songs and styles that defy precise definition. Mountain-born musicians still make music in great profusion at home, in church, at community gatherings, and in professional venues. Exhibiting great diversity, their music illustrates the continuing interrelationship of their region with the rest of the world. The old ballads and love songs that so enthralled Cecil Sharp are now rare, but they live in the performances of such singers as Jean Ritchie, Betty Smith, Ginny Hawker, and Sheila Adams (the grandniece of the Madison County balladeer Dellie Chandler Norton). Other musicians consciously preserve the banjo, fiddle, dulcimer, autoharp, and other string-band styles of earlier mountain stylists. Old Regular Baptists still sing their hymns in congregational style—unadorned, unaccompanied, and unharmonized—led by a song leader who lines out the songs in chanting fashion. No style of music is more traditional or more rooted in mountain culture. Students of Appalachian music, and other folk expressions, can learn elements of Old Regular Baptist singing and other vocal and instrumental styles at Sacred Harp songfests; annual workshops, such as those held each year in West Virginia at the Augusta Heritage Center on the campus of Davis and Elkins College; or from people such as Wayne Erbsen, who instructs students on Appalachian instrumental styles from his base in Asheville, North Carolina.[46]

The Appalachian-born musicians who inhabit contemporary country and bluegrass music perform in a broad range of styles. Ralph Stanley and Hazel Dickens convey a rough-hewn and unaffected rural sound, whereas Dwight Yoakam and Kenny Chesney sing with rock-inflected mannerisms and butt-wiggling theatrics. Loretta Lynn, Dolly Parton, Ricky Skaggs, and Patty Loveless sing with the high, pristine clarity that is often associated with mountain music. But Skaggs's onetime singing partner, the late Keith Whitley who also grew up in eastern Kentucky, sang plaintively in a low vocal register, and Doc Watson, the quintessential Appalachian musician, sings in a warm, expressive baritone. In their choice of musical material, these singers have roamed all over the map, singing and playing everything from traditional murder ballads to pop, jazz, and rock.

The diversity displayed by Appalachian-born musicians is impressive, but in many people's minds it is overshadowed by the romance that clings to the concept of mountain music. Appalachian music conjures up simpler and time-honored notions of purity and ancient moorings, appealing to those who envision a culture unspoiled by urban conceits and machine technology. Among musicians and fans in the highly commercial and urban-based genres known as country and bluegrass, one finds frequent assertions that their music was born in Appalachia (an idea that is often coupled with the thesis of Celtic identity).[47] Rather than acknowledging that these styles of music were born in many places, including Appalachia, it is more tempting to claim exclusively the seemingly pristine origins identified with mountain life (even though the music made by Appalachian people themselves occurred as often in bars, honky-tonks, radio stations, and recording studios as in churches and homes). If such presumptions encourage an appreciation for old-time musical styles and songs and a desire to preserve them, we can forgive the narrow understanding that they convey of Appalachian history and music. However, it is less easy to tolerate those who glibly describe as "Appalachian" any expression of music that seems old or based on traditional rural sounds, whether it be the homespun pop songs written by the California convert to old-time music Gillian Welch or the classical adaptations of old-time material performed by Mark O'Connor, Edgar Meyer, Bela Fleck, and Yo-Yo Ma. O'Connor and his colleagues commented in one of their several CDs dealing with presumed Appalachian material that they proposed to celebrate American "roots," "folk," and "traditional" songs (thereby suggesting that such descriptions were synonymous with the word "Appalachian").[48]

Welch, O'Connor, and Yo-Yo Ma may be simply using a shorthand and appealing way of labeling their music, knowing full well that hosts of fans and critics are more than ready to accept any acoustic "rural" sound as Appalachian. More likely, these sophisticated musicians themselves may have succumbed to the romance of Appalachia. After all, it has happened many times in the past and will continue to do so in the future. As America continues its irreversible journey down the road toward industrial and technological hegemony, many of us will cling to the visions of another time and another place. The reality of our lives may not change significantly, but at least for the duration of a song or a concert, our immersion in Appalachian music—either real or imagined—will link us once again to a land of presumed simplicity, moral rectitude, and honest emotion.

NOTES

1. Richard Harrington assessed the effects of the movie and soundtrack in "Mountain Music's Moment in the Sun," *Washington Post*, August 12, 2001.

2. Guthrie T. Meade Jr., Dick Spottswood, and Douglas S. Meade, *Country Music Sources: A Biblio-Discography of Commercially Recorded Traditional Music* (Chapel Hill, N.C.: Southern Folklife Collection, 2002).

3. Jean Ritchie, *Singing Family of the Cumberlands* (New York: Oak Publications, 1955), 73–75.

4. Emma Bell Miles, *The Spirit of the Mountains* (New York: J. Pott, 1905), 69.

5. *Musical Traditions* is published in Great Britain and available online at http://www.mustrad.org.uk/.

6. Olive Dame Campbell and Cecil J. Sharp, *English Folk Songs from the Southern Appalachians* (New York: Knickerbocker Press, 1917), viii–ix.

7. Francis James Child, *The English and Scottish Popular Ballads*, 5 vols. (Boston: Houghton Mifflin, 1882–1898).

8. *Songcatcher*, the popular movie of 2001, was a very loose and highly romanticized version of the role played by settlement schoolteachers in the discovery of balladry in the southern mountains and Cecil Sharp's arrival on the scene.

9. Cecil Sharp, *The Country Dance Book* (London: Novelle, 1918), pt. 5.

10. All of the recordings made by these performers are listed in Meade, Spottswood, and Meade, *Country Music Sources*.

11. Charles Wolfe's notes to *The Bristol Sessions* (CMF Records-011-1); Nolan Porterfield, *Jimmie Rodgers: The Life and Times of America's Blue Yodeler* (Urbana: University of Illinois Press, 1979), 105–14; Ivan M. Tribe, *The Stonemans: An Appalachian Family and the Music That Shaped Their Lives* (Urbana: University of Illinois Press, 1993), 56–62.

12. Charles Wolfe and Richard Weize, *In the Shadow of Clinch Mountains* (Bear Family BCD 15865).

13. *White Country Blues: A Lighter Shade of Blue* (Columbia/Legacy C2K 47466).

14. Cecelia Conway, *African Banjo Echoes in Appalachia: A Study of Folk Traditions* (Knoxville: University of Tennessee Press, 1995).

15. Bill C. Malone, *Singing Cowboys and Musical Mountaineers: Southern Culture and the Roots of Country Music* (Athens: University of Georgia Press, 1993).

16. Loyal Jones, *Radio's "Kentucky Mountain Boy," Bradley Kincaid* (Berea, Ky.: Appalachian Center, Berea College, 1980).

17. Pete Stamper, *It All Happened in Renfro Valley* (Lexington: University Press of Kentucky, 1999).

18. Lily May Ledford, *Coon Creek Girl* (Berea, Ky.: Appalachian Center, Berea College, 1991); William E. Lightfoot, "Belle of the Barn Dance: Reminiscing with Lulu Belle Wiseman Stamey," *Journal of Country Music* 12, no. 1 (1987): 2–16.

19. Loyal Jones, *Minstrel of the Appalachians: The Story of Bascom Lamar Lunsford* (Boone, N.C.: Appalachian Consortium Press, 1984).

20. Annabel Morris Buchanan, "The Function of a Folk Festival," *Southern Folklore Quarterly* 1, no. 1 (March 1937): 29–34.

21. David E. Whisnant, *All That Is Native and Fine: The Politics of Culture in an American Region* (Chapel Hill: University of North Carolina Press, 1983).

22. See *Anglo-American Ballads*, vol. 1 (Rounder 1511; originally recorded in 1942 by the Archive of Folk Song, Library of Congress); *Anglo-American Ballads*, vol. 2 (Rounder 1516; originally recorded in 1943); *Texas Gladden: Ballad Legacy* (Rounder 116611; originally recorded in 1941 and 1946).

23. Jones, *Minstrel of the Appalachians*, 71–73.

24. Archie Green, notes to Sarah Ogan Gunning's *Girl of Constant Sorrow* (Folk-Legacy Records FSA-26).

25. Jim Garland, *Welcome the Traveler Home: Jim Garland's Story of the Kentucky Mountains* (Lexington: University Press of Kentucky, 1983); John Greenway, *American Folksongs of Protest* (Philadelphia: University of Pennsylvania Press, 1953); Robbie Lieberman, *My Song Is My Weapon: People's Songs, American Communism, and the Politics of Culture, 1930–1950* (Urbana: University of Illinois Press, 1995); Richard Reuss, "American Folklore and Left-Wing Politics, 1927–1957" (PhD diss., Indiana University, 1971); Shelly Romalis, *Pistol Packin' Mama: Aunt Molly Jackson and the Politics of Folksong* (Urbana: University of Illinois Press, 1999).

26. Jacquelyn Dowd Hall, *Like a Family: The Making of a Southern Cotton Mill World* (Chapel Hill: University of North Carolina Press, 1987).

27. Richard D. Smith, *"Can't You Hear Me Callin'": The Life of Bill Monroe* (Boston: Little, Brown, 2000).

28. Neil Rosenberg, *Bluegrass: A History* (Urbana: University of Illinois Press, 1985).

29. Tribe, *Stonemans*, 86–88.

30. Neil V. Rosenberg, ed., *Transforming Tradition: Folk Music Revivals Examined* (Urbana: University of Illinois Press, 1993).

31. Jean Ritchie's instruction manual *The Dulcimer Book* (New York: Oak Publications, 1963) went through numerous printings in the ten years after its first issuance.

32. Ritchie deserves a comprehensive biography. Her *Singing Family of the Cumberlands* (New York: Oak Publications, 1955) is an excellent account of her youthful experiences. She is the subject of a video documentary, *Mountain Born: The Jean Ritchie Story*, produced by Kentucky Educational Television.

33. The anthology was reissued in 1997 on six compact discs by Smithsonian Folkways Recordings, *Anthology of American Folk Music* (SF 251, SF 252, SF 253).

34. Greil Marcus, *Invisible Republic: Bob Dylan's Basement Tapes* (New York: Henry Holt, 1997).

35. New Lost City Ramblers, *The Early Years, 1958–1962* (Smithsonian Folkways SF 40036).

36. Mike Seeger, *The New Lost City Ramblers Song Book* (New York: Oak Publications, 1964), 22.

37. Bill Clifton, *150 Old-Time Folk and Gospel Songs* (Privately printed ca. 1956).

38. *Doc Watson Legacy* (High Windy Audio, Fairview, N.C.).

39. *The High Lonesome Sound* (Smithsonian Folkways CD SF-40104).

40. Rod Amberg, *Sodom Laurel Album* (Chapel Hill: University of North Carolina Press, 2002), and the companion CD, *Appalachian Ballads from Madison County, North Carolina*; Tommy Jarrell, *Sail Away Ladies* (County 756); John Hartford, *Wild Hog in the Red Brush* (Rounder 0392) and *The Speed of the Long Bow: A Tribute to the Fiddle Music of Ed Haley* (Rounder 0438).

41. Mary Battiata, "A High and Lonesome Sound," *Washington Post Magazine*, June 24, 2001, 8–15, 21–25; Hazel Dickens and Bill C. Malone, *Working Girl Blues: The Life and Music of Hazel Dickens* (Urbana: University of Illinois Press, 2008).

42. Alan Lomax, "Bluegrass Background: Folk Music with Overdrive," *Esquire* 52, no. 4 (Oct. 1959): 103–109.

43. *Mountain Music Bluegrass Style* (Smithsonian Folkways CD SF-40038).

44. Robert Cantwell, *Bluegrass Breakdown: The Making of the Old Southern Sound* (Urbana: University of Illinois Press, 1984).

45. John Wright, *Traveling the High Way Home* (Urbana: University of Illinois Press, 1993); *Short Life of Trouble: Songs of Grayson and Whitter* (Rebel CD-1735); *Ralph Stanley* (DMZ/Columbia CK 86625).

46. Niki Denison, "A Mountain Music Master," *On Wisconsin* 104, no. 1 (Spring 2003): 40–45.

47. It is amusing but irritating to learn that although the spurious doctrine of Anglo-Saxonism has been largely abandoned by students of mountain music, it is being replaced by the equally shadowy thesis of Celticism.

48. Gillian Welch, *Time (the Revelator)* (Acony 0103). For examples of the romantic classical depiction of presumed Appalachian themes, see Yo-Yo Ma, Edgar Meyer, and Mark O'Connor, *Appalachian Journey* (Sony Classical 66782) and *Appalachia Waltz* (Sony Classical 68460).

CHAPTER 13

ELVIS, COUNTRY MUSIC, AND THE SOUTH

I have presented varying versions of this essay to two or three different audiences, including the First Annual International Elvis Presley Conference in Oxford, Mississippi, in August 1995. The crux of the article included here, though, was published in 1979 in Jac L. Tharpe, ed., *Elvis: Images and Fancies* (Jackson: University Press of Mississippi). My views have changed considerably in the sixty years since I first saw Elvis, and readers will consequently find contradictions in my judgments. Some readers may interpret the essay's remarks as an anguished effort to rationalize or gloss over my earlier positions. I prefer to think of them as examples of my academic maturation. But I must confess that I am still angry at Elvis for cutting in on Hank Snow's stage time at that concert in Austin many years ago!

This is in many ways a highly personal essay, and many readers may not want to trust all of the details that are presented. Happily, published works exist that can illuminate the life of Elvis and place him in his proper social context. Peter Guralnick has written the definitive biography in two volumes, entitled *Last Train to Memphis: The Rise of Elvis Presley* (New York: Little, Brown, 1994) and *Careless Love: The Unmaking of Elvis Presley* (New York: Little, Brown, 1999). Joel Williamson has written a one-volume interpretation called *Elvis Presley: A Southern Life* (New York: Oxford University Press, 2015). Along with Ernst Jorgenson, Guralnick has compiled a meticulous account of Presley's early personal appearances and other activities in *Elvis Day by Day: The Definitive Record of His Life and Music* (New York: Ballantine, 1999). Because of this work, I now know that I saw Elvis in Austin on January 18, 1956. Other indispensable works that help to round out the history of rockabilly and other related forms of music are Guralnick, *Sam Phillips: The Man Who Invented Rock 'n' Roll* (New York: Little, Brown, 2015), and Rick Bragg, *Jerry Lee Lewis: His Own Story* (New York: HarperCollins, 2014). If the reader is reluctant to tackle a ream of formidable biographies, he or she might want to read an excellent and probing essay by Louis Menand called "The Invention of Rock and Roll," in the *New Yorker*, November 16, 2015, 80–87. Basically a review of Guralnick's biography of Sam Phillips, the essay raises questions that should make us all reevaluate our assumptions about Elvis, American youth, and the emergence of rock and roll.

SOMETIME IN EARLY 1956 I ATTENDED A CONCERT FEATURING HANK SNOW, AT THE OLD CITY COLISEUM on the south side of Austin, Texas. To my chagrin the concert was cut short, and Hank was reduced to giving an abbreviated medley of his songs so that a second show could be scheduled for the accommodation of the large throng clamoring to get into the arena. The multitude was not there to see my hero, Hank Snow, nor to hear "old-time" country music. They had come to see the rising new sensation, Elvis Presley. He was just beginning his stint with RCA Victor, and the company had not yet released his first smash national hit, "Heartbreak Hotel." Stylistically, he was neither fish nor fowl and, consequently, his managers had not yet determined how to package or label him. To a rock-ribbed country traditionalist like me, it was bad enough to be given only a condensed version of my favorite kind of music. Even more appalling was the tumultuous, and even frenzied, response of the audience to Presley who, in my opinion, was not good and, more significantly, was not country. He came out in his red sports coat (or was it pink?) wearing his pompadour and long sideburns, and twisting his lips into that peculiar shy sneer. After one verse and a chorus of "That's All Right, Mama," he shoved his guitar to one side of his body, set his left leg to quivering, and began the pelvic thrusts that any stripper would have envied. With each bump and grind his young women listeners came unglued until, unable to resist any longer, they stormed to the foot of the stage shrieking their pleasure and reacting in a manner allegedly alien to most proper southern girls. I do not know whether my discomfort arose most acutely from my puritanism or from my musical conservatism. Whatever the source, I felt that Presley was a disrupter and that, as evidenced by the response given to him, the future of country music was dim.

In retrospect, although I did not take up the guitar and become a rockabilly, Elvis's Austin concert did serve as a kind of transforming experience for me. It seemed to be a barometer marking both the beginning of a revolution in American music and my own loss of innocence. I actually had become familiar with Elvis earlier, in the summer of 1954 when his first Sun releases were played on Tom Perryman's radio show out of Gladewater, Texas, only thirty miles or so from my home in Tyler. I probably sensed then, well before the Austin concert, that the stirrings of a musical revolution were under way, and that southern boys and girls were already ripe for transformation. Rhythm and blues songs had begun to dominate the jukebox in the Wigwam, the student center at Tyler Junior College, before Elvis's first records were released, and my classmates had already discovered the joys of "Dirty Bop" and the suggestive lyrics of such songs as "Fever" and "Work with Me Annie." Nevertheless, until that evening in Austin, when the upstart Elvis upstaged the veteran Hank Snow, I had not fully recognized the physical dimensions of the social and musical revolution that was underway in America, nor had I actually witnessed the stirrings of feminine revolt, as young women tentatively recognized and openly displayed their own sexual feelings.

While my affection for Elvis's music is not much stronger than it was sixty years ago, time and reflection have made my response more nuanced, perhaps more historical than hysterical, and I feel that I now have a more balanced view of his place in the country music continuum. And Elvis *was* country, as much as he was anything, and it is in country music that one must look to find the roots of his style, if not his appeal. Much has been made of Elvis's successful exploitation of the black musical idiom, as if he and Sam Phillips, the director of Sun Records, were the first to stumble upon such an idea. On the contrary, Elvis's fusion of black and white music in the mid-1950s was merely the most recent phase in a process of interaction that extends back to the earliest contacts between blacks and whites in the early seventeenth century and has been manifested in American professional entertainment since at least the appearance of the blackface minstrels after 1830.

Since the early 1920s, when commercial country music first began to emerge, its musicians have demonstrated a strong and continuing fascination with black sounds, songs, styles, and images. Most people are at least dimly aware of the influence exerted by African American styles upon the

The young Elvis in one of his dynamic sensual performances.
Photograph courtesy the Raymond H. Pulley Collection (P-20422), Southern
Folklife Collection, Louis Round Wilson Special Collections Library,
University of North Carolina, Chapel Hill.

music of such major performers as Jimmie Rodgers, Bob Wills, Bill Monroe, Hank Williams, and Charlie Rich, but it may not be quite so well known that the music of a host of other country performers has been tarred with the African brush. Even Louisiana's famous singing governor, Jimmie Davis of "You Are My Sunshine" fame, known for his policy of racial segregation and his soulful singing of gospel songs, got his professional music start in the early 1930s by singing versions of sexually suggestive tunes like "Red Night Gown Blues" and "Tom Cat and Pussy Blues." Western swing musicians, who were principally country boys from Texas and Oklahoma who loved to experiment with jazz and other African American musical idioms, were not above drifting into what they perceived as black pronunciations and dialects. Nevertheless, it is important to stress that these entertainers succeeded because they were able to "mix" or appropriate racial styles, not because they made themselves into replicas of black performers (although, ironically, the Allen Brothers, white musicians from Chattanooga, were greatly irritated when they found their music listed in record brochures alongside "race" performers because they sang and played blues tunes so convincingly). Similarly, Elvis did not sound like an African American, despite Sam Phillips's search for such a performer; he sounded like a white boy from the Deep South who was familiar with and fond of black musical idioms. That alone was enough to make him unusual in the bland, homogenized atmosphere of American popular music at the end of the 1950s. His exploitation of black material, in any case, has been greatly exaggerated; it was, rather, part of an eclectic and, in fact, largely undisciplined approach to music.

Although country music was once considered the hayseed stepchild of the American popular music industry and perceived solely as a regional genre of limited appeal, it had begun to launch out into the world at large long before Elvis made his first test recordings in the Sun studio in 1954. Much of its expansion occurred during World War II when the migrations of defense workers and servicemen promoted musical interchange, but the music's first commercial boom came after 1946 when, freed from war-imposed scarcities and motivated by a consumer-driven economy, Americans launched into an unprecedented pursuit of entertainment. With over 650 radio stations carrying live and recorded "hillbilly" talent and a proliferation of small record labels promoting all kinds of grassroots musical material (Cajun, Tex-Mex, gospel, blues), the music began entering homes where it had never before been admitted. While they seldom appeared on the major pop music charts—musical forms were still rigidly segregated until the mid-fifties—singers like Eddy Arnold, Carl Smith, Lefty Frizzell,

Kitty Wells, Webb Pierce, Hank Snow, and Hank Williams gained a name recognition in American popular culture that earlier country entertainers would have envied. And, increasingly, songs of country origin *did* begin to appear on the popularity charts, but usually when performed by such pop singers as Patti Page ("Tennessee Waltz"), Rosemary Clooney ("Half as Much"), and Tony Bennett ("Cold Cold Heart").

The covering of country songs by pop singers is a well-known fact of the early fifties; the parallel utilization of other forms of music by country singers has been insufficiently recognized. Since the twenties country musicians had exhibited a major preoccupation with the cluster of black-derived musical forms that included ragtime, blues, boogie, and hot dance rhythms. In the late forties and early fifties when Elvis would have been warehousing sounds he would later exploit, Hank Williams, for instance, did songs such as "My Bucket's Got a Hole in It"; Red Foley had smash hits with "Chattanoogie Shoe Shine Boy" and "Hearts Made of Stone"; and the Delmore Brothers (Alton and Rabon), who had been performing country boogie tunes since the mid-thirties, had great success with songs like "Freight Train Boogie" and "Blues Stay Away from Me." Furthermore, many of the instrumental clichés that would later characterize early rock and roll could be heard distinctly in country music during the immediate postwar years. As an inveterate radio listener Elvis could scarcely have avoided hearing such musicians as Moon Mullican and the Maddox Brothers and Rose (billed as "the most colorful hillbilly band in the land") whose exuberant and jivey songs featured hot electric guitar solos, slapped bass playing, and an energetic style of singing similar to and anticipatory of rockabilly music. Nick Tosches, in *Country: The Biggest Music in America*, calls the Maddox Brothers and Rose's "Hangover Blues," recorded in 1952, "pure gutter-rock."

Elvis's derivative style, then, was a composite drawn in great measure, but not exclusively, from earlier country music. One could hear in his performances echoes of country boogie pianist Moon Mullican, the Maddox Brothers, Hank Williams, Red Foley, and others like the bluegrass patriarch, Bill Monroe, whose music he had long loved and absorbed. Nevertheless, it is almost a certainty that his career would never have experienced its rapid ascent had he not unleashed his own charismatic combination of sensuality, high energy, and rollicking bad boyishness in tapping a brand-new audience, the youth, which was ready for the music he purveyed, and whose musical interests could not be confined to the traditional country music format.

The social demographics of the era explain the expansion of country music and other grassroots forms, as well as the emergence of Elvis and the Youth Culture that nourished him and the rockabilly phenomenon. Although the contours of change were already present in the rural South before the coming of the great conflict, World War II unleashed a social revolution in the region. Massive population shifts within the area, from agriculture to industry and from farms to cities, and to cities in the industrial Midwest and on the West Coast, promoted economic improvement, altered lifestyles, and new attitudes. Change, though, did not occur instantly, and the habits and assumptions of the rural past receded slowly. Millions of rural southerners changed their residences and occupations, but they found that folkways, values, or expectations could not change as rapidly.

Americans in the mid-fifties became increasingly aware of a new subculture, that of the teenager, a product of postwar affluence and Depression-spawned guilt. As late Depression babies came of age, joined by the Baby Boom generation of the mid-forties, these teenagers became a large and important body of culture consumers who, significantly, had money to spend. The new prosperity, marked by the emergence of the two-car economy and coupled with relaxed parental standards, contributed to a sense of liberation that had not previously animated American youth. Still mindful of their Depression experiences, parents were ready to provide their children with material comforts that older generations had only dreamed of.

Radio, jukeboxes, the movies, the automobile, and television brought the nation's popular culture into the lives of all southern working people. Not only did these innovations integrate working folk more firmly into the socioeconomic processes of the nation, they also contributed to the making of a self-conscious youth culture. Like young people elsewhere in the nation, southern youth experienced the moods of confusion and uncertainty that gave rise to the famous "rebels without a cause."

While the earlier heroes of the American people (Babe Ruth, Charles Lindbergh, Will Rogers, and the like) had been revered by both the young and old, this new youth culture demanded youthful role models. Peer-group heroes had seldom been available in earlier decades, but the mass media of the fifties popularized those who were immediately and readily available everywhere in the nation: the method actors (James Dean, Marlon Brando, Montgomery Clift) and pop music entertainers (Johnny Ray, Pat Boone, Fats Domino, Chuck Berry). The vaunted sexual revolution described by the Kinsey Reports may have involved more talk than action, and young people may not have always understood their long-repressed feelings that were struggling to gain expression. Nonetheless, they often found outlets for these emotions by identifying with media heroes, a preoccupation that was reflected in the music to which they listened. Anticipations of the moral revolt of the sixties could be heard in such songs as "Work with Me Annie," "Fever," and "Annie Had a Baby." Bored with mainstream pop music, young people began searching for and experimenting with alternative music forms such as country and, especially, rhythm and blues. Armed with transistor radios and the little 45 rpm records that became available after 1948, young people now had ample opportunities to create their own musical culture.

White adults may not have known the names of their children's heroes, but an increasing number of young whites bought records in sufficient quantities to make "crossover" stars of black singers like Fats Domino, Clyde McPhatter, Lloyd Price, Little Richard, Chuck Berry, and the Platters. While Elvis began as a member of this audience, sharing its desires and frustrations; overnight, he soon became one of its heroes and spokesmen. Up to a point, his biography resembles my own and that of millions of southern working-class youth. Like many of our generation born on farms or in small hamlets during the Depression, there was, during the war and its immediate aftermath, a move to the city—in Elvis's case, Memphis. This migration brought into focus a confrontation of values both generational and social. Many people readily conformed to the city, welcoming its hastened pace as well as its economic enticements. Others never really abandoned their inherited rural scheme of values even though they became permanently domiciled in urban homes and occupations. Elvis participated in both sides of this equation. He found himself attracted to exciting urban temptations while remaining culturally rooted to his family's values, absorbing them both into his music.

Like Jerry Lee Lewis, the wild man of rockabilly music, Elvis was reared in the Pentecostal faith. Pentecostalism embodies a wondrous mixture of otherworldly vision and earthly abandon that contributed heavily to the building of modern gospel music and to the molding of an impressive body of musicians ranging from Mahalia Jackson and Sister Rosetta Tharp to James Blackwood. No musical instrument was ever taboo in Pentecostal services, and church members felt free to express a joyous emotionalism that was often closed to them in secular life. Elvis did his first public singing in church, and his style certainly bears the marks of this experience. However, he has alluded more directly to the influence upon his life of the ministers, that zealous and often flamboyant breed of men and women who intrigued him with their theatrical flair and platform choreography.

The white gospel quartets were also powerful shapers of Elvis's music, and the greatest of them all, the Blackwood Brothers, were Mississippians who made their headquarters in Memphis when he was still a teenager. The rather affected and throaty vibrato that he used on his slower songs probably came from the quartet singers, and Elvis usually recorded or performed with two of the best groups, the Jordanaires and the Stamps Quartet. Elvis never abandoned his affection for gospel music. Even at the peak of his professional career, when mainstream pop music was his primary expression and Las Vegas his principal arena of action, he usually sang religious songs during his private moments offstage. Gospel music remained one of the few safe retreats available to him during those lonely days of isolation at the end of his life and a mark of loyalty to the culture of his mother.

Immersed in the traditional culture and music of his parents, yet drawn by the liberating musical trends of his own era, Elvis, like his southern contemporaries, was torn by conflicting impulses. His eclecticism seems to have been his way of resolving this conflict. In addition to the church music he had heard all his life, he listened to any and every kind of music that was available on the radio. Much of his musical experimentation was a trial-and-error search for a successful commercial formula; in his Sun auditions he tried a sampling of everything he knew, from Dean Martin–style pop music to gut-bucket blues.

His first Sun recording included, on one side, "Blue Moon of Kentucky," a bluegrass song by Bill Monroe, and on the other, "That's All Right, Mama," a rhythm and blues tune from the repertory of Arthur "Big Boy" Crudup. By successfully wedding the music of the poor whites and poor blacks of the South, Elvis had, unconsciously, established a new folk consensus that proved commercial enough to alter the course of American popular music as no other singer, from Al Jolson to Frank Sinatra, had ever done. His impact on the larger popular music world has been explored elsewhere; my emphasis will be, instead, on Elvis's effect on the music from which he had first drawn sustenance, the music of his origins, the country music of the South.

His rapid ascent as a pop-culture icon should not obscure the fact that his early years as an entertainer were spent within the boundaries of country music. Although he pushed those boundaries farther than anyone had previously taken them, Elvis, in a sense, never strayed very far from the sensibilities of the little ten-year-old boy who sang "Old Shep" at the Mississippi-Alabama Fair and Dairy Show in Tupelo. As an adult performer, Elvis often sang this Red Foley classic, about an aging and dying dog, and never burlesqued nor made fun of it. He offered, instead, one of his most sincere and unaffected performances.

Except for the occasional national television engagement, most of Elvis's early professional appearances occurred at country venues, and usually with other country performers like Faron Young, Slim Whitman, and Hank Snow. Despite the initial exposure given to "That's All Right, Mama" on Dewey Phillips's Memphis rhythm and blues show in July 1954, Elvis's other recordings generally played on country disc jockey programs. The publicity won through country radio, in turn, generated public appearances in areas blanketed by the stations' transmitters. Elvis was particularly popular in the region reached by the powerful transmission of KWKH (Shreveport) and the Louisiana Hayride—east and west Texas, western Louisiana, and Arkansas. And it was there that he exerted his most immediate and dramatic influence, when other young country boys with guitars, like Buddy Holly, Sonny Curtis, Mac Davis, Roy Orbison, Bob Luman, and Johnny Cash, abandoned the traditional styles of country music (or so it seemed) and embraced the musically and socially liberating sounds popularized by the Hillbilly Cat.

Elvis's recording success inspired a similar exploitation of other young singers who could perform his kind of music. Some, like Bob Luman, were directly inspired by Elvis; others, like Carl Perkins, Johnny Cash, Charlie Rich, and Jerry Lee Lewis, had been waiting in the wings with rocking styles developed independently of Presley. Elvis opened the commercial doors for all of these young singers, many of whom made their recording debuts on the Sun label. Whether they came from the Mississippi Delta or from the Texas Plains, they were generally described as rockabillies because of their alleged fusion of blues and hillbilly music. But again, it would be a gross misinterpretation to view the rockabillies as nothing more than white boys doing black music even if they did "cover" a considerable amount of black songs; more often they just applied their high-energy styles to country music. The term "rockabilly" means just that: hillbilly music with a rocking beat.

Although it occupied only a brief moment in American popular music history, the rockabillies' success marked the first important intrusion made by southern whites into mainstream music. The rockabillies made their southernness known by their accents and dialects, but they also projected a hedonistic, even macho, strain that had always been part of southern working-class culture, the wild devil-may-care abandon that had helped to fling their earlier counterparts and ancestors onto the battlefields of the Civil War (but more likely today to lure them into barroom fights or into stock car races). If W. J. Cash had lived, he might have recognized them as the simple "men-at-the-center" whom he discussed in his 1941 classic, *Mind of the South*—men who felt rather than thought and who embodied, without hypocrisy, both hedonistic and puritanical traits (and, as Jerry Lee Lewis has repeatedly demonstrated, the distance from the honky-tonk to the revival mourner's bench, and back again, is short indeed).

Jack Kirby, in *Media-Made Dixie*, describes country musicians as conveyors of the myth of "the visceral white Southerner," a character who is "languid, innocent of caprice and wisdom in handling money, moonstruck, and often drunk." He would have been more accurate if he had centered his discussion on the rockabillies. The hedonistic strain had always been present in southern rural culture, but seldom had it been so blatantly displayed in the white man's music. Country singers like Jimmie Rodgers, Charlie Poole, Hank Williams, and George Jones had often conveyed the image in their songs about drinking and rambling, and on occasion someone like Prince Albert Hunt, the Texas fiddler who was shot to death outside a Dallas tavern in 1931 by a jealous husband, could even act out the fantasy. Performing styles, though, have rarely been so uninhibited. A singer like Little Jimmie Dickens might bounce around the stage like a whirling dervish, and a Bill Carlisle could amuse an audience with his jumping antics, but no white country singer prior to Elvis and the other rockabillies had ever fused so closely physical action and sexual suggestion.

To argue that Elvis drew upon cultural and musical sources common to the other rockabillies is not to deny his uniqueness. Roy Orbison projected a "cool" image with his black-leather jacket and dark sunglasses; the Everly Brothers and Buddy Holly exuded the boyish innocence of a high school sock hop; Carl Perkins came across as a rustic hep cat; Jerry Lee Lewis was definitely macho, but almost manic, in his appeal. Elvis embodied all of these. And unlike the others, with his appealing combination of vulnerability and aggressive suggestiveness, he brought a frank sexuality to both country and pop music. His pouting leer and heavy-lidded bedroom eyes made him fascinating to many people, but his boyish appeal also evoked the motherly instinct in many of his women fans. His physicality, his crucial contribution to country and popular music, was distasteful to many people, especially to the ministers of his own religious denomination (at least in his early nonestablishment days), but he was careful never to offend public tastes as did, say, Jerry Lee Lewis (that is, no hell-raising in public, no marrying his thirteen-year-old cousin, no outrageous interviews).

For two or three years after 1957, "traditional" country music suffered as a result of the rock and roll revolution. Except for bluegrass music, which has always led an alternative if not underground existence, fiddles almost disappeared from country recordings, and the mainstay of the honky-tonk genre, the electric steel guitar, became even rarer. The "rural" sound was discouraged, and everywhere one encountered a tremendous emphasis on youth, vitality, and modernity. Recording companies, booking agents, and other music promoters began a rather frantic search for talent that, hopefully, could equal Elvis's appeal among American youth. Under intensive prodding older country singers added rock and roll songs to their repertories or, often with pathetic results, adapted their performing styles to the new phenomenon. Even Bill Monroe, the veteran bluegrass star, sped up his version of "Blue Moon of Kentucky" after Elvis hit with the song. The most traditional mountain-oriented bluegrass group, the Stanley Brothers, recorded a rhythm and blues tune, Hank Ballard's "Finger Popping Time," and hard-core honky-tonk singer George Jones recorded a few rock and roll songs under the name of Thumper Jones. There was also a great profusion of singers who, if not fully rock and roll, at least souped up their styles to appeal to young listeners.

Television introduced Elvis to America. Steve Allen's and Ed Sullivan's efforts to tame the young singer merely made him more fascinating and irresistible to millions of Americans. He turned increasingly toward the pop music that had always appealed to him, and he won an audience that lay far beyond the bounds of his native South. He never severed his connections with country music, however. Nashville replaced Memphis as his chief locus of recording, and the vocal backing of gospel quartets and the instrumental support of Floyd Cramer, Chet Atkins, and other session musicians became indispensable and permanent ingredients of his performances. The sound heard on Elvis's recordings, in fact, closely approximated the country-pop compromise that Chet Atkins, ironically, fashioned to preserve country music's viability after the upsurge of rock and roll had sapped its strength.

The rock and roll inundation of country music nevertheless proved to be short-lived, and by the end of the fifties, the mainline country styles were making vigorous comebacks. Led by such entertainers as Merle Haggard, Loretta Lynn, Charley Pride, and Buck Owens, these styles were experiencing a remarkable resurgence by the end of the sixties. Nonetheless, rock and roll left permanent marks on country music. High-powered electronics remained as an enduring facet of country music, and young guitarists who had begun their careers as rock and roll musicians came back into country bands bringing their instrumental licks with them (Waylon Jennings provided dramatic evidence of this in the seventies; virtually any top forty band in our own time exhibits the lingering effects of the revolution wrought by Elvis). Rock and roll songs like "Johnny B. Goode" have repeatedly resurfaced in the repertories of country singers. Disc jockeys who had grown up listening to rock and roll, or who had sometimes been rock and roll musicians, often found employment on country radio stations, especially after 1960 when the number of such stations greatly proliferated. As powerful tastemakers, they did much to alter both the style and audience of country music. The country music industry reacted to the rock and roll threat (and to the recognition that a vast new audience had emerged) by creating a form of music that would be inoffensive to listeners who had not grown up in a southern rural environment or who wanted to forget that they had. The result was a so-called compromise that would supposedly preserve the flavor and ambience of country music while projecting a more urban image. Chet Atkins and the other architects of this country-pop blending, sometimes called the "Nashville Sound," seemed to assume that the "old" country music audience would remain loyal regardless of the changes (they after all had little choice); the "compromise" obviously was designed to attract a new audience.

The rockabillies faded rather quickly from the national consciousness, and rock and roll gave way to an even more hard-driving and defiantly urban form of musical expression: the rock culture that knows no regional identity or bounds. The rockabillies, however, never disappeared from American music; they, and their successors, remained as a fringe of country music. Some, such as Conway Twitty, became very successful mainstream country singers; others, like Jerry Lee Lewis and Waylon Jennings, effectively combined country and rock music in their repertories. Then again, a few, such as Billy Swan and Crash Craddock, adhered closely to the sounds of the fifties. Several singers dressed in costumes reflective of Elvis's flamboyant Las Vegas period, with tight, flared bell-bottom pants (usually white or some bright color) and sequined shirts open to at least the third button, strutting or swaggering around the stage and singing with a great deal of acrobatic vigor: Crash Craddock, Narvel Felts, Joe Stampley, Roy Head, T. G. Sheppard, Ray Griff, Gene Kurtz, Ronnie McDowell, to name only a few. In addition to these successful professional singers, many others too numerous to name (including the host of Elvis imitators) have kept his legacy alive in nightclub performances or at Saturday night barn dances. Their dynamic stage routines, replete with often grotesque displays of leering and bumping-and-grinding, reinforce the faith of an audience who still think that Elvis is king and who enthusiastically welcome any performer who seems reminiscent of him.

In evaluating Elvis's impact on American music, some writers assess him as a conscious rebel who deliberately set out to offend public sensibilities and overthrow both conventional musical tastes and societal standards. Like the motorcycle hellion portrayed by Marlon Brando in the movie *The Wild Ones*, Elvis, in this view, was an indiscriminate rebel against anything that society had to offer (Questioner: "What are you rebelling against?" Brando: "What've you got?). But those who would interpret Elvis as an anarchistic iconoclast merely project their own consciousness upon him, much in the way that ideologues interpret earlier revolutionaries to fit their own political agendas. If Elvis was a revolutionary, he was a mostly unconscious one who distanced himself from the musical Jacobins, that is, the protest singers and the acid rock singers, who came later.

From the time he decked himself out in flamboyant clothing and ducktail hairstyle as a Memphis teenager, to the rather aimless search for commercial material in the Sun studio that led to his first hit record, and on through his fabulous career, Elvis never rejected his origins or his essential southernness. Nor did he reject that larger world from which his family had long been excluded. Rather than thumb his nose at the middle-class mainstream, he actively sought to enter it, as the children of humble origins have inevitably tried to do. He succeeded in his quest but was imprisoned, tightly sheltered from the adoring public that had given him his success. Some would say that his music also became similarly constricted and that his RCA recordings never achieved the vitality and individuality of those early Sun performances.

Although his musical managers tried to blunt it, Elvis's southernness remained an essential and defining aspect of the man. He always adhered to his gospel origins, even if some of the musical energy of his Pentecostal background was dissipated. Elvis was almost a parody of southern courtesy with his deference toward women and older people. By serving unquestioningly in the U.S. Army, and in offering his services to the FBI as an informer against scandalous behavior by rock musicians, he exhibited those stereotypically southern male responses that also surfaced in his love of guns, high-speed automobiles, and karate: the physical, loyal, and thoroughly masculine man. He reportedly viewed the Beatles as bad examples for American youth because of their flaunting deprecation of that which he valued: patriotism and Christian morality. If he ever recognized the English musicians as his cultural offspring, there seems to be little evidence for it. Despite his own indebtedness to black musicians, he never openly questioned the racial values of his region. His fascination with big cars, fine mansions, jewelry, and expensive clothes, which he enjoyed displaying and magnanimously sharing with others, affirmed his endorsement of that capitalistic world that had long been closed to him and his poor white ancestors.

More than twenty years after I first encountered Elvis in that abbreviated Hank Snow concert in Austin, I once again saw Hank in a setting that brought back some of those old memories. In May 1978, I attended the Jimmie Rodgers' Memorial Festival in Meridian, Mississippi, and heard Hank Snow who, thankfully, looked and sounded much as he did twenty years earlier. He received vigorous applause, but the singers who caused pandemonium in the audience were the rockabillies Ray Griff and T. G. Sheppard. Griff, one of the finest songwriters in country music, wore a mod leisure suit with musical notes embroidered upon it, and when he went through his sexy undulations many of the women in the audience squealed the same way the young women in Austin had done for Elvis back in 1956. Since some of them appeared to be in their forties (and older) they may very well have been the same women reliving the fantasies that King Elvis had aroused in them years before.

Apart from the sense of déjà vu that swept over me as I watched the Meridian performances, I was most impressed by the contrasting and seemingly ambivalent strains that fans were willing to accept as *country*. Despite my earlier fears, country music had not died, and its composition at that time seemed flexible and responsive enough to contain both the older (Hank Snow) and the newer (Elvis-derived) entertainers. The tensions I felt at the sensual superimposed upon the traditional made the issues Elvis interjected as alive and controversial as they seemed to be many years ago. The persistence of such contradictory strains indicates the conflicting Saturday night/Sunday morning impulses that have defined and continue to propel country music. Like Elvis himself, the music simultaneously clings to tradition and exhibits its own take on modernity.

Most country singers in the late twentieth and early twenty-first centuries incorporated elements of Elvis and the rockabillies into their performances, not as a conscious imitation but merely as part or a synthesis of sound drawn from all of the musical forms that have been available to them. Like Elvis, they are a part of all they have heard. Most of these musicians would probably be surprised to hear that controversy once swirled around the rockabilly genre, not merely because Elvis's music seems so innocent today, but because his once innovative style has been so thoroughly integrated into today's country music. The influence of the later Elvis, with its patterned and highly choreographed Las Vegas style, can be seen and heard in a host of modern country performers, ranging from Tanya Tucker to Sawyer Brown, Billy Ray Cyrus, and the Oak Ridge Boys. But, ironically, it is the early Elvis—the one who seemed to be destroying traditional country music—that remains most attractive to today's country singers. Buck Owens, for example, along with his indispensable electric guitarist, Don Rich, were hailed in the 1960s as saviors of traditional country music, even though their hard-edged honky-tonk sound received its punch and vigor from an infusion of rockabilly. Owens's most ardent disciple, Dwight Yoakam, has fashioned a similar fusion of sounds, along with an array of sinuous and sexy stage movements, while becoming one of the most successful and outspoken neotraditionalists of our own time. To singers like Yoakam, Marty Stuart, Dale Watson, Rosie Flores, and Travis Tritt, rockabilly is a vital traditional country style that merits preservation.

Elvis certainly did not single-handedly unleash the changes that swept across America in the two decades following his emergence, but to a remarkable degree he became emblematic of America's social transformation. Perceived as a threat in the fifties because he and his music fundamentally endangered the consensual social order of generational, gender, racial, class, and even regional relationships, Elvis and his music truly represented the emerging dominance of youth culture, the growing importance and sexual self-awareness of women, the attractiveness of black culture, the assertiveness of working-class culture, and movement of the southern version of that culture into the national mainstream. Elvis, in short, challenged the very idea of culture that had been supreme in the United States.

Elvis should be remembered and valued for many reasons, not the least being his role in the redefinition of culture in our country. Because of him we may have inched a bit closer toward an appreciation of the varied strands and multicolored hues that brighten our cultural tapestry. And we may have come closer to an understanding that our popular culture is not a national embarrassment, but one of America's great contributions to the world. I would like to think that Elvis also contributed to the dissipation of one of America's most enduring prejudices, that directed against the southern white working class. He and the other rockabillies introduced their versions of culture, and their "good time" vision of life, to a receptive world at a time when only bigots and racists seemed to dominate the mental landscape of the South. Along with Fats Domino, Little Richard, Ray Charles, and other southern exponents of rhythm and blues, they not only enriched the music of the world, they also reminded us, at a time of growing racial polarities, of the affinities of southern white and black culture.

CHAPTER 14

THE RURAL SOUTH
MOVES NORTH
Country Music since World War II

This essay was first published in *The Rural South since World War II* (1998), edited by R. Douglas Hurt. The dates and details mentioned in this essay have not been substantially changed since it was first written. A careful revision and updating might find many of my conclusions severely challenged. The suburbanization of America has wrought significant changes in the identity and sound of the music that I loved. The reader can decide whether the music now heard on Top Forty country radio merits the description of "country" or, indeed, whether it deserves to be listened to or not.

Although the endnotes cover most of the important sources dealing with the history of the South and country music during this period, a few more recent books merit inclusion: James Noble Gregory, *The Southern Diaspora: How the Great Migration of Black and White Southerners Transformed America* (Chapel Hill: University of North Carolina Press, 2005); Joel Williamson, *Elvis Presley: A Southern Life* (New York: Oxford University Press, 2014); Chris Willman, *Rednecks and Bluenecks: The Politics of Country Music* (New York: New Press, 2005); and Bill C. Malone, *Don't Get Above Your Raisin': Country Music and the Southern Working Class* (Urbana: University of Illinois Press, 2006).

IN THE FIFTY YEARS FOLLOWING THE END OF WORLD WAR II, MUSICAL STYLES BORN IN THE SOUTH—gospel (black and white), blues, rhythm and blues, country, Cajun, to name only a few—moved into the nation's musical mainstream. While shaping the musical contours of the nation, southern styles have also become some of America's most valuable cultural exports. Although inseparable from the historic poverty, discrimination, and racial injustice of the South, and surviving as living testaments of the abilities of poor people to sustain themselves and to assert their cultural worth, these styles did not flourish commercially until the time of World War II.

The form of music that has best represented the ever-changing social topography of the South—the music that is now called "country"—was not so described until about 1948. The search for an appropriate label reflected the commercial maturation of the genre and the desire among many musicians to abandon the term "hillbilly" that had often been used to describe it. *Country*, however, obscured the fact that the music by 1948 was sustained by people who lived in towns and cities and was disseminated among them by urban forms of communication. The music had begun its commercial evolution in the 1920s at a time of rapid urban growth and had always owed its existence to a peculiarly American blending of urban technology and rural folkways. The massive migration of rural southerners in the 1940s to cities in the South and throughout the nation contributed both to the commercial burgeoning of this music and to its nationalization. Country music endured as the major voice of people who longed nostalgically for a disappearing way of life and who were struggling to adjust to urban industrial life.[1]

Country music in the immediate postwar years conveyed a distinctly regional and rural flavor. Country musicians, of course, could be found throughout North America, and a few of them, such as the Canadian-born Hank Snow and Bob Nolan, were among the best-loved entertainers in the United States. Nevertheless, most of the singers and musicians who attained national public visibility and who dominated the jukeboxes and popularity charts came overwhelmingly from the South. The music as a whole conveyed a strong southern flavor in the accents and dialects of its performers and in the themes of its songs. Even the most sophisticated of the country singers could scarcely avoid an identification with the rural southern imagery shared by their fans, nor could they easily avoid the performance of songs that embodied such symbolism. Eddy Arnold, for example, the predominant country singer of the mid-1940s, whose smooth style and receptivity to pop innovations soon carried him into nightclubs and on to the leading network radio and television series of the era, called himself the "Tennessee Plowboy." His first widely circulated song, recorded in March 1945, "Mommy, Please Stay Home with Me," was the story of a child who died while his mother was out drinking at a party. This was the kind of song that had been deeply loved by traditional country music fans, but it was far removed from the songs with which Arnold eventually became identified.[2]

Although most country musicians came from rural southern homes, they and their audience should more properly be described as working people with middle-class aspirations. Although many of the musicians had grown up on farms and could recall milking cows or picking cotton, most had spent their young adult lives in military service or as cotton mill workers, coal miners, truck drivers, automobile mechanics, beauticians, or workers in some other blue-collar occupation. The widespread fame attained by a few country entertainers encouraged young amateurs to try their hands at the music business. For example, the commercial success attained in the late 1920s by Jimmie Rodgers, the "Singing Brakeman" from Mississippi who moved from railroad work to a recording career with RCA Victor, and in the 1930s by Gene Autry, the Oklahoma railroad telegrapher who became the first and most famous Hollywood Singing Cowboy, suggested not only that music could be an escape from manual labor but that it could also be a source of material wealth and comfort. Few musicians, though, could free themselves from wage labor (or "day jobs," as such work is described by country musicians), so most of them performed music at night or on weekends and hoped that a successful record or radio show would launch them into a full-time career in entertainment.[3]

As working people from rural backgrounds who nevertheless yearned for acceptance in middle-class urban America, country musicians were understandably ambivalent about themselves, the stage personas they hoped to convey, and the success they hoped to attain. Few country entertainers stressed their blue-collar backgrounds in their stage presentations or in their promotional material; instead, they identified most often with a place—a county, state, region, or local landmark. Even Jimmie Rodgers, who did exploit his railroad experiences, stressed the glamorous, rambling aspects of railroading and not the labor that dominated it. He and his promoters emphasized his Mississippi origins as often as his railroading background. Neither the musicians nor their promoters (radio and recording executives, movie producers, booking agents, advertisers) could be certain what the mood of the American public would be at any given moment or what image would be the most effective moneymaker. Should the musicians wax nostalgic about their presumed rural or mountain pasts and dress accordingly in overalls, sunbonnets, and gingham dresses? The public mood certainly inspired such a posture from time to time. Even in the big northern city of Chicago, where the WLS National Barn Dance played to capacity audiences each Saturday night at the Eighth Street Theatre, the hunger for Kentucky Mountain Boys, Arkansas Woodchoppers, and Cumberland Mountain Folk seemed to be insatiable. The fascination with rube hillbillies, which had been a staple in American entertainment long before country music's commercial birth, was also apparent all over America, and most country musicians showed no hesitation in exploiting that comic depiction of their culture for commercial purposes.[4]

Some early performers (but usually not their promoters) felt that success would be more attainable and more widespread if they abandoned the hillbilly image for a more urbane persona combined with a "progressive" music approach. Texas fiddler and bandleader Bob Wills had already proved in the late 1930s that large audiences could be won through the fusion of jazz and country styles, and Gene Autry had seen his audiences grow larger when he abandoned his early nasal hillbilly sound and replaced it with the smooth, mellifluous tones of the crooner. During the war, though, the Tennessee Mountain Boy, Roy Acuff, had demonstrated that a huge audience could be won by a musical style suggesting the image and morality of rural Appalachia. Most country performers, however, did not adopt the tradition-oriented and backwoods flavor of the mountains. To a remarkable degree, they instead embraced the romantic, liberating ideal of the cowboy, and from the Canadian Maritime Provinces to California, from the West Virginia hills to the Texas plains, most country entertainers adopted some semblance of cowboy attire and often gave themselves a western moniker. Consequently, Eddy Arnold could call himself the "Tennessee Plowboy" while wearing cowboy stage garb and using "Cattle Call" as his theme song, and Bob Wills could successfully project the persona of a prosperous rancher while performing a jazz-inflected style of rural music that had nothing to do with cowboys or the West.[5]

Whatever the style or image, country music entered its first great phase of national and international expansion in the years following World War II. As American popular culture invaded the world after the war, country music prospered as an integral ingredient of that invasion. The Armed Forces Radio Network introduced the music to Europeans during the occupation period, and American servicemen carried elements of the music all over the world (one of them, Marshall Louis "Grandpa" Jones, sang with his army buddies in a band called the Munich Mountaineers). At home, many factors fueled the music's postwar boom: the end of rationing and war-imposed scarcity, the prosperity that accompanied full employment, a sense of rising expectations, the movement to the cities, and the maturing sophistication of the American media and advertising complex that skillfully engineered a revolution in consumer purchasing. The recording industry returned to vigorous life, and such older companies as Columbia, RCA Victor, and Decca were joined by a host of newer and smaller labels that aggressively recorded grassroots forms like hillbilly, Cajun, gospel, and rhythm and blues and made them available to the American public. Close to four hundred thousand coin-operated automatic music machines, known as jukeboxes, provided a powerful market for the record industry, while also providing an inexpensive form of entertainment for thousands of dance halls, cafes, bowling alleys, and other public centers of amusement. The beautifully decorated jukebox, with its bright chrome-and-plastic exterior, neon illumination, and openly displayed record-changing mechanisms became not only a central focus for musical and social experience but also a ready reminder to displaced country folk of American capitalistic ingenuity and success in the postwar era. In many respects, too, the jukebox became a vehicle for and a symbol of country music's dramatic commercial surge during those years.[6]

Records, of course, also became standard fare for radio stations throughout the nation, as disc jockeys steadily replaced the older forms of broadcast programming. Despite the growing allure of "canned music" on radio, live broadcasting continued to be common throughout the United States on the powerful fifty-thousand-watt, clear-channel stations and on the hosts of smaller stations that had only limited coverage. Hillbilly acts appeared on early morning and noontime shows and on Saturday night variety shows that were described variously by such evocatively nostalgic names as barn dances, hoedowns, jamborees, shindigs, or frolics. One of the oldest of these shows, the Grand Ole Opry, obtained network affiliation on NBC in 1939 and by the early 1950s was well on the way toward making Nashville the premier city of country music in the United States. Nashville's ascendancy was by no means assured, however, in the years immediately following the war. Other "barn dances" competed favorably in such cities as Shreveport, where the Louisiana Hayride held sway; Dallas, the home of the Big D Jamboree; Knoxville, the locus of the Mid-Day-Merry-Go-Round; Atlanta, the site of the Cross Roads Follies; and Wheeling (West Virginia), the location of the Wheeling Jamboree.

All of these shows attracted multitudes of adoring and faithful fans, but in some ways, the most instructive experience exhibited by a country radio show was that of the Renfro Valley Barn Dance. Located about sixty miles southeast of Lexington, Kentucky, the Renfro Valley show lay in a little community that did not exist until after 1939, when John Lair began broadcasting his homespun shows from a big barn that was newly constructed near his old home place. Lair had preserved his affection for the area during his several years as staff member and music librarian at WLS in Chicago. The throngs who came to the barn dance each Saturday night or who heard the broadcasts of that show and the Sunday Morning Gathering were engaged, like Lair, in a trip down memory lane to a rural home that no longer existed or that, in some cases, had never been more than an imaginative construct.[7]

As country music became a national phenomenon with a remarkable commercial appeal, it continued to exhibit its southernness and working-class identity. The music that prevailed from roughly 1945 to 1955 was as transitional in nature as the society that sustained it. Rural southerners were changing their residences and occupations but were not so quickly abandoning their folkways. The crowds who attended the Renfro Valley Barn Dance or the Grand Ole Opry or who otherwise demonstrated their affection for country music did so for a wide variety of reasons. Some of them had no actual experience with rural life but nevertheless identified with musical forms they believed were representative of an older America. More often, though, they were transplanted rural people who were trying to come to terms with lives now spent permanently in cities. Styles of adjustment varied, of course, depending on such variables as the size of the place to which they moved, age, gender, income, education, and race. Some fled the land as if it were a curse and enthusiastically embraced the city and its promises. Others abandoned rural life reluctantly, while more than a few moved with the expectation that urban residence would be only temporary. Women probably made the transition to urban life more easily and willingly than men, welcoming the innovations that made life more bearable. Children also adjusted in varying ways, but ultimately, they became the most willing converts to urban society.[8]

Dramatic changes in perceptions and worldviews certainly did not occur immediately. In the immediate postwar years, country entertainers, promoters, and fans shared an unspoken, and probably unconscious, assumption that the traditional social relationships that had prevailed in society and were endorsed in the music would endure. Material conditions could be dramatically altered and improved, it was believed, without an alteration of the gender, racial, generational, class, and regional relationships that had long defined American society. Traditional hierarchies, however, had been undermined during the war and were weakened further by the prosperity and accelerated social changes that came in the late 1940s and early 1950s. Ultimately, the consumer revolution did the most to transform an already fragile social structure. While promising "things" to people at an unprecedented volume and rate, it obscured the presence of class in American life, denied the need for structural change in capitalism, accentuated embarrassment about rural origins, and encouraged (but did not easily create) homogeneity in American society. Country music could not help but be dramatically transformed by such changes, as money flowed into the hands of music purchasers and as women, young people, and African Americans became more assertive of their rights and needs.[9]

It is difficult to pinpoint precisely the moment when country music crossed the threshold into modernity. Well into the age of television, country musicians were still appearing live on early morning radio shows, hawking their picture-songbooks, and making strings of one-night stands on the so-called kerosene circuit in school auditoriums, American Legion halls, movie theaters, churches, and tents. No show was complete without

Bob McCoy and Ernest Tubb and band on stage at Carnegie Hall,
New York, September 18–19, 1947. Country music had truly gone "uptown."
Photograph courtesy the Music Division, Library of Congress,
Washington, D.C. (LC-GLB23-0875 DLC)

the performance of a hoedown fiddle tune, one or more religious songs, a moralistic recitation, a comedy routine presented by a comedian in baggy pants, floppy hat, and blacked-out teeth, and perhaps a buck-and-wing dance. Country shows were a blend of ingredients that came from virtually every rural music performance idiom of the nineteenth century: minstrel theater, medicine show, circus, religious camp meeting, and tent vaudeville. Some shows, such as those presented by Roy Acuff, the Bailes Brothers, the Louvin Brothers, Molly O'Day and the Cumberland Mountain Folk, and Brother Claude Ely were almost evangelistic in their use of religious material. At the other extreme, a Grand Ole Opry duo called Jamup and Honey performed in blackface in a tent show that traveled through the South until the late 1940s. Fans and performers enjoyed a close relationship during these years that was never again achieved in country music's later history. Bill Monroe, for example, sometimes scheduled baseball games between his own team (composed partially of his own musicians) and teams assembled in the towns where his Blue Grass Boys made music. The Bailes Brothers were not unique in often accepting invitations to eat dinner in the homes of fans who lived in the small towns of western Louisiana, eastern Texas, and southern Arkansas where they often performed.[10]

Although radio programming and musical recording became increasingly uniform, mechanized, and impersonal in the 1950s, disc jockeys with highly personal styles and contrived hayseed demeanors remained common on large and small stations alike. On the powerful Mexican border station XERF, announcer Paul Kallinger, who called himself "your good neighbor along the way," won the confidence of his listeners with down-home charm and folksy patter. Kallinger made sophisticated use of the airwaves, and his shrewd understanding of his listeners sold country music to a national audience while also marketing with great skill the baby chicks, laxatives, and chill tonics of his sponsors. Elsewhere, other DJs built close relationships with fans by reading their cards and letters and by playing requests from listeners, and with performers by interviewing them on their programs. It was not uncommon for a big-name performer like Red Foley to drop by a tiny station in Brookhaven, Mississippi, or for a complete unknown to visit a station and succeed in having his self-produced record played on the daily broadcast. Because of their intimate relationships with fans and performers, disc jockeys often acted as successful booking agents. Elvis Presley, for example, won his first loyal coterie of fans in East Texas through the active booking of DJ Tom Perryman of KSIJ in tiny Gladewater, Texas. Presley was still playing such one-night stands throughout the South as late as 1956 while his manager, Colonel Tom Parker, hawked the star's photographs outside in time-tested carnival fashion.[11]

The music heard in the immediate postwar era also illustrated the transitional nature of country music and its audience. Jazz, blues, and pop sounds often intruded into the music of country performers, but old-time fiddle breakdowns, novelty songs of minstrel parentage, ancient ballads, love songs, and gospel songs from paperback hymnals appeared with great frequency in the repertoires of such performers as the Blue Sky Boys, Grandpa Jones, and Mainer's Mountaineers. Roy Acuff still sang "Wabash Cannon Ball" and "Precious Jewel" each Saturday night on the Grand Ole Opry, and country gospel singers still spoke to their listeners in stark, fundamentalist terms about declining morals, a dying world, and the imminent Second Coming of Christ. Nowhere do we find better examples of the divided thinking of that postwar southern generation that, only freshly uprooted from its rural past, was reaching out to embrace the material fruits of the new society while still not sure that it would all last, than in such songs as "This World Can't Stand Long," "Whiskey Is the Devil (in Liquid Form)," "The Drunken Driver," "They Locked God outside the Iron Curtain," "Lord Give Me a Cabin in Glory Land," and an extensive body of songs that commented on the atomic bomb as an agent of God's wrath and a sign of the soon coming end of the world.[12]

Gradually, though, visions of cabins in glory land gave way to dreams of mansions in heaven and here on earth. An abundant society challenged the fatalistic assumptions of the past, the burgeoning consumer economy weakened the once deeply held conviction of limits, and the city promised opportunities that had never been available in the older rural-village society. Understandably, then, country music continued to reflect the simultaneous impulses of tradition and innovation exhibited in the larger society.[13]

Hank Williams reigned as the king of country music during those first great prosperous years in the early 1950s. His death on January 1, 1953, on first impression, might appear to have been a demarcation point in country music history, a symbol of the similar demise, or coming demise, of the older southern rural society and the music that reflected it. On closer examination, however, Hank's career is best understood as an embodiment of the tensions and contradictions found in country music and as both the fulfillment of traditional country music and the precursor of the modernization that came with great rapidity after his death. Hank was a country boy but never a farmer, who came of age in south Alabama during the unsettling years of World War II. He named his band the Drifting Cowboys, although neither he nor they ever rode the range or sang its rhythms. His intense vocal style rang with the inflections and drawl of the Deep South and was as strongly rooted in the singing of the rural Baptists of his boyhood church as in any other source. Hank's songs ran the gamut from the blues to gospel, and his stage shows included every type of material with which rural southerners were familiar: moralistic recitations, corny humor, fiddle tunes, love songs (both tragic and happy), blues tunes, and sacred songs.[14]

The overall sound and ambience of Hank Williams's music, however, suggested the influence of the country honky-tonks, the bars where strong drink, dancing, noise, and the hints of violence and illicit sex combined to spawn a style of music that seemed consonant with southerners' evolution from rural to urban blue-collar culture. The honky-tonk was a kind of halfway house between rural and urban life. For some people it provided nothing more than a temporary release from the anxieties of work and daily responsibilities. For others it was an introduction to a world that seemed far more dangerous and sordid than the older rural society. The old-time frolic of rural America (a dance held in rural homes) had virtually disappeared, so many working people sought the honky-tonk as an urban equivalent of that older social diversion. "Honky-tonking" (having a good time on Saturday night and perhaps going to more than one dance hall during the night) became a pastime that provided enjoyment for dancers and listeners while also shaping the tone and sound of country music. In this atmosphere, rustic or pastoral themes became obsolescent—and the beat and volume of country instrumentation changed to accommodate the needs of dancers. Obviously necessary in such an environment, the electric guitar was well on the way to becoming the dominant instrument of country music.[15]

Hank's rural and compelling vocal sound and his charismatic stage presence made him the leading performer of country music in the early 1950s. His beautifully crafted compositions such as "Honky Tonking," "Your Cheating Heart," "Cold, Cold Heart," and "I'm So Lonesome I Could Cry" moved across the parameters of song genre and audience taste into the repertoire of such pop musicians as Tony Bennett and Rosemary Clooney. Country singers and songwriters never abandoned the dream of having their songs adopted by pop singers or of having their own recordings accepted by the large pop audience. Hank's death at the age of twenty-nine contributed to the creation of the aura of romance that now surrounds his memory, while also suggesting several presumed legacies that later musicians and fans have freely exploited. His talented son, Hank Jr., has sought to legitimize his own highly publicized rebellion against musical or societal conventions by describing his father as the original country music "outlaw." Other musicians try to emulate the lifestyle of the great country singer, by living fast, loving hard, and dying young. Still others refer to him as an early rockabilly—a precursor of Elvis Presley—and point to his recording of a few songs such as "Rootie Tootie," a country boogie tune, as evidence. A few allude to the pop success enjoyed by some of Hank's songs and speculate that not only would he have been pleased with the country-pop style of music that emerged in the 1960s but would also have been a willing participant in the making of such music. An even larger number of fans believe contrarily that, if Hank had lived, he would have remained faithful to his traditional roots and would have resisted the tide of pop homogenization.[16]

Less than one year after Hank Williams died, another southern country boy, Elvis Aaron Presley, unleashed a revolution that did more than simply lure thousands of youth away from traditional country music; it changed the face of American music. Elvis's early success—before television made him a pop icon of international dimensions—was rooted in the same demographic transformations that subtly changed Hank Williams's music and made country music a national phenomenon. Like other southern working-class youth of his age, Elvis felt the stirrings of change and embraced the promise of the better life that had eluded his parents. His family's move to Memphis in 1948, from his birthplace in Tupelo, Mississippi, certainly did not remove them from the necessity of dealing with an uncertain hardscrabble life. In Memphis, however, Elvis saw glimpses of a brighter and more prosperous existence. Elvis was a child of popular culture and a part of all that he saw and heard. The movies, the hot-rod culture, all forms of popular music, including the country and gospel sounds loved by his parents, and ultimately, television, all bound him to other young people of his age while also providing arenas for a quiet rebellion against the world of his parents. Not untypically, Elvis sought both distinctiveness and conformity. From his parents' lives, if not from their reassuring words, he probably received the message that typified a working-class southern view: that one should be aware of limits in this life. In contrast, the American consumer culture defined the pursuit of happiness as the acquisition of material goods and promised liberation and fulfillment in such a quest.[17]

The story of Elvis's emergence as a professional singer in July 1954 and his consequent ascent to international stardom is too well known to be repeated here. But his swift rise to fame should not obscure his role in country music history. His career and musical style are as deeply rooted in southern working-class history as are those of Hank Williams, and his effects on country music may ultimately be seen as having been far more profound than the influence exerted by the young Alabama singer. Hank had opened up new windows of opportunity for aspiring country singers, and he had attracted younger audiences to country music. But though he could sometimes sing with abandon and delight his listeners with songs of honky-tonking, rambling, and hedonistic glee, Hank Williams could never fully escape the fatalistic vision of his rural forebears or his own sense of personal foreboding. The tragic dimensions of Hank's lifestyle colored both the lyrics and style of his music. Greil Marcus called him a "poet of limits, fear, and failure" and said that "he went as deeply into one dimension of the country world as anyone could, gave it beauty, gave it dignity."[18]

Although Elvis revolutionized American music, no revolution was ever begun so innocently. Early interviews reveal a young man who seemed genuinely surprised, but delighted, at the almost delirious enthusiasm evoked by his music. Probably neither Elvis nor his young female fans fully understood the sexual dimension of their relationship or the degree to which such conduct challenged the social orthodoxy of the South. Although Elvis skillfully exploited the relationship and, consequently, enjoyed extraordinary commercial success, he never intended to defy his parents' culture or the larger one to which he aspired.[19]

Elvis was a part of, and prophet to, the youth community that emerged after World War II. Although this community did much to fuel the growth of the modern consumer economy, its rise and influence were disquieting to the nation's moral arbiters and cultural custodians. They resented Elvis's role as the first powerful musical representative of the youth culture. Not only did his music and stage act suggest a loosening of traditional moral standards but he also represented and encouraged a new assertiveness among young people, African Americans, women, and working-class southerners. As a white southerner of blue-collar parentage who successfully fused elements of black and white music, Elvis seemed to be redefining American culture in an alarming way.

The young southern men and women who emulated Elvis when they took up guitars and pursued musical careers or who did so through the encouragement of their record companies have usually been described as rockabillies. Like Elvis, most of them adapted black or black-sounding music to country string instruments or otherwise made their music palatable to youthful audiences by blending the traditions of African American and white country music. Although a few women, such as Wanda Jackson, Charlene Arthur, Janis Martin, and Rose Maddox, could rock with the best of the singers, rockabilly was essentially a musical genre performed by white men, and it provided an outlet for impulses that were embedded deeply in the culture of the working-class South. Carl Perkins, Jerry Lee Lewis, Charlie Rich, Gene Vincent, Johnny Cash, Bob Luman, Roy Orbison, Buddy Holly, the Everly Brothers, and a host of other performers projected aggressive, sexually tinged styles that captured not only the modern cravings of youth everywhere but also the hedonism that too often served as a legitimization of manhood in the rural South. It is difficult to accept the assertion that their traits in any way "expressed contempt for the American dream," but Stanley Booth is otherwise right on target when he compares the young southern workingmen of Elvis's generation with the rebels of 1861: "You even see their sullen faces, with a toughness lanky enough to just miss being delicate, looking back at you out of old photographs of the Confederate Army."

For the most part, however, the rockabillies' aggressiveness was contained in their music, and as was true of other "Good Old Boys" in the South, a strong streak of religious guilt infused their character and value system. Few singers so strongly embodied the contest between piety and hedonism (with the latter usually winning) as did Jerry Lee Lewis, the extraordinarily talented singer and pianist from Ferriday, Louisiana, but virtually all of the rockabilly men and women gravitated as easily toward the church as toward the dance hall. If their dress, hairstyles, demeanor, and musical styles often seemed menacing to polite, middle-class society, the rockabillies nevertheless were not rebelling against the larger society that had always excluded them. And for a brief moment in American history, these singers carried the music of the working-class South into the mainstream of American life.[20]

No facet of American popular music remained unaffected by the rock and roll revolution. The style of music performed by such singers as Bing

Crosby, Frank Sinatra, Perry Como, and Jo Stafford lost its dominance. By 1957 Elvis's impact on traditional country music seemed equally devastating. Except for an occasional song, such as the versions of "Crazy Arms" and "Fraulein" recorded respectively by Ray Price and Bobby Helms, fiddles and steel guitars virtually disappeared from the music heard on jukeboxes and radio shows and from the industry popularity charts. In the quest for a new Elvis, or for someone who could command the same popularity among young people, the record companies emphasized youth and sex appeal as much as talent. Older performers, male and female, had once appeared frequently in country music; it now seemed inconceivable that someone like Uncle Dave Macon, who had first recorded when he was fifty-six years old, could ever again obtain a recording contract. By the end of the 1950s, it also seemed doubtful that any singer could thrive commercially unless he or she demonstrated the ability to rock. Consequently, almost every singer, including such hard-core honky-tonkers as George Jones, recorded a few songs that contained the rollicking beat of rockabilly.[21]

Elvis and the rockabillies evoked a variety of responses among country musicians, most of which have had permanent consequences. Many fans and performers of traditional country music bitterly opposed the rockabilly genre, perceiving it as a threat to both conventional morality and musical purity, but elements of the style nevertheless moved into country music and have remained there ever since. Many former rockabilly musicians and fans eventually became sidemen or singers in country bands, disc jockeys on country radio stations, or journalists for country music publications. Country music became a haven for aging or failed rockabilly singers, and a few of them, such as Jerry Lee Lewis and Conway Twitty, became major country entertainers. More interesting, though, were the even younger musicians and singers such as Gary Stewart, Tanya Tucker, Marty Stuart, Travis Tritt, Dwight Yoakam, and Dale Watson who came to country music long after the exciting period surrounding Elvis's Sun sessions and for whom rockabilly conveyed no hint of scandal or controversy. They were too young to have heard preachers denounce Elvis from their pulpits or to have read the condescending or outraged remarks of establishment critics. To these singers, rockabilly was nothing more than a "traditional" form of country music.[22]

The country music industry initially responded to the rock and roll threat by trying to produce a body of music that would preserve a country ambience while employing pop instrumental sounds and group vocal backing. Sometimes described as the "Nashville Sound" because it was engineered in that city by producers such as Chet Atkins and crafted by a small group of session musicians there, or as "country-pop" because of its fusion of down-home informality and urbane smoothness, the style seemed designed for people who cared for neither rock and roll nor the older varieties of country music. With the fiddle and steel guitar temporarily abandoned and vocal groups supplying background support for the featured singers, the architects of country-pop produced a body of music that was politically and stylistically middle-of-the-road. Ironically, this music sounded much like that performed by Elvis Presley after he moved to RCA in the late 1950s. The country-pop "compromise," as it was also described, won great commercial success for the record companies that produced it, while also solidifying Nashville's reputation as "Music City, U.S.A." At its best, country-pop resulted in the superb music of such singers as Jim Reeves and Patsy Cline. At its worst, it produced a bland, predictable, and over-stylized product that was neither good nor country.[23]

While the country music industry made its various accommodations with rock and roll and the youth market, certain country performers made their own adjustments, often oblivious to market considerations and with little conscious effort either to revive or to alter traditional musical forms. They merely made the music they wanted to make. We have learned to describe their styles as "traditional," but in some cases their contributions were intensely innovative, and in every case their music reflected all of the broad currents of sound that swirled around them in modern America. Throughout the rock and roll period and during the country-pop phase that followed, strongly individualistic singers and musicians managed to create or preserve styles that differed markedly from the sounds heard on Top Forty radio. The quintessential honky-tonk singer George Jones preserved his hard-edged, soulful vocal style through every successive change and instrumental variation in country music. Another veteran of the Texas honky-tonk scene, Ray Price, competed favorably with the country-pop singers by combining his smoky tenor voice with a highly electrified instrumental sound that fused country fiddling and pedal steel guitar phrasing with the shuffle beat of jazz. A few years later, a transplanted Texan named Alvis Edgar "Buck" Owens took the style popularized by Price, added the vigorous beat of rockabilly, and made his own name and Bakersfield, California (where he established a mini-empire), synonymous with that of honky-tonk revivalism.[24]

Long before the modern honky-tonkers began making their vital innovations and well before Elvis launched his revolution, Bill Monroe from Rosine, Kentucky, had been building his own staunchly individualistic style of country music. Since 1939, he had been a fixture on the Grand Ole Opry with a band called the Blue Grass Boys, named in honor of his home state of Kentucky. This was a string band with a difference—the sky-high tenor of Monroe and a hard-driving ensemble instrumental sound powered by his blues-inflected mandolin playing. Exhibiting the influence of Jimmie Rodgers, black blues, gospel, minstrel, and old-time string band music, Monroe clung resolutely to the acoustic sound throughout the 1940s and 1950s when almost everyone else was adopting electrified instruments. He and his music were already virtually sui generis when in 1944 and 1945 guitarist Lester Flatt and banjoist Earl Scruggs joined the Blue Grass Boys. Flatt's supple singing and guitar backup style were widely copied, while Scrugg's sensational syncopated, three-finger banjo style made the Blue Grass Boys even more distinctive and attracted a growing legion of fans all over the nation. This was the band the young Elvis Presley heard and from whom he borrowed "Blue Moon of Kentucky."[25]

By the end of the 1950s, the term "bluegrass" was being attached to any band whose musicians had once played with Monroe or whose sound resembled that of Monroe's seminal band. Preserving the acoustic sound, singing in the high-lonesome style of the backwoods, and featuring old or old-sounding songs, the proliferating bluegrass style was soon perceived as the most "traditional" subgenre of country music. But bluegrass dates from as recently as the mid-1940s, and one need only compare the bluegrass version of a song with its original hillbilly counterpart (e.g., Monroe's and Charlie Poole's versions of "White House Blues") to discern how much bluegrass music diverged from earlier country styles. It is no wonder that Monroe did not seem particularly displeased in 1954 when Elvis recorded his supercharged and radically altered version of "Blue Moon of Kentucky." After all, Monroe had also tampered with older hillbilly songs when he forged his own dynamic sound.[26]

Whatever Monroe's motives may have been, the musical style that he and the Blue Grass Boys created became a retreat for old-time country music fans and musicians. It must have been surprising to Monroe, Flatt, Scruggs, and other pioneer bluegrass performers to learn that their fans did not live solely in the towns and hamlets of the South where the early bands played or where their radio broadcasts reached. Bluegrass music also touched the lives of young people in other parts of the nation who were attracted by the musicianship they heard or by the mistaken belief that bluegrass was a traditional Appalachian form of musical expression. By the end of the 1950s, the style was being heard on college campuses and in folk clubs and parks well outside the South, and as early as 1957 bluegrass began to spawn "progressive" offshoots when a group of young musicians in Washington, D.C., the Country Gentlemen, extended the repertoire of bluegrass into the realms of jazz, blues, pop, rock and roll, and urban folk music.[27]

Bluegrass profited commercially from its association with the urban folk music revival of the late 1950s and early 1960s. Folk music had made inroads into the North, especially New York City, as early as the 1930s when such southern rural singers as Woody Guthrie, Leadbelly, and Aunt Molly Jackson captured the hearts of young, socially conscious intellectuals and singers such as Pete Seeger and Cisco Houston. Periodically, self-styled folksingers like Burl Ives, the Weavers, and Harry Belafonte made the nation conscious of ballads and folk songs, but no flurry of interest came close to equaling that which followed the emergence of the Kingston Trio in 1958 and their widely popular recording of an old North Carolina murder ballad, "Tom Dooley."[28]

The Trio's performance of "Tom Dooley" was essentially a smooth, pop interpretation of traditional material, and the song reached the number one position on the pop music charts. It generated a national enthusiasm for folk and folk-like material, most of it performed by young singers who had no experience with the traditions about which they sang. The folk revival, as it was soon called, won adherents in every segment of society and was particularly strong on college campuses around the nation. To most singers and fans, folk music was an innocent diversion that provided pleasure and little intellectual absorption. A small number of people, though, both in and outside of academia, soon became dissatisfied with the poppish and often sanitized interpretations of folk songs heard on radios and jukeboxes, and they began searching for both authentic representations and sources of such music. Above all, they yearned for faithful re-creation of the styles of older musical forms.

Earlier, in 1952, the prolific West Coast collector, Harry Smith, had persuaded Moe Asch and the Folkways label in New York City to release a large sampling of the 78 rpm records that he collected through the years. The result was a boxed collection of six LPs called *The Anthology of American Folk Music*, consisting of blues, hillbilly, Cajun, gospel, cowboy, and other southern grassroots songs originally recorded commercially in the 1920s and 1930s. For many young Americans, who usually discovered the collection in college or public libraries, the *Anthology* was their first introduction to the recorded music of the grassroots South. Distributed by the prestigious Folkways label and described as "folk" music, the songs reached an audience that otherwise would have had no contact with them. The term "folk" lent the music respectability among educated listeners who otherwise might have rejected music described as "hillbilly" or "country."[29]

The circulation of the *Anthology* and the burgeoning of the folk revival had enormous consequences for country music. The revival did not simply provide a forum for bluegrass musicians and a consequent entrée to a national audience; it also contributed directly to a renewed interest in the roots of country music. Mainstream country songwriters began dabbling with story songs about real or pseudo-historical events, and a few singers, such as Johnny Cash, became active on the folk revival circuit. Cash began building a relationship with young non-country fans that surpasses that of any other country singer and lasts until this day.[30]

More important, perhaps, were the musicians who styled themselves as folksingers and who performed songs from the repertoires of Uncle Dave Macon, the Carter Family, Charlie Poole, and other musicians featured in the *Anthology*. Spurred by the *Anthology*, musicians, fans, collectors, and scholars began dipping into other recorded collections while also trying to persuade the recording industry to release such material from its vaults. If it was exciting to hear this music for the first time, it was even more exhilarating to learn that some of these performers were still alive. Buell Kazee, Mississippi John Hurt, Maybelle Carter, Tom Ashley, Dock Boggs, and other pioneer hillbillies and blues singers were rediscovered and introduced to revival audiences throughout the country. The search for these performers had other unexpected but fortuitous consequences. While looking for Tom Ashley, a banjo player and singer from Tennessee, two northern enthusiasts, Ralph Rinzler and Eugune Earle, found Arthel "Doc" Watson, a young blind musician from Deep Gap, North Carolina, whose extraordinary talents as a singer and guitarist have dazzled audiences ever since.[31]

Country music survived not only the emergence of rock and roll and the often agonizing readjustments of the late 1950s; it evolved in the succeeding decades as a force of great economic power. Some purists, of course, have argued that country music died with Hank Williams or that it did not survive the movement to the cities. The insistence that country music still lives is not merely an acknowledgment that a body of music continues to be commercially marketed under such a title but also an indication of the organic evolution of the music and of its intimate relationship to the lives of an evolving southern working-class culture.[32]

It is not easy, however, to generalize about a body of music whose dimensions have become so vast and whose audience now resides in every corner of the globe. On one hand, country music has become an industry whose leaders speak of producing a "product" for a mass market. Their goal is a commodity shorn of regional identification and class connotations that will appeal to the broadest spectrum of listeners and move readily across the barriers that supposedly separate musical categories. This quest for new audiences has been accompanied by the movement into country music of performers who have had no experience with southern, rural, or working-class life. Country music now embraces pop has-beens, former rock and roll stars, and alumni of the folk revival, therefore adding new dimensions while simultaneously making it a genre much more difficult to define.[33]

On the other hand, neither industry leaders nor entertainers could always accurately gauge public tastes or determine what music would sell. The homogenized sound of country-pop sometimes evoked boredom or discontent, as did the corporate, almost assembly-line methods of modern record making and merchandising. The realization emerged frequently not only that markets could be found in various age and demographic segments of American life but also that songs about working-class life, rowdiness, the South, cowboys, and even rednecks could be commercial. Even more surprising, perhaps, was the realization that many younger listeners, many of whom had been weaned on rock music, were among the most passionate of the fans of the older varieties of country music.[34]

Nashville never lost its economic dominance, and the Grand Ole Opry remained an almost holy mecca for multitudes of fans. Nevertheless, alternative centers of musical production emerged in the 1960s and 1970s that provided Nashville with healthy competition while also injecting vital and divergent musical strains into American life. A few, like Memphis and Muscle Shoals, Alabama, and Macon, Georgia, became vital recording centers that demonstrated the pervasive role of the blues in the making of southern music. Austin, Texas, did not become a recording capital, but in the early 1970s it became a thriving haven of live music making where the traditions of rock, blues, and country music became intertwined under the romantic canopies of the Texas Mystique and cowboy imagery. When music legend Willie Nelson arrived in 1972, he found a scene that was already booming and experimental and one in which the styles of western swing, honky-tonk, blues, and rock all coexisted comfortably and intermingled freely.[35]

Amid country music's commercial revitalization and in large part as a consequence of it, there came an unprecedented politicization. By the early 1970s country music had gained a widespread reputation as the voice of the "Silent Majority," or of conservative Middle America. While many earlier songs had conveyed a workingman's populism, country music as a whole had expressed no explicit political agenda or ideology. The new conservative political identification arose from certain preoccupations strongly identified with southern history, especially racism, and from others generated by perceived threats to traditional moral values and the old hierarchical structure that had defined life and preserved order. These concerns gradually intersected with similar anxieties felt by other Americans. When some country singers endorsed or attached themselves to George Wallace in the late 1950s, they were endorsing the racial values upheld by the Alabama governor and also linking themselves to a feisty, populistic southerner who talked and behaved as they did. Even though the virulently racist and under-the-counter songs that came out of Crowley, Louisiana, with such titles as "Nigger Hating Me" and "Kajun Klu Klux Klan" (*sic*), had only regional circulation, as the 1960s dawned, the racism explicit in southern society began to match the mood of many dissatisfied white northerners as well.[36]

The challenge to traditional lifestyles, racial values, older moral presumptions, and masculine dominance posed by Supreme Court decisions and Great Society legislation gradually provoked a conservative backlash that lacked clear regional connotations. The polarization inspired by the Vietnam War and student protests only strengthened the conviction that America was threatened by a breakdown of authority and disintegration of moral values. The country songs that attacked the protesters, such as Merle Haggard's "Okie from Muskogee" and "Fighting Side of Me," or that ridiculed welfare recipients ("Welfare Cadillac") or called for a revival of patriotism ("God Bless America Again") won enthusiastic audiences all over the nation and provided functional forums in which middle-class conservatives and working-class populists could unite in a common complaint against elitists, intellectuals, and well-to-do students. Jingoistic defenses of war and militant attacks against critics of U.S. foreign policy—from Vietnam to the Persian Gulf—provided public and acceptable ways for musicians like Hank Williams Jr. and Charlie Daniels to impart their machismo apart from the normal avenues of boozing, fighting, and womanizing.[37]

Cultural anxieties explain much of country music's drift to the right, but a quest for public acceptance also prompted the actions of a music community that wanted simultaneously to be working-class and middle-class, southern and American. That craving for legitimacy could translate into support for a southerner and Democratic candidate for president in 1976 but more often has gravitated toward Republicans in the elections that followed. The conservatism in country music cut across stylistic categories and, seemingly incongruously, was represented by the poles of musical expression, whether that of Hank Jr.'s hedonism or Ricky Skaggs's pietism.[38]

As the political stridency of the Vietnam years subsided, the corresponding tone also diminished in country music. An enduring legacy of that prior political involvement, however, and one widely repeated in the popular press and in country music journalism was the explicit linking of country music with the patriotism and conservative moral values of working-class Americans. Popularly depicted as "poets of the common man," such singer-songwriters as Tom T. Hall and Merle Haggard lent to the music an identification that was proudly accepted by the country music industry and echoed by many writers. Consequently, the music became more explicitly working-class in its self-depiction than ever before in its history. Throughout the 1980s and 1990s, songs like Alabama's "Forty-Hour Week for a Living," Travis Tritt's "Lord Have Mercy on the Working Man," and Aaron Tippin's "Working Man's Ph.D." praised the worker's pride and independence and complained about the burdens under which he labored as a wage earner and family man. Some of these songs seemed little more than reassertions of masculine authority, and one usually had to look beyond the ranks of the male country stars, and even outside of country music (to such rock singers as Bruce Springsteen, John Cougar Mellencamp, and Billy Joel), to find expressions of a more inclusive compassion for working people. Dolly Parton, for example, sang about all kinds of workers in her album *9 to 5 and Odd Jobs*, and Hazel Dickens, the great but sadly under-recognized singer from West Virginia, sang about women's issues and the problems of coal miners and other industrial workers with a biting commentary not heard in American music since the days of Woody Guthrie. But there were no Woody Guthries in the commercial country music of the 1990s.[39]

Country music's identification with working people was accompanied by a heightened reassertion of southernness. The Civil Rights Acts of 1964 and 1965 and the eruption of racial turmoil in the North may have permitted a renewed glorification of the South without the accompanying guilt that had existed earlier. The national mood of conservatism also may have inspired a rediscovery of the mythic South as a region of contentment, stability, and bucolic values. But the equally old fascination exhibited by Americans for eccentric southern characters and exotic southern places may have done more to fuel the fad for the down-home humor and gothic backwoods drama that appeared so often in movies and on television in the 1970s and 1980s.

Since the 1960s, country singers and songwriters have turned often to southern themes, sometimes resurrecting Confederate imagery to express an aggressive southern nationalism or a personal mode of machismo. They often submit willingly to the stereotypes of a simple and fun-loving people with songs and humor about "Good Old Boys" and rednecks but more frequently revive the revered idea—first voiced by Stephen Foster and the poets of Tin Pan Alley—of a warm, harmonious, and placid rural region. Most of these songs steered clear of politics, but on occasion a veiled plea for racial tolerance could be heard, as in "Catfish John," and at least one song, "The South's Gonna Rise Again," envisioned a modern South barren of cotton fields and filled with skyscraper-dominated cities where the children of poor whites and blacks lived in harmony. A few songs even touched lightly on the theme of class consciousness, as did Johnny Russell's "Rednecks, White Socks, and Blue Ribbon Beer," which noted that "we don't fit in with that white collar crowd."

Southern cities appeared occasionally in country songs, but more often the songs called singers and listeners back to the society described in "Mississippi, You're on My Mind" or "Sunday in the South," a region of small towns and villages where life was lived simply, close to the healing balm of nature and amid the reassuring warmth of friends, family, and church. Such songs have obvious appeal to southerners, but Americans everywhere can identify with the simple charms celebrated in their lyrics. Living in a highly competitive society, where neither abundance nor progress seems any longer assured, Americans can easily embrace the fantasies conveyed by "Rocky Top, Tennessee," and "Luckenbach, Texas," where life is lived free from smoggy smoke and telephone bills and where "ain't nobody feeling no pain."[40]

Country music has remained alive in the seventy years since the end of World War II because it addresses, with evocative language, singable melodies, and danceable rhythms, the basic longings, frustrations, aspirations, and prejudices of America's working people. It has not simply prevailed; it has become a powerful economic entity in the most intensely urban nation in the world. Its endurance gives testament to the survival strength of rural folkways through successive generations of urban change and adjustment and to the power of the rural myth among a people who have persistently moved to cities while never fully accepting their adopted domain.

Country music speaks in many languages and dialects, but its central voice is that of the South, and many people judge its authenticity by the degree to which southernness endures. The young performers of today come principally from the South or from regions to which southerners have migrated. Many are the grandchildren of the people who left the rural South seventy years ago to take up new residences and occupations in the region's urban centers or in industrial areas elsewhere in America. Transformation came slowly, and the marks of the rural past endured on the automobile assembly line and in the steel mill and at other sites where industrial or blue-collar work was done. And they persisted in the housing projects and even in the suburban developments when economic opportunities permitted the move to more comfortable residences. Education and exposure to the national media blunted but could not completely obliterate the imprints of those rural beginnings, and traces lingered among later generations.[41]

The young descendants of the rural South grew up hearing the music of that older society, usually as performed by professional musicians but sometimes in the singing and playing of their parents or grandparents. Often they rejected what they heard and embraced instead the musical styles fashionable among youth everywhere in America. Among those who have chosen to follow country music careers one still hears, amid the elements borrowed from Merle Haggard, Lefty Frizzell, George Jones, Willie Nelson, or other traditional country stars, strains absorbed from Bob Dylan, the Rolling Stones, the Eagles, Motown, Billy Joel, the Allman Brothers, or other rock influences.[42]

The country musicians of today pay homage to the rural past, or show evidence of it, in a variety of ways. Many of them have supported Farm Aid, the movement launched and sustained by Willie Nelson to generate financial aid and legislative support for the nation's endangered family farmers. In supporting this cause, they link themselves to America's most cherished myth and one that conveys no hint of controversy. Similar crusades for the nation's equally embattled steelworkers and coal miners have not been forthcoming. Endangered country styles have also evoked support from a large number of country singers who, since the early 1980s, have been described as "neotraditionalists." A few of these performers, such as Emmylou Harris, Ricky Skaggs, Dwight Yoakam, Alan Jackson, Marty Stuart, Iris DeMent, and Dale Watson have consciously articulated defenses of older styles and the veteran musicians who personified them while also performing music that honored these sources. Most of the neotraditionalists, however—such as George Strait, who contributed to the revival of western swing, or Randy Travis, whose vocals recall the sound of Lefty Frizzell—have preserved the older styles and demonstrated their commercial viability without crusading or drawing invidious distinctions between the various approaches available to country musicians. Nevertheless, they have all demonstrated that a hunger for the older styles exists and that such performances can be commercial.[43]

We should understand, however, that the southernness of country music is not defined by the rhetorical postures assumed by performers, or by the symbolism and imagery that surround the music, or even by the style of music that is played. Neither support for Farm Aid nor neotraditionalism, for example, really defines either ruralness or southernness, nor does the wearing of a cowboy hat prove that its singer had a western or country origin. Musical nostalgia for the South, the western plains, or the old rural home place have been staples of American popular music for well over a century, and such feelings have often been purveyed by writers and singers who have never been south of the Mason-Dixon line, never been near a horse, and have no familiarity with rural society. The love for traditional music similarly has not been confined to southerners with a rural heritage. Some of the best performers of old-time music—like Mike Seeger—have been northern-born musicians of urban origin. Country music, in contrast, displays its southernness in the lifestyles of its performers, most of whom are southern-born and southern-bred, and in the values they convey through their songs. While they sometimes succumb to nostalgia about a way of life they have never known or reverentially revive older songs and styles, most modern country singers and songwriters concentrate on the problems and concerns of today. Their accents and dialects betray their southern origins, and their songs often reflect preoccupations and values, such as individualism, religiosity, home-centeredness, the sense of place, and a faith in simple solutions, that are rooted in the rural past.[44]

When country music began its impressive national expansion after World War II, it spoke as the voice of people who were moving away from agriculture and rural life to take up lives as wage earners in the towns and cities of America. In many ways, it was the "language of a subculture." It now speaks to—and for—a vast constituency of people who have no memories of tenant farms, coal camps, mill villages, Farm Security camps, or even housing projects. Many of its fans have left the ranks of blue-collar labor. But even though the specific loci of country music support can no longer be precisely determined, the music still carries the imprints of its earlier history. As the music of people torn between tradition and modernity, who have struggled to make sense of their experiences, country music has bequeathed a style and message that finds resonance in the hearts of millions of Americans everywhere who are still trying to understand and come to terms with a complex society that increasingly seems beyond control.[45]

NOTES

1. According to the longtime radio personality Hugh Cherry, the term "country and western" was first used in 1943 by Steve Sholes to describe the hillbilly songs circulated on the V-Discs produced for the American Forces Network program in Europe. Sholes, who had been a longtime producer for RCA Victor before he entered military service, may have been primarily responsible for the decision made by RCA *Victor Record Review* 10 (April 1948): 12, to use "country and western" to advertise similar recordings; see Hugh Cherry, "Joe Allison, AFRTS, Topsy and How They Grew," *Music City News* 7 (April 1970): 28. In June 1949, the national music trade journal, *Billboard* magazine, began using the same designation to describe its hillbilly popularity charts.

2. Arnold's dominance in the late 1940s and early 1950s is documented in the *Billboard* listing of "top ten" country songs, which began in 1948. The listings for the years from 1948 to 1963 appeared in *The World of Country Music* (New York: Billboard, 1963), 187, 189–99. Despite Arnold's prominence in American entertainment, he had never received much attention from writers who specialize in country or any other field of American music, until Michael Streissguth wrote *Eddy Arnold: Pioneer of the Nashville Sound* (Jackson: University Press of Mississippi, 1997). Arnold himself has written a highly unsatisfactory autobiography, *It's a Long Way from Chester County* (New York: Pyramid Books, 1969).

3. Rodgers's story is well told in Nolan Porterfield, *Jimmie Rodgers: The Life and Times of America's Blue Yodeler* (Urbana: University of Illinois Press, 1979). Autry has written an autobiography, with Mickey Herskovitz, called *Back in the Saddle Again* (New York: Doubleday, 1978), but the best account of his impact on American

music is Holly George-Warren, *Public Cowboy No. 1: The Life and Times of Gene Autry* (New York: Oxford University Press, 1997). See also Douglas B. Green, "Gene Autry," in *Stars of Country Music: Uncle Dave Macon to Johnny Rodriguez*, ed. Bill C. Malone and Judith McCulloh (Urbana: University of Illinois Press, 1976).

4. Lewis Atherton long ago noted the popularity of the National Barn Dance among midwesterners in *Main Street on the Middle Border* (Bloomington: Indiana University Press, 1954). John Lair's role in establishing a down-home, and even southern, ambience on the show has not properly been acknowledged, but Wayne Daniel is now working on a book on Lair and his influence in both Chicago and at Renfro Valley, Kentucky. The National Barn Dance's history has been well presented in a PBS documentary, *The Hayloft Gang*. Additional useful information on the show's relationship to midwestern broadcasting can be found in James F. Evans, *Prairie Farmer and WLS: The Burridge Butler Years* (Urbana: University of Illinois Press, 1969).

5. Fortunately, Bob Wills's career and influence have received impressive treatment in Charles Townsend, *San Antonio Rose: The Life and Music of Bob Wills* (Urbana: University of Illinois Press, 1976). Wills's onetime musical partner and co-founder of western swing has been well portrayed by Cary Ginell in *Milton Brown and the Founding of Western Swing* (Urbana: University of Illinois Press, 1994). Gene Autry was unquestionably the most popular country singer of the war years even though his career was interrupted by military service. The best treatment of Acuff is Elizabeth Schlappi, *Roy Acuff, the Smoky Mountain Boy* (Gretna, La.: Pelican, 1978). I have discussed the search for usable symbols among country musicians in *Singing Cowboys and Musical Mountaineers: Southern Culture and the Roots of Country Music* (Athens: University of Georgia Press, 1993).

6. The music's commercial expansion had actually begun in the 1930s with the fifty-thousand-watt radio stations; the national advertising on hillbilly shows of such products as Crazy Water Crystals and Alka-Seltzer; radio transcriptions, which permitted performers to tour while their shows were being broadcast; and, of course, the powerful transmission of the "Mexican border" stations, which could be heard all over North America. See Bill C. Malone, *Country Music, U.S.A.* (Austin: University of Texas Press, 1985), chaps. 4–6; Gene Fowler and Bill Crawford, *Border Radio* (Austin: Texas Monthly Press, 1987); Gene Fowler, *Crazy Water: The Story of Mineral Wells and Other Texas Health Resorts* (Fort Worth: Texas Christian University Press, 1991), 40–42; and Louis M. Jones, with Charles Wolfe, *Everybody's Grandpa: Fifty Years behind the Mike* (Knoxville: University of Tennessee Press, 1948). One of the best accounts of the postwar boom and its effects on American habits and assumptions is Godfrey Hodgson, *America in Our Time* (Garden City, N.Y.: Doubleday, 1976). For discussions of jukeboxes, see Vincent Lynch and Bill Henkin, *Jukebox: The Golden Age* (Berkeley: Lancaster-Miller, 1981); Christopher Pearce, *Vintage Jukeboxes* (Secaucus, N.J.: Chartwell Books, 1988); Lewis Nichols, "The Ubiquitous Juke Box," *New York Times Magazine*, October 5, 1941, 22; and John Morthland, "Jukebox Fever," *Country Music* 6 (May 1978): 35–36.

7. Useful surveys of radio barn dances include Charles Wolfe, *A Good-Natured Riot*; Tracey E. W. Laird, *Louisiana Hayride: Radio and Roots Music Along the Red River* (New York: Oxford University Press, 2004); Stephen R. Tucker, "The Louisiana Hayride 1948–54," *North Louisiana Historical Journal* 8 (Fall 1977): 187–201; Ivan Tribe, *Mountain Jamboree: Country Music in West Virginia* (Lexington: University Press of Kentucky, 1984); and Linnell Gentry, *A History and Encyclopedia of Country, Western, and Gospel Music* (Nashville: McQuiddy Press, 1961). Wayne Daniel has authored many articles on country music and a fine book on the country scene in Atlanta, Georgia, entitled *Pickin' on Peachtree: A History of Country Music in Atlanta, Georgia* (Urbana: University of Illinois Press, 1990).

8. A fine case study of a Virginia mountain family who moved to Washington, D.C., and whose members made country music over a period of seventy years is Ivan Tribe, *The Stonemans: An Appalachian Family and the Music That Shaped Their Lives* (Urbana: University of Illinois Press, 1993). Also excellent is Henry Glassie, Clifford R. Murphy, and Douglas Dowling Peach, *Olabelle Reed and Southern Mountain Music on the Mason-Dixon Line* (Dust-to-Digital, 2015). While the topic deserves further serious academic treatment, Harriet Arnow, in her impressive novel about a Kentucky mountain family who moved to Detroit during the war years, *The Dollmaker* (1954; rpr., New York: Collier Books, 1970), paints a vivid portrait of a woman who never lost her longing for the hills of home. Evidence that is admittedly anecdotal, including the recollections of my mother and other women relatives, suggests that women strongly embraced the alternatives presented by city life.

9. George Lipsitz, *Rainbow at Midnight: Labor and Culture in the 1940s* (1981; rpr., Urbana: University of Illinois Press, 1994), presents a good nuanced analysis of the ambivalence felt by men and women after the war.

10. The evidence of the simultaneous coexistence of traditional and contemporary material in country music programming is found in "The Grand Ole Opry, 1944–45: A Radio Log Kept by Dick Hill, of Tecumseh, Nebraska," *Journal of Country Music* 5 (Fall 1974): 91–122; and in the transcriptions of Hank Williams's Health and Happiness radio shows (Mercury 314512862-2, originally produced in 1949 by the makers of the patent medicine Hadacol), and in Hank's Mother's Best shows. A few radio transcriptions survive that capture the mood of evangelism. The best are the Bailes Brothers (Old Homestead OHCS 103 and 104) and the Louvin Brothers, *Songs That Tell a Story* (Rounder 1030). Brother Claude Ely's recordings from that period are clearly evangelistic and are wonderful representations of rural Pentecostal music. Some of his songs were recorded at revival meetings near Whitesburg, Kentucky, in 1953 and 1954 and can be heard on Brother Claude Ely, *Satan Get Back* (King CDCHD456). The Bailes Brothers' Old Homestead recordings (CS-103, originally recorded in 1948 and 1949) contain commercials, dedications to their "shut-in" listeners, and announcements of personal appearances.

11. Fowler and Crawford, *Border Radio*; Peter Guralnick, *Last Train to Memphis: The Rise of Elvis Presley* (Boston: Little, Brown, 1994), 150–52, 250, 303, 430.

12. These songs are not collected in a single recording, or in a single publication, but see Charles Wolfe, "Nuclear Country: The Atomic Bomb in Country Music," *Journal of Country Music* 7 (January 1978): 4–21, for a discussion of one genre of topical songs. These songs are placed in a larger perspective by Paul Boyer, *By the Bomb's Early Light* (New York: Pantheon, 1985).

13. Curtis Stewart's "Lord, Build Me a Cabin in Glory," published in 1944 while he was a corporal in the U.S. Army and printed in numerous paperback hymnals, is a classic statement of rural gospel humility. Such songs are very rare today in gospel music, as are the philosophy and theology that once motivated them. Songs about mansions in heaven are, in contrast, abundant in the gospel repertoire.

14. The best biography of Williams is Paul Hemphill, *Lovesick Blues: The Life of Hank Williams* (New York: Viking Penguin, 2005). Other useful accounts are Colin Escott, with George Merritt and William MacEwen, *Hank Williams: The Biography* (Boston: Little, Brown, 1994); Roger Williams, *Sing a Sad Song: The Life of Hank Williams* (Garden City, N.Y.: Doubleday, 1970); and Chet Flippo, *Your Cheating Heart: A Biography of Hank Williams* (New York: Simon and Schuster, 1981). George William Koon has provided a very useful assessment of the literature on Hank, while also correcting a few false impressions, in *Hank Williams: A Bio-Bibliography* (Westport, Conn,: Greenwood Press, 1983). The lyrics of Hank's own compositions (without music) have been compiled by Don Cusic in *Hank Williams: The Complete Lyrics* (New York: St. Martin's Press, 1993). Most of Hank's recordings are available, but the most useful album is probably *Hank Williams: The Original Singles Collection* (three compact discs, Polygram 847 194-2).

15. The emergence of the honky-tonk as a factor in country music culture is discussed in Malone, *Country Music, U.S.A.*, chap. 5, and in the *Encyclopedia of Southern Culture*, ed. Charles Reagan Wilson and William Ferris (Chapel Hill: University of North Carolina, 1989), 1014–16. Rich Kienzle provides a good discussion of the electrification of the country guitar in "The Electric Guitar in Country Music: Its Evolution and Development," *Guitar Player* 13 (November 1979): 30, 32–34, 36–37, 40–41.

16. While paying tribute to his hero, Waylon Jennings nevertheless says to Hank, "It's no thanks to you that I'm still living today," heard in "Hank Williams Syndrome," in the CD collection, *Too Dumb for New York City/Too Ugly for L.A.* (Epic CD 48982). Hank Williams Jr.'s various incantations of his father's name include "Standing in the Shadows," on *Fourteen Greatest Hits* (Polydor 0518); "Are You Sure Hank Done It This Way," on *Rowdy* (Elektra 6E-330); and "Family Tradition," on *Greatest Hits* (Elektra 60193-1). There are probably thousands of "amateur" singers in America, performing on weekends in some friend's house or at the VFW hall or some other local venue, who are still singing Hank's songs as close to the "original" style as they can achieve.

17. Peter Guralnick has written a great two-volume biography of Elvis Presley: *Last Train to Memphis* and *Careless Love: The Unmaking of Elvis Presley* (Boston: Baybooks, 1999). Joel Williamson puts Elvis in southern historical perspective in

Elvis Presley: A Southern Life (New York: Oxford University Press, 2014). Greil Marcus, *Mystery Train: Images of America in Rock 'n' Roll Music*, 2d rev. ed. (New York: E. P. Dutton, 1982), devotes a lengthy section to Presley and contains a fine analysis of those southern cultural tensions that gave rise to both Presley and Hank Williams.

18. Elvis Presley was not finally named to the Country Music Hall of Fame until 1998.

19. Guralnick, *Last Train to Memphis*, 162.

20. Probably the single best summary of these musicians is Nick Tosches, "Rockabilly," in *The Illustrated History of Country Music*, ed. Patrick Carr (New York: Country Music Magazine Press, 1979), 217–37. See Robert K. Oermann and Mary A. Bufwack, "Rockabilly Women," *Journal of Country Music* 8 (May 1979): 65–94. The classic exposition of that dualism in southern working-class men is still W. J. Cash, *Mind of the South* (New York: Knopf, 1941). Ted Ownby discusses the efforts made by the evangelicals in the late nineteenth century to tame the wild side of southern masculinity in *Subduing Satan: Religion, Recreation, and Manhood in the Rural South, 1865–1920* (Chapel Hill: University of North Carolina Press, 1990). See also Stanley Booth, *Rhythm Oil: A Journey through the Music of the American South* (New York: Pantheon, 1991), 61. Lewis has attracted a fairly large number of chroniclers, but Nick Tosches has written the best account of him in *Hellfire: The Jerry Lee Lewis Story* (New York: Delacorte, 1982) and in *Country: The Biggest Music in America* (New York: Stein and Day, 1977), 57–84.

21. Malone, *Country Music, U.S.A.*, 251–52, 480–81.

22. Several contemporary singers, such as Dwight Yoakam, Marty Stuart, Travis Tritt, and Hank Williams Jr. move freely and easily from rockabilly to honky-tonk and perform creditably in either genre. A very instructive article is Karen Schoemer's "Marty Stuart Doesn't Need a Big Hat to Be Country," *New York Times*, July 12, 1992, 22.

23. Malone, *Country Music, U.S.A.*, chap. 8. Bill Ivey defended the country-pop genre in "Commercialization and Tradition in the Nashville Sound," in *Folk Music and Modern Sound*, ed. William Ferris and Mary Hart (Jackson: University Press of Mississippi, 1982), 129–41, and in his essay "Chet Atkins," in *Stars of Country Music: Uncle Dave Macon to Johnny Rodriguez*, ed. Bill C. Malone and Judith McCulloh (Urbana: University of Illinois Press, 1976), 283–87.

24. Biographies and autobiographies of country musicians have proliferated since the 1970s. Their worth and reliability vary widely, but the more creditable ones include Dolly Carlisle, *Ragged but Right: The Life and Times of George Jones* (Chicago: Contemporary Publications, 1984); Bob Allen, *George Jones: The Saga of an American Singer* (Garden City, N.Y.: Doubleday, 1984); Merle Haggard with Peggy Russell, *Sing Me Back Home* (New York: Quadrangle, 1981); Loretta Lynn with George Vecsey, *Loretta Lynn: Coal Miner's Daughter* (Chicago: Henry Regnery, 1976); Tammy Wynette with Joan Dew, *Stand by Your Man* (New York: Simon and Schuster, 1978); Hank Snow with Jack Ownbey and Bob Burris, *The Hank Snow*

Story (Urbana: University of Illinois Press, 1994); and Steve Eng, *A Satisfied Mind: The Country Music Life of Porter Wagoner* (Nashville: Rutledge Hill Press, 1992). The immensely influential Ray Price and Buck Owens have not yet been the subjects of biographies or autobiographies. Their work lives on, however, in the performances and repertoires of singers like Dwight Yoakam, Darrell McCall, and Alan Jackson, and of course, in the singing of countless unknown musicians throughout America.

25. The best short treatment of Bill Monroe is Ralph Rinzler, "Bill Monroe," in *Stars of Country Music: Uncle Dave Macon to Johnny Rodriguez*, ed. Bill C. Malone and Judith McCulloh (Urbana: University of Illinois Press, 1976), 202–22. The best full-scale biography is by Steven Smith. Neil Rosenberg, of course, devotes extensive attention to Monroe in his comprehensive *Bluegrass: A History* (Urbana: University of Illinois Press, 1985). Another excellent and provocative treatment of bluegrass music is Robert Cantwell, *Bluegrass Breakdown: The Making of the Old Southern Sound* (Urbana: University of Illinois Press, 1984). See also Guralnick, *Last Train to Memphis*, 121–22.

26. The phrase "high lonesome sound" was apparently coined by John Cohen, who produced and filmed a documentary of the same name, dealing with Roscoe Holcomb and other mountain singers in Kentucky. Charlie Poole and the North Carolina Ramblers recorded their influential version of "White House Blues" for Columbia in 1927. It can be heard today on *Charlie Poole and the North Carolina Ramblers* (County 505). Monroe's version was recorded for Decca in 1954 and can be heard on *The High, Lonesome Sound of Bill Monroe* (Decca DL 4780).

27. Guralnick, *Last Train to Memphis*, 121–22; Rosenberg, *Bluegrass*, 158–61.

28. The best overall survey of the folk revival is Ronald Cohen, *Rainbow Quest: The Folk Music Revival and American Society, 1940–1970* (Amherst: University of Massachusetts Press, 2002). Works that emphasize the southern origins of the folk revival include R. Serge Denisoff, *Great Day Coming: Folk Music and the American Left* (Urbana: University of Illinois Press, 1971); Joe Klein, *Woody Guthrie* (New York: Knopf, 1980); Archie Green, notes to Sara Ogan Gunning, *Girl of Constant Sorrow* (Folk-Legacy FSA-26); Neil Rosenberg, ed., *Transforming Tradition: Folk Music Revivals Examined* (Urbana: University of Illinois Press, 1993); Norm Cohen, *Folk Song America: A 20th Century Revival* (Smithsonian Collection of Recordings RD 046). The most influential early attempt to link bluegrass music with the folk revival was Alan Lomax's article "Bluegrass Background: Folk Music with Overdrive," *Esquire* 52 (October 1959): 103–109.

29. *The Anthology of American Folk Music*, 3 vols. (Folkways Records FA 2951-FA 2953), included recordings taken from the private collection of Harry Smith. The folk revival was paralleled by the emergence of a group of scholars, many of them in folklore, who began probing the origins of such commercial southern grassroots styles as country, Cajun, blues, and gospel. Such scholars as D. K. Wilgus, Archie Green, John Greenway, Ed Kahn, and Norm Cohen were sometimes described as the "hillbilly folklorists." The first significant compilation of their research appeared in a special issue of the *Journal of American Folklore* (the "Hillbilly Issue") 78

(July–September 1965). The relationship between the folk revival and academic scholarship is explored in several essays in Rosenberg, ed., *Transforming Tradition*, but the best book-length account of the revival is Robert Cantwell, *When We Were Good* (Cambridge Mass.: Harvard University Press, 1995).

30. Malone, *Country Music, U.S.A.*, 283–85; Johnny Cash's CD collection of 1994, featuring the singer alone with his acoustic guitar and simply entitled *Cash* (American 45520-2), inspired a renewed interest in his music among youthful and rock-oriented fans.

31. Doc Watson was first introduced to folk music fans on an album released in 1961, *Old Time Music at Clarence Ashley's* (Folkways FA2355). The most influential revival string band, the New Lost City Ramblers, recorded several albums for Folkways and made many early hillbilly songs available through Mike Seeger and John Cohen, eds., *The New Lost City Ramblers Songbook* (New York: Oak Publications, 1964). See Ray Allen, *Gone to the Country: The New Lost City Ramblers and the Folk Revival* (Urbana: University of Illinois Press, 2010).

32. A young collector from Australia, John Edwards, popularized the idea of "the golden age of country music," the period running roughly from 1920 to 1940. After his death in 1960, his extensive collections of early country recordings and related materials became the basis for the John Edwards Memorial Foundation, a repository of American grassroots music, originally housed at UCLA and now located at the University of North Carolina at Chapel Hill. The trustees of the foundation have been much more catholic in their musical tastes than Edwards ever was.

33. The most prominent "converts" to country music have included John Denver, Kenny Rogers, Anne Murray, Emmylou Harris, Mary Chapin Carpenter, Nanci Griffith, Donna Summer, and Neil Diamond. Some of them, of course, like Summer, have made only occasional experiments with the genre.

34. Gram Parsons is probably the best example. Before he assumed his stage name, Parsons grew up in Florida as Cecil Ingram Connors, an heir to great wealth who was nonetheless attracted to the music of the Louvin Brothers, Merle Haggard, and other working-class musical heroes. As the leader of the country-rock band the Flying Burrito Brothers, Parsons strove to incorporate country music into a rock format and to attract other young people to the old-time country sound. Excellent examples of his musical style can be heard in the Byrds' *Sweetheart of the Rodeo* (Columbia CS9670), the Flying Burrito Brothers' *The Gilded Palace of Sin* (A&M SP4175), and his own collection, *GP* (Warner Brothers 0598). See also Ben Fong-Torres, "Gram Parsons: The Spirit of Country," *Esquire* 96 (December 1981): 96–98.

35. The Austin music scene has been much written about. See, for example, Jan Reid, *The Improbable Rise of Redneck Rock* (Austin: Heidelberg Press, 1974); Archie Green, "Austin's Cosmic Cowboys: Words in Collision," in *And Other Neighborly Names: Social Process and Cultural Image in Texas Folklore*, ed. Richard Bauman and Roger D. Abrahams (Austin: University of Texas Press, 1981), 152–94; Nick Spitzer, "Bob Wills Is Still the King: Romantic Regionalism and Convergent Culture

in Central Texas," *John Edwards Memorial Foundation Quarterly* 2 (Winter 1975): 191–97; Clifford Endres, *Austin City Limits* (Austin: University of Texas Press, 1987); and Willie Nelson, with Bud Shrake, *Willie: An Autobiography* (New York: Simon and Schuster, 1988).

36. Malone, *Country Music, U.S.A.*, 317–19; Neil Maxwell, "The Bigotry Business: Racist Records, Books Are Hits in the South," *Wall Street Journal*, April 20, 1967, 1, 12; Dan Carter, *The Politics of Rage: George Wallace, the Origins of the New Conservatism, and the Transformation of American Politics* (New York: Simon and Schuster, 1995), 314–16.

37. The disaffection of many traditional Democrats from their party's liberal orientation began as early as World War II. Three articles in the *Journal of American History* describe the disintegration of the New Deal liberal consensus: Arnold R. Hirsch, "Massive Resistance in the Urban North: Trumbull Park, Chicago, 1953–1966"; Thomas J. Sugrue, "Crabgrass Politics: Race, Rights, and the Reaction against Liberalism in the Urban North, 1940–1964"; and Gary Gerstle, "Race and the Myth of the Liberal Consensus" 82 (September 1995): 522–87. Merle Haggard, "Okie from Muskogee" (Capitol 2626); Haggard, "Fighting Side of Me" (Capitol ST 451); Guy Drake, "Welfare Cadillac" (Royal American 1); Hank Williams Jr., "Don't Give Us a Reason" (Warner/Curb 26453-2); Charlie Daniels, "Simple Man" (Epic EK 45316).

38. Although his songs have consistently voiced right-wing political positions, Hank Jr. has made few explicit political endorsements. Ricky Skaggs, in contrast, has been a vocal supporter of the religious right and of Pat Robertson's quests for the presidency. Skaggs has also become a prominent performer of contemporary Christian songs.

39. See, for example, John Buckley, "Country Music, American Values," *Popular Music and Society* 6 (Fall 1979): 293–301; Paul DiMaggio, Richard A. Peterson, and Jack Esco Jr., "Country Music: Ballad of the Silent Majority," in *The Sounds of Social Change*, ed. R. Serge Denisoff and Richard A. Peterson (Chicago: Rand McNally, 1972), 38–55; Richard A. Peterson and Paul DiMaggio, "From Region to Class, the Changing Focus of Country Music: A Test of the Massification Hypothesis," *Social Forces* 53 (March 1975): 497–506. Dolly Parton, *9 to 5 and Odd Jobs* (RCA AAL1-3852); Hazel Dickens, *Hard Hitting Songs for Hard Hit People* (Rounder 0126).

40. Larry King discussed, with reservations, the attempts to convert the redneck into a romanticized pop figure in "Redneck!" *Texas Monthly* 2 (August 1974): 50–64. The contemporary fascination with the South and the consequent embodiment of that impulse in various styles of music is discussed by Paul Harvey in "'Sweet Home Alabama': Southern Culture and the American Search for Community," *Southern Cultures* 1 (Spring 1995): 321–34. A good overview of southern themes in country songs lyrics is Melton A. McLaurin, "Songs of the South: The Changing Image of the South in Country Music," in *You Wrote My Life: Lyrical Themes in Country Music*, ed. Melton A. McLaurin and Richard A. Peterson (Philadelphia: Gordon and Breach, 1992), 15–35. Unfortunately, these songs are not readily available in any one place. The interested reader or listener must search for them in individual collections:

"Catfish John" and "Red Necks, White Socks, and Blue Ribbon Beer," for example, can be heard on Johnny Russell, *Greatest Hits* (Dominion 3141-2); Tanya Tucker sang "The South Is Gonna Rise Again" (Columbia KC33355); Stoney Edwards sang "Mississippi, You're on My Mind" (Capitol ST-11401); the vocal group Shenandoah recorded "Sunday in the South" (Columbia 386892); the Osborne Brothers' hit recording of "Rocky Top" (Decca 32242); Waylon Jenning's "Luckenback, Texas" (RCA 10924).

41. James Gregory has ably discussed the transplantation of country music in one of these areas, southern California, in *American Exodus: The Dust Bowl Migration and Okie Culture in California* (New York: Oxford University Press, 1989).

42. Examples of these influences can be heard in a variety of tribute albums recorded by country singers: *Common Thread: The Songs of the Eagles* (MCA 924531-3); *Skynyrd Frynds* (a tribute to the southern rock band Lynyrd Skynyrd; MCAD 11097); *Come Together: America Salutes the Beatles* (Liberty CDP 31712); and *Rhythm Country and Blues* (songs performed by soul and country singers; MCAD 10965).

43. The first significant discussion of the neotraditionalists appeared as "The Old Sound of New Country: A JCM Special Report," *Journal of Country Music* 11 (Spring 1986): 2–25.

44. Mike Seeger, for example, the son of the famous ethnomusicologists Charles and Ruth Crawford Seeger and brother of the legendary Pete Seeger, has been an indefatigable champion, scholar, and performer of traditional country music. One of his most representative albums is *Tipple Loom and Rail: Songs of the Industrialization of the South* (Folkways FH 5273). Excellent discussions that assay the relationship of modern country musicians to the South can be found in *You Wrote My Life*, ed. McLaurin and Peterson; see Melton A. McLaurin, "Songs of the South: The Changing Image of the South in Country Music," 15–35; Richard A. Peterson, "Class Consciousness in Country Music," 35–63; and James C. Cobb, "From Rocky Top to Detroit City: Country Music and the Economic Transformation of the South," 63–81.

45. Gregory, *American Exodus*. Bruce Feiler describes modern country music as the voice of the suburbs in "Gone Country: The Voice of Suburban America," *New Republic* 214 (February 1996): 19–24. Of about thirty entertainers mentioned in the article, however, twenty-five come from the South.

CHAPTER 15

COUNTRY MUSIC AND THE ACADEMY

I have always been quick to acknowledge that I was an enthusiastic fan of country music long before I became a historian of the phenomenon. And I've tried to be honest in admitting that close and passionate association with the music may have marred my interpretation of it. My formal scholarship began in the early 1960s when debates concerning the music's identity began to erupt. Personal artistic preferences undoubtedly influenced the judgments that made their way into my published works. The essay presented here was first given to an academic conference at the University of North Carolina in Chapel Hill in 1989. It was intended to show how my scholarship had evolved and to suggest that other students of country music may have been similarly influenced in their work. Although I have not modified the arguments presented here, it has now been almost thirty years since the conference was held, and over fifty years since my scholarship began!

Since this article first appeared, there has been a burgeoning of interest in country music, even in some academic music departments. Jocelyn R. Neal, for example, who joined me in the 2008 revision of *Country Music, U.S.A.*, is a member of the Music Department at UNC–Chapel Hill, and the author of a textbook on country music, *Country Music: A Cultural and Stylistic History* (New York: Oxford University Press, 2012). Scholars and popular enthusiasts alike meet annually in Nashville to address both the history of the music and its current manifestations at the International Country Music Conference (ICMC). In 2015 the *Journal of American Folklore* 127, no. 504, devoted an entire issue to one of my central theses, "the Southernness" of country music, and I was asked to supply an essay responding to my critics. Otherwise, I had earlier fulfilled my promise to write an interpretive history of country music in *Don't Get above Your Raisin': Country Music and the Southern Working Class* (Urbana: University of Illinois Press, 2002).

MANY OF US HAVE SPENT A LIFETIME COLLECTING, DOCUMENTING, AND EVALUATING the varying strains of traditional American music, or what is now called "roots" music. Our role has not been simply reportorial; in a multitude of ways, both overt and subtle, we have done much to define, and even to mold, the music that we study. Like the recording director or festival promoter who influences the repertories of performers, the songbook or record-jacket illustrator who links the music to certain visual images, or the radio-barn-dance entrepreneur who determines the stage dress and names of his entertainers, scholars and writers of all stripes have participated in shaping public perception of and response to America's grassroots musical forms. The mere decision to discuss the music of a particular performer instead of another is a choice that can influence popular perceptions. Only rarely, however, have we paused to admit or evaluate the motives and perceptions that have influenced our work. The performers and their music should not be the sole objects of our concern. We need to bring into our purview the full range of people who have collected, promoted, advertised, disseminated, interpreted, and written about traditional and country music.

As a modest contribution to this task of self-evaluation, I will discuss my own personal odyssey as a scholar of country and southern music—the process by which I became involved, the limitations under which I have labored, and also my strengths, intellectual growth, and efforts to transcend those early limitations. Perhaps this undertaking will illuminate some of the problems that have accompanied the evolving country music scholarship and will provoke questions concerning the roles played by non-performers in the making of American folk music.

Intellectual immersion in a subject to which one has an emotional attachment is obviously a perilous enterprise. I have been acutely aware of the pitfalls of such an undertaking, for it has been my fate to be a student of my own culture. The academic phase of my research did not commence until about 1961, near the end of my PhD program in history at the University of Texas in Austin, when I embarked upon a dissertation on commercial country music. Unconsciously, though, my education had begun virtually at birth. When I began my dissertation research, I carried into the project nothing more than the passionate enthusiasm of a lifetime fan of country music, an amateur's knowledge of the subject gleaned from song magazines, gossip, and untold hours of radio listening, a repertory of perhaps a thousand songs that I could sing passably well, and a whole welter of presumptions absorbed since childhood from both home experiences and popular culture.

I had completed a program of coursework in history, with a concentration on the South, but I had no training in folklore, anthropology, sociology, ethnomusicology, or music theory, or in any other discipline that one might presume would be indispensable for a proper understanding of the topic I had chosen. I began my investigation under the supervision of a professor, Joe B. Frantz, whose specialty was business history and who knew less about the subject of country music than I did. He nevertheless had a receptivity to unorthodox subjects that was then unusual. During this same period he was supervising Ronald Davis's dissertation on opera in the West. His initial suggestion was that I should do a history of the music publishing business in Nashville, but he permitted an expansion of the subject soon after the project got underway. There were as yet no repositories of country music material, and no journals devoted to the subject. Except for D. K. Wilgus's master's thesis at Ohio State, which dealt with American folksongs on commercial records, almost no academic work ever touched upon the subject of country music.[1] Nor was country music the subject of any books except for a few fan-oriented items such as Mrs. Jimmie Rodgers' romanticized biography of her famous husband and George D. Hay's paperback reminiscence of the Grand Ole Opry.[2]

I did carry with me the cultural baggage of my childhood years—a panorama of impressions that has ever since shaped my view of country music. Life on a cotton tenant farm in East Texas, at the end of the 1930s, was almost defined by deprivation and scarcity. But music was a constant positive in our lives. Mama was the first singer I ever heard. I can still hear her clear alto voice raised in harmony at the old Tin Top Pentecostal Church, but my most vivid recollections are of those private moments at home when, nursing a disappointment or slight, she sang something like "Farther Along" or "Take Your Burden to the Lord and Leave It There."

Although I was much too young to understand or empathize with her emotion, as an impressionable young boy I was struck by the powerful intensity conveyed as she rebelled, through song, against the isolation and confinement of her life.

Although gospel songs were the most common items of music in our household, my mother also sang the old-fashioned sentimental songs like "The East Bound Train," "Two Little Orphans," and "Little Rosewood Casket," numbers that I have since heard described as parlor songs. Ours was largely an oral tradition, but it was reinforced by a variety of commercially distributed written materials: paperback gospel hymnals, songs copied in school tablets, clippings from magazines or newspapers that were pasted in old grammar books. I cannot now say with assurance where my mother learned those old pop songs, for that is what they were. She learned some of them as a young girl, but the radio hillbillies, to whom we were introduced at the end of the 1930s, also included these same songs in their repertories.

Radio, that wondrous link to the outside world, first came into our lives in 1939, when Daddy bought a little Philco battery set. Many of the songs we heard were old favorites, but they were joined by a growing number of new songs and styles, as well as by a new means of preservation and documentation—the song magazines and the picture-songbooks hawked by the performers (and by the phonograph records, which came into our house considerably later than the radio broadcasts). The radio also introduced into our household a new group of participants, enlarging our musical world, because once in our home, they actively became part of our lives. These performers carried monikers like Tex, Slim, Hank, Zeke, and Lulu Belle. The shows that reached us from Dallas, Fort Worth, Shreveport, Tulsa, the Mexican border, Chicago, and Nashville created a world of intimacy and fantasy, much like that of the soap operas, where music provided escape, diversion, and emotional release. It was a world of old cabin homes, lone prairies, isolated mountain coves, east-bound freight trains, little country churches, and of course that promised home in Heaven. It was populated by cowboys, mountaineers, rambling men, hoboes, railroaders, dying orphans, and sainted mothers. Even though the Carter Family came to us each night amid the tawdry commercial advertising of XERF, for the brief fifteen minutes of their program we were transported to those "green fields of Virginia far away." And when Gene Autry sang "Empty Cot in the Bunkhouse," his lonesome lament about the old cowboy who gave his life to save a young calf from the icy blasts of winter, I easily imagined myself chilled by the norther's winds far out on the Texas plains.

The musicians also played dual roles. While they were fantasy figures, they were also in a sense part of our extended family, almost like brothers and sisters. While we elevated them and made them our heroes, we also identified with them and imagined that we could do what they were doing. Country music was still relatively new as an industry in 1939, but Bradley Kincaid and Jimmie Rodgers had already demonstrated in the early thirties, as Gene Autry and Bob Wills did at the end of the decade, that one could make a comfortable living from performing. The music had become, so it seemed, an economic outlet for working-class boys and girls, an exotic escape from the cotton fields, the coal mines, the textile mills, the diners and beauty shops. Armed with a Sears-Roebuck guitar, a few chords, and a little luck, we too might have our transcriptions played on XEG, and we too might become part of what we perceived as an exciting and glamorous life. All of this music, then, whether in the form inherited from my mother or in the styles learned from the radio hillbillies or Hollywood Cowboys, converged and became enmeshed in my total music and cultural world. I forever carried with me the conviction that music was a major sustaining force in the lives of people like my own. Regardless of the forms that country music might one day assume, or of the far-flung audiences that it might eventually win, country music for me would always be bound up with my boyhood experiences on that little cotton farm in the late 1930s.

Although I was not then aware of it, the years from 1954 to 1960 at the University of Texas and in Austin provided a nurturing context for my doctoral dissertation on commercial country music. The music I loved, and which to me constituted the bedrock core of country music—that of Hank Williams Sr. and his contemporaries—had been battered and almost driven from the radio and jukebox by rock and roll, or by country-pop, the so-called Nashville "compromise" that was designed to win a new audience by smoothing out country music's rough and rural edges. To put it mildly, I was no friend of either rock and roll or country-pop and was not then prepared to see either as an extension of country music, nor did I then recognize rockabilly music as still another expression of the working-class South. When a package of RCA country entertainers appeared in Austin sometime in 1955, I went to see Hank Snow, not the headliner Elvis Presley, who offended me not only with his unorthodox performing style but also with what I perceived to be his threat to traditional country music. By early 1961, when my formal research began, the country-music industry had gained renewed commercial vigor and was experiencing one of its periodic revivals. I welcomed any sign of revitalization and thought that I heard it in bluegrass and in the styles of performers like George Jones, Ray Price, and Buck Owens.

The most obvious example of traditional resurgence in those years was the music of the urban folk revival. Like most of my "hillbilly" friends— graduate-school buddies who liked the same kind of country music I did and who either sang it or listened to it—I delighted in pointing out the phoniness and inauthenticity of the music and in laughing at the earnest- ness of its young middle-class converts, people who grew up with neither the music nor purple-hull peas and white gravy, and who knew nothing of Sears catalogs in the little brown shack out back.

In retrospect, I realize that we were as phony as they, but that our "pho- niness" was of a different stripe. Whatever my reservations, I got caught up in the revival too, as did the country-music business as a whole, and I welcomed the refreshing reorientation that some of the revival musicians emphasized. Led by Mike Seeger and the New Lost City Ramblers, a few of the revivalists began resurrecting hillbilly songs from the 1920s and 1930s, which they reproduced with literal stylistic faithfulness. Although it was easy to mock the rural pretensions of this trio of city boys, I never- theless bought their albums and valuable songbook and learned the songs that they revived.[3] My singing buddies and I generally stayed clear of the campus folk-song club and instead spent most of our time at a hillbilly bar on the north side of Austin called Threadgill's. Housed in a onetime filling station, Threadgill's was a typical hillbilly joint run by a genial proprietor, Kenneth Threadgill, who sang and yodeled Jimmie Rodgers's songs. The bar was almost a microcosm of the changes then occurring in popular music, and Threadgill's musical scene was a portent of the kind of cultural fusion that developed in Austin later in the 1970s. Transformed by a few graduate students like myself, who were looking for old-time music, both the atmosphere and musical ambience of the bar were altered even further when spillovers from the campus folk-music club began arriving with their songs and instruments.

Tolerance of unorthodox musical expressions or cultural styles was not my strong suit back in those days, and so I was not particularly impressed when a student wearing a sheepskin coat and tattered jeans joined us one night with her autoharp and a little group of companions known as the Waller Creek Boys. Of course, neither Janis Joplin nor the rest of us realized the full musical or cultural import of what we were witnessing, and none of us could have known the directions that she and American popular music would travel just a few short years later. (The most embarrassing confession I should make is that on the first night she came in with her group she looked across the room at where I was sitting with my guitar, and she said, "He doesn't want us here." Her perception was probably correct. Although I soon came to admire Janis's spirited renditions of Carter Family and Rose Maddox tunes, my initial reaction must have been, "Well, here come the beatniks and their fake folk music.")

The folk revival was accompanied by at least a slight stirring of interest in old-time country music by a few folklorists. My own introduction to these scholars came through the work of Alan Lomax, who had made at least stray references to hillbillies in his published folk-song collections. His most explicit statement linking traditional music to modern commercial forms was his famous 1959 *Esquire* article "Bluegrass Background: Folk Music with Overdrive."[4] About two years later I began to learn about the interests of men like D. K. Wilgus, John Greenway, Ed Kahn, and that indefatigable champion of vernacular music, Archie Green. The whole field of folklore scholarship became acquainted with these men in 1965, when the *Journal of American Folklore* published a series of articles by them in its "Hillbilly Issue."[5] These folklorists generally demonstrated interest only in the commercial music of the pre-1941 era, and their research was concentrated on the persistence of tradition in such music. Furthermore, like their more literary predecessors in folklore scholarship, the hillbilly folklorists were preoccupied with the Appalachians as the seedbed and preserve of white American folk music.

My introduction to the hillbilly folklorists came almost simultaneously with my discovery, in the Austin Public Library, of that remarkable body of recordings, the Folkways *Anthology of American Folk Music.*[6] Much of the material there, which had come from Harry Smith's private collection of old 78 rpm recordings, was new to me. But I also found selections by such old friends as Uncle Dave Macon and the Carter Family, a revelation that reinforced my belief that commercial country music and folk music were inextricably linked. I later learned that a rather extensive number of folk-music fans were making a similar discovery. These sources directly affected my scholarship, and the perceptions that lay behind it. I leaned heavily upon the hillbilly folklorists because theirs was about the only available academic material that ever touched upon country music. I spent an inordinate amount of time trying to establish country music's folk roots, and like the folklorists, I was perhaps too concerned with "mountain" origins. My fascination with the southern mountains long preceded my introduction to either folklore or country music scholarship. The novels of John Fox Jr., the movie "Sergeant York," a multitude of songs like "The Trail of the Lonesome Pine," "Blue Ridge Mountain Blues," and "Carry Me Back to the Mountains," and musicians with names like the Smoky Mountain Boys and the Clinch Mountain Clan, all conspired to invest the southern Appalachians with the misty haze of romance and to reinforce in my mind the archetypical image of mountain hollows populated by a peculiarly musical people.

When my research began, the central question I faced was how to properly document and evaluate a topic as massive as the history of country music, and one about which so little had been written. The proper answer, of course, was that one should not undertake such a project, but no one gave me such advice. I looked at anything I could find—scholarly journals and books, folk-song collections, hillbilly picture-songbooks, popular magazines, song magazines like *Country Song Roundup*, Sears-Roebuck and Montgomery Ward catalogs, record-industry catalogs and brochures, record liner notes, newspapers, and radio and entertainment-industry publications. For instance, I may have been the first person to do extensive research in *Billboard* magazine, concentrating on the years running from 1928 to 1964. My interviews were done in a rather scatter-gun fashion, first in Nashville in early 1961with the help of Jo Walker, the executive secretary of the fledgling Country Music Association, and later with anyone I could contact among industry people and both active and inactive musicians and their offspring. Having neither a car nor a tape recorder during those first few years of research, my "interviews" were often nothing more than a set of hastily scribbled notes written on the performer's touring bus or backstage during intermission.

Probably the greatest boon to my early investigations, and an incalculable resource for all students of country music, was the exhaustively documented research done by the network of record collectors in the United States and around the world. I learned about some of them through their advertisements in the song magazines and record catalogs, and about others in conversations with Archie Green and Ed Kahn. Through the efforts of these collectors I was introduced to the wondrous science of discography and to the auction lists, mimeographed newsletters, and printed magazines, such as *Disc Collector, Country Directory, Record Research*, and *Country and Western Spotlight*, where their quiet and diligent research had been appearing for years. The greatest revelation of all, perhaps, was that the collection of American grassroots music was a worldwide enterprise and that an Australian, John Edwards, was one of the great collectors of American hillbilly music. My naïveté and newness to the field of discography were undoubtedly irritating to some of the collectors, and a few of them only reluctantly provided assistance. I will therefore always have a special place in my heart for Bob Pinson, who sought me out and unselfishly provided assistance when I was floundering. (Bob soon thereafter became employed by the Country Music Foundation, but at that time his private collection was one of the largest in the world.) Although some of the collectors exhibited interest only in the music of the pre-1941 period, or what John Edwards called "the Golden Age of Hillbilly Music," many of these specialists tended to be catholic in their approach to country music. The fascination with western swing, for example, which many of them demonstrated, brought some balance to a field too often dominated by an emphasis on the Southeast or by an Appalachian fixation. (The western swing advocates, however, also sometimes ride their hobby horse too far, and they similarly have to be reminded of country music's diversity.)

As I looked around for academic companionship in the early 1960s, I therefore found some support among folklorists and popular culturists and, of course, among collectors, fans, and ardent "amateurs." I found, though, that even among some of these devotees "commercial" music was suspect. History, my own academic discipline, had usually ignored music or had dealt only with its High-Art manifestations. In southern history, and in southern-oriented scholarship generally, one found little recognition of the role played by music in the lives of plain white people. It is beyond the scope of this paper to explore the reasons for the differing responses made by intellectuals to black and white musical styles, but the interest accorded to white folk music had been minimal compared to that given to black music. At best, one found a tendency to take seriously only the quaint, anti-quated, or romantic forms of white folk music. For example, historian Tom Clark provided wonderful vignettes of nineteenth-century fiddlers in *The Rampaging Frontier*, but in referring to the "hillbilly rabble on the radio" in another book on the Kentucky River, he implied that folk musicians lost their credibility or authenticity when they tried to make money from their talents.[7] Indeed, his larger implication was that they were no longer "folk" at all.

The famous literary Southern Agrarians of the early 1930s made some comments about the "frolic" music of an older rural South but said nothing about the rural music that surrounded them in their own time, or the music that could be heard from the stage of the Grand Ole Opry in the same city where many of them pursued their scholarship. One suspects that country music was a bit too crass and commercial to fit the status image of folk art that the Agrarians envisioned. In their famous manifesto *I'll Take My Stand*, Andrew Lytle was the only Agrarian who devoted any attention to the culture of the plain folk, and his discussion was highly romanticized. He lists, for example, a number of fiddle tunes and then says, "With a list of such dances as a skeleton, some future scholar could reconstruct with a common historical accuracy the culture of this people."[8] By 1930, when his essay was published, the "folk" had already gone far beyond the skeleton of fiddle tunes to which he referred, and despite his advice that they should "throw out the radio," people everywhere had incorporated that remark-able communications device into their everyday culture.

Ignoring, or at best romanticizing, folk music, in both its traditional and commercialized forms, was part of a more general neglect—among scholars of all stripes—of plain folk culture. Since the 1920s a rash of monographs and statistical studies had been appearing, many of them produced by Howard Odum and his students at the University of North Carolina, or inspired by the New Deal's rediscovery of the folk. However, except for Frank Owsley's *Plain Folk of the Old South*, a work also marred by a tendency to romanticize its subjects, no general historical survey of the southern folk was available when my own research got underway.[9]

Why the long scholarly neglect of commercial country music? Long before my academic research began, I perceived that "respectable" people disliked country music because of its associations with disreputable, uneducated social and economic failures—that is, rednecks, holy rollers, and denizens of honky-tonks. This perception was reaffirmed once I became part of the world of academic scholarship. Country music did not fit the images that scholars had of folk culture, and most important, the genre's intense commercialism seemed to set it starkly apart from "real" folk music. Apparently, real folk musicians did not travel in sordid surroundings, nor did they traffic in the world of commerce. The "purer" varieties of mountain music, and even bluegrass, won slow and often grudging acceptance from the scholars; Jimmie Rodgers, Hank Williams, and George Jones did not.

Although I shared some of the preconceptions of my colleagues in folklore and no doubt many of their misconceptions, I also had my own agenda when I first began to write *Country Music, U.S.A.* My first priority, I believed, was simply to tell country music's story; hence my emphasis on narrative at the expense of interpretation. While insisting on the persistence of tradition in country music, arguing that "the folk musician did not cease to be folk merely because he stepped in front of a microphone," I was just as determined to validate the music's commercial history and to show that folk music and commercial intent were age-old partners.[10] Commercialization, I argued, had been linked to folk music well back into the Middle Ages. The early ballad hawkers, broadside vendors, and tavern fiddlers had been the ancestors of Johnny Cash and Merle Haggard and, indeed, of ASCAP, BMI, and RCA. Commercialization was valuable because it permitted and encouraged the wide dissemination of grassroots forms, and it was just one additional means by which working-class people found economic alternatives to farming, coal mining, and industrial labor. Most important, it was a fact of American life.

While maintaining that country music was a reflection of societal changes and of a changing folk—a conservative people whose long history had been marked by migration and incessant economic transformation—I was particularly determined to demonstrate that the music was far from being simply a mountain-derived form that accompanied the mountaineers' move to the industrial cities. Mountain musicians had certainly made vital contributions to commercial country music. The culture that surrounded them, as well as the music they played, as pointed out elsewhere, had always exerted a powerful romantic appeal for many Americans. Country music, however, was a remarkably eclectic, "impure" mix that showcased the influence of many styles of music, both commercial and folk, and it was a peculiar blending of urban and rural elements. My own southwestern origins may have made me acutely conscious of the unique cultural confluence found in that region, for one could scarcely listen to the radio during my youthful growing up days without hearing the jazz-inflected dance tunes of bands like the Light Crust Doughboys and Bob Wills's Texas Playboys. These musicians were no less "folk" in origin than those who came from the mountains, and their earliest performing experiences came in the fiddle bands and house parties of the rural Southwest. The form of music they created, later described as western swing, was an amalgam of city and rural styles allied with the western image.

Country Music, U.S.A., the first published product of my personal and professional odyssey, appeared in 1968. Written by a historian, and perceived by him as history, it nevertheless carried the imprint of the American Folklore Society. The book received generally favorable reviews, and at least a moderately successful commercial reception. It has since remained in print through several different book jackets, three paperback editions, and a thorough revision in 1985. I am aware that a variety of phenomena, both cultural and commercial, contributed to the original publication and continued sales of my book. The burgeoning of the country-music industry, and its aggressive expansion through the leadership of the Country Music Association; the widespread public exposure prompted by the founding of

The original cover of the first edition of Country Music, U.S.A. *in 1968.*
Image courtesy the University of Texas Press, Austin.

television's Nashville Network; the short-lived Urban Cowboy craze; the political conservatism of the last thirty years and more; Jimmie Carter's presidency and the rediscovery of the South—all have prompted and preserved interest in a music that is presumed to be socially conservative and southern.

Still, I would like to think that my book has also succeeded on its own merits. I hope that it has contributed in some measure to the acceptance and legitimacy of country music among scholars. It has been particularly gratifying to see the appearance of academic courses on country music, particularly in the once restrictive music departments of major universities. Most of these courses, however, seem to have been offered in curricula outside of the history profession.

What has been the reaction within my own discipline? *Country Music, U.S.A.* was reviewed favorably in most of the historical journals (although the *Journal of American History* has never reviewed it), and I have given programs or participated in sessions of the Organization of American Historians, the Southern Historical Association, and other academic organizations. Country music has been the theme of two opening sessions of the Southern Historical Association (in 1977 and 1989). Nevertheless, a reference to the music in a history text or journal article is still rare. Histories of the 1920s invariably refer to "Jazz"; almost none speak of "Hillbilly," which began its commercial existence in that decade, and which mirrored the thinking and values of millions of Americans. Studies of the cultural ferment and rebellion of the 1960s usually mention Bob Dylan, the Beatles, or Woodstock; none of them makes even a passing reference to Merle Haggard, one of the musical messengers of Middle America. Textbooks and other studies of southern history, where one might expect to find discussions of country music, have been surprisingly barren in their treatments of the subject.

It is encouraging to note, however, that a gradual awakening of interest in the southern plain folk and their culture has been underway for the past fifteen years or so—much of it influenced and informed by the "new social history" and by those who have been concerned with the story of the "inarticulate." The field is still tiny compared to what has been done on black history, and there is as yet nothing in the realm of white plain folk history comparable to Lawrence Levine's *Black Culture and Black Consciousness.*[11] One deterrent has been the relative paucity of source materials and repositories to house the material and make it available to scholars. Happily, indispensable information is now available in the Library and Media Center at the Country Music Foundation in Nashville and at the University of North Carolina in the John Edwards Memorial/ Southern Folklife Collection, allied with the oral history material in the Southern Historical Collection. Gradually, the raw materials for a study of the music and its relationship to the larger culture are becoming available to scholars.

Although little attention has been devoted to the subject of country music in the discipline of history or related fields of scholarship, a few recent works do deserve special mention. Jack Temple Kirby in *Media-Made Dixie*, for instance, argues that country musicians have contributed to the image of a "visceral South."[12] J. Wayne Flynt in *Dixie's Forgotten People* and *Poor but Proud* made a valiant effort to integrate music into the social history of his subjects—arguing rightly that music was a sustaining force and a means of communication—but he seemed unable to rid himself of romantic speculation about the music's origins and about its means of dissemination.[13] He emphasized dulcimers, which were rarely used by the people he discusses, but said very little about fiddles, which were omnipresent among the folk. Grady McWhiney's *Cracker Culture* similarly described the centrality of music in the lives of the people and was correct in emphasizing continuity between their lives today and their historical past but was too preoccupied with Celtic themes.[14] When McWhiney heard the fiddle, he heard the strains of an ancient bagpipe; someone else might discern a different influence, including vaudeville or ragtime, that went into the making of the music.

Among the more successful of the recent books have been David Whisnant's *All that Is Native and Fine*, Jacquelyn Hall's *Like a Family*, and James Gregory's *American Exodus*.[15] Whisnant refuted some of the romantic shibboleths associated with "mountain music" and demonstrated that the dulcimer and many of the songs and dances considered to be the "purest" expressions of Appalachian music were in fact relatively recent imports brought in by cultural missionaries. The Hall and Gregory books, which deal respectively with Piedmont cotton-mill culture and the Okie culture of California, do wonderful jobs of demonstrating the central role played by music in creating an identity for people and in sustaining a form of community during periods of stress and adversity. In Gregory's words, country music was "the language of a sub-culture," an effective instrument used by the Okies, a supposedly inarticulate people, to express their experience to themselves and to the world at large.

In conclusion, I shall not spare my own work a final measure of criticism and will discuss where I am trying to go next and where all of us in the field of folk and country-music scholarship should be headed. I hope that I have learned and matured over the years, and that my mistakes and false emphases have not misled or lured other people down the wrong roads. The 1985 revision of *Country Music, U.S.A.* was, I think, much better than the original of 1968, but, given the volatile nature of popular culture, the 1985 revision was almost outdated by the time it appeared.

I have always felt that my book was never adequately reviewed. Reviewers did freely point out both strengths and weaknesses, but almost no one engaged in the kind of dialogue that would have been useful to me and to the larger world of folk scholarship. Ardent country-music fans were so pleased to find a serious book on their favorite kind of music that they overlooked mistakes and simplifications and tended to be displeased only if their heroes were omitted from the story. Critics, however, should not have been so tolerant. While noting errors of fact, they should also have questioned some of the assumptions on which the book was based or, at least, should have demanded greater clarification or proof. Is the music southern in either origin or ultimate meaning?[16] Does it really make sense to discuss both "country" and "western" styles as part of a common entity? Is country music a direct outgrowth of folk music? Or is the music preeminently a product of commercial developments and decisions? And is country music truly a reflection of the society in which it exists? Too often, the answers to such questions have been presented simply and accepted with little challenge, and only rarely have they inspired the kinds of rigorous debate that any field of serious scholarship deserves.

The recognition of country music's diversity has sharpened my awareness of both the South's cultural pluralism, and the interrelatedness of musical forms.[17] This music, like the culture that produced it, is neither socially, ethnically, nor stylistically pure. As argued in a separate essay, the music is neither Celtic nor Anglo-Saxon. Like African American music—with which it has always had a fruitful interrelationship—it is an eclectic musical product developed on American soil and out of American experiences. While this form of music has often reflected the realities of people's lives, it has just as often appealed to their desire for release, escape, fantasy, and romance. And it has often embodied the confusions and contradictions of the people who have nourished and preserved it. The ongoing dialectic within country music—witnessed both in the industry and among the fans who sustain it—is basically a question of identity and ultimate goal. The music began its commercial existence as a working-class expression, but through almost seventy years of development both it and the people who cherished it have persistently sought entrance into American's cultural mainstream. One finds, therefore, an unending pattern of ambivalence in a music that would be simultaneously working-class and middle-class, hedonistic and pious, ruggedly individualistic and patriotic, both southern and American. Industry leaders in the recent past have tried to market a musical product that is all things to all people and have instead disseminated a music that in its attempts to be popular is often lacking in either distinctiveness or substance.

The cultural ambivalence, or what I have described as an ongoing dialectic in country music, is merely the most recent manifestation of a similar complex of tensions, conflicts, and paradoxes that have lain at the heart of southern folk culture throughout 350 years of American history. This conviction has drawn me inexorably toward a thorough study of the relationship between country music and southern folk culture, an analysis not found or only hinted at in *Country Music, U.S.A.* This project will take the form of a cultural interpretation of the music of the southern working class, treated thematically and chronologically, from pre-twentieth-century folk roots to the present. The power asserted by myth, symbol, and fantasy in creating the music that I love and study will occupy a major portion of my research, as will the efforts exerted by the folk themselves to utilize music for a wide variety of purposes, including survival itself. These emphases, however, will not blind me to the role played by the commercial process. As argued earlier, one of my basic intents always was to demonstrate that country music, as a *commercial* phenomenon, was worth taking seriously, and that this commercialization was part of a process that long predated the settlement of the southern frontier. My romantic bent, however—the desire to believe that the folk themselves controlled the making and preservation of their music—may have inhibited my ability to recognize the full implications of commercialization.

The most recent phase of commercialization has attracted few serious students of country music or the folk process: that is, the role played by promoters, businessmen, record producers, merchandisers, and studio engineers. Bill Ivey made a similar criticism of my work in his review of the 1985 revision of *Country Music, U.S.A.*[18] His chief complaint was that I still clung to the romantic folk emphasis, that I wanted desperately to believe that "the people" really controlled country music, that singers sang what they wanted to sing, and that what they sang was what people wanted to hear. Ivey's point was that the process had been so transformed by commercialization that country music is virtually defined by the people who control the studios, by the engineers and sessions directors who produce the records, and by the decision makers who determine which songs will be played on Top Forty radio or the eight-in-a-row stations. It is admittedly difficult for someone with a background such as mine, who grew up in a culture where music was a part of daily life and was a part of the emotional fabric of growth and development, to think that the music is controlled by a small group of powerful commercial men in a few music centers around the country. Nevertheless, this is a topic that we all ought to take into account. My historical understanding informs me that something similar to the process that Ivey describes has always been at work in both country music and its folk musical ancestors.

On the other hand, I also know that regardless of its origins or original intent, music often takes on a life and meaning of its own that may be far different from the designs of those who made and commercially disseminated it. At heart I will always be that little boy of long ago, clinging to the Philco battery radio and thrilling to the sounds of singers like Roy Acuff, the Bailes Brothers, and Gene Autry. I do not know why Autry chose to sing "Empty Cot in the Bunkhouse," or what sordid merchandising methods may have underlain the marketing of his performance. I only know that the song brought joy into our simple little farmhouse and that it transported me to a world of enchantment and romance that still sometimes glimmers through the murky haze of commerce that now surrounds the country-music business.

NOTES

1. D. K. Wilgus, "A Catalogue of American Folksongs on Commercial Records" (M.A. thesis, Ohio State University, Columbus, 1947).

2. Mrs. Jimmie (Carrie) Rodgers, *My Husband, Jimmie Rodgers* (Nashville: Ernest Tubb Publications, n.d.); George D. Hay, *A Story of the Grand Ole Opry* (copyright George D. Hay, 1953).

3. Mike Seeger and John Cohen, eds., *The New Lost City Ramblers Song Book* (New York: Oak Publications, 1964).

4. Alan Lomax, "Bluegrass Background: Folk Music with Overdrive," *Esquire Magazine* 52 (Oct. 1959): 108.

5. D. K. Wilgus, ed., "Hillbilly Issue," *Journal of American Folklore* 78 (1965): 195–288.

6. Harry Smith, ed., *Anthology of American Folk Music*, 3 vols. (Folkways Records FA2951–FA2953).

7. Thomas D. Clark, *The Rampaging Frontier: Manners and Humors of Pioneering Days in the South and the Middle West* (Indianapolis and New York: Bobbs-Merrill, 1939); Thomas D. Clark, *The Kentucky* (New York: Rinehart & Co., 1942), 127.

8. *I'll Take My Stand: The South and the Agrarian Tradition*, by Twelve Southerners (New York and London: Harper, 1930), 233.

9. Frank Owsley, *Plain Folk of the Old South* (1949; Baton Rouge: Louisiana State University Press, 1982).

10. Bill C. Malone, *Country Music, U.S.A.: A Fifty-Year History* (Austin: University of Texas Press for the American Folklore Society, 1968), 45.

11. Lawrence Levine, *Black Culture and Black Consciousness: Afro-American Folk Thought from Slavery to Freedom* (New York: Oxford University Press, 1977).

12. Jack Temple Kirby, *Media-Made Dixie: The South in the American Imagination* (Baton Rouge: Louisiana State University Press, 1978; rev. ed., 1986).

13. J. Wayne Flynt, *Dixie's Forgotten People: The South's Poor Whites* (Bloomington: Indiana University Press, 1979) and *Poor but Proud: Alabama's Poor Whites* (Tuscaloosa: University of Alabama Press, 1989).

14. Grady McWhiney, *Cracker Culture: Celtic Folkways in the Culture of an American Region* (Tuscaloosa: University of Alabama Press, 1988).

15. David Whisnant, *All That Is Native and Fine: The Politics of Culture in an American Region* (Chapel Hill: University of North Carolina Press, 1983); Jacquelyn D. Hall et al., *Like a Family: The Making of a Southern Cotton Mill World* (Chapel Hill: University of North Carolina Press, 1987); James N. Gregory, *American Exodus: The Dust Bowl Migration and Okie Culture in California* (New York: Oxford University Press, 1989).

16. Such scholars as Peter Narvaez and Neil Rosenberg have discussed the important country music tradition in Canada, but the most published student of non-southern country music is Simon J. Bronner. For example, see his *Old-Time Music Makers of New York State* (Syracuse: Syracuse University Press, 1987).

17. Along with David Stricklin, I have explored the relationship between the South and American music in *Southern Music/American Music* (Lexington: University Press of Kentucky, 1979).

18. Bill Ivey, review of *Country Music, U.S.A.* (rev. ed., 1985) in *The Journal of Country Music* 11 (1986): 91–93.

CHAPTER 16

MEMORIES OF AUSTIN
AND THREADGILL'S

This essay was inspired by an earlier article, "Old-Time Music Austin Style," written by Alice Gerrard for *The Old-Time Herald* 4, no. 1 (1993) after she had visited Austin and played music with some of her old-time music friends there. While I believed that her essay made important contributions to our understanding of the modern music scene, I wanted the readers of her influential journal to be aware of an Austin old-time music scene that preceded by at least fifteen years the one she discussed. The seminal old-time string band the New Lost City Ramblers (which included Alice's onetime husband, Mike Seeger) had in fact played at Threadgill's on one occasion in 1962. I feel a particular obligation to memorialize the sessions at Threadgill's Bar because they, and my active participation in them, did much to shape my understanding of country music and its relationship to the urban folk music revival.

ALICE GERRARD'S RECENT ESSAY "OLD-TIME MUSIC AUSTIN STYLE" BROUGHT BACK FOND MEMORIES of a somewhat earlier period that I would like to share. When I went to Austin in 1954 as an undergraduate at the University of Texas, the music "scene" was encompassed largely by several honky-tonks in or near the city, such as the Split Rail, Big Gil's, Dessau Hall, and the Skyline Club (where Hank Williams allegedly gave his last performance before his death), and an arena across the Colorado River where I saw Elvis Presley sometime in 1955.

The few hillbilly fans and pickers at the university had no trouble finding each other in the mid-1950s, because most students had joined Elvis and the rock and roll bandwagon. I remained at the university after graduation in 1956 to pursue work toward a PhD, but I never let studies interfere with my passion for country music. I spent many more hours than I should have picking and singing with friends in the home or apartment of anyone who was willing to sponsor a session. Actually, I did a lot more singing than picking, because I was still laboring earnestly to master a few chords on my first guitar, a blonde Stella, purchased from Bill Casey, an English graduate student and budding novelist. I was popular at these parties because I knew so many old songs, but I usually sang to the guitar accompaniment of two good friends and fellow graduate students, Tom Crouch and Willie Benson. Willie was one of the most enthusiastic guitar players and hillbilly music fans I've ever known. He became very excited when he thought of an old song that I might know, but he could also become violently infuriated when a guitar resisted precise tuning. I saw him throw a guitar against a wall one night when he could not get it into tune.

Guitar players were usually the only musicians present at these jam sessions, so any fiddler, banjoist, or other instrumentalist who wandered on to the scene was eagerly welcomed. When Ed Mellon joined our sessions with his mandolin, our horizons were greatly expanded. Although we all loved Bill Monroe and the style he pioneered, Ed, the son of an Austin symphonic musician, was the first bluegrass fanatic I ever met. Ed loved Bill Monroe so much that he sometimes sent out Christmas cards signed "Bill Monroe and Ed Mellon." We often gathered in Ed's garage apartment to listen to his favorite bluegrass records, and such songs as "The River of Death," "Little Cabin Home on the Hill," and "Little White Church" will always be linked in my mind to those wonderful moments when Ed eagerly pointed out to us a particularly exciting guitar run, mandolin break, or vocal inflection.

Stan Alexander came along at about this time, and the two of us found an immediate affinity in the kind of music we liked, the blend of our voices, and in the backgrounds that we shared. Stan was a Texas country boy like me, and he knew a lot of old country songs, such as "Breeze," some which he had learned from his father. These were the pre-revival days of American folk music, but most students who were interested in old-time music dipped periodically into the immense collections recorded by Moe Asch for his Folkways label. Stan and I made a simultaneous discovery of the great songs in Harry Smith's *Anthology*, along with those borrowed from the occasional newly released LPs of the Carter Family, Jimmie Rodgers, and other early hillbilly stars, and they began to move into our own repertoires. Stan had a particular fondness for the country blues and for traditional balladry, but the Folkways *Anthology* lured him back to the singing of the hillbilly songs that had been a part of his own personal tradition, that of growing up on a central Texas farm.

Willie Benson introduced us all to Threadgill's. This was a hillbilly bar out on the edge of Austin's north side, which had been converted from a filling station, and which claimed to have received the city's first beer license when prohibition was repealed in 1933. Willie had been making individual forays there for awhile and had begun accompanying the proprietor, Kenneth Threadgill, who periodically halted his bartending long enough to sing and yodel his favorite Jimmie Rodgers's songs. Until the end of the 1950s Threadgill's clientele was exclusively working-class, except for the occasional stray student like Willie who was drawn there by both the beer and the music. The chief contingent of musicians were Threadgill (who played no instrument), Willie, and Shorty Zieger who played sock rhythm on the guitar while Willie surrounded it with some of the most dynamic bass runs I've ever heard. Shorty had a set patter, which included "this one's in the Key of A. A as in AIG," or "this one's in G, as in Gnat."

As far as I can recall, Ed, Willie, Stan, and I were the first university students to perform regularly at Threadgill's. The place had no stage, no electrical amplification, and certainly no formal sets. We merely sat for hours around the big round wooden tables, played our instruments, and sang one song after another. We did bluegrass, traditional country, and occasional songs from the Folkways collections of the pre-revival days. When I sang by myself, the songs came mostly from Ernest Tubb, Roy Acuff, and Hank Williams, but scarcely a night went by without me doing "The Knoxville Girl," "Mary Dear," or "Amelia Earhart's Last Flight." Stan lent his strong, resonant baritone voice to solos like "Rambling Gambler," "East Colorado Blues," "Old Dog Blue," and other traditional material. One drunken regular invariably requested that Stan do "the sailor song," which happened to be Stan's version of "The Golden Vanity." Together, he and I sang Carter Family songs, bluegrass tunes, Mainer's Mountaineer numbers like "Run Mountain" and "Maple on the Hill," or an occasional gospel song like "Mansions for Me." Best of all, once Threadgill got caught up on his beer sales, he would set everyone up with beer or Big Orange drinks, walk over to the group with his apron on and, beer in hand, would launch into a Jimmie Rodgers song like "Carolina Sunshine Girl," "Land of My Boyhood Dreams," or "Sailor's Plea," or he would reach back and do a parlor song learned from his older brother Frank, "Down in the Old Cherry Orchard." Threadgill typically ended each evening session with the Stuart Hamblen religious song, "It Is No Secret," a tribute perhaps to the memory of his father, a highly revered Nazarene preacher in northeast Texas.

Our "audiences" at Threadgill's, right at the end of the 1950s and during the first years of the 1960s, tended to be composed of friends, relatives, wives, and the usual contingent of working-class customers who had kept the bar alive during the previous decades. Then came the folk revival. The most active fans at the University of Texas organized a folk music club, sponsored by singer and folklorist Roger Abrahams, which held weekly jam sessions at the University Center and invited folk singers to perform in concert at the university. Gradually, little contingents of students began to journey to Threadgill's—looking for local musicians who seemed more real and "authentic" than the Kingston Trio and other revival luminaries.

My recollection may be faulty, but I think that the first student who made the transition from the folk music club to Threadgill's was John Clay, a passionate young man with intense eyes and a stammering style of speaking. In those days I had a habit, which many people probably found disconcerting, of bursting into song in the most unlikely places. One day I began singing "Man of Constant Sorrow" in a restroom at the University Center, and Clay, whom I had not previously met, heard me and began a highly animated explication of his own liking for the song and others like it. We thereafter began sharing information about our mutual music interests; I loaned him some of my Stanley Brothers and Mainer's Mountaineers records and invited him to come to Threadgill's. John loved old songs, but he will always be best-remembered for the performances, with banjo, of his own topical ballads.

Arriving at Threadgill's almost simultaneously with Clay was another coterie of university musicians that included guitarist Tary Owens (I have a theory that everyone named Owens is musical), banjoist Lanny

Kenneth Threadgill, singer, yodeler, and mentor to countless young singers and fans.
Photograph courtesy the Collection of Bill C. Malone, Madison, Wisconsin.

Wiggins, French harpist Powell St. John, and singer Janis Joplin. Many details from those years have vanished from my memory, but I still have a vivid recollection of the night these musicians first came to Threadgill's. I think that we all felt, at least in the very beginning, a bit suspicious of each other's feelings and motives. The young newcomers could not have felt too comfortable bringing their music into a redneck bar, and they must have wondered whether they were welcomed by any of us who made music there. My buddies and I, on the other hand, probably doubted whether these "folkies" could appreciate or adequately perform hillbilly music. We found a common ground in the broad range of old-time music, however, and the suspicions were quickly overcome. Tary Owens became virtually a disciple of Willie Benson and could soon replicate his bass runs note for note. We learned songs from each other and often performed together in various combinations (I have bragged often about singing "Silver Threads and Golden Needles" with Janis Joplin). No one at the time, however, could have known that these early 1960s sessions at Threadgill's were microcosms of the kinds of cultural and musical mixing that made Austin famous in the following decade. Nor could anyone have prophesied the fate that would ultimately follow the lives of some of the musicians there. We all knew that Janis Joplin was a powerful singer, and with a distinctive style unlike any we had heard before, but no one could have foreseen either the triumph or the tragedy that awaited her in San Francisco.

Janis was not the only alumnus of Threadgill's who left Austin in the early 1960s. Her own colleagues went their separate ways (with Powell St. John joining her in San Francisco as part of the rock band Mother Earth), and my own musical partners took their PhDs in hand—Ed Mellon in chemistry, Stan Alexander in English, Willie Benson in psychology, and I in history—and we soon built new lives outside of Austin in academia or in business. The scene at Threadgill's, however, got bigger and bigger as the years went by. A constantly self-renewing audience of students made the bar one of their weekly recreation outlets, while also making Kenneth Threadgill a local celebrity. Threadgill eventually sold his bar (the building now houses a chicken fried steak restaurant) and began making frequent concerts at other Austin nightspots and at the Kerrville Folk Festival with his inelegantly named band, Velvet Cowpasture. He became almost a household word in Texas music circles, particularly during the 1970s when his earlier association with Janis Joplin became widely known and when Austin won national notoriety as a music center. Willie Nelson's movie, *Honeysuckle Rose*, introduced him to an even larger audience, but, unfortunately, Threadgill was never recorded at the peak of his performing powers—during the early 1960s—when his voice was at its strongest and his yodeling was at its clearest and crispest range.

Although my friends and I have ventured far from Threadgill's, and our own paths in fact seldom cross, I am sure that none of us have ever forgotten those days in Austin. It was an unusual period of both loss and renewal, when older forms of music were being transformed and newer forms were coming into existence. Later life has brought its own rewards and a sense of fulfillment that a struggling graduate student could never hope to possess, but I know that the exciting sense of discovery that accompanied those days of musical experimentation and performance can never be recovered. While I do not wish to return to those days at Threadgill's, I do hope that they, and the people who filled them with song, will be remembered.

INDEX

Page numbers in italics indicate illustrations.

"Clinch Mountain Home," 247
"Cocaine Blues," 115, 244
Coe, David Allen, 118
Cohen, John, 255–56
"Cold, Cold Heart," 269, 292
Confederate Veteran magazine, 66n10, 83
"The Constitution as It Is. The Union as It Was," 93
Conway, Cecelia, 47n, 85
cotton mills and country music, 126
"A Country Boy Can Survive," 118
country music: and politics, 302–3; first usage of term "country," 283
Country Music, U.S.A., 327–30, *329*, 332–34
Country Music Association (CMA), 33, 217, 325, 328
country music discography, 325
country-pop, 297
Country Song Roundup magazine, 324
"Cowboy Blues," 177
"Cowboy Jack," 173
cowboy myth, 225–28
"Crazy Arms," 203, 296
Crazy Barn Dance (WBT, Charlotte, N.C.), 129
Crazy Hickory Nuts, 129
Crazy Water Crystals, 129
"Cripple Creek," 127
Crouch, Tom, 29, 197, 338

Dallas Semi-Weekly Farm News, 228
dancing, 51; interrelationship between blacks and whites, 73–76; solo, 70; square, 52–53; step, 53
Daniels, Charlie, 303
Davis, Jimmie, 191, 267
Davis, Ronald, 319
"The Day Is Past and Gone," 67

"Dear Companion," 254
Delmore Brothers (Alton and Rabon), 269
Dickens, Hazel, 257, 304
"Did You Ever Go Sailin'," 160
"Dill Pickle Rag," 50, 52
disc jockeys, 290
Divine Praise (Frank Stamp), 157–58
"Dixie," 50, 91, 102
Dixie Chicks (Natalie Maines, Martie Erwin, Emily Erwin), 234–35
"Do Not Turn Me from Your Door," 94
Dorsey, Thomas, 154
"Down in the Old Cherry Orchard," 340
"Dreaming of a Little Cabin," 149, 160, 162
"Driftwood on the River," 31
"The Drummer Boy of Shiloh," 92
"The Drunken Driver," 291
Dunn, Bob, 212
"Durang's Hornpipe," 52–53
"Dust on the Bible," 139

Earle, Steve, 121–22, 233
"The East Bound Train," 320
"East Colorado Blues," 339
East Texas Serenaders, 210
"Echoes from the Burning Bush," 194
Edwards, Don, 233
Edwards, John, 314n32, 325
"The Eighth of January," 52
"Empty Cot in the Bunkhouse," 321, 334
"Empty Mansion," 178
"Engine 143," 30
"Evangeline," 89, 91
"Everybody Will Be Happy Over There," 151

"Faded Love," 215
"The Faithful Engineer," 88

Malone, Patrick Cleburne, 10–11, 14
"Mama's Hand," 257
"Man of Constant Sorrow," 239, 340
"Mansion on the Hill," 31
"Mansions for Me," 340
"Maple Leaf Rag," 229
"Maple on the Hill," 339
Marcus, Greil, 294
Martin, Lecil Travis. *See* Boxcar
    Willie
"The Martins and the Coys," 247
"Mary Dear," 339
"Matthew 24," 23
McAuliffe, Harry (Big Slim), 117
McFarland, Lester, 131
McWhiney, Grady, 331
Meeting in Heaven—The Chuck
    Wagon Gang Sings the Songs of
    Marty Stuart (album), 194
Mellon, Ed, 338
Mendoza, Lydia, 230
Merlefest (Wilkesboro, N.C.), 255
Mexican border radio stations, 230,
    251, 290
"Midnight on the Stormy Deep," 145
migration, of Southerners to the
    North and within the South, 251
Miles, Emma Bell, 44, 240–41
"A Mill Mother's Lament," 250
Mind of the South (W. J. Cash), 34
"Mississippi, You're on My Mind," 305
"Mollie Darling" (also "Molly
    Darling"), 88, *95*–96
"Mommy, Please Stay Home with Me,"
    284
Monroe, Bill, 252–53, 289–90, 298–99
Monroe Brothers (Charlie and Bill),
    252
Moore, Thomas, 89, 96–97
"Mother's Prayer," 185
Mountain Dance and Folk Festival
    (Asheville, N.C.), 249

Mountain Music Bluegrass Style
    (album), 258
"Move It On Over," 120
Mull, J. Bazzel, 180, 187–88
Munde, Alan, 235
Murphey, Michael Martin, 233
"My Bucket's Got a Hole in It," 269
My Kind of Music (album), 218
"My Southern Sunny Home," 90, 93

Nashville Sound, 203, 277, 297
Neal, Jocelyn R., 317
Nelson, Willie, 233, 302
neotraditionalists, 306–7
"The New Frontier," 173, 177
New Lost City Ramblers, 31, 255, 337
"Nickety Nackety Now Now Now," 128
"Nigger Hating Me," 303
Niles, John Jacob, 248
9 to 5 and Odd Jobs (album), 304
"Nobody Answered Me," 160
"Nobody's Darling on Earth," 94
No Depression (as a synonym for
    alternative music style), 120
"No Name," 94
"Nora O'Neill," 95

Oak Ridge Quartet, 185
Oberstein, Eli, 132
O Brother, Where Art Thou? 184, 240,
    259
O'Daniel, Wilbert Lee "Pappy," 231
Odum, Howard, 41, 56n13, 57n30
Ogan, Sarah, 251
"Oh, Sam," 94
"Okie from Muskogee," 303
"Old Black Joe," 68
"Old Dan Tucker," 68
"Old Dog Blues," 339
"Old Familiar Songs" (Columbia
    label), 99
"Old Love Letters," 175